STRATEGY AND POLICY FORMATION
a multifunctional orientation

WILEY SERIES IN MANAGEMENT

STRATEGY AND POLICY FORMATION
a multifunctional orientation

SECOND EDITION

Robert C. Shirley
Central College

Michael H. Peters
Louisiana State University

Adel I. El-Ansary
George Washington University

John Wiley & Sons
New York □ Chichester □ Brisbane □ Toronto

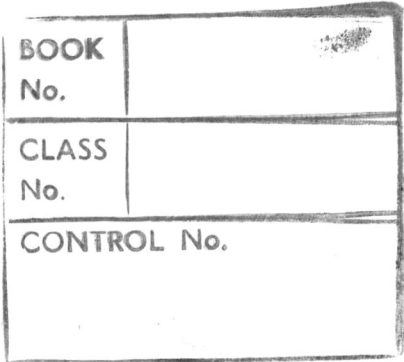

Copyright © 1976, 1981 by John Wiley & Sons, Inc.

All rights reserved. Published simultaneously in Canada.

Reproduction or translation of any part of
this work beyond that permitted by Sections
107 and 108 of the 1976 United States Copyright
Act without the permission of the copyright
owner is unlawful. Requests for permission
or further information should be addressed to
the Permissions Department, John Wiley & Sons.

Library of Congress Cataloging in Publication Data:

Shirley, Robert C.
   Strategy and policy formation.

   (Wiley series in management)
   Includes bibliographical references and index.
   1. Industrial management—Decision making.
2. Industrial management. I. Peters, Michael H.,
joint author. II. Ansary, Adel I., joint author. III. Title.
HD30.23.S54   1981   658.4'03   80-13551
ISBN 0-471-06510-2

Printed in the United States of America

10 9 8 7 6 5 4 3 2 1

To Our Wives

ABOUT THE AUTHORS

ROBERT C. SHIRLEY received his Ph.D. in policy from Northwestern University. He has taught at Northwestern, Louisiana State University, University of Houston, and S.U.N.Y.–Albany. He has also served as Director of Planning at University of Houston and as Associate Vice-President for Academic Affairs at S.U.N.Y.–Albany. Presently, he is a member of the faculty at Central College in Pella, Iowa. Articles by Dr. Shirley have appeared in the *Academy of Management Journal*, *MSU Business Topics*, *Journal of General Management*, *Long Range Planning*, *Journal of Higher Education*, and other journals. He is a former Vice-President of the Southwest Division, Academy of Management, and an active member in other professional groups. His current research interest is strategic planning for business and for nonprofit institutions.

MICHAEL H. PETERS received his D.B.A. and M.B.A. degrees in production management from Indiana University. He also holds a B.M.E. from General Motors Institute. At present, he is an associate professor at Louisiana State University and has had many years of industrial experience, including consultation projects with various profit and nonprofit organizations. Articles by Dr. Peters have appeared in academic journals and proceedings, and he is co-author of a forthcoming textbook on operations/production management. Dr. Peters is a member of numerous professional and honorary associations. His current research interests include aggregate scheduling, quality control, and design of management information systems.

ADEL I. EL-ANSARY is a professor of business administration at George Washington University, as well as a consultant and an owner of international joint ventures in the Middle East. He received his M.B.A. and Ph.D. degrees from The Ohio State University. His areas of interest include corporate strategy, international business and marketing, marketing management, marketing channels, and retailing. Widely published, Dr. El-Ansary has written articles appearing in the *Journal of Retailing*, *Journal of Marketing Research*, and *Journal of Marketing*, where he serves as a member of the Board of Reviewers. His textbook, *Marketing Channels*, was published in 1977 by Prentice-Hall.

PREFACE

The second edition of *Strategy and Policy Formation: A Multifunctional Orientation* incorporates the helpful suggestions of many of the adopters of the first edition and of reviewers of the present book. The original structure is retained, but rewriting has helped to clarify and update the substantive content.

The book still presents a general management, or holistic, view of organizational decision making that covers both strategy formulation and functional area interrelationships. The "general management perspective" is now recognized as being quite different from a functional or elemental perspective on organizational problems; this is because the unit of analysis that concerns a general manager is the *total* organization, not any specialized part of it. The general manager is confronted with problems and issues that transcend functional area boundaries and that cannot be neatly categorized as, for example, purely marketing or purely financial in nature. This multifunctional approach of the general manager derives from the job's two major tasks: (1) definition of the relationship between the total organization and its environment (external oriented), and (2) coordination and control of total organizational activities to effectuate a defined strategy (internal oriented). A specialist or elemental view of an enterprise is obviously inappropriate to these tasks.

This text is intended for use in policy courses that utilize either case analysis or computer simulation exercises as primary learning tools. Chapter 1 develops a framework that identifies the major parts of the organization and the nature of their "linkages" through various decision processes. The remainder of the book elaborates on the major elements of that framework. Chapters 2 and 3 cover the subject of corporate strategy in some detail, with greater emphasis in this edition on environmental analysis and the impact of societal values on strategic decision making. Numerous examples of strategic behavior have been added to these two chapters. Although not all of the various models and techniques of strategy and planning are covered, these chapters provide students with good exposure to the complexities of decision making at this level.

Chapters 4, 5, and 6 discuss finance, marketing, and production, respectively, with emphasis on the *interactions* that occur across the functional areas. A strong decisional orientation is taken in these chapters in order to keep students focused on the integrative character of general management. The chapter on finance has been revised to explain more fully the uses (and limitations) of financial statements and to provide more examples of how financial considerations affect strategic decision making. The popular section on financial analysis in business policy cases has also been strengthened to convey better the role of ratio analysis and other techniques in the diagnosis of policy problems. The Dun and Bradstreet ratios for manufacturing industries have been updated, and more ratios have been provided to cover wholesaling and retailing.

The marketing and production chapters have also been substantially revised. In the marketing area, more attention is given to environmental challenges to market planning and to new diagnostic tools and techniques (e.g., a detailed marketing audit is included). In general, much greater emphasis is placed on the development of marketing plans and controls from a policy perspective. Similarly, the revisions in the production chapter place greater emphasis on production planning in the face of environmental uncertainties and the internal impact of new technological developments. The production chapter also contains more examples of real-life situations to illustrate these concepts.

Chapter 7 still concentrates primarily on organizational structure and strategy, but much information has been added about the contingency approach and organizational adjustments to environmental uncertainties. New material is also provided on the role of the informal organization. Chapter 8 discusses the subject of organizational change at some length, since students are always faced with the problem of developing recommendations for strategy *implementation* as well as formulation. This chapter has been revised to put greater emphasis on the interrelationship of strategic, structural, and behavioral changes. More examples of these interrelationships are provided, and some new material is offered on how to overcome resistance to such changes.

Three supplementary readings (Mintzberg, Buchele, and Skinner) from the original edition are included, each of which is rapidly approaching the status of a "classic" article. Three new readings have been added to add depth to the discussion of particular issues.

All the material necessary to address and resolve fully the numerous issues related to strategy and policy formation is *not* provided. No single volume can accomplish that end; the nature of policy courses presumes—and, indeed, usually demands—that students complete prerequisites in management, organizational behavior, marketing, finance, economics, accounting, production/operations, and quantitative methods. Consequently, this book formulates a structure for analysis so that students can approach the complex and multidimensional field of policy. This structure facilitates the resolution of problems from a general manager's perspective and prevents students from becoming hopelessly enmeshed in the many details usually found in policy cases. We have frequently found it necessary to deal with some issues in a broad fashion in order to develop a comprehensive scheme.

However, the approach is consistent with the assumption that students in a policy course have completed the prerequisites previously cited.

Many individuals have contributed to the development of this book. We especially thank Raymond V. Kinnunen, now an associate professor at Northeastern University in Boston, for his contributions in the areas of strategy, organizational structure, and marketing. Many colleagues, both adopters and nonadopters, have made invaluable comments and suggestions for improvement of the original edition. In particular, Bernard Rieman, Cleveland State University, and J. David Hunger, University of Virginia, provided helpful reviews of the first edition. It is both humbling and gratifying to receive so many useful ideas but, of course, we remain responsible for what appears on these pages. Finally, we are indebted to our wives who were understanding and encouraging throughout the process of revision.

Robert C. Shirley
Michael H. Peters
Adel I. El-Ansary

CONTENTS

1 STRATEGY AND POLICY a framework for analysis   1

    CASE STUDIES AND COMPUTER SIMULATIONS   2
    The Analysis of Cases   2
    Use of This Text in Case Analysis   2
    AN OVERVIEW OF THE FRAMEWORK   3
    STAGE 1: CLASSIFICATION OF CASE DATA   5
    Environmental Dimension   5
    Strategic Dimension   6
    Program Dimension   7
    Structural Dimension   7
    Behavioral Dimension   7
    Additional Remarks   8
    STAGE 2: ANALYSIS OF CASE DATA   9
    The Class 1 and Class 2 Decision Variables   11
    The Class 3 and Class 4 Decision Variables   13
    Additional Remarks   14
    STAGE 3: IDENTIFICATION OF PROBLEMS AND/OR ISSUES   15
    STAGE 4: FORMULATION OF RECOMMENDATIONS   16
    SUMMARY   17
    Reading: Raymond E. Miles, Charles C. Snow, Alan D. Meyer, and Henry D. Coleman, Jr., "ORGANIZATIONAL STRATEGY, STRUCTURE, AND PROCESS"   19

2 STRATEGIC DECISIONS the impact of environmental forces   35

    THE CONCEPT OF STRATEGY   37
    The Strategic Decisions   38
    Determinants of Strategy   39
    The Relationship of Strategy Formulation to Implementation   40
    THE STRATEGY FORMULATION PROCESS   40
    Environmental Forces   41
        Economic Forces   41
        Competitive Forces   44
        Structure of the Industry   45
        Social Forces   46
        Technological Forces   48
        Political/Legal Forces   50
    Environmental Research: Its Role and Forms   51
    SUMMARY   54
    Reading: Henry Mintzberg, "STRATEGY-MAKING IN THREE MODES"   55

3 STRATEGY FORMULATION relating environmental forces to internal capabilities and values 68

THE ASSESSMENT OF CAPABILITIES	69
The Capability or Resource Audit	69
Human Resources	69
Financial Resources	70
Physical Resources and Production	70
Marketing	70
Research and Development	70
Organizational	70
Present Strategic Posture	70
Environmental Research Capabilities	71
Establishing a Competitive Advantage	71
The Concept of Synergy	74
THE INFLUENCE OF PERSONAL VALUES ON STRATEGY	77
Culturally Derived Values	77
Organizationally Derived Values	80
Cases of Conflicting Values	81
The Resolution of Conflicting Values	83
SUMMARY	84
Reading: Robert B. Buchele, "HOW TO EVALUATE A FIRM"	85

4 FINANCIAL ANALYSIS process and techniques 102

FINANCIAL ANALYSIS IN BUSINESS POLICY CASES	103
Analysis of the Situation	103
Evidence of Financial Objectives	103
Basic Financial Statements	104
Evidence of External Effectiveness	105
Profitability Indicators	105
Liquidity Indicators	105
Leverage Indicators	105
Overall Ability to Obtain Funds	105
Evidence of Internal Efficiency	108
Further Analysis of Financial Indicators	108
DIAGNOSIS OF PROBLEMS	109
DEVELOPMENT OF PLANS OF ACTION	117
BREAK-EVEN ANALYSIS	124
FINANCE FUNCTION	128
FINANCE DECISION VARIABLES	129
Level of Working Capital	129
Level of Dividend Payment	132
FUNCTIONALLY INDEPENDENT FINANCE VARIABLES	136
SUMMARY	136

5 MARKETING the interdependent nature of decision making 138

A MULTIDIMENSIONAL VIEW OF MARKETING	139
Marketing's Core Elements	139
Themes of Analysis and Integration	140
A Basic Approach to Marketing	140

	Tools of Analysis for Marketing	142
	MARKETING MANAGEMENT: ENVIRONMENT AND CHALLENGES	142
	MARKETING MANAGEMENT: STRATEGY AND TASKS	144
	Marketing Planning	144
	Marketing Organization	149
	Marketing Controls	149
	MARKETING DECISION VARIABLES	156
	Product Research and Development (R&D)	157
	Marketing Research and Information Systems	159
	Distribution Channel Structure	162
	Price	164
	Discounts: Type and Structure	165
	Promotion	165
	Credit	167
	Physical Distribution and Inventory Levels	168
	FUNCTIONALLY INDEPENDENT MARKETING VARIABLES	170
	SUMMARY	171
	APPENDIX	172
	Reading: George S. Day, "A STRATEGIC PERSPECTIVE ON PRODUCT PLANNING"	179
6	**PRODUCTION/OPERATIONS** a multifunctional view	**198**
	TYPES OF PRODUCTION/OPERATIONS SYSTEMS	200
	PRODUCTION/OPERATIONS DECISION VARIABLES	201
	Plant Location and Capacity	201
	Facilities Layout	208
	Process Planning and Job Design	211
	Planning of Aggregate Output	214
	Raw Materials and Work-in-Process Inventory Levels	216
	FUNCTIONALLY INDEPENDENT PRODUCTION/OPERATIONS DECISION VARIABLES	218
	SUMMARY	218
	Reading: Wickham Skinner, "MANUFACTURING—MISSING LINK IN CORPORATE STRATEGY"	220
7	**ORGANIZATIONAL STRUCTURE** a general management perspective	**232**
	A MULTIDIMENSIONAL VIEW OF ORGANIZATIONAL STRUCTURE	233
	ORGANIZATIONAL DESIGN	234
	Characteristics of Formal Organizations	235
	Structuring Formal Organizational Relationships	237
	THE FORMAL ORGANIZATION: ALTERNATIVE STRUCTURAL FORMS	238
	The "Small" Structure	238
	The Functional Structure	240
	The Divisional Structure	242
	Product Departmentation	243
	Territorial Divisionalization	243
	Basic Advantages	244
	Project Management	244
	The Matrix Organization	246

Hybrid Designs: Committees and Task Forces	249
THE INFORMAL ORGANIZATION	251
Keys to Linking the Formal and Informal Organizations	251
Needs and Motivation	252
Leadership	252
SUMMARY	253
Reading: Mack Hanan, "REORGANIZE YOUR COMPANY AROUND ITS MARKETS"	254

8 ORGANIZATIONAL CHANGE an integrated approach — 266

THE CONCEPT OF ORGANIZATIONAL CHANGE	267
STRATEGY, STRUCTURE, AND BEHAVIOR: A CASE STUDY OF INTERRELATEDNESS	268
THE ORGANIZATIONAL CHANGE PROCESS	270
Forces Toward Change	270
Perception of Forces	271
Development of Change Goals	272
Determination of Change Targets	274
Organization for Implementation	274
Determination of Change Tactics and Channels of Influence	275
Results of Change and Intervening Variables	276
Additional Remarks	277
RESISTANCE TO CHANGE	277
Openness to Change	277
Method of Implementation of Change	279
Other Factors Affecting Acceptance of Change	280
SUMMARY	283

INDEX 285

STRATEGY AND POLICY FORMATION
a multifunctional orientation

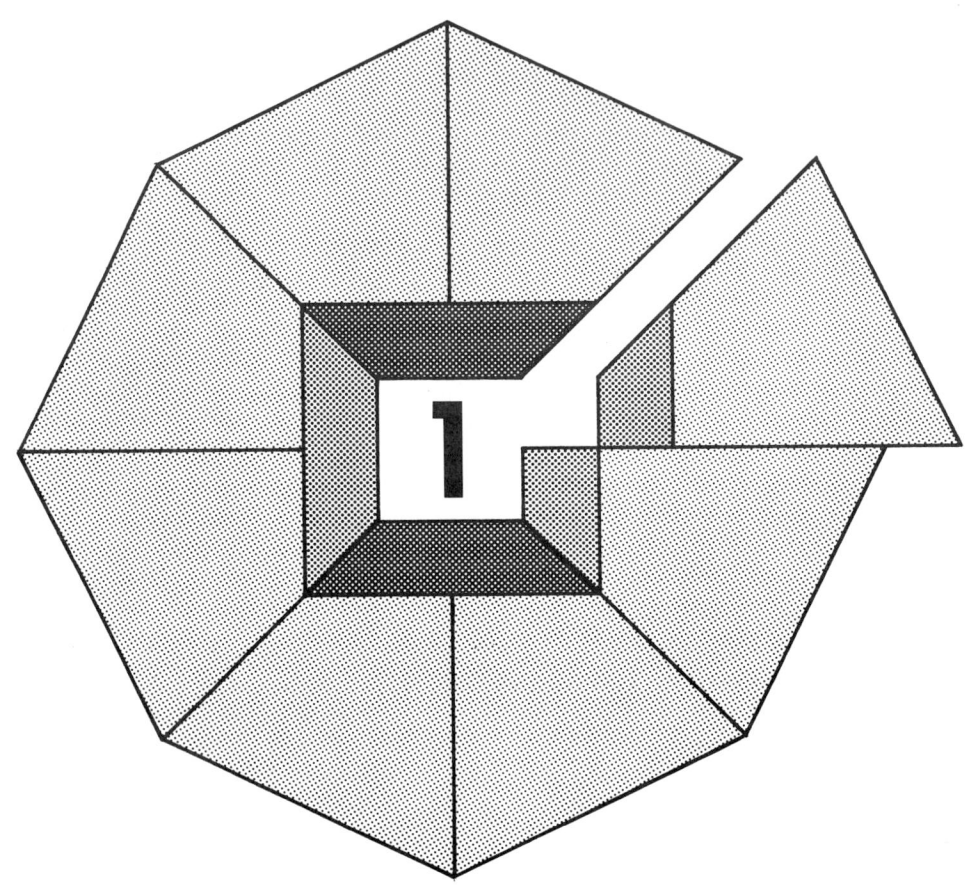

STRATEGY AND POLICY
a framework for analysis

In the past few years, the field of corporate strategy and policy has received increasing attention. Many undergraduate and graduate business curricula now include a required integrative course in policy.[1] These courses focus on the application of broad, diverse skills to the solution of complex business problems that transcend traditional functional area boundaries. Because of this, most students must complete courses in marketing, finance, accounting, economics, quantitative methods, production/operations, organization behavior, and general management before they can enter a policy course. This allows the course to focus on problems and issues that are *multifunctional* in nature—those problems and issues that cannot be neatly categorized as, for example, purely financial or purely marketing in nature. Emphasis is placed on viewing the firm as a complex system and on seeing the relations between the various functional areas from the perspective of a general manager. Consequently, the nature of policy courses requires an integrative view of the various academic disciplines involved. Otherwise, the unique purposes and attributes of policy courses would be lost, and discussions would revert to purely financial, marketing, production, or organizational behavior problems.

The field of strategy and policy represents the study of top or general management decision making. Consequently, analysis must focus on the organization as a complete entity rather than on a specific area or department. The emphasis on functional area interrelationships and the integration of all organizational activities in a policy course is derived from the two basic tasks that face all general managers: they must understand the interplay between the organization and its environment (external oriented) and must integrate and direct the efforts of the total organization toward reaching predetermined objectives (internal oriented).[2] It is obvious that a specialist or elemental view of an organization is inappropriate to these two general tasks. This text focuses on the analytical constructs and methods that are useful for solving the multifunctional problems encountered in policy courses.

---

[1] The American Assembly of Collegiate Schools of Business requires that undergraduate curricula include "a study of administrative processes under conditions of uncertainty, including integrating analysis and policy determination at the overall management level." Although the phraseology of this requirement may change, all indications are that the substance will remain the same for the foreseeable future.

[2] As used here, the term "general manager" refers not only to the president or chief executive officer of an organization, but also to those individuals charged with the overall management and direction of the major units of a firm. Such units may be either subsidiaries or major product divisions of the larger organization. Thus a "general manager" is one who manages and coordinates a variety of production, marketing, and financial activities in pursuit of the overall objectives of the unit or larger organization.

CASE STUDIES AND COMPUTER SIMULATIONS

Varied approaches to learning have been used to accomplish the integrative purpose of a policy course: computer simulation "games," case analyses, various experiential exercises, and more traditional lecture/discussion sessions. These approaches all have one thing in common when used in a policy course: they are directed toward solving problems and resolving issues from a general management perspective since, by definition, such a perspective *must* be multifunctional and integrative in nature. Case analysis is the most widely used vehicle for instilling this perspective in students and for developing a capacity for solving complex problems, although the other techniques mentioned (especially computer simulation exercises) have become more and more popular in recent years. This book has been designed to assist students who are engaged in either case analysis or computer simulation exercises. For convenience, the word "cases" is used throughout the text, although the material should be of equal benefit to students using computer simulation as their primary learning tool.

The Analysis of Cases

The use of cases exposes the student to the real experiences of existing companies. This provides the opportunity to assess the past failures and successes of well-known firms in order to evaluate why certain actions or decisions were desirable and why others were not. Case analysis is frequently criticized because complete information is not usually available to students—especially where company names are disguised and students cannot do outside research on the firm in question. But, when well-written cases that include most of the information relevant to understanding the total firm situation are available, this ceases to be true. In addition, much important out-of-class research *can* be done on the industry or industries in which a particular firm operates. Besides, no one, not even the chief executive who actually experienced the events described in a case, ever has as much information as would be desirable in resolving matters of strategy and policy.

Thus cases as well as many simulation exercises are realistic in that some desirable information may be missing. This is characteristic of top management decision making; consequently, the student is also exposed to some of the frustration and chagrin that is frequently experienced in the "real world." It is important that the student (1) recognize and delineate what desirable information is missing from a case and treat this as a constraint on, or a limitation of, the analysis, and (2) be willing to "stick his or her neck out" under conditions of uncertainty in order to make a decision—not hastily, but after a thorough and informed analysis.

Use of This Text in Case Analysis

This text has been designed as a comprehensive guide to the analysis of corporate strategy and policy. Specifically, it provides an approach to analysis and decision making that emphasizes functional interrelationships and focuses on the kinds of functional area analyses that should be performed from a general management perspective. Because of this, the book may be used in conjunction with traditional casebooks on policy or computer-simulation materials. Its analytical framework provides a foundation that will help the student to make the transition from a somewhat elemental view of an organization to a total systems or top-management approach.

The rest of this chapter takes the first step toward developing an analytical framework by constructing its "skeleton." Subsequent chapters "put the meat on the bones" by discussing functional area interrelationships in more detail. In this way the material focuses on integrative, multifunctional approaches to analysis, and a systemic rather than an elemental perspective is stressed throughout.

There are no quick and easy formulas available for the solution of policy issues. A good deal of considered judgment is required to isolate complex problems and to develop workable recommendations for future action. Thus, although the analytical framework and integrative material in this book will help the student to structure and focus his or her efforts, it can provide no ready answers to many questions and issues encountered in policy cases and in computer simulations. Similarly, the student should recognize that there is very rarely only *one* desirable answer to questions of strategy and policy. The ability to reason through the limited information available and to support one's conclusions with facts and/or logic must be the primary criteria for evaluating work of this kind. Therefore one should not be dismayed to learn that he or she has developed an analysis that is quite different from that of fellow students. Frequently, the unique and creative solution is the most desirable one, but *only* if it can be supported with hard facts (where available), incisive logical reasoning, and the proper assessment of the implications of recommended courses of action. With this in mind, the student should be prepared to stretch and exercise imagination and analytical ability—not in the sense of "wild" or "far-out" conclusions under the guise of creativity, but by thorough and careful analysis of the information presented in order to develop sound, supportable conclusions.

AN OVERVIEW OF THE FRAMEWORK

Figure 1-1 presents an overview of the integrative framework for the analysis of strategy and policy cases. Stage 1 of the framework requires that all relevant case information be sifted and sorted along the five basic dimensions of any organization: environmental, strategic, program, structural, and behavioral. These basic organizational dimensions are explained more fully below. They represent a comprehensive set of categories for classifying all of the relevant information to be found in any case.

Stage 2 is where the process of *analysis* of the data really begins. Note that, in each area, analysis is conducted from the integrative total systems perspective of general or top management—as opposed to the more elemental perspective of a vice president of marketing, for example. Just how this may be accomplished is, of course, the basic subject matter of this book.

Stage 3 involves the identification of the problems and/or decision issues facing the firm. The analysis conducted in Stage 2 should indicate the major

Figure 1-1 An integrative framework for the analysis of strategy and policy cases.

Stage 1
Classification of Case Information
Organizational Dimensions

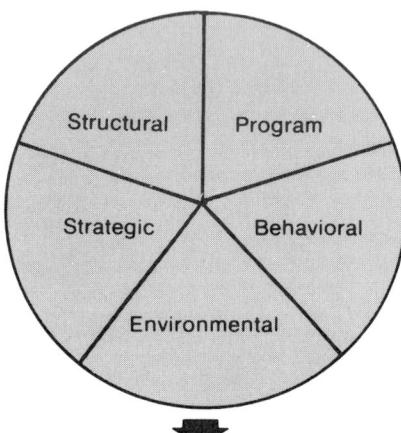

- Structural
- Program
- Strategic
- Behavioral
- Environmental

Stage 2
Analysis of Case Information
General Management Perspective

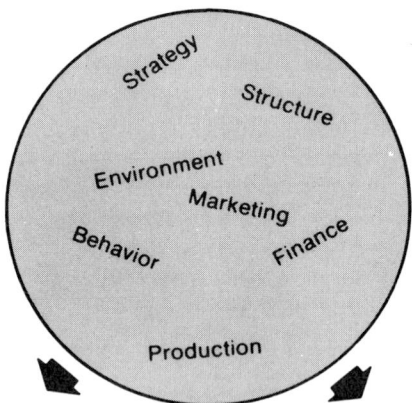

- Strategy
- Structure
- Environment
- Marketing
- Behavior
- Finance
- Production

Stage 3
Identification of Problems and/or Issues

What are the underlying causes of observed difficulties?

What major issues must be resolved to ensure future viability?

Stage 4
Formulation of Recommendations

Elimination of problems

Resolution of issues

areas in which the firm is experiencing difficulties or facing unresolved issues. If difficulties exist, Stage 3 will require a decision as to *why* the difficulties are occurring. Where there are unresolved issues, the student will have to pinpoint the *specific* issues that must be resolved in order to ensure the future viability of the firm.

Finally, Stage 4 requires the student to either eliminate the problems or resolve the issues with appropriate recommendations.

This brief overview provides a basic background for a more detailed discussion of each major stage of the process.

STAGE 1: CLASSIFICATION OF CASE DATA

Because of the multifunctional nature of policy study, cases used in this course are necessarily very complex. They generally are somewhat longer than cases to which students have been exposed in functional area courses such as marketing and include descriptions of all the facets of a firm's operations, making it necessary to have some mechanism for *organizing* the case information. Without some attempt at organization before beginning the actual analysis, the student will likely become lost in a maze of seemingly unrelated incidents, issues, and problems. The following paragraphs delineate the elements of a comprehensive scheme that may be used to sift, sort, and classify all case data. Note that not all of the types of information discussed will be present in every case. Our task at this point, however, is to develop a comprehensive framework that will serve for all policy cases.

As discussed earlier, five basic categories of information may be found in any case. These categories correspond to the basic dimensions or parts of any organization. Each dimension is discussed separately. As the student reads through the case, he or she should attempt to classify all relevant information into one or more of these five categories.

Environmental Dimensions

First, every organization has an *environmental dimension* within which it operates. The particular external conditions faced by any firm always may be further classified into one of six major (although obviously interrelated) categories. Each category is now outlined:

1. *Economic.* Includes information in the case related to general economic conditions, volume of demand for the firm's products, overall market trends, lines of credit available, tax credits, money markets, capital markets, and other information that is economic in nature *and* external to the firm.
2. *Competition.* Includes all information related to the firm's competitors: their strengths and weaknesses, relative market shares, strategies and tactics, and other items of importance.
3. *Structure of the industry.* Includes information related to the type of skills required for success in the industry, the productive capacity of the industry in relation to total market demand, labor conditions, size

requirements, geographical characteristics, nature of governmental controls, and similar information.
4. *Social.* Includes larger societal values, ethical customs, consumer behavior, minority group influences, various demographic data of concern to the firm, the general issue of social responsibility, and similar phenomena.
5. *Technological.* Includes information about technological developments in the industry or elsewhere that have an impact on new product development, improvement of production processes, and the like.
6. *Political/Legal.* Includes information related to legislation, regulatory agencies, court decisions, executive acts, foreign policy, tariffs, policies of other countries toward foreign investment, and similar matters that may either present new opportunities to the firm or act as constraints on its operations.

Taken together, these six sectors comprise the total set of environmental conditions faced by any firm. The dynamic nature of their influence on strategy formation and on internal operations is discussed more fully in Chapters 2 and 3. However, the various types of environmental forces present a firm with *both* opportunities and constraints. The basic task of top management is to develop an overall strategy for the firm that fully exploits available opportunities, subject to the constraints placed on it by the environment and by internal capabilities and resources.

Strategic Dimension

The *strategic dimension* of the firm refers to its basic product/market scope and objectives, both present and projected. Stated simply, every firm has a basic strategic posture that requires determination of, or decisions about, the following:

1. *Customer Targets.* The market segment(s) of concern to the firm.
2. *Product Mix.* The products to be produced and distributed to the market segments defined as targets.
3. *Geographic limits of the market(s) to be served.* The boundaries of principal concern to the firm (i.e., the areas where efforts to sell the products or services will be concentrated).
4. *Competitive Emphasis.* Some distinctive competence of the firm that gives it an edge over competitors.
5. *Objectives.* Targets and performance criteria for the firm as a whole with regard to profitability, growth, market share, and survival.

Regardless of whether management has formulated a specific and *explicit* strategy, the student usually can infer the firm's present product/market scope, although future strategy may or may not be as evident. If it is not clear-cut, this would be dealt with in the subsequent stages of analysis and problem identification, to be discussed later. Similarly, specific objectives (e.g., profitability, growth, market share, survival) for a given firm being studied may or may not be evident. The student should attempt to develop as much information about present and future strategy as possible at this stage that will utilized in subsequent analyses of issues and problems. Chapters 2 and 3 discuss the process of strategy formulation in detail in order to aid the student in analysis.

Program Dimension

The *program dimension* of an organization comprises the plans developed by a firm to effect its overall strategy. This refers to information about the *technical specifics* of programs in terms of objectives, processes, and techniques to be utilized in each implementation area in order to accomplish the firm's objectives. Included here would be the detailed plans for marketing, finance, production, research and development (R & D), engineering, purchasing, personnel administration, and other major task areas. The four major programs of any firm are:

1. *Finance*. Information about liquidity, leverage, profitability, and other elements of the firm's overall fiscal situation and methods of financial management would be classified here.
2. *Marketing*. This would include the structure of distribution channels, promotional programs and techniques, market research, salespeople and their territories, and similar information.
3. *Production*. Information about plant and equipment, the technology of production, materials utilized, inventory management, scheduling, and similar matters would be classified here.
4. *Research and Development*. Information about the firm's efforts to develop new products and/or production processes would be included here.

Finance, marketing, and production are covered in detail (from a general management perspective) in Chapters 4, 5, and 6, respectively. Research and development is also given attention in Chapters 5 and 6.

Structural Dimension

The *structural dimension* of a firm refers to the formal arrangements, both horizontal and vertical, that have been established to coordinate the total activities involved in the implementation of a given strategy. In a sense, this dimension reflects the "anatomy" of a firm through its focus on mechanisms and processes that *link* (again, both vertically and horizontally) the various parts of an organization. For purposes of analysis it is useful to classify the major elements of organizational structure as follows:

1. *Distribution of Functions Throughout the Organization*. Includes definition of functions to be performed, groupings of functions, and the vertical and horizontal task relationships among functions.

2. *Vertical and Horizontal Authority Relationships.* Who has the authority to do what and in which areas.
3. *Reporting Relationships.* Definition of superior/subordinate relationships and spans of control.
4. *Communication/Decision Processes.* The manner in which formal decisions are made and by whom, supporting informational inputs, and the information systems established to provide the inputs to decision makers.
5. *Policies.* The decision rules or guidelines established in finance, marketing, production, personnel, purchasing, research and development, and other areas; these guidelines tie the performance of specific functions to the firm's overall strategy and objectives.
6. *Formal Incentive Systems.* Compensation plan characteristics, fringe benefits, incentive or bonus plans, promotion criteria, and other features of the organization's formal reward system.

Taken together, these structural elements establish the basic conditions under which organizational members perform their various roles. Information about each element should be gleaned from the case data and recorded for reference in accomplishing Stages 2 and 3. The major focus for analysis of structure from a general management perspective is discussed in Chapter 7.

Behavioral Dimension

Finally, the *behavioral dimension* comprises various considerations related to human behavior in organizations. For the purpose of sorting and classifying case information, it is useful to subdivide this dimension as follows:

1. *The Individual.* All relevant information related to individual beliefs, values and attitudes should be recorded here as well as overt behavior that seems to be dysfunctional; also includes considerations of abilities, satisfaction, personalities, and other behavioral phenomena of an individualistic nature.
2. *Interpersonal Relationships.* Whereas the preceding focus was on the individual, the appropriate information in this category relates to the interactions between two persons in accomplishing tasks. Any evidence of difficulties in personal interactions not of a group nature should be noted here (e.g., constant friction between the heads of production and marketing).
3. *Group Behavior.* All information related to the work group as a unit of analysis should be recorded here—presence or absence of group cohesiveness; informal group goals, leaders, and members; influence of the group over individuals; group norms; processes utilized by the group to maintain itself; and other behavioral phenomena that are of a group nature.
4. *Intergroup Behavior.* Whereas the preceding focus was on the single work group, the appropriate information in this category relates to the

interactions of two or more work groups in accomplishing tasks. Any evidence of difficulties in group interactions that are not purely individualistic or interpersonal in nature should be noted here (e.g., constant friction between all personnel in marketing and all personnel in production as a result of differing goal and value orientations across these two groupings).

The major focus for analysis of behavior from a general management perspective is discussed in Chapters 7 and 8.

Additional Remarks   The five basic dimensions and their components provide a comprehensive set of reference points for the student. Sorting and classifying information into the categories presented is the first step in "getting a handle" on a particular firm's characteristics and overall situation, both externally and internally. Figure 1-2 summarizes these categories. Once this step is completed, some order has been introduced into the process of analysis, and the student can proceed to Stage 2. As a final note, it should be emphasized that the student is assumed to have completed the various functional area course requirements before embarking on a course in policy. Such a background should permit the student to distinguish between relevant and irrelevant information in this first stage of the process.

STAGE 2: ANALYSIS OF CASE DATA   Once the student has completed the "sifting and sorting" just described, he or she is ready to begin Stage 2 of the process. This is where analysis really begins, since Stage 1 has provided only the framework within which analysis may proceed. As depicted in Figure 1-1, the analysis is prepared from a "general management perspective" and focuses on the five major dimensions previously discussed (see Figure 1-2). The "program dimension" in Stage 2 has been subdivided into production, marketing, and finance to emphasize the importance of analysis in these three program areas. The remainder of the book provides much material to help the student in the analysis of all the areas shown. The material is *integrative* in nature, in keeping with the purposes of a policy course and the multifunctional nature of the general manager's job. For example, Chapter 5 focuses primarily on the marketing decision variables that are concerned with inputs received from other functional areas such as production or research and development. This approach should prevent the student from becoming hopelessly enmeshed in the innumerable marketing details that may be appropriate for consideration in a marketing problems course but not in a policy course. Furthermore, focusing on multifunctional decision variables necessarily means that they are the decisions of concern to the general manager who, by definition, is concerned with *coordinating* the numerous and diverse activities of a firm.

Figure 1-2 The five major dimensions and their components.

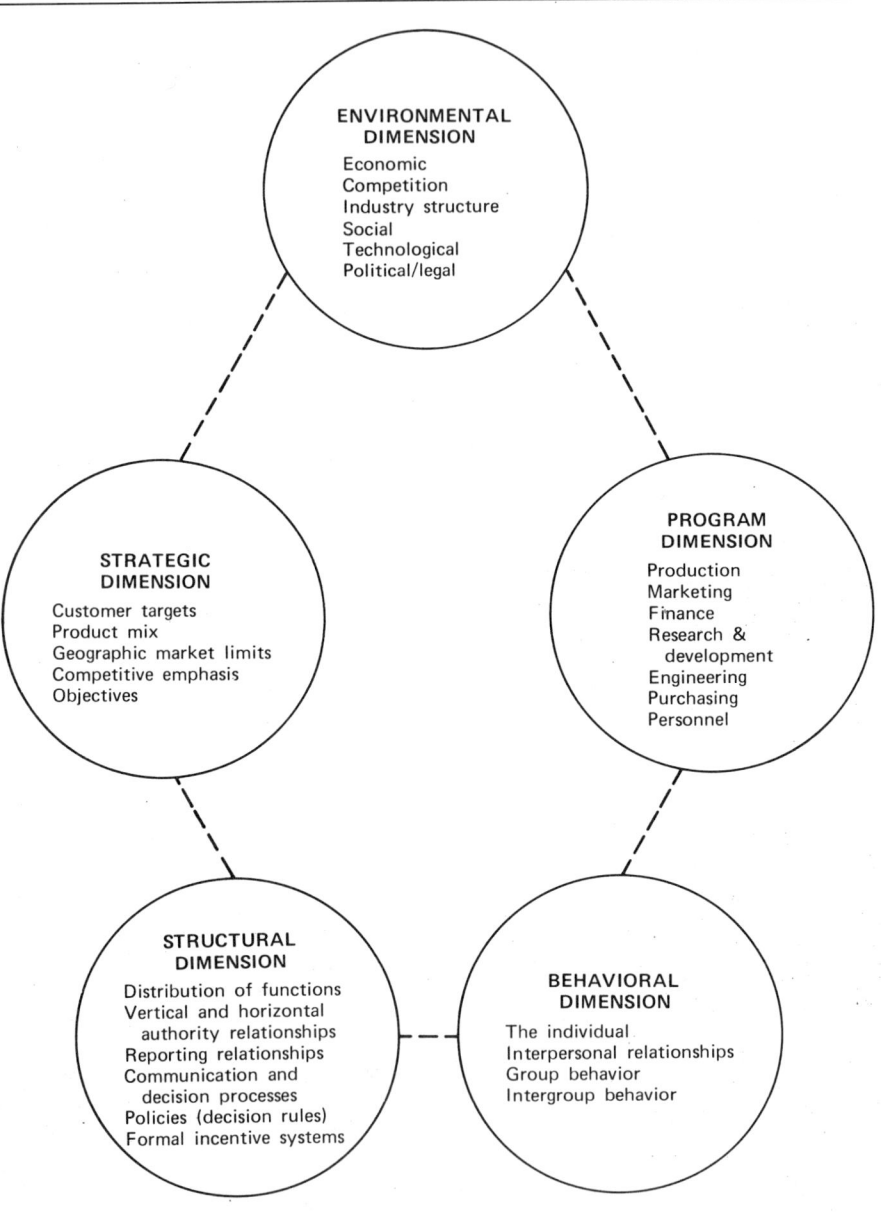

Figure 1-3 has been prepared to lend some clarity to what this general management perspective entails. It distinguishes among four major classes of organizational decision variables: strategic (C_1), multifunctional coordinative (C_2), functionally dependent (C_3), and functionally independent (C_4). The types of decisions included in each class and the interrelationships of the four classes are discussed next.

The Class 1 and Class 2 Decision Variables

The C_1 decision class includes decisions on the major strategic variables identified earlier: customer targets, product mix, geographic limits of the market, competitive emphasis, and objectives. These decisions define the basic relationship between the firm and its environment and also the kind of business to be engaged in by the company. Furthermore, once these decisions are made, they provide overall direction for decision making throughout the firm. For example, decisions made in the marketing area concerning distributors for a firm's products must be congruent with the strategic decisions about geographic boundaries of the market. The distributors must also be sufficiently attractive to the kinds of customers who have been selected as the primary target audiences for the firm's products. In general, the C_1 decisions are the *first-order* decisions of the firm, since they define the basic directions for all activities and tasks to be performed by the organization. Obviously, a great deal of thought must be given to these decisions because of their cruciality to future survival. Just as obviously, students in a policy course should spend a great deal of analytic effort in determining whether or not a firm has chosen a viable strategy for future development.

The second class of decisions shown in Figure 1-3 has been labeled "multifunctional coordinative decisions" because, like the C_1 variables, they are total-firm oriented and usually are finally made by top management. In relation to the C_1 decisions, the C_2 decisions are *implemental* in nature and provide the basic set of major policies or conditions to guide lower-level organizational decisions and activities. Decisions here include the basic organizational structure (e.g., definition of functions and their interrelationships, authority relationships, basic information flow processes to provide data for decision making); the allocation of resources (both for operating and capital budgets) to various divisions, departments or projects; manpower development programs, compensation plans, fringe benefit programs; financing policy, including sources of funds and desired capital structure; overall pricing policies; and basic operating objectives for various units of the firm.

The latter two C_2 decision variables deserve further elaboration. Overall pricing policy does *not* refer to specific decisions about the prices of individual items produced by a particular firm. Instead, it includes the basic policies developed by general or top management that guide the more specific marketing decisions on exact prices and discounts. Broad policies are necessary to ensure that specific product prices are consistent with overall firm objectives and resources. For example, Gulf Oil Corporation once had a company policy that banned participation in local gasoline "price wars"—a decision that obviously had ramifications for the total firm and not just for its marketing activities.

Figure 1-3 Classes of organizational decision variables.

Decision Variables
Class 1
Strategic decisions

Objectives	Customer mix
Product mix	Competitive emphasis
Geographic limits of market	

Class 2
Multifunctional coordinative decisions

Organizational structure, including information flows
Resource allocation (operating and capital budgets)
Manpower development and compensation policies
Financing policy
Functional area objectives
Pricing policy

Class 3
Functionally dependent decisions
PROGRAM AREAS

PRODUCTION	MARKETING	FINANCE
Examples:	Examples:	Examples:
Plant capacity	Distribution channels	Dividend policy
Production schedules	Prices and discounts	Working capital needs

Class 4
Functionally independent decisions

PRODUCTION	MARKETING	FINANCE
Examples:	Examples:	Examples:
Quality control techniques	Advertising media	Accounting procedures
Equipment maintenance schedules	Sales territories and routes	Cost analysis techniques

Basic operating objectives for the various units of the firm necessarily must be derived from and be consistent with the overall objectives of the firm. Thus, if a firm's return on investment (ROI) objective is 13%, the particular sales volume objective for the marketing group must make a 13% ROI possible. Similarly, the firm's strategy with regard to product quality (an element of the product mix decision) must be translated into specific quality control objectives for the production area, such as "a 95% probability that no more than .001% of the units produced are defective." Regardless of whether these area or departmental objectives are determined unilaterally by top management or formulated through a consultative, mutual influence process with departmental heads, they represent the "link" between strategy formulation and implementation. Subsequent, lower-order decisions on methods to *implement* the area objectives then may be made by the functional areas affected. For example, quality control sampling techniques and inspection procedures can be decided on by lower-level personnel charged with that responsibility.

To summarize, the C_2 multifunctional coordinative decisions link the overall strategy of a firm to actual operational activities. They provide, in conjunction with the strategic decisions, a basic set of constraints for production, marketing, finance, research and development, and the other basic task areas. The work in all the task areas *must* reflect and be consistent with the basic C_1 and C_2 decisions or the firm is headed toward a path of suboptimization and faulty implementation of overall strategy.

The Class 3 and Class 4 Decision Variables

Two basic types of organizational decisions depicted in Figure 1-3 remain to be discussed. Decisions included in the C_3 and C_4 classes actually operationalize a firm's strategy (C_1) and major coordinative policies (C_2); that is, given the C_1 and C_2 decisions already made, various task areas (especially production, marketing, and finance) are provided with the necessary guidance for what work has to be done and under what basic conditions or constraints. Deciding *how* to do the work and how to coordinate with other task areas, however, are generally the responsibilities of the heads of the various task areas. Much of the work to be done or decisions to be made in each area require little, if any, consultation with other functional areas. On the other hand, much of the work to be done or decisions to be made affects, or is affected by, the work or decisions of other areas. This basic distinction provides the criterion for developing the final two classes of organizational decisions.

Class 3 decisions are generally associated *primarily* with one particular functional area, but these decisions depend heavily on inputs from the other areas. For example, a major production decision variable is that of plant capacity; however, this decision depends heavily on, among other things, long-range sales forecasts and the structure of distribution channels (marketing inputs), forecasted developments in production technology (a research and development input), and the firm's cost of capital (a finance input), as well as on production inputs such as operating costs.

Finally the Class 4 decisions, termed "functionally independent," are those that can be made by a particular task area in a virtually autonomous fashion, given the C_1 and C_2 constraints. In the marketing sphere, for example, decisions on advertising media to be utilized, sales territories and routes, and similar matters require virtually no interaction with other task areas. The same is true of production area decisions such as quality control techniques and scheduling equipment maintenance. These C_4 decisions receive virtually no attention (only a detailed listing in appropriate chapters) in this book.

Additional Remarks

Several clarifications are in order at this point. The C_1 decision variables establish the strategic posture of the firm at any point in time. That is, decisions on these variables establish the relationship between the firm as a whole and its environment by specifying the types of products and markets to be served, the basis on which the firm will compete, and the criteria by which success will be measured. Once decisions are made here, a set of coordinative policies must be developed (the C_2 decisions) to provide guidance and direction to task performance and interactions *throughout* the enterprise. The C_3 (functionally dependent) variables represent decisions of a third order that are implemental in nature and are generally the responsibility of a particular functional area. The fact that the C_3 decisions are highly dependent on other functional area inputs, however, means that, regardless of the locus of decision-making authority, they are worthy of inclusion in the general management perspective. This is because general managers, by definition, are concerned with the overall coordination of activities that interrelate in a cross-functional fashion. Finally, it follows that the C_4 (functionally independent) variables are not included in the general management perspective. As noted these types of decisions require little if any consultation across functional areas. Such decision variables in marketing, for example, are very worthy of study in a marketing problems course but not in a policy course.

The Class 1, 2, and 3 variables thus constitute the focus of this book. By definition, then, the material presented in subsequent chapters shows interrelationships of the various functional areas and focuses on decisions of major importance to the firm. It should provide the student with the analytical framework necessary to identify key problems or issues facing the firm, as discussed in Stage 3.

It should be recognized that the decision framework presented in Figure 1-3 is *not* intended as an exhaustive list of the various problems and concerns of top management. Rather, the framework delineates those major organizational decisions which define the overall strategy of the firm and the *types* of lower-order decisions which have to be monitored for purposes of overall integration and coordination of organizational activities. *It is thus a device for structuring one's view of the total decision making system of an organization.* General managers obviously have responsibilities and obligations both inside and outside the organization related to public relations, maintenance of ethical standards, and other matters which are not depicted in Figure 1-3.

STAGE 3: PROBLEMS AND/OR ISSUES

As shown in Figure 1-1, the analysis conducted in Stage 2 should culminate in the identification of basic problems and/or key decision issues facing the firm. The term "problem" is used here to mean the underlying *cause* of some observed difficulty within the firm. It must be distinguished from the term "symptom," which is actually synonymous with the difficulty itself. Thus, if an observed difficulty (symptom) within the firm is high employee turnover, one must search for and analyze all relevant information to determine *why* this exists. Similarly, a declining profit margin is never a problem, it is only a symptom of some problem that is causing the reduced margin. The reason for making this distinction between symptoms (difficulties) and problems (causes) is to insure that the student's point of attack for case solution is poised at the proper level. Unless the underlying cause of the observed difficulty is eliminated, similar difficulties may arise again in the future.

In addition to the identification of problems, the student frequently finds that there are key issues facing a firm. What should be the firm's future strategy? What steps must be taken to *prevent* problems from occurring in various aspects of the firm's operations? How could the firm better standardize its production operations without sacrificing the desires of marketing personnel for more flexibility in product design? These and similar issues are not really "problems" in the sense in which we are using the term. Instead, they represent focal points for action that might improve the firm's effectiveness or efficiency in relating to environmental demands, even though no real or apparent difficulty in present operations seems to exist.

In arriving at conclusions concerning what problems and/or issues are facing the firm, the student is urged to utilize the framework presented earlier in Stage 1. Recall that Stage 1 involves sorting and classifying all the case information along the various dimensions and their components. The analytical process begun in Stage 2 focuses on those same dimensions from a general management perspective. In effect, the student is trying, throughout Stage 3, to determine what the key problems and/or issues are. The multifunctional nature of the problems and issues in a policy case forces one to abandon any inherent marketing, production, or financial bias, as all matters to be focused on generally will be either Class 1, 2, or 3 in nature.

STAGE 4: FORMULATION OF RECOMMENDATIONS

Once the student is confident that the underlying causes of difficulties and any key decision issues have been pinpointed, he or she is ready to proceed to the recommendations stage. This basically involves the formulation of alternative solutions to the problems identified in Stage 3. It is extremely important for the student to consider more than one possible solution (or set of solutions) to the problems identified. Otherwise, the tendency is to select the first idea that comes to mind and to ignore the fact that there usually are several feasible points of attack and that one's first idea is not necessarily the best approach. Beyond this admonition, there are four equally important points to bear in mind. The recommendations formulated must:

1. Eliminate all problems identified in Stage 3 and resolve all significant issues.
2. Be *feasible*.
3. Avoid the creation of *new* problems in the process of solving old ones.
4. Be *justified*.

The first item needs no elaboration except to say that recommendations must be specific and provide appropriate guides for action. The second point, however, is worth exploring. To begin with, the recommendations must be feasible in a *financial* sense. Students frequently prepare proposals with only one thought in mind: to eliminate the problems or to resolve the issues. Often, however, the recommendations would require large amounts of funds which the firm may not have available. Also, the firm's debt ratio and other indicators of credit worthiness may preclude the obtaining of outside funds. Therefore one must estimate to the extent possible the cost of implementing the proposals; these costs then must be evaluated in light of the firm's financial capabilities.

The recommendations also must be feasible in the *human* sense. This means that not only the necessary quantity and quality of manpower skills must be available, but also that any potential resistance to change must be recognized. For example, the recommendation to fire a company president who is a member of the family who owns controlling interest in a firm may make sense based on a rational assessment of company difficulties; however, its feasibility may be seriously questioned. In such situations, it is necessary to "back off" from the ideal and treat such a phenomenon as a *constraint* on any proposals that may be developed. The student must understand that the ideal solution simply may not be feasible in light of the constraints on the situation. Similarly, all recommendations must be congruent with the value systems of key personnel, a subject covered more fully in Chapter 3.

The student's recommendations must minimize the creation of *new* difficulties in the process of solving old ones. Each proposal must be thoroughly examined not only to establish its effectiveness in solving existing problems but also to establish that no long-run dysfunctional consequences may occur. For example, a recommendation to alter the product mix in light of changing market trends may promise to arrest a previous decline in sales. However, it may be that existing distribution channels and sales methods are inadequate to the new requirements. This illustrates the need to evaluate thoroughly all proposals to determine their effects throughout the organization. In this sense, the process of formulating recommendations should be viewed as iterative in nature, since proposals are continually recycled and refined until the most desirable one is found. Once the most desirable recommendation or set of recommendations is finally developed, the student must *justify* the final proposals, the fourth point listed. Why is the proposal better than the other alternatives considered? On what grounds did the student choose one solution over another?

SUMMARY   This chapter has provided the student with a general framework for the analysis of corporate strategy and policy. It has focused on developing the means for directing one's analysis toward those decisions or problems of most concern to general managers. The remaining chapters and readings provide the student with a great deal of detail on functional area interrelationships and on the integrative, multifunctional nature of top-management decision making. Chapters 2 and 3 discuss the process of strategy formation and evaluation in depth, including consideration of the external and internal forces (and values) that impinge on strategic decisions. Chapters 4, 5, and 6 discuss the major decision variables in finance, marketing and production, respectively, *with emphasis on functional area interrelationships*. Chapter 7 considers the development of organizational structure for the total firm, with emphasis on alternative structural arrangements and their relationship to corporate strategy. Finally, Chapter 8 discusses some behavioral problems that may be encountered when implementing corporate strategy. It is appropriate to emphasize this subject in a separate chapter, since recommendations for problem solution *always* necessitate behavioral change on the part of affected organizational members. Chapter 8 also discusses the overall process of change, various change techniques, and factors commonly associated with resistance to change.

Finally, it should be emphasized that there is no step-by-step approach that will guide students through the analysis of complex policy cases. However, the framework in this chapter should provide some structure for the process. Also, the material in subsequent chapters and in the readings will illuminate potential problem areas by emphasizing total-firm oriented decisions and interactions. It also should restrict analysis in a policy case to matters of general management concern: relating the firm to its environment and coordinating the numerous internal activities in pursuit of overall corporate objectives.

The following reading, "Organizational Strategy, Structure, and Process," will give the student additional insights into the major tasks faced by top management. The authors present a "theoretical framework that managers and students of management can use to analyze an organization as an integrated and dynamic whole—a model that takes into account the interrelationships among strategy, structure, and process."

ORGANIZATIONAL STRATEGY, STRUCTURE, AND PROCESS

Raymond E. Miles
University of California, Berkeley
Charles C. Snow
The Pennsylvania State University
Alan D. Meyer
University of Wisconsin, Milwaukee
Henry J. Coleman, Jr.
University of California, Berkeley

Organizational adaptation is a topic that has received only limited and fragmented theoretical treatment. Any attempt to examine organizational adaptation is difficult, since the process is highly complex and changeable. The proposed theoretical framework deals with alternative ways in which organizations define their product-market domains (strategy) and construct mechanisms (structures and processes) to pursue these strategies. The framework is based on interpretation of existing literature and continuing studies in four industries (college textbook publishing, electronics, food processing, and health care).

An organization is both an articulated purpose and an established mechanism for achieving it. Most organizations engage in an ongoing process of evaluating their purposes—questioning, verifying, and redefining the manner of interaction with their environments. Effective organizations carve out and maintain a viable market for their goods or services. Ineffective organizations fail this market—alignment task. Organizations also constantly modify and refine the mechanism by which they achieve their purposes—rearranging their structure of roles and relationships and their managerial processes. Efficient organizations establish mechanisms that complement their market strategy, but inefficient organizations struggle with these structural and process mechanisms.

For most organizations, the dynamic process of adjusting to environmental change and uncer-

SOURCE: The Academy of Management Review, Vol. III, No. 3, July, 1978. Reprinted by permission.

tainty—*of maintaining an effective alignment with the environment while managing internal interdependencies*—is enormously complex, encompassing myriad decisions and behaviors at several organization levels. But the complexity of the adjustment process can be penetrated: by searching for patterns in the behavior of organizations, one can describe and even predict the process of organizational adaptation. This article presents a theoretical framework that managers and students of management can use to analyze an organization as an integrated and dynamic whole—a model that takes into account the interrelationships among strategy, structure, and process. [For a complete discussion of the theoretical framework and research studies, see (15)]. Specifically, the framework has two major elements: (a) a general model of the process of adaptation which specifies the major decisions needed by the organization to maintain an effective alignment with its environment, and (b) an organizational typology which portrays different patterns of adaptive behavior used by organizations within a given industry or other grouping. But as several theorists have pointed out, organizations are limited in their choices of adaptive behavior to those which top management believes will allow the effective direction and control of human resources (4, 5, 6). Thus the theoretical framework to prevailing theories of management is also related. An increased understanding of the adaptive process, of how organizations move through it, and of the managerial requirements of different adjustment patterns can facilitate the difficult process of achieving an effective organization-environment equilibrium.

In the following sections, a typical example of organizational adaptation drawn from one of our empirical research studies is first presented. Second, a model of the adaptive process that arose from this research is described and discussed. In the third section, four alternative forms of adaptation exhibited by the organizations in our studies are described. Finally, the relationship between the organizational forms and currently available theories of management is discussed.

AN EXAMPLE OF ORGANIZATIONAL ADAPTATION

As an example of the problems associated with the adaptive process, consider the experience of a subsidiary of one of the companies in our studies.

> Porter Pump and Valve (PPV) is a semi-autonomous division of a medium-sized equipment-manufacturing firm, which is in turn part of a large, highly diversified conglomerate. PPV manufactures a line of heavy-duty pumps and components for fluid-movement systems. The company does most of its own castings, makes many of its own parts, and maintains a complete stock of replacement parts. PPV also does special-order foundry work for other firms as its production schedule allows.
>
> Until recently, Porter Pump and Valve had defined its business as providing quality products and service to a limited set of reliable customers. PPV's general manager, a first-rate engineer who spent much of his time in the machine shop and foundry, personified the company's image of quality and cost efficiency. In the mid-seventies corporate management became concerned about both the speed and direction of PPV's growth. The management and staff at corporate headquarters began considering two new product and market opportunities, both in the energy field. Fluid-movement systems required for nuclear power generation provided one of these opportunities, and the development of novel techniques for petroleum exploration, well recovery, and fluid delivery provided the second. PPV had supplied some components to these markets in the past, but it was now clear that opportunities for the sale of entire systems or large-scale subsystems were growing rapidly.
>
> PPV's initial moves toward these new opportunities were tentative. The general manager discovered that contract sales required extensive planning,

field-contact work, and careful negotiations—activities not within his primary area of interest or experience. Finally, in an effort to foster more rapid movement into these new markets, executives in the parent organization transferred the general manager to a head-office position and moved into the top spot at PPV a manager with an extensive background in both sales and engineering and who was adept at large-scale contract negotiations.

Within a year of the changeover in general managers, PPV landed several lucrative contracts, and more appeared to be in the offing. The new business created by these contracts, however, placed heavy coordination demands on company management, and while the organization's technology (production and distribution system) has not been drastically revised over the past two years, workflow processes and the operational responsibilities of several managers have changed markedly. Materials control and scheduling, routine tasks in the past, are now complex activities, and managers of these operations meet regularly with the executive planning committee. Moreover, a rudimentary matrix structure has emerged in which various line managers undertake specific project responsibilities in addition to their regular duties. Key personnel additions have been made to the marketing department and more are planned, with particular emphasis on individuals who are capable of performing field planning and supervising and who can quickly bring new fluid systems to full operation. Budgets of some of the older departments are being cut back, and these funds are being diverted to the new areas of activity.

As illustrated, Porter Pump and Valve experienced changes in its products and markets, in the technological processes needed to make new products and serve new markets, and in the administrative structure and processes required to plan, coordinate, and control the company's new operations. None of the usual perspectives which might be used to analyze such organizational changes—for example, economics, industrial engineering, marketing, or policy—appears to address all of the problems experienced by Porter Pump and Valve. Therefore, how can the adaptive process which occurred at PPV be described in its entirety?

THE ADAPTIVE CYCLE

We have developed a general model of the adaptive process which we call the *adaptive cycle*. Consistent with the strategic-choice approach to the study of organizations, the model parallels and expands ideas formulated by theorists such as Chandler (9), Child (10), Cyert and March (11), Drucker (12, 13) Thompson (18), and Weick (19, 20). Essentially, proponents of the strategic-choice perspective argue that organizational behavior is only partially preordained by environmental conditions and that the choices which top managers make are the critical determinants of organizational structure and process. Although these choices are numerous and complex, they can be viewed as three broad "problems" of organizational adaptation: the entrepreneurial problem, the engineering problem, and the administrative problem. In mature organizations, management must solve each of these problems simultaneously, but for explanatory purposes, these adaptive problems can be discussed as if they occurred sequentially.

The Entrepreneurial Problem

The adaptive cycle, though evident in all organizations, is perhaps most visible in new or rapidly growing organizations (and in organizations which recently have survived a major crisis). In a new organization, an entrepreneurial insight, perhaps only vaguely defined at first, must be developed into a concrete *definition of an organizational domain: a specific good or service and a target market or market segment*. In an ongoing organization, the entrepreneurial problem has an added dimension. Because the organization has already obtained a set of "solutions" to its engineering and administrative problems, its next attempt at an entrepreneurial "thrust" may be difficult. In the example of Porter Pump and Valve, the company's attempt to modify its products and markets was constrained by its present production process and by the fact that the general manager and his staff did not possess the needed marketing orientation.

In either a new or ongoing organization, the solution to the entrepreneurial problem is marked by management's acceptance of a particular product-market domain, and this acceptance becomes evident when management decides to commit resources to achieve objectives relative to the domain. In many organizations, external and internal commitment to the entrepreneurial solution is sought through the development and projection of an organizational "image" which defines both the organization's market and its orientation toward it (e.g., an emphasis on size, efficiency, or innovation).

Although we are suggesting that the engineering phase begins at this point, the need for further entrepreneurial activities clearly does not disappear. The entrepreneurial function remains a top-management responsibility, although as Bower (7) has described, the identification of a new opportunity and the initial impetus for movement toward it may originate at lower managerial levels.

The Engineering Problem

The engineering problem involves the creation of a system which *operationalizes management's solution to the entrepreneurial problem*. Such a system requires management to select an appropriate technology (input-transformation-output process) for producing and distributing chosen products or services and to form new information, communication, and control linkages (or modify existing linkages) to ensure proper operation of the technology.

As solutions to these problems are reached, initial implementation of the administrative system takes place. There is no assurance that the configuration of the organization, as it begins to emerge during this phase, will remain the same when the engineering problem finally has been solved. The actual form of the organization's structure will be determined during the administrative phase as management solidifies relations with the environment and establishes processes for coordinating and controlling internal operations. Referring again to Porter Pump and Valve, the company's redefinition of its domain required concomitant changes in its technology—from a pure mass-production technology to more of a unit or small-batch technology (21).

The Administrative Problem

The administrative problem, as described by most theories of management, is primarily that of reducing uncertainty within the organizational system, or, in terms of the present model, of rationalizing and stabilizing those activities which successfully solved problems faced by the organization during the entrepreneurial and engineering phases. Solving the administrative problem involves more than simply rationalizing the system already developed (uncertainty reduction); it also involves formulating and implementing those processes which will enable the organization to continue to evolve (innovation). This conception of the administrative problem, as a pivotal factor in the cycle of adaptation, deserves further elaboration.

Rationalization and Articulation. In the ideal organization, management would be equally adept at performing two somewhat conflicting functions: it would be able to create an administrative system (structure and processes) that could smoothly direct and monitor the organization's current activities without, at the same time, allowing the system to become so ingrained that future innovation activities are jeopardized. Such a perspective requires the administrative system to be viewed as both a *lagging* and *leading* variable in the process of adaptation. As a lagging variable, it must rationalize, through the development of appropriate structures and processes, strategic decisions made at previous points in the adjustment process. As a leading variable, the administrative system must facilitate the organization's future capacity to adapt by articulating and reinforcing the paths along which innovative activity can proceed. At Porter Pump and Valve, management modified its planning, coordination, and control processes substantially in order to pursue the company's newly chosen areas of business (the "lagging" aspect of administration). At the same time, key personnel were added to the marketing department; their duties included product development, market research, and technical consulting. These activities were designed to keep PPV at the forefront of new product and market opportunities (the "leading" aspect of administration).

THE STRATEGIC TYPOLOGY

If one accepts the adaptive cycle as valid, the question becomes: How do organizations move through the cycle? That is, using the language of our model, what strategies do organizations employ in solving their entrepreneurial, engineering, and administrative problems? Our research and interpretation of the literature show that there are essentially three *strategic types* of organizations: Defenders, Analyzers, and Prospectors. Each type has its own unique strategy for relating to its chosen market(s), and each has a particular configuration of technology, structure, and process that is consistent with its market strategy. A fourth type of organization encountered in our studies is called the Reactor. The Reactor is a form of strategic "failure" in that inconsistencies exist among its strategy, technology, structure, and process.

Although similar typologies of various aspects of organizational behavior are available (1, 2, 3, 15, 16, 17), our formulation specifies relationships among strategy, technology, structure, and process to the point where entire organizations can be viewed as integrated wholes in dynamic interaction with their environments. Any typology is unlikely to encompass every form of organizational behavior—the world of organizations is much too changeable and complex to permit such a claim. Nevertheless, every organization that we have observed appears, when compared to other organizations in its industry, to fit predominantly into one of the four categories, and its behavior is generally predictable given its typological classification. The "pure" form of each of these organization types is described below.

Defenders

The Defender (i.e., its top management) deliberately enacts and maintains an environment for which a stable form of organization is appropriate. Stability is chiefly achieved by the Defender's definition of, and solution to, its entrepreneurial problem. Defenders define their *entrepreneurial* problem as *how to seal off a portion of the total market in order to create a stable domain*, and they do so by producing only a limited set of products directed at a narrow segment of the total potential market. Within this limited domain, the Defender strives aggressively to prevent competitors from entering its "turf." Such behaviors include standard economic actions like competitive pricing or high-quality products, but Defenders also tend to ignore developments and trends outside of their domains, choosing instead to grow through market penetration and perhaps some limited product development. Over time, a true Defender is able to carve out and maintain a small niche within the industry which is difficult for competitors to penetrate.

Having chosen a narrow product-market domain, the Defender invests a great deal of resources in solving its *engineering* problem: *how to produce and distribute goods or services as efficiently as possible*. Typically, the Defender does so by developing a single core technology that is highly cost-efficient. Technological efficiency is central to the Defender's success since its domain has been deliberately created to absorb outputs on a predictable, continuous basis. Some Defenders extend technological efficiency to its limits through a process of vertical integration—incorporating each stage of production from raw materials supply to distribution of final output into the same organizational system.

Finally, the Defender's solution to its administrative problem is closely aligned with its solutions to the entrepreneurial and engineering problems. The Defender's *administrative* problem—*how to achieve strict control of the organization in order to ensure efficiency*—is solved through a combination of structural and process mechanisms that can be generally described as "mechanistic" (8). These mechanisms include a top-management group heavily dominated by production and cost-control specialists, little or no scanning of the environment for new areas of opportunity, intensive planning oriented toward cost and other efficiency issues, functional structures characterized by extensive division of labor, centralized control, communications through formal hierarchical channels, and so on. Such an administrative system is ideally suited for generating and maintaining efficiency, and the key characteristic of stability is as apparent here as in the solution to the other two adaptive problems.

Pursued vigorously, the Defender strategy can be viable in most industries, although stable industries lend themselves to this type of organization more than turbulent industries (e.g., the relative lack of technological change in the food-processing industry generally favors the Defender strategy compared with the situation in the electronics industry). This particular form of organization is not without its potential risks. The Defender's *primary risk* is that of *ineffectiveness*—being unable to respond to a major shift in its market environment. The Defender relies on the continued viability of its single, narrow domain, and it receives a return on its large technological investment only if the major problems facing the organization continue to be of an engineering nature. If the Defender's market shifts dramatically, this type of organization has little capacity for locating and exploiting new areas of opportunity. In short, the Defender is perfectly capable of responding to today's world. To the extent that tomorrow's world is similar to today's, the Defender is ideally suited for its environment. Table 1 summarizes the Defender's salient characteristics and the major strengths and weaknesses inherent in this pattern of adaptation.

Prospectors

In many ways, Prospectors respond to their chosen environments in a manner that is almost the opposite of the Defender. In one sense, the Prospector is exactly like the Defender: there is a high degree of consistency among its solutions to the three problems of adaptation.

Generally speaking, the Prospector enacts an environment that is more dynamic than those of other types of organizations within the same industry. Unlike the Defender, whose success comes primarily from efficiently serving a stable domain, the Prospector's prime capability is that of finding and exploiting new product and market opportunities. For a Prospector, maintaining a reputation as an innovator in product and market development may be as important as, perhaps even more important, than high profitability. In fact, because of the inevitable "failure rate" associated with sustained product and market innovation, Prospectors may find it difficult consistently to attain the profit levels of the more efficient Defender.

Defining its *entrepreneurial* problem as *how to locate and develop product and market opportunities*, the Prospector's domain is usually broad and in a continuous state of development. The systematic addition of new products or markets, frequently combined with retrenchment in other parts of the domain, gives the Prospector's products and markets an aura of fluidity uncharacteristic of the Defender. To locate new areas of opportunity, the Prospector must develop and

Table 1 Characteristics of the Defender

Entrepreneurial Problem	Engineering Problem	Administrative Problem
Problem How to "seal off" a portion of the total market to create a stable set of products and customers.	**Problem** How to produce and distribute goods or services as efficiently as possible.	**Problem** How to maintain strict control of the organization in order to ensure efficiency.
Solutions 1. Narrow and stable domain. 2. Aggressive maintenance of domain (e.g., competitive pricing and excellent customer service). 3. Tendency to ignore developments outside of domain. 4. Cautious and incremental growth primarily through market penetration. 5. Some product development but closely related to current goods or services.	**Solutions** 1. Cost-efficient technology. 2. Single core technology. 3. Tendency toward vertical integration. 4. Continuous improvements in technology to maintain efficiency.	**Solutions** 1. Financial and production experts most powerful members of the dominant coalition; limited environmental scanning. 2. Tenure of dominant coalition is lengthy; promotions from within. 3. Planning is intensive, cost oriented, and completed before action is taken. 4. Tendency toward functional structure with extensive division of labor and high degree of formalization. 5. Centralized control and long-looped vertical information systems. 6. Simple coordination mechanisms and conflict resolved through hierarchical channels. 7. Organizational performance measured against previous years, reward system favors production and finance.
Costs and Benefits It is difficult for competitors to dislodge the organization from its small niche in the industry, but a major shift in the market could threaten survival.	**Costs and Benefits** Technological efficiency is central to organizational performance, but heavy investment in this area requires technological problems to remain familiar and predictable for lengthy periods of time.	**Costs and Benefits** Administrative system is ideally suited to maintain stability and efficiency but it is not well suited to locating and responding to new product or market opportunities.

SOURCE: Raymond E. Miles and Charles C. Snow, *Organizational Strategy, Structure, and Process* (New York: McGraw-Hill, 1978) Table 3-1.

maintain the capacity to survey a wide range of environmental conditions, trends, and events. This type of organization invests heavily in individuals and groups who scan the environment for potential opportunities. Because these scanning activities are not limited to the organization's current domain, Prospectors are frequently the creators of change in their respective industries.

Change is one of the major tools used by the Prospector to gain an edge over competitors, so Prospector managers typically perceive more environmental change and uncertainty than managers of the Defender (or the other two organization types).

To serve its changing domain properly, the Prospector requires a good deal of flexibility in its technology and administrative system. Unlike the Defender, the Prospector's choice of products and markets is not limited to those which fall within the range of the organization's present technological capability. The Prospector's technology is contingent upon both the organization's current *and* future product mix: entrepreneurial activities always have primacy, and appropriate technologies are not selected or developed until late in the process of product development. Therefore, the Prospector's overall engineering problem is *how to avoid long-term commitments to a single type of technological process*, and the organization usually does so by creating multiple, prototypical technologies which have a low degree of routinization and mechanization.

Finally, the Prospector's *administrative* problem flows from its changing domain and flexible technologies: *how to facilitate rather than control organizational operations*. That is, the Prospector's administrative system must be able to deploy and coordinate resources among numerous decentralized units and projects rather than to plan and control the operations of the entire organization centrally. To accomplish overall facilitation and coordination, the Prospector's structure-process mechanisms must be "organic" (8). These mechanisms include a top-management group dominated by marketing and research and development experts, planning that is broad rather than intensive and oriented toward results not methods, product or project structures characterized by a low degree of formalization, decentralized control, lateral as well as vertical communications, and so on. In contrast to the Defender, the Prospector's descriptive catchword throughout its administrative as well as entrepreneurial and engineering solutions is "flexibility."

Of course, the Prospector strategy also has its costs. Although the Prospector's continuous exploration of change helps to protect it from a changing environment, this type of organization runs the *primary risk of low profitability and overextension of resources*. While the Prospector's technological flexibility permits a rapid response to a changing domain, complete efficiency cannot be obtained because of the presence of multiple technologies. Finally, the Prospector's administrative system is well suited to maintain flexibility, but it may, at least temporarily, underutilize or even misutilize physical, financial, and human resources. In short, the Prospector is effective—it can respond to the demands of tomorrow's world. To the extent that the world of tomorrow is similar to that of today, the Prospector cannot maximize profitability because of its inherent inefficiency. Table 2 summarizes the Prospector's salient characteristics and the major strengths and weaknesses associated with this pattern of adaptation.

Analyzers

Based on our research, the Defender and the Prospector seem to reside at opposite ends of a continuum of adjustment strategies. Between these two extremes, a third type of organization is called the Analyzer. The Analyzer is a unique combination of the Prospector and Defender types and represents a viable alternative to these other strategies. A true Analyzer is an organization that attempts to minimize risk while maximizing the opportunity for profit—that is, an experienced Analyzer combines the strengths of both the Prospector and the Defender into a single system. This strategy is difficult to pursue, particularly in industries characterized by rapid market and technological change, and thus the word that best describes the Analyzer's adaptive approach is "balance."

The Analyzer defines its *entrepreneurial* problem in terms similar to both the Prospector and

Table 2 Characteristics of the Prospector

Entrepreneurial Problem	Engineering Problem	Administrative Problem
Problem How to locate and exploit new product and market opportunities.	**Problem** How to avoid long term commitments to a single technological process.	**Problem** How to facilitate and coordinate numerous and diverse operations.
Solutions 1. Broad and continuously developing domain. 2. Monitors wide range of environmental conditions and events. 3. Creates change in the industry. 4. Growth through product and market development. 5. Growth may occur in spurts.	**Solutions** 1. Flexible, prototypical technologies. 2. Multiple technologies. 3. Low degree of routinization and mechanization; technology embedded in people.	**Solutions** 1. Marketing and research and development experts most powerful members of the dominant coalition. 2. Dominant coalition is large, diverse, and transitory, may include an inner circle. 3. Tenure of dominant coalition not always lengthy; key managers may be hired from outside as well as promoted from within. 4. Planning is comprehensive, problem oriented, and cannot be finalized before action is taken. 5. Tendency toward product structure with low division of labor and low degree of formalization. 6. Decentralized control and short-looped horizontal information systems. 7. Complex coordination mechanisms and conflict resolved through integrators. 8. Organizational performance measured against important competitors; reward system favors marketing and research and development.
Costs and Benefits: Product and market innovation protect the organization from a changing environment, but the organization runs the risk of low profitability and overextension of its resources.	**Costs and Benefits:** Technological flexibility permits a rapid response to a changing domain, but the organization cannot develop maximum efficiency in its production and distribution system because of multiple technologies.	**Costs and Benefits:** Administrative system is ideally suited to maintain flexibility and effectiveness but may underutilize and misutilize resources.

SOURCE: Raymond E. Miles and Charles C. Snow, *Organizational Strategy, Structure, and Process* (New York: McGraw-Hill, 1978), Table 4–1.

the Defender: *how to locate and exploit new product and market opportunities while simultaneously maintaining a firm core of traditional products and customers.* The Analyzer's solution to the entrepreneurial problem is also a blend of the solutions preferred by the Prospector and the Defender: the Analyzer moves toward new products or new markets but only after their viability has been demonstrated. This periodic transformation of the Analyzer's domain is accomplished through imitation—only the most successful product or market innovations developed by prominent Prospectors are adopted. At the same time, the majority of the Analyzer's revenue is generated by a fairly stable set of products and customer or client groups—a Defender characteristic. Thus, the successful Analyzer must be able to respond quickly when following the lead of key Prospectors while at the same time maintaining operating efficiency in its stable product and market areas. To the extent that it is successful, the Analyzer can grow through market penetration as well as product and market development.

The duality evident in the Analyzer's domain is reflected in its *engineering* problem and solution. This type of organization must learn *how to achieve and protect an equilibrium between conflicting demands for technological flexibility and for technological stability*. This equilibrium is accomplished by partitioning production activities to form a dual technological core. The stable component of the Analyzer's technology bears a strong resemblance to the Defender's technology. It is functionally organized and exhibits high levels of standardization, routinization, and mechanization in an attempt to approach cost efficiency. The Analyzer's flexible technological component resembles the Prospector's technological orientation. In manufacturing organizations, it frequently includes a large group of applications engineers (or their equivalent) who are rotated among teams charged with the task of rapidly adapting new product designs to fit the Analyzer's existing stable technology.

The Analyzer's dual technological core thus reflects the engineering solutions of both the Prospector and the Defender, with the stable and flexible components integrated primarily by an influential applied research group. To the extent that this group is able to develop solutions that match the organization's existing technological capabilities with the new products desired by product managers, the Analyzer can enlarge its product line without incurring the Prospector's extensive research and development expenses.

The Analyzer's administrative problem, as well as its entrepreneurial and engineering problems, contains both Defender and Prospector characteristics. Generally speaking, the *administrative* problem of the Analyzer is *how to differentiate the organization's structure and processes to accommodate both stable and dynamic areas of operation*. The Analyzer typically solves this problem with some version of a matrix organization structure. Heads of key functional units, most notably engineering and production, unite with product managers (usually housed in the marketing department) to form a balanced dominant coalition similar to both the Defender and the Prospector. The product manager's influence is usually greater than the functional manager's since his or her task is to identify promising product-market innovations and to supervise their movement through applied engineering and into production in a smooth and timely manner. The presence of engineering and production in the dominant coalition is to represent the more stable domain and technology which are the foundations of the Analyzer's overall operations. The Analyzer's matrix structure is supported by intensive planning between the functional divisions of marketing and production, broad-gauge planning between the applied research group and the product managers for the development of new products, centralized control mechanisms in the functional divisions and decentralized control techniques in the product groups, and so on. In sum, the key characteristic of the Analyzer's administrative system is the proper differentiation of the organization's structure and processes to achieve a balance between the stable and dynamic areas of operation.

As is true for both the Defender and Prospector, the Analyzer strategy is not without its costs. The duality in the Analyzer's domain forces the organization to establish a dual technological core, and it requires management to operate fundamentally different planning, control, and reward systems simultaneously. Thus, the Analyzer's twin characteristics of stability and flexibility limit the organization's ability to move fully in either direction were the domain to shift dramatically. Consequently, the Analyzer's *primary risks* are both *inefficiency and ineffectiveness* if it does not maintain the necessary balance throughout its strategy-structure relationship. Table 3 summarizes the Analyzer's salient characteristics and the major strengths and weaknesses inherent in this pattern of adaptation.

Reactors

The Defender, the Prospector, and the Analyzer can all be proactive with respect to their environments, though each is proactive in a different way. At the extremes, Defenders continually attempt to develop greater efficiency in existing operations while Prospectors explore environmental change in search of new opportunities. Over time, these action modes stabilize to form a pattern of response to environmental conditions that is both *consistent* and *stable*.

A fourth type of organization, the Reactor, exhibits a pattern of adjustment to its environment that is both *inconsistent* and *unstable*; this type lacks a set of response mechanisms which it can consistently put into effect when faced with a changing environment. As a consequence, Reactors exist in a state of almost perpetual instability. The Reactor's "adaptive" cycle usually consists of responding inappropriately to environmental change and uncertainty, performing poorly as a result, and then being reluctant to act aggressively in the future. Thus, the Reactor is a "residual" strategy, arising when one of the other three strategies is improperly pursued.

Although there are undoubtedly many reasons why organizations become Reactors, we have identified three. First, *top management may not have clearly articulated the organization's strategy*. For example, one company was headed by a "one-man" Prospector of immense personal skills. A first-rate architect, he led his firm through a rapid and successful growth period during which the company moved from the design and construction of suburban shopping centers, through the construction and management of apartment complexes, and into consulting with municipal agencies concerning urban planning problems. Within ten years of its inception, the company was a loose but effective collection of semi-autonomous units held together by this particular individual. When this individual was suddenly killed in a plane crash, the company was thrown into a strategic void. Because each separate unit of the company was successful, each was able to argue strongly for more emphasis on its particular domain and operations. Consequently, the new chief executive officer, caught between a number of conflicting but legitimate demands for resources, was unable to develop a unified, cohesive statement of the organization's strategy; thus, consistent and aggressive behavior was precluded.

A second and perhaps more common cause of organizational instability is that *management does not fully shape the organization's structure and processes to fit a chosen strategy*. Unless all of the domain, technological, and administrative decisions required to have an operational strategy are properly aligned, strategy is a mere statement, not an effective guide to behavior. One publishing company wished, in effect, to become an Analyzer—management had articulated a direction for the organization which involved operating in both stable and changing domains within the college textbook publishing industry. Although the organization was comprised of several key Defender and Prospector characteristics

Table 3 Characteristics of the Analyzer

Entrepreneurial Problem	Engineering Problem	Administrative Problem
Problem 　How to locate and exploit new product and market opportunities while simultaneously maintaining a firm base of traditional products and customers.	Problem 　How to be efficient in stable portions of the domain and flexible in changing portions.	Problem 　How to differentiate the organization's structure and processes to accommodate both stable and dynamic areas of operation.
Solutions 1. Hybrid domain that is both stable and changing. 2. Surveillance mechanisms mostly limited to marketing; some research and development. 3. Steady growth through market penetration and product-market development.	Solutions 1. Dual technological core (stable and flexible component). 2. Large and influential applied engineering group. 3. Moderate degree of technical rationality.	Solutions 1. Marketing and engineering most influential members of dominant coalition, followed closely by production. 2. Intensive planning between marketing and production concerning stable portion of domain; comprehensive planning among marketing, engineering, and product managers concerning new products and markets. 3. "Loose" matrix structure combining both functional divisions and product groups. 4. Moderately centralized control system with vertical and horizontal feedback loops. 5. Extremely complex and expensive coordination mechanisms; some conflict resolution through product managers, some through normal hierarchical channels. 6. Performance appraisal based on both effectiveness and efficiency measures, most rewards to marketing and engineering.
Costs and Benefits: 　Low investment in research and development, combined with imitation of demonstrably successful products, minimizes risk, but domain must be optimally balanced at all times between stability and flexibility.	Costs and Benefits: 　Dual technological core is able to serve a hybrid stable-changing domain, but the technology can never be completely effective or efficient.	Costs and Benefits: 　Administrative system is ideally suited to balance stability and flexibility, but if this balance is lost, it may be difficult to restore equilibrium.

SOURCE: Raymond E. Miles and Charles C. Snow, *Organizational Strategy, Structure, and Process* (New York: McGraw-Hill, 1978), Table 5-1.

such as functional structures and decentralized control mechanisms, these structure-process features were not appropriately linked to the company's different domains. In one area where the firm wished to "prospect," for example, the designated unit had a functional structure and shared a large, almost mass-production technology with several other units, thereby making it difficult for the organization to respond to market opportunities quickly. Thus, this particular organization exhibited a weak link between its strategy and its structure-process characteristics.

The third cause of instability—and perhaps ultimate failure—is a *tendency for management to maintain the organization's current strategy-structure relationship despite overwhelming changes in environmental conditions*. Another organization in our studies, a food-processing company, had initially been an industry pioneer in both the processing and marketing of dried fruits and nuts. Gradually, the company settled into a Defender strategy and took vigorous steps to bolster this strategy, including limiting the domain to a narrow line of products, integrating backward into growing and harvesting, and assigning a controller to each of the company's major functional divisions as a means of keeping costs down. Within recent years, the company's market has become saturated, and profit margins have shrunk on most of the firm's products. In spite of its declining market, the organization has consistently clung to a Defender strategy and structure, even to the point of creating ad hoc cross-divisional committees whose sole purpose was to find ways of increasing efficiency further. At the moment, management recognizes that the organization is in trouble, but it is reluctant to make the drastic modifications required to attain a strategy and structure better suited to the changing market conditions.

Unless an organization exists in a "protected" environment such as a monopolistic or highly-regulated industry, it cannot continue to behave as a Reactor indefinitely. Sooner or later, it must move toward one of the consistent and stable strategies of Defender, Analyzer, or Prospector.

MANAGEMENT THEORY LINKAGES TO ORGANIZATIONAL STRATEGY AND STRUCTURE

Organizations are limited in their choices of adaptive behavior to those which top management believes will allow the effective direction and control of human resources. Therefore, top executives' theories of management are an important factor in analyzing an organization's ability to adapt to its environment. Although our research is only in its preliminary stage, we have found some patterns in the relationship between management theory and organizational strategy and structure.

A theory of management has three basic components: (a) a set of assumptions about human attitudes and behaviors, (b) managerial policies and actions consistent with these assumptions, and (c) expectations about employee performance if these policies and actions are implemented (see Table 4). Theories of management are discussed in more detail in Miles (14).

During the latter part of the 19th Century and the early decades of the 20th, mainstream management theory, as voiced by managers and by management scholars, conformed to what has been termed the *Traditional* model. Essentially, the Traditional model maintained that the capability for effective decision making was narrowly distributed in organizations, and this approach thus legitimized unilateral control of organizational systems by top management. According to this model, a select group of owner-managers was able to direct large numbers of employees by carefully standardizing and routinizing their work and by placing the planning function solely in the hands of top managers. Under this type of management system, employees could be expected to perform up to some minimum standard, but few would be likely to exhibit truly outstanding performance.

Beginning in the twenties, the Traditional model gradually began to give way to the *Human Relations* model. This model accepted the traditional notion that superior decision-making competence was narrowly distributed among the

Table 4 Theories of Management

Traditional Model	Human Relations Model	Human Resources Model
Assumptions	**Assumptions**	**Assumptions**
1. Work is inherently distasteful to most people.	1. People want to feel useful and important.	1. Work is not inherently distasteful. People want to contribute to meaningful goals which they have helped establish.
2. What workers do is less important than what they earn for doing it.	2. People desire to belong and to be recognized as individuals.	2. Most people can exercise far more creative, responsible self-direction and self-control than their present jobs demand.
3. Few want or can handle work which requires creativity, self-direction, or self-control.	3. These needs are more important than money in motivating people to work.	
Policies	**Policies**	**Policies**
1. The manager's basic task is to closely supervise and control his (her) subordinates.	1. The manager's basic task is to make each worker feel useful and important.	1. The manager's basic task is to make use of his (her) "untapped" human resources.
2. He (she) must break tasks down into simple, repetitive, easily learned operations.	2. He (she) should keep his (her) subordinates informed and listen to their objections to his (her) plans.	2. He (she) must create an environment in which all members may contribute to the limits of their ability.
3. He (she) must establish detailed work routines and procedures and enforce these firmly but fairly.	3. The manager should allow his (her) subordinates to exercise some self-direction and self-control on routine matters.	3. He (she) must encourage full participation on important matters, continually broadening subordinate self-direction and control.
Expectations	**Expectations**	**Expectations**
1. People can tolerate work if the pay is decent and the boss is fair.	1. Sharing information with subordinates and involving them in routine decisions will satisfy their basic needs to belong and to feel important.	1. Expanding subordinate influence, self-direction, and self-control will lead to direct improvements in organizational performance.
2. If tasks are simple enough and people are closely controlled, they will produce up to standard.	2. Satisfying these needs will improve morale and reduce resistance to formal authority—subordinates will willingly cooperate and produce.	2. Work satisfaction may improve as a "by-product" of subordinates making full use of their resources.

SOURCE: Raymond E. Miles, *Theories of Management* (New York: McGraw-Hill, 1975), Figure 3–1.

employee population but emphasized the universality of social needs for belonging and recognition. This model argued that impersonal treatment was the source of subordinate resistance to managerial directives, and adherents of this approach urged managers to employ devices to enhance organization members' feelings of involvement and importance in order to improve organizational performance. Suggestion systems, employee counseling, and even company unions had common parentage in this philosophy. The Depression and World War II both acted to delay the development and spread of the Human Relations model, and it was not until the late forties and early fifties that it became the prime message put forth by managers and management scholars.

Beginning in the mid-fifties, a third phase in the evolution of management theory began with the emergence of the *Human Resources* model which argued that the capacity for effective decision making in the pursuit of organizational objectives was widely dispersed and that most organization members represented untapped resources which, if properly managed, could considerably enhance organizational performance. The Human Resources approach viewed management's role not as that of a controller (however benevolent) but as that of a facilitator—removing the constraints that block organization members' search for ways to contribute meaningfully in their work roles. In recent years, some writers have questioned the extent to which the Human Resources model is applicable, arguing for a more "contingent" theory emphasizing variations in member capacity and motivation to contribute and the technological constraints associated with broadened self-direction and self-control. The Human Resources model probably still represents the leading edge of managment theory, perhaps awaiting the formulation of a successor model.

Linking the Strategic Typology to Mangement Theory

Are there identifiable linkages between an organization's strategic type and the management theory of its dominant coalition? For example, do top executives in Defenders profess Traditional beliefs about management and those in Prospectors a Human Resources philosophy? The answer to this question is, in our opinion, a bit more complex than simply "yes" or "no."

One of our studies investigated aspects of the relationship between organizational strategy-structure and management theory. Although the results are only tentative at this point, relatively clear patterns emerged. In general, Traditional and Human Relations managerial beliefs are more likely to be found in Defender and Reactor organizations, while Human Resources beliefs are more often associated with Analyzer and Prospector organizations. But this relationship appears to be *constrained in one direction*; it seems highly unlikely that a Traditional or Human Relations manager can function effectively as the head of a Prospector organization. The prescriptions of the Traditional model simply do not support the degree of decentralized decision making required to create and manage diversified organizations. It is quite possible for a Human Resources manager to lead a Defender organization. Of course, the organization's planning and control processes under such leadership would be less centralized than if the organization were managed according to the Traditional model. Using the Human Resources philosophy, heads of functional divisions might either participate in the planning and budgeting process, or they might simply be delegated considerable autonomy in operating their cost centers. (In Defender organizations operated according to the Human Resources philosophy, human capabilities are aimed primarily at cost efficiency rather than product development.)

The fit between management theory and the strategy, structure, and process characteristics of Analyzers is perhaps more complex than with any of the other types. Analyzer's as previously described, tend to remain cost efficient in the production of a limited line of goods or services while attempting to move as rapidly as possible into promising new areas opened up by Prospectors. Note that the organization structure of the Analyzer does not demand extensive, permanent delegation of decision-making authority to division managers. Most of the Analyzer's products or services can be produced in functionally structured divisions similar to those in Defender organizations. New products or services may be developed in separate divisions or departments created for that purpose and then integrated as quickly as possible into the permanent technology and structure. It seems likely to us, although our evidence is inconclusive, that various members of the dominant coalition in Analyzer organizations hold moderate but different managerial philosophies, that certain key executives believe it is their role to pay fairly close attention to detail while others appear to be more willing to delegate, for short periods, moderate amounts of autonomy necessary to bring new products or services on line rapidly. If these varying managerial philosophies are "mismatched" within the Analyzer's operating units—if, for example, Traditional managers are placed in charge of innovative subunits—then it is unlikely that a successful Analyzer strategy can be pursued.

Holding together a dominant coalition with mixed views concerning strategy and structure is not an easy task. It is difficult, for example, for managers engaged in new product or service development to function within planning, control, and reward systems established for more stable operations, so the Analyzer must be successfully differentiated into its stable and changing areas and managed accordingly. Note that experimentation in the Analyzer is usually quite limited. The exploration and risk associated with major product or service breakthroughs are not present (as would be the case in a Prospector), and thus interdependencies within the system may be kept at a manageable level. Such would not be the case if Analyzers attempted to be both cost-efficient producers of stable products or services and active in a major way in new product and market development. Numerous organizations are today being led or forced into such a mixed strategy (multinational companies, certain forms of conglomerates, many organizations in high-technology industries, etc.), and their struggles may well produce a new organization type and demands for a supporting theory of management. Whatever form this new type of organization takes, however, clearly its management-theory requirements will closely parallel or extend those of the Human Resources model (15).

CONCLUSIONS

Our research represents an initial attempt: (a) to portray the major elements of organizational adaptation, (b) to describe patterns of behavior used by organizations in adjusting to their environments, and (c) to provide a language for discussing organizational behavior at the total-system level. Therefore, we have offered a theoretical framework composed of a model of the adaptive process (called the adaptive cycle) and four empirically determined means of moving through this process (the strategic typology). In addition, we have related this theoretical framework to available theories of management (Traditional, Human Relations, Human Resources). Effective organizational adaptation hinges on the ability of managers to not only envision and implement new organizational forms but also to direct and control people within them.

We believe that managers' ability to meet successfully environmental conditions of tomorrow revolves around their understanding of organizations as integrated and dynamic wholes. Hopefully, our framework offers a theory and language for promoting such an understanding.

REFERENCES

1. Anderson, Carl R., and Frank T. Paine. "Managerial Perceptions and Strategic Behavior." *Academy of Management Journal*, Vol. 18 (1975), 811–823.

2. Ansoff, H. Igor. *Corporate Strategy* (New York: McGraw-Hill, 1965).

3. Ansoff, H. Igor, and Richard Brandenburg. "A Language for Organizational Design," *Management Science* Vol. 17 (1971), B717–B731.

4. Ansoff, H. Igor, and John M. Stewart. "Strategies for a Technology-Based Business," *Harvard Business Review*, Vol. 45 (1967), 71–83.

5. Argyris, Chris. "On Organizations of the Future," *Administrative and Policy Study Series*, Vol. 1, No. 03-006 (Beverly Hlls, Calif.: Sage Publications, 1973).

6. Beer, Michael and Stanley M. Davis. "Creating a Global Organization: Failures Along the Way." *Columbia Journal of World Business*, Vol. 11 (1976), 72–84.

7. Bower, Joseph L. *Managing the Resource Allocation Process* (Boston: Division of Research, Harvard Business School, 1970).

8. Burns, Tom, and G. M. Stalker. *The Management of Innovation* (London: Tavistock, 1961).
9. Chandler, Alfred D., Jr. *Strategy and Structure* (Garden City, N. Y.: Doubleday, 1962).
10. Child, John. "Organizational Structure, Environment, and Performance—The Role of Strategic Choice," *Sociology*, Vol. 6 (1972), 1–22.
11. Cyert, Richard, and James G. March. *A Behavioral Theory of the Firm* (Englewood Cliffs, N. J.: Prentice-Hall, 1963).
12. Drucker, Peter F. *The Practice of Management* (New York: Harper & Brothers, 1954).
13. Drucker, Peter F. *Management: Tasks, Responsibilities, Practices* (New York: Harper & Row, 1974).
14. Miles, Raymond E. *Theories of Management* (New York: McGraw-Hill, 1975).
15. Miles, Raymond E., and Charles C. Snow. *Organizational Strategy, Structure, and Process* (New York: McGraw-Hill, 1978).
16. Rogers, Everett M. *Communication of Innovations: A Cross-Cultural Approach*, 2nd ed. (New York: Free Press, 1971).
17. Segal, Morley. "Organization and Environment: A Typology of Adaptability and Structure," *Public Administration Review*, Vol. 35 (1974), 212–220.
18. Thompson, James. D. *Organizations in Action* (New York: McGraw-Hill, 1967).
19. Weick, Karl E. *The Social Psychology of Organizing* (Reading, Mass.: Addison-Wesley, 1969).
20. Weick, Karl E. "Enactment Processes in Organizations," in Barry M. Staw and Gerald R. Salancik (Eds.), *New Directions in Organizational Behavior* (Chicago: St. Clair, 1977), pp. 267–300.
21. Woodward, Joan. *Industrial Organization: Theory and Practice* (London: Oxford University Press, 1965).

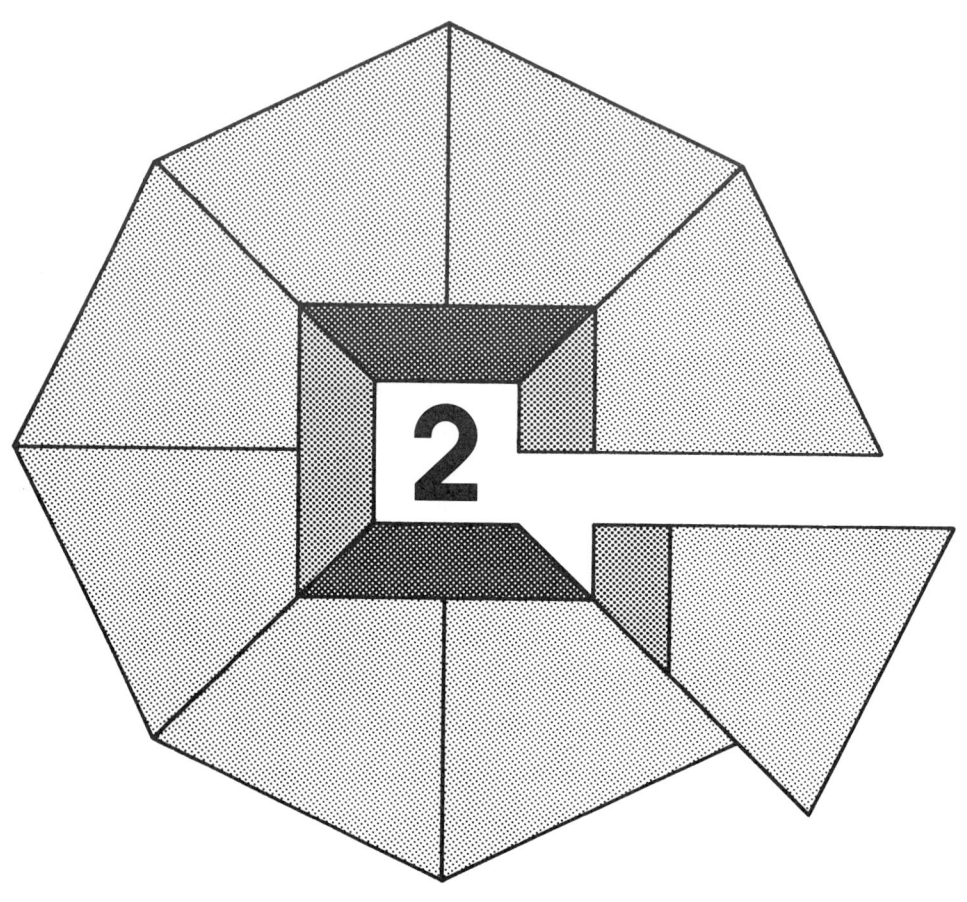

STRATEGIC DECISIONS
the impact of environmental forces

Chapter 1 has delineated the elements of a comprehensive scheme for the analysis of corporate strategy and policy cases. This chapter explores the concept of strategy formulation and the numerous variables relevant to that process in more detail and thus focuses on the strategic decision class (C_1) referred to briefly in Chapter 1. It clarifies the somewhat ambiguous notion of strategy and provides an understanding of the numerous factors involved in strategy formulation.

THE CONCEPT OF STRATEGY

Strategy can be defined in many ways. As generally used, the term refers to the overall purposes, goals, and scope of a firm's operations. There is a tendency to attach identical meanings to the words "strategic" and "important." Just because a decision is important to the success of a firm, however, does not mean that it is necessarily an element of the firm's overall strategy. What is needed is a conceptualization of the strategy phenomenon that will enable one to consistently distinguish strategic decisions from other types, regardless of the particular firm being examined.

What then is a strategic decision? The issue may be clarified by understanding the purpose of strategy—to define the nature of the relationship between a firm and its environment and to specify the types of businesses to be engaged in by the firm. Given this comprehensive definition, it is possible to identify the five key decisions that comprise the overall strategy of any firm.

1. Customer mix.
2. Product mix.
3. Geographic limits of the market to be served.
4. Competitive emphasis.
5. Objectives (performance criteria).

Each decision will be discussed in more detail later. However, it is important to emphasize that these decisions are formulative, not implemental. They *define* the nature of the firm's relationship to its environment but do not indicate *how* the relationship will be effectuated. They are the "first-order" decisions of any firm and, once clearly delineated, provide direction to lower-order implemental considerations in production, marketing, finance, research and development, engineering, and other areas. Consequently, very important decisions on channels of distribution, methods of financing, pricing, resource allocation, type of production process, and similar matters are not regarded as a part of a firm's strategy. As discussed shortly, these and other considerations greatly influence strategy and help determine its nature; however, they are only *inputs* to the definition of strategy through an iterative, analytical process of decision making. Before moving to the subject of strategy determinants, a more detailed look at the strategic decisions themselves is necessary.

The Strategic Decisions

The five basic strategic decision areas are obviously interrelated. For example, a definition of the customer mix (target group[s] of customers) of the firm cannot be accomplished without deciding on the product mix, and vice versa. *Similarly, quantifiable objectives concerning desired profitability, growth, and market share cannot be formulated independently of decisions on the other elements of strategy, simply because what may be a feasible objective in some industries may not be in others.* Note that the term "objectives" is not used here to refer to general, nonoperational types of statements—for example, "maximize profits," "become the leader in the industry." Instead, the term is used to refer to measurable performance criteria that can operationalize subunit or functional area objectives as well as serve as evaluation criteria in assessing the degree of success of a firm's strategy. With the exception of a new firm just beginning operations, it is impossible for the setting of objectives to precede the determination of the product mix and the other elements of strategy just indicated. Established firms are generally constrained by physical, human, and financial resources that limit the setting of feasible objectives independently of their influence. For example, it probably would be unrealistic for a food retailer to establish a profit margin objective of 10% on sales when the characteristics of the industry are such as to preclude, at the present time, a margin of much over 2 or 3%. On the other hand, in the dynamic electronics industry a much larger margin is generally the case and is essential for continued investment in new product development. Thus we must recognize that the development of corporate strategy is an iterative, interdependent process, not a sequential one.

In one instance, a particular and unique resource base possessed by a firm (i.e., the competitive advantage that is stressed by the firm—perhaps its product design ingenuity) may be the major influence on a decision to enter a new product market, given a reasonable projection of potential volume. Another firm, however, may consider entering a new market because of the overwhelming opportunities that exist in terms of perceived consumer needs and only later attempt to develop a unique competitive advantage. In the first instance, we see that the determination of competitive advantage was *followed* by a change in the product and customer mixes of the firm, while in the second instance the reverse was true. Consequently, it is impossible to state that the determination of one element of strategy precedes the determination of another. The process is not simple; it is not subject to an explicit sequence of decisions, nor is it susceptible to a generic algorithm. The decisions are made in a complex and iterative process characterized by much subjective evaluation. In this sense we reason that it is better to approach such a complex and ambiguous problem area with some structure for analysis than with none at all. Recognizing these limitations, this chapter and the following one provide such a framework for analysis.

A useful starting point in building this overall framework is the identification of the *specific* decisions that must be made with respect to the five major components of strategy. These decisions are listed here in the form of questions that any firm must answer in determining its strategy.

What is our target group(s) of customers? What are their needs and wants? What segmentation criteria appear to be appropriate? What geographic market areas will we cover? What will be our market niche(s)?

What specific products, or services, should we produce? Which products will receive the greatest emphasis? What will be the price/quality relationships of our various lines? What are the basic characteristics of the products? Can the characteristics be differentiated from those of similar products offered by our competitors? What end uses do the products serve? At what point in time should new products be introduced?

What factor(s) will we stress to provide us with a unique competitive advantage? Is it our price? Quality? Service? Design? Differentiated product? Other? What can we do better than our competitors?

What are our basic objectives? What return on investment (ROI) do we seek? What should be our profit margin on sales? What are our growth objectives with regard to total assets, total sales, net worth, or number of employees? What share of the market do we seek and in what time period? What is the minimum return we must achieve to avoid liquidation and/or redeployment of our assets?

As will be seen later, there are many factors to be assessed (both externally and internally) before a firm can ever begin to answer these questions or before it can ever finally decide on its basic strategy. Note, however, that answers to these questions define specifically the product mix, customer mix, geographic limits of the market, competitive emphasis, and objectives of the firm. In general, the total set answers the overall question "What business are we in?" The firm then has, in effect, defined the relationship desired between itself and the environment. It then can focus on implementation considerations, which are concerned with *how* to achieve the corporate strategy. Final decisions on financing methods, supplier sources, marketing programs, production processes, organization structure, control systems, and so forth can be effected *only* after decisions are reached on the basic strategy. As will be seen later, such considerations are obviously analyzed before the final strategy is developed to ensure its feasibility. We should not let this fact distort the basic notion that the implementation of strategy follows its formulation.

Determinants of Strategy

As mentioned, the process of strategy formulation is extremely complex and iterative, involving consideration of numerous external and internal forces that impinge on the five basic decision areas. The process basically involves a *matching of external opportunities and constraints with internal values and capabilities at an acceptable level of economic and personal risk.*[1] The

---

[1]The inspiration for this concise description of the process is derived from C. R. Christensen, K. R. Andrews, and J. L. Bower's discussion of the concept of corporate strategy. See Christensen et al., *Business Policy: Text and Cases* (Homewood, Ill.: Richard D. Irwin, 1973), pp. 107–111.

four major components of the strategy formulation process are readily identifiable: (1) external opportunities, (2) external constraints, (3) internal capabilities, and (4) personal values, including propensity to assume risk. The environment, composed of economic, social, technological, and political/legal sectors, presents various opportunities to the firm. However, the firm's capabilities (human, physical, and financial resources) limit the extent to which it may capitalize on such opportunities, as do environmental constraints (laws, highly effective competitors, and the like). Moreover, the final strategy must be congruent with the value structures of key personnel in order to inspire commitment. Final decisions on the five basic strategic variables result from a dynamic assessment and evaluation of the environment in relation to organizational skills, resources, and values. This "matching process" is discussed in greater detail in Chapter 3.

One important point pertinent to this section is that, with respect to internal influences, strategy is a *multifunctional* phenomenon. This means that decisions on the five basic variables are dependent on inputs from *all* functional areas of the firm. Even though a consumer-need orientation may be of the highest priority in strategy formation, decisions on customer and product mixes are *not* marketing decision variables. The fact that decisions on these variables establish direction, constraints, and operating modes for *all* functional areas necessitates their finally being made by the top or general management of the firm.

The Relationship of Strategy Formulation to Implementation

It was noted earlier that the formulation of strategy should be distinguished from its implementation. Figure 2-1 further clarifies this distinction. The left side of the figure depicts the basic ingredients of strategic planning. The complex and iterative process of assessing environmental factors in relation to internal capabilities and values culminates in decisions on the five basic strategic variables. Once decisions are made concerning overall strategy, detailed implementation plans can be developed for the various functional areas of operation, as shown on the right side of Figure 2-1. Consequently, "strategic planning" may be thought of as the basic, analytical process of strategy formulation. On the other hand, "implementation planning" is the basic process of developing internal plans for operationalizing a given strategy. The feedback loop emphasizes the need to assess implementation plans and performance results continually in order to determine any needed changes in strategy. Environmental forces also must be continually monitored in order to anticipate needed shifts in strategy. This point is elaborated more fully later.

THE STRATEGY FORMULATION PROCESS

As discussed, strategy is a function of four major types of variables: external opportunities, external constraints, internal capabilities, and personal values. The remainder of this chapter will explore more fully the influence of external opportunities and external constraints on strategy. Chapter 3 will then consider the dynamic process of relating these environmental forces to internal capabilities and values of the firm.

Figure 2-1 The process of strategy formulation and implementation.

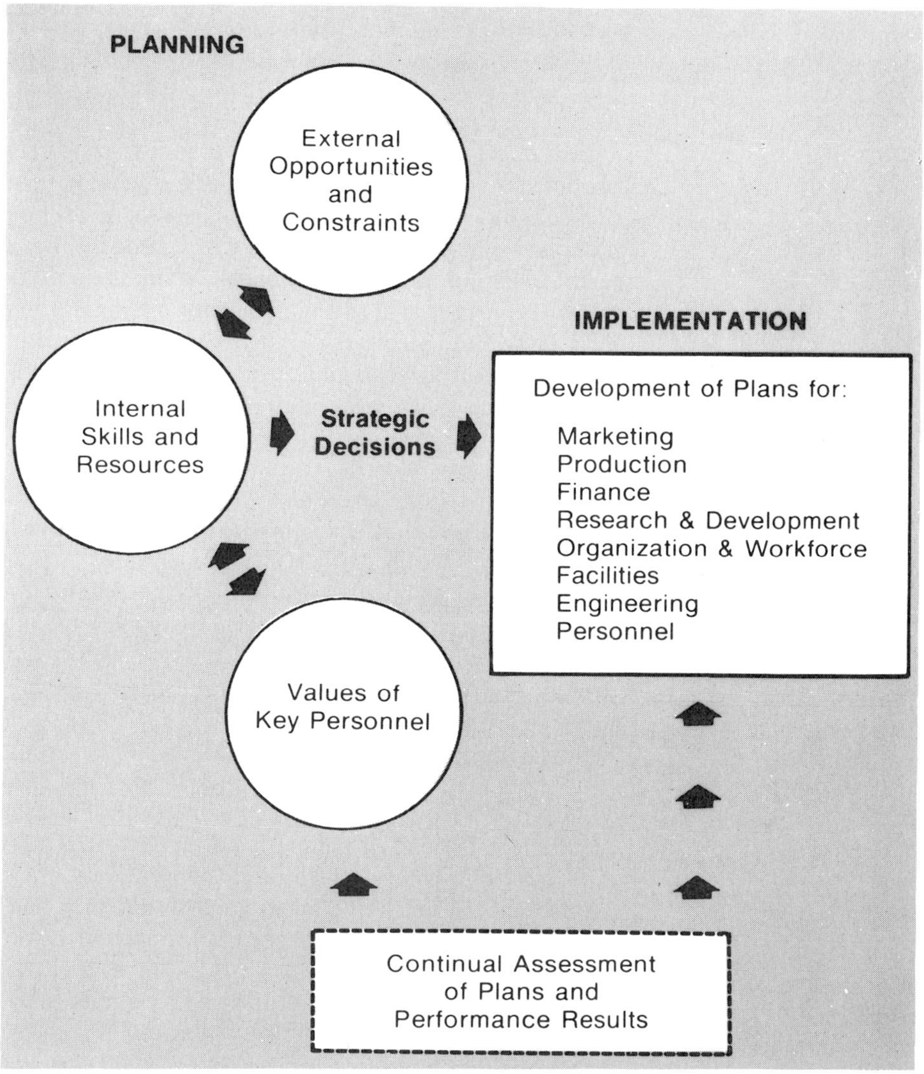

```
                          PLANNING

                    ┌─────────────────┐
                    │    External     │
                    │  Opportunities  │
                    │       and       │
                    │   Constraints   │
                    └─────────────────┘
                            ⇅
                                              IMPLEMENTATION
    ┌─────────────┐                    ┌──────────────────────────────┐
    │  Internal   │     Strategic      │  Development of Plans for:   │
    │  Skills and │ ⟹  Decisions  ⟹   │    Marketing                 │
    │  Resources  │                    │    Production                │
    └─────────────┘                    │    Finance                   │
            ⇅                          │    Research & Development    │
                                       │    Organization & Workforce  │
                                       │    Facilities                │
    ┌─────────────┐                    │    Engineering               │
    │  Values of  │                    │    Personnel                 │
    │Key Personnel│                    └──────────────────────────────┘
    └─────────────┘                              ⇑
                                                 ⇑
                   ⇑                  ⇑
              ┌ ─ ─ ─ ─ ─ ─ ─ ─ ─ ─ ─ ─ ─ ─ ─ ─ ┐
                  Continual Assessment
              │      of Plans and                │
                  Performance Results
              └ ─ ─ ─ ─ ─ ─ ─ ─ ─ ─ ─ ─ ─ ─ ─ ─ ┘
```

Environmental Forces

When analyzing the environment within which a given firm operates, it is useful to think in terms of six distinct (although obviously interrelated) environmental forces: economic, competitive, industry structure, technological, social, and political/legal. They present opportunities and constraints to a firm.

Economic forces. As noted in Chapter 1, economic forces in a given firm's environment include overall market trends for present and potential products or services, lines of credit available, tax credits, supplier characteristics, stockholder characteristics and investment motivation, and similar phenomena. General economic conditions also are important to specific firms, including growth of gross national product, disposable personal income, money markets, capital markets, and other phenomena of a macronature. Detailed analysis by a given firm tends to concentrate on the microforces, however, because they tend to exert the greatest *direct* influence on desirable product and customer mix and overall strategy.

Insofar as the analysis of overall market trends for present and potential products or services is concerned, one is usually provided with a good deal of "demand" information in a policy case. A note of caution is appropriate here, however, since the tendency is to assume that a given firm should attempt to exploit the area of greatest volume potential in the market. This ignores the fact that a given firm may not have the resources necessary to meet larger and stronger competitors head-on in the marketplace. Witness American Motors' classic decision to concentrate on the small car segment of the automobile market in the middle of the 1950s, while the "Big 3" concentrated on appealing to the then faster-growing large automobile segment. American Motors, realizing it could not hope to match the strengths of the larger firms, developed its own competitive advantage and was very successful. Since that time, the company has had varying degrees of success and now has dropped to fifth place among U. S. automobile producers. Ironically, the problem may be that the federal fuel-economy laws have pushed larger competitors (General Motors, Ford, Chrysler) into American Motors' specialized niche of small cars! However, American Motors is now capitalizing on the success of its Jeep four-wheel-drive vehicles and made a profit in 1978 after having lost money in the three previous years.

International Multifoods presents another example of a firm that has carefully concentrated its efforts so as to avoid head-to-head competition with a larger firm. This company entered the cheese market in 1971 through acquisition. Instead of competing directly with Kraft and Borden, however, the firm chose to concentrate on the relatively uncrowded specialty snack segment of the market. The strategy to date has had positive results. Similarly, Blount, Inc., a general contractor and farm equipment manufacturer, seeks to acquire companies in various niches of the $15 billion farm equipment industry that are not dominated by giants such as John Deere and International Harvester.[2]

On the other hand, many firms have fallen prey to the lure of high-potential markets without sufficient recognition of the strengths of competitors. For example, during the past few years, Bell and Howell, a highly successful pioneer in home movie equipment, attempted to move into growth fields such as printing, aerospace equipment, and copiers and soon found itself up against companies like Kodak and Xerox. The result was rapidly declining earnings per share in the late 1960s and a subsequent trimming of many product lines.

---

[2]"Blount: Building More Than Buildings to Broaden Its Base," *Business Week*, April 23, 1979, p. 108.

Closely associated with this point is the fact that it may be more feasible and more profitable to capture a larger share of a declining market than to pursue what inevitably may be only a very small share of an expanding market because of the larger number of competitors involved. This only accentuates the need for assessment of opportunities *not* in an idealistic vacuum but in relation to what the firm is capable of accomplishing. A good example of this is the product-mix and customer-mix strategy of Fisher-Price Toys in the 1970s. While Mattel, Ideal Toy and other firms in the industry have expanded their strategy to include toys, games, and hobbies for all ages, Fisher-Price has concentrated on toys for the preschool child, which make up only about 10% of the total toy market. A quality product is stressed, and promotional efforts are aimed at young mothers. As a result, Fisher-Price has now become the number one growth company in the industry. Because the U. S. birthrate has slowed considerably, one could argue that Fisher-Price is concentrating on a declining market. However, their success has resulted from their strong reputation as *the* producer of preschool toys. They have clearly exploited a specialized market.

As indicated, most firms place their greatest emphasis on analyzing the external forces (e.g., market demand) that impinge most directly on day-to-day operations. On the other hand, the deterioration of the U.S. economy during the late 1970s has caused more and more companies to be concerned with macroeconomic phenomena such as inflation, the purchasing power of the dollar, the propensity of consumers to spend more and save less, the increasing balance-of-trade deficits, the huge increases in short-term interest rates, and rising unemployment. Although economists have varying opinions concerning the best solutions to such economic problems, they do tend to agree on the *cause* of the economy's deterioration in the late 1970s: the productive capacity of U.S. business has simply failed to keep pace with the rapid increase in consumer demand for all types of products. One burden placed on government, therefore, is how to create the conditions that will make it desirable (profitable) for businesses to expand their capacity within a new mosaic of tax laws, rules, and regulations. In turn, businesses must do their part to influence the design of appropriate legislation that will help to overcome these economic woes. Government must attend to other elements of the problem (e.g., how to direct more disposable income of consumers into savings accounts) in order to stem the inflationary tide, of course; the main task of business seems to be the stimulation of increased productivity from existing employees and plants. To the extent that "productive capacity" in this sense can be increased, the U.S. economy will stand a much greater chance of regaining its position of leadership in the world setting.

It should be evident from this discussion that as conditions worsen in the larger economy, these macroforces demand more and more attention from those who shape corporate strategy. Roundtable discussions between top business leaders, government officials, and academicians have become quite common during the 1970s as solutions are sought for the economic difficulties. Yet even in these times, the primary concern of the architects of strategy must continue to be the future strength and viability of their *individual* firms. Consequently, macroeconomic forces will always receive less attention than the analysis of competition, market demand, and similar external forces that have greater direct impact on the firm.

Competitive forces. Regardless of one's relative share of the market, every firm operating today *must* have thorough knowledge of who its competitors are and their basic operating characteristics. The following key questions must be asked.

1. What is the strategic profile of each major competitor (i.e., what decisions have been made by competitors with regard to customer targets, product mix, geographic areas to be served, and competitive emphasis)? What are the areas of overlap with our company?
2. What are the major strengths of each competitor (i.e., what do they do better than us)?
3. What are the major weaknesses of each competitor (i.e., what can we do better than them)?
4. What is the overall reputation or image of each competitor?
5. What are the relative market shares of competitors?
6. How do our products (or services) compare insofar as quality, price, cost, style, design, image, and utility?
7. What are the *future* strategic profiles of each competitor likely to be? How do these profiles compare with our own thinking about future requirements for success in the industry?

Once a firm has reasonably sound knowledge about each of its competitors, it can begin to predict the probable reactions to its own tactics related to price, advertising, inventory expansion, or other competitive moves. Most important, a firm can begin to assess *when* it should take bold, dramatic moves to improve its position in the marketplace versus when it should assume a more passive, reactive posture. Thus the *timing* of competitive moves is extremely important, as illustrated by the following examples.

Perhaps the most visible example of the importance of timing in the late 1970s is found in the automobile industry. In response to the federally mandated regulations on gasoline consumption, General Motors decided to use its vast resources and be first among automobile manufacturers in the shift to smaller cars. General Motors proceeded to make its plant conversions at a rate that Ford and Chrysler could not hope to match. By 1979, the strategy had resulted in General Motors having nearly 60% of the market for domestic cars and nearly 50% of the worldwide automobile market. Clearly, being there *first* in this instance has resulted in an even stronger position of leadership for General Motors.

As another successful example of proper timing, consider the case of Stanley Works, the company that was *first* to move heavily into the homeowners' do-it-yourself market in the early 1970s. Tools were redesigned for amateurs by the firm, yet its long-standing reputation for quality remained intact. Most of the customers in the do-it-yourself market are between the ages of 25 and 44, an age group that is predicted to expand during the next two decades. Other companies have found it extremely difficult to overcome Stanley Works' lead, which resulted from aggressive movement into a new target market.

Although the evidence is not yet in, it may be that Fleetwood Enterprises is about to establish a similar advantage by being the first mobile home manufacturer to move aggressively into "subdivision" development. Sensing that the rapidly escalating prices for conventional housing is leaving many young families out in the cold, Fleetwood plans to develop up to three prototype mobile home subdivisions and market them on a subdivision basis, just like conventional homes.[3] The company will develop its own land, since conventional developers are not yet persuaded of the approach. If Fleetwood is successful, it will be because it parted company with the conservative approach of most mobile home manufacturers to address the needs of a new and possibly major market.

As a final example of the importance of competitive timing, consider what has happened to the U.S. apparel industry as a result of its failure to time its efforts properly. American companies used to dominate the wholesale apparel market, and imports were generally regarded as noncompetitive, low-quality products. Imports have doubled since 1975, however, and in 1979 are expected to account for 22% of the U.S. apparel market.[4] The products from abroad are of much higher quality than before, yet U.S. manufacturers have been extremely slow to recognize this circumstance as a genuine competitive threat. The U.S. companies are now awake to the threat and are trying to move quickly toward greater mechanization, more exports, diversification, and other tactics. *But* these moves may all be too late to constitute an effective counterstrategy.

The examples in this section have all shown the importance of *timing* in relation to the actions of one's competitors. The larger question of how to go about establishing a "competitive advantage" on grounds other than timing will be addressed in Chapter 3.

Structure of the industry. The nature of the competition is, of course, a key characteristic of the industry to be analyzed. The *structure* of the industry refers, however, to fundamental operating characteristics such as:

1. What is (are) the requirement(s) for success in the industry? Is it product design? Low cost of manufacturing? Control of scarce raw materials? Vertical integration of operations? Strong dealerships?

---

[3] "A Mobile Home Maverick," *Business Week*, February 19, 1979, p. 63.
[4] "Apparel's Last Stand," *Business Week*, May 14, 1979, p. 60.

2. What is the rate of technological innovation in the industry? Is a strong focus on research and development required? Are existing plants soon to be outmoded and thus require replacement?
3. What is the overall productive capacity of the industry in relation to market demand? Is there excess capacity?
4. What are the existing labor conditions in the industry? Is the industry strongly unionized? Is labor in short supply or relatively plentiful?
5. What are the effects of economies of scale? Does one have to be huge in order to be successful?
6. What are the effects of the "learning curve?" Does success in the industry require a long period of experience and learning?
7. What is the geographic scope of the industry? Is it worldwide, national, regional, state, or local?
8. What is the nature of governmental regulation in the industry?
9. What "barriers to entry" exist (i.e., how difficult is it for new firms to enter the industry)?
10. What is the *future* outlook for the industry on all of the dimensions listed? Does our company have the wherewithal to compete successfully in the future?

Each of these 10 areas represents a key focal point for assessing the firm's capabilities in relation to the requirements of the industry. This analysis, when combined with the analyses of economic forces and competitive requirements, will give the architect of corporate strategy a strong grasp of the "market" components of the environment. Just as important, however, are analyses of the social, technological, and political/legal sectors.

Social forces. Perhaps the most important contemporary social influence on the process of strategy formation is the doctrine of social responsibility, which emphasizes the consideration of social criteria along with the more familiar economic criteria in the development of corporate strategy. Many scholars, most notably Milton Friedman, argue vigorously that business has no social obligation whatsoever other than to make as much money for their stockholders as possible.[5] This implies that business has no obligation other than conformity to law and ethical custom and that the impetus for social action programs must emanate from the governmental sector of the economy in a democratic society. On the other hand, advocates of the doctrine say that technological progress in the pursuit of profit has had dysfunctional consequences for the ecological "quality of life," not to mention other aspects of social welfare that have suffered from an overemphasis on profits, such as equality of hiring and promotional opportunity, product quality, and fair pricing.

---

[5]Milton Friedman, *Capitalism and Freedom* (Chicago: The University of Chicago Press, 1962), p. 133.

Regardless of one's particular *philosophy* concerning the social obligations of business, the practical implications of the social responsibility doctrine cannot be ignored.

> Carl A. Gerstacker, chairman of Dow Chemical Co., wastes no time on flowery phrases about "social responsibility" and "commitment to a cause" when telling why his company has undertaken costly antipollution and product safety programs. Rather, he states baldly: "Our motive is profit."
>
> With just that in mind, Dow is putting into effect a program that it calls "product stewardship," under which it assumes total responsibility for how its products affect people. Indeed, more and more industrial companies are looking beyond their immediate commercial customers and into the marketplace to make sure that their products will not have an adverse effect on the environment or the end-user. Dow, for its part, thinks it has come up with an effective marketing tool as well: It will offer a virtual guarantee of harmlessness. "If we do a better job of product stewardship than our competitors," Gerstacker says, "we believe it will be recognized in the marketplace."[6]

The following indicates that the "product stewardship" program at Dow Chemical is not mere window dressing.

> A number of important findings have come out of the program already. One product, an organic arsenical, was thought by the company to have considerable potential as an ingredient in paint for the bottoms of ships, since it would bleed slowly out of the paint and retard the growth of barnacles and other organisms. Doubts about the product's effect on the marine environment over a long period, however, and the need for additional costly research led to a "kill" decision—despite an urgent need by customers for such a product.[7]

Organized movements are under way for "social accounting" and "social auditing" of business firms. In marketing, the "consumerism" and "societal marketing" emphases are exerting influence in both academic and industry circles. In general, the increased attention being given to the subject of "business and society," whatever the particular variation, has resulted in a great deal of publicity and public debate. Even if one's basic philosophy precludes the use of other than economic criteria in strategic decision making, top management must recognize and adjust for the societal value shift that the doctrine implies. The particular impact of the doctrine will vary for each firm, depending on the desires of stockholders, values and attitudes of top management, the firm's location and community influence, its "pollution propensity," and other matters.

Closely associated with these "social responsibility" movements are the changing general views about business among the larger public. For exam-

---

[6]"Dow's Big Push for Product Safety," *Business Week*, April 21, 1973, p. 82.
[7]Ibid.

ple, there seems to have been a negative view of "big business" during the past decade, and the negativism shows no sign of abating in the near future. As an illustration of the influence of this negative view, consider the hearings being conducted as of this writing by the U.S. Senate Judiciary Committee. The hearings are on a bill being pushed by the chairman of the committee, Senator Edward M. Kennedy. Senator Kennedy's bill would limit conglomerate mergers drastically, since it would outlaw all mergers between companies with more than $2 billion in sales or assets.[8] In addition, the bill would force other sizable companies to prove that there will be a "significant social advantage" to their acquiring any other company with a similar degree of power in the marketplace.[9] Without such proof, the merger would be forbidden. This is a landmark set of hearings; prior to this time antitrust considerations were based primarily on economic criteria. Clearly, a shift in societal values is reflected by these Senate committee hearings.

At the individual company level, the effects of social values are becoming more and more apparent. The Dow Chemical case has already been mentioned. Consider also the well-known (and justified) concerns of U.S. tobacco companies about the future sales of cigarettes. It is interesting to note that producers in the industry ascribe the sales decline not to the issue of bodily harm, but to the efforts of nonsmokers to make smoking socially unacceptable! A moral dilemma is posed here as well, particularly for key executives in tobacco companies. As noted by one such executive in a candid moment: "There is no loyalty to the industry outside of those of us who benefit from it financially. I think that all smokers really want to quit and that they are secretly for the other guy to win."[10]

As a final point, it is important to note that a prevailing social attitude of today is that business firms should be held responsible for the *extended effects* of their products, even though the products themselves may be harmless. For example, Nestlé has encountered significant problems in its sales of powdered infant formula in less developed countries. The poor and illiterate peoples of such countries buy the formula, partially because it is prestigious to do so. The problem arises as a result of the formula being mixed with contaminated water in these countries, the consequence being the alleged deaths of many babies. Nestlé now faces a hard decision on whether or not to continue distribution of the product because of pressure brought to bear by the Infant Formula Action Coalition. The company has engaged in educational efforts to little avail, and advertising programs have not been successful in informing parents of the potential dangers.

Technological forces. The fifth major type of environmental force that must be reckoned with is the phenomenon of technological developments outside the firm. The firm constantly must be aware of new discoveries,

---

[8]"Social Goals Become an Antitrust Weapon," *Business Week*, April 9, 1979, p. 42.
[9]Ibid.
[10]"The Long, Slow Stunting of Cigarette Sales," *Business Week*, May 7, 1979, p. 41.

both in its own industry and in others, that may impinge on its future viability. Technological developments are important for the firm in two major areas: product development and process improvement. As an example of the importance of continued assessment insofar as product development is concerned, one only has to consider the hundreds of products that either have become technologically obsolete or have lost consumer utility in the past few years. In addition, product improvement is frequently contingent on the incorporation of new components or other features made possible by expanding technology. For example, Magnavox's failure to anticipate the need to develop color televisions with solid-state circuitry left it at a distinct competitive disadvantage in the early 1970s vis à vis Zenith, RCA, and Motorola. As a result, the company lost several major distribution outlets, such as Marshall Field, the Chicago department store chain, and suffered a loss of momentum with others.

In some industries, of course, companies have no choice but to be actively and directly engaged in research and development activities. This is perhaps most obvious in electronics-related firms where technological breakthroughs seem to occur almost on a monthly basis. For example, Texas Instruments, Inmos, and other companies are currently competing to develop the 64K random access memory (RAM), the next generation semiconductor that presumably will make up the on-line memory system of large, mainframe computers. Such a development will enable the storage of 64,000 bits of data on a single silicon chip, or four times the capacity of the largest memory circuit now in mass production.[11]

On another front, Winnebago Industries has found it necessary to become actively engaged in research to respond to the rising price of gasoline which, in turn, has caused a drastic decline in the sale of recreational vehicles. Winnebago has introduced an optional fuel system that will allow motor homes to run on liquefied propane gas, a fuel that is much more plentiful (and cheaper) than gasoline. Similarly, the external developments in the apparel industry that led to increased competition from imports has placed a premium on research and development efforts among U.S. companies. Cluett Peabody, maker of Arrow shirts and other lines, has taken the lead in automation efforts to combat the lower-cost imports and has a jump on its competitors in this regard. The Cluett Peabody case is an example of *process* improvement, which is necessary to compete on the basis of price.

The importance of research and development is not always as evident as it seems to be in these illustrations. However, many forward-looking firms recognize that their long-term viability depends on a strong program of technological development. For example, Texas Instruments' extensive experience with semiconductor technology led it quite naturally into research

---

[11]"Inmos: The British Dream of Semiconductor Technology," *Business Week*, April 23, 1979, p. 112.

on solar energy systems. As a result, the firm announced in 1979 that a startling breakthrough had occurred: the company's scientists had devised a self-contained photovoltaic system in which sunlight could be captured and converted into a fuel suitable for producing electricity around the clock.[12] This result would solve the problem of how to store energy collected from the sun and thus provide Texas Instruments with a significant competitive advantage for future systems development. Two years of research by its top technical experts have been invested so far by the company; the project clearly has had worthwhile results, even though no guarantees of success were available in the beginning.

Many firms recognize the need for research and development but cannot afford the huge investments that are sometimes necessary. Others may become "followers," as is the case with Olivetti, Italy's giant office equipment manufacturer. Olivetti has a team of technicians located in the United States in order to follow technological developments more closely. The hope is to enhance the company's shift from traditional office equipment into the faster-growing markets for electronic office systems. The company evidently hopes to accomplish this shift by adopting technological advances created by others.

In general, the more stable the outlook for a product or industry, the less the need to actively search the technological environment, and vice versa. Certainly, an active, product-oriented research and development group is *relatively* more important in the electronics industry than in steel. It is also important to note that technological developments may present either opportunities or constraints to a firm. If a firm is active either in its own research and development and/or in obtaining intelligence about developments in other organizations, the chances are much greater that new technologies will present opportunities and not constraints. This is because of the importance of *timing* in capitalizing on new developments, as illustrated by the Magnavox example.

Political/legal forces. External forces in this category include legislation, executive acts, court opinions, regulatory agencies, foreign policy developments, fiscal policy, monetary policy, and other political/legal phenomena that impinge on the firm's operations. Obviously, some pieces of legislation, such as the Robinson-Patman Act, affect all firms, while others may involve only specific industries or product areas. By the same token, the role and authority of regulatory agencies may be either universal or industry or product specific.

As in the other major types of external forces, it is important to realize that political/legal phenomena present *both* opportunities and constraints to a firm with regard to strategy determination. Although the tendency is to classify or view phenomena such as the regulatory power of the Federal

---

[12] "TI Breaks a Barrier in Solar Energy," *Business Week*, June 4, 1979, p. 64.

Trade Commission or the Food and Drug Administration as constraints, at the same time these political/legal forces can operate to present significant opportunities for some firms. Consider the profitable opportunities now existing for efficient manufacturers of antipollution equipment who service the various industries now subject to legal constraints on products or processes. In this case, the same legal phenomenon—antipollution laws and control standards—has created an opportunity for some firms and a constraint for others. Also consider the impact of foreign policy developments on strategy formulation. Multinational firms have alternately prospered or suffered, depending on government decisions concerning tax treatment, accounting practices, antitrust provisions, and other matters. Thus it is now necessary, in the case of multinationals, to extend one's political/legal analysis to the policies and decisions of foreign governments as significant factors in shaping strategy.

Some concrete examples of the pervasive impact of political/legal forces will highlight their importance. First, consider how passage of the Airline Deregulation Act of 1978 has virtually restructured the whole airline industry. The act makes possible entry into new markets that were previously unavailable to certain carriers. For example, the "regional" airlines (Allegheny, Frontier, Ozark) can now expand their routes, and several have jumped into the Florida market. Also, airlines can now engage in significant price-cutting tactics, and early indications are that most will be implementing radical changes in their pricing policies. All of these changes are a result of the 1978 act. Note also that this act is unique in that it focuses on *deregulation*.

Political or legal forces can also have negative effects, however, as indicated by the experience of many oil companies in Alaska during the late 1970s. The oil industry seems to be reluctantly turning away from Alaska, primarily because of state taxes, environmental laws, and high operating costs. State taxes on oil companies rose 900% in the 1970s! This factor plus the others mentioned have led Gulf to close its exploration office, Exxon to trim its Alaska staff by more than 25%, and Standard of Ohio to reevaluate its commitment seriously. In all, 21 energy-related companies have "backed away" from Alaska since 1971.[13] When one considers that Alaska's potential oil reserves are more than one-third of the U.S. total, it is obvious that the constraints being placed on the companies are indeed serious and debilitating.

Environmental Research: Its Role and Forms

As just implied, whether or not a particular environmental force constitutes an opportunity or a constraint depends in many cases on the firm itself, particularly the adequacy of its externally oriented research efforts. Many critics of external research have argued that the typical state of uncertainty associated with most environmental variables—the inability to accurately

---

[13] "The Great Alaskan Oil Freeze," *Business Week*, February 26, 1979, p. 74.

forecast future values of the variables—works against even attempting to do so. There is a basic contradiction in this argument, precisely because the role of environmental research is to provide the firm wth a larger degree of *control* over the uncertain environmental forces.

To illustrate the preceding point, it is useful to visualize for any given environmental variable a continuum such as the one in Figure 2-2. Obviously, very few environmental variables are ever completely controllable by the firm. Where a firm has a long-term contract for supplying a consumer (e.g., Whirlpool's agreement for many years with Sears), it may be construed as having gained almost complete control (although perhaps only temporarily) over the important external variable of consumer demand. Quite obviously, however, an overwhelming majority of all businesses are faced with environmental forces that are at, or very near, the uncontrollable end of the continuum. For example, coffee processors such as General Foods, Procter and Gamble, Hills Brothers, and Chase and Sanborn are extremely vulnerable to the volatility of green coffee prices. The 1975 Brazilian frost hit these companies particularly hard; the dramatic increases in green coffee prices caused the supermarket price to rise beyond the level consumers were willing to pay. Consequently, the companies were left with high-cost inventories that ate into working capital and eroded earnings. Recently, however, the effect of these "uncontrollable forces" has been just the opposite: green coffee prices have been falling faster than the wholesale prices charged by General Foods and the other coffee processors! As a result, the companies have improved their profit margins considerably in 1979.[14]

The coffee processing example demonstrates why many companies may have lean years even though they may be efficient producers or distributors of certain products. But the fact that such uncertainty may exist does *not* mean that a firm should not attempt to forecast, for example, the future price of green coffee beans. The essential point here is that the more information a firm gains about an environmental variable, the greater the degree of "control" the firm has over that same variable. Thus, even though a firm very rarely achieves a large degree of control over, say, consumer demand, (as in the captive outlet case just referred to or in a monopoly situation), in effect it is able to influence the future state or value of the variable by fore-

Figure 2-2 "Control" continuum for environmental variables.

```
           Environmental variable X
|←─────────────────────────────────────→|
| Completely                  Completely |
| uncontrollable              controllable|
```

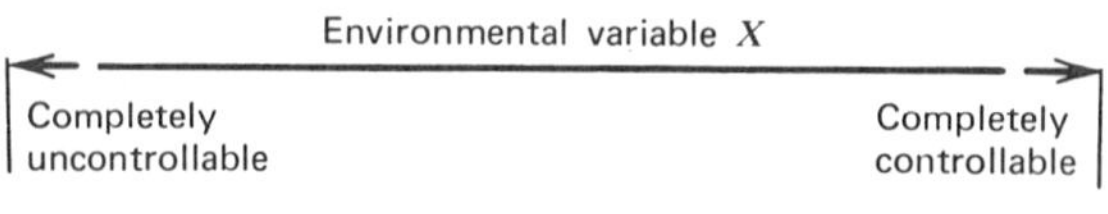

[14]"Falling Coffee Prices Boost Profit Margins," *Business Week*, March 5, 1979, p. 26.

casting. The increased information about a given force enables the firm to predict more accurately the effect of that force on strategy and operations, providing advance opportunity to adjust for such effects. In this sense, the firm obtains a measure of control over the environment and over changes in the environment by having already activated response mechanisms to cope with such changes.

Based on the preceding discussion, it follows that firms may be readily distinguished on the basis of their attempts to influence and control environmental forces. On the one hand, there are very "active" firms that seek—through economic forecasting, market research, lobbying, or other means—to influence the environment and to control, to the extent possible, their own destiny. On the other hand, many "passive" firms merely respond to shifts in the environment as they occur, with little if any attempt to predict or plan strategy adjustments *in advance* of the changes. Such firms frequently find themselves fighting fires and engaged in "crisis management" because of their failure to formulate future-oriented strategy on a rational, although always imperfect and incomplete, base. As an example, consider the case of American Brands, for years the number one company in cigarette sales. Failing to monitor changing market trends actively, American was slow to respond to the "filter revolution" within the industry. Consequently, American Brands now ranks fourth in the industry in cigarette sales, behind Reynolds, Philip Morris, and Brown & Williamson.

There are several forms of environmental research. Perhaps the most familiar type is frequently referred to as *market research*. This is generally restricted, however, to the economic and social sectors of the environment, focusing on customer needs, demand trends, competitor strengths and weaknesses, industry characteristics, demographic aspects of the market, and similar factors that impinge directly on present and future sales. A second form of environmental research—*economic forecasting*—tends to "fill out" the firm's assessment of the economic sector. This usually focuses on the macro-variables affecting the firm's success (e.g., gross national product, disposable personal income, and inventory accumulation in the economy) as well as on the firm's capital and money markets. Very large firms may have completely separate groups to perform the market research and economic forecasting functions.

A third form of environmental research is known as *research and development*. Although this function is frequently internally oriented and concerned with product and/or process innovation, its successful accomplishment requires continuing surveillance of the technological sector of the firm's environment. Finally, *political/legal research* constitutes an increasingly important form of external analysis. This is generally performed by legal departments or by a retained attorney and, in the case of large firms, also by lobbyists who attempt not only to influence the legislative process but also to discern important political and legal developments in advance of their formal announcement.

In many firms, a general coordinative and/or technical staff exists to assume responsibility for overall environmental assessment. Most commonly known as *long-range planning* groups, they perform two major functions: (1) overall coordination of the various forms of environmental research (usually participating in one or more forms of the research themselves), and (2) relating externally identified opportunities and constraints to corporate goals and capabilities for the purpose of recommending strategic realignments to top management.

Although the exact nature of, and organization for, environmental research varies from firm to firm, it is useful to think in terms of the basic forms of environmental research noted here. Very large and profitable firms may have separate groups of people, one group for each of the major forms. On the other hand, very small firms may have only one group, or perhaps only one person, charged with "scanning" the total environment. Of course, the "passive" type of firm discussed earlier may perform no environmental research at all, under the erroneous assumption that the firm is a closed system.

The ultimate goal of *all* the forms of environmental research is the identification and analysis of opportunities and constraints that are operative in the firm's environment. As mentioned earlier, however, this is only the first step in the process of strategy formation. Once the opportunities and constraints are identified, they must be related in some systematic fashion to the firm's internal capabilities and resources. Unless this analytical process occurs, the firm can never rationally assess the strategic implications of environmental forces. This "matching" of external opportunities and constraints with internal capabilities and resources is the subject of the next chapter.

The reading immediately following this chapter discusses on the process of strategy formation in more detail, with emphasis on the varying approaches utilized by different firms.

SUMMARY

The first part of this chapter discussed the general concept of corporate strategy. It identified five key decision areas as strategic issues: customer mix, product mix, geographic limits of the market to be served, competitive emphasis, and objectives. The chapter discussed the interrelationship of these five decision areas and the major inputs to such decisions. Environmental inputs were emphasized with several examples to illustrate how organizations have responded to various economic, competitive, social, technological, and political/legal forces. The last part of the chapter concentrated on the various types of environmental research that are conducted by firms in order to maintain effective strategies in the face of changing conditions.

STRATEGY-MAKING IN THREE MODES

Henry Mintzberg

How do organizations make important decisions and link them together to form strategies? So far, we have little systematic evidence about this important process, known in business as *strategy-making* and in government as *policy-making*. The literature of management and public administration is, however, replete with general views on the subject. These fall into three distinct groupings or "modes." In the *entrepreneurial* mode, found in the writings of some of the classical economists and of many contemporary management writers, one strong leader takes bold, risky actions on behalf of his organization. Conversely, in the *adaptive* mode, described by a number of students of business and governmental decision-making, the organization adapts in small, disjointed steps to a difficult environment. Finally, the proponents of management science and policy science describe the *planning* mode, in which formal analysis is used to plan explicit, integrated strategies for the future.

I shall begin by describing each mode as its proponents do, in simple terms and distinct from the other two. Considered in this way, each may appear to be a naive reflection of the complex reality of strategy-making. But taken as a set of three, as I shall do in subsequent sections, to be combined and alternated by managers acting under different conditions, these modes constitute a realistic and useful description of the strategy-making process. To illustrate this point, I shall cite studies of the strategy-making behaviors of a number of very different kinds of organizations—hotels, hospitals, car dealerships, modeling agencies, airports, radio stations, and so on. Finally, I shall discuss some important implications for strategic planning.

THE ENTREPRENEURIAL MODE

The entrepreneur was first discussed by early economists as that individual who founded enterprises. His roles were essentially those of innovation, of dealing with uncertainty, and of brokerage. The entrepreneur found capital which he brought together with marketing opportunity to form, in the words of Joseph Schumpeter, the well-known Harvard economist, "new combinations."

In a recent book called *The Organization Makers*, Orvis Collins and David Moore present a fascinating picture of those independent entrepreneurs, based on a study of 150 of them. The authors trace the lives of these men from childhood, through formal and informal education, to the steps they took to create their enterprises. Data from psychological tests reinforce their analysis. What emerges are pictures of tough, pragmatic men driven from early childhood by a powerful need for achievement and independence. At some point in his life, each entrepreneur faced disruption ("role deterioration"), and it was here that he set out on his own:

> What sets them apart is that during this time of role deterioration they interwove their dilemmas into the projection of a business. In moments of crisis, they

SOURCE: Henry Mintzberg, "Strategy-Making in Three Modes." © 1973 by The Regents of the University of California. Reprinted from *California Management Review*, Vol. XVI, No. 2, pp. 44–53, by permission of The Regents.

did not seek a situation of security. They went on into deeper insecurity....[1]

A number of management writers view the entrepreneurial mode of strategy-making not only in terms of creating new firms but in terms of the running of ongoing enterprises. Typical of these is Peter Drucker, who writes in a recent article:

> Central to business enterprise is . . . the entrepreneurial act, an act of economic risk-taking. And business enterprise is an entrepreneurial institution. . . . Entrepreneurship is thus central to function, work and performance of the executive in business.[2]

What are the chief characteristics of the entrepreneurial mode of strategy-making as described by economists and management writers? We can delineate four:

1. *In the entrepreneurial mode, strategy-making is dominated by the active search for new opportunities.* The entrepreneurial organization focuses on opportunities; problems are secondary. Drucker writes: "Entrepreneurship requires that the few available good people be deployed on opportunities rather than frittered away on 'solving problems'."[3] Furthermore, the orientation is always active rather than passive. Robert McNamara, when he was Secretary of Defense, stressed the active role for the government administrator:

    > *I think that the role of public manager is very similar to the role of a private manager; in each case he has the option of following one of two major alternative courses of action. He can either act as a judge or a leader. In the former case, he sits and waits until subordinates bring to him problems for solution, or alternatives for choice. In the latter case, he immerses himself in the operations of the business or the governmental activity . . .*
    > *I have always believed in and endeavored to follow the active leadership role as opposed to the passive judicial role.*[4]

2. *In the entrepreneurial organization, power is centralized in the hands of the chief executive.* Collins and Moore write of the founder-entrepreneur: "The entrepreneurial personality . . . is characterized by an unwillingness to 'submit' to authority, an inability to work with it, and a consequent need to escape from it."[5] In the entrepreneurial mode, power rests with one man capable of committing the organization to bold courses of action. He rules by fiat, relying on personal power and sometimes on charisma. Consider this description of an Egyptian firm:

    > *The great majority of Egyptian-owned private establishments . . . are organized closer to the pattern of the Abboud enterprises. Here the manager is a dominant individual who extends his personal control over all phases of the business. There is no charted plan of organization, no formalized procedure for selection and development of managerial personnel, no publicized system of wage and salary classifications.*
    > *. . . authority is associated exclusively with an individual. . . .*
    > *Abboud is the kind of person most people have in mind when they discuss the successful Egyptian entrepreneur.*[6]

But while there may be "no charted plan of organization," typically one finds instead

---

[1] O. Collins and D. G. Moore, *The Organization Makers* (New York: Appleton, Century, Crofts, 1970), p. 134.
[2] P. F. Drucker, "Entrepreneurship in the Business Enterprise," *Journal of Business Policy* (1:1, 1970), p. 10.
[3] Ibid.
[4] Quoted in C. J. Hitch, *Decision-making for Defense* (Berkeley: University of California Press, 1967).
[5] Collins and Moore, op. cit., p. 45.
[6] F. Harbison and C. A. Myers, *Management in the Industrial World* (New York: McGraw-Hill, 1959), pp. 40–41.

that strategy is guided by the entrepreneur's own vision of direction for his organization—his personalized plan of attack. Drucker writes:

Every one of the great business builders we know of—from the Medici and the founders of the Bank of England down to IBM's Thomas Watson in our days—had a definite idea, indeed a clear "theory of the business" which informed his actions and decisions.[7]

3. *Strategy-making in the entrepreneurial mode is characterized by dramatic leaps forward in the face of uncertainty.* Strategy moves forward in the entrepreneurial organization by the taking of large, bold decisions. The chief executive seeks out and thrives in conditions of uncertainty, where his organization can make dramatic gains. . . . The entrepreneurial mode is probably most alive in the popular business magazines such as *Fortune* and *Forbes* which each month devote a number of articles to the bold actions of manager-entrepreneurs. The theme that runs through these articles is what has been referred to as the "bold stroke," the courageous move that succeeds against all the odds and all the advice.

4. *Growth is the dominant goal of the entrepreneurial organization.* According to psychologist David McClelland, the entrepreneur is motivated above all by his need for achievement. Since his organization's goals are simply the extension of his own, we can conclude that the dominant goal of the organization operating in the entrepreneurial mode is growth, the most tangible manifestation of achievement. *Fortune* magazine came to this conclusion in a 1956 article about the Young Presidents' Organization entitled "The Entrepreneurial Ego":

Most of the young presidents have the urge to build rather than manipulate. "Expansion is a sort of disease with us," says one president. "Let's face it," says another. "We're empire builders. The tremendous compulsion and obsession is not to make money, but to build an empire." The opportunity to keep on pushing ahead is, indeed, the principal advantage offered by the entrepreneurial life.[8]

In summary, we can conclude that the organization operating in the entrepreneurial mode suggests by its actions that the environment is malleable, a force to be confronted and controlled.

THE ADAPTIVE MODE

The view of strategy-making as an adaptive process has gained considerable popularity since the publication of two complementary books in 1963. Charles Lindblom and David Braybrooke wrote *A Strategy of Decision* about policy-making in the public sector, while Richard Cyert and James March published *A Behavioral Theory of the Firm* based on empirical studies of decision-making.

Lindblom first called this approach "the science of 'muddling through'," later "disjointed incrementalism."[9] The term "adaptive" is chosen here for its simplicity. As described by Lindblom, the adaptive policy-maker accepts as given a powerful status quo and the lack of clear objec-

---

[7]Drucker, op. cit., p. 5.

[8]S. Klaw, "The Entrepreneurial Ego," *Fortune* (August 1956), p. 143.

[9]See C. E. Lindblom, "The Science of 'Muddling Through'" *Public Administration Review* (19, 1959), pp. 79–88; C. E. Lindblom and David Braybrooke, *A Strategy of Decision* (New York: Free Press, 1963); C. E. Lindblom, *The Intelligence of Democracy* (New York: Free Press, 1965); and C. E. Lindblom, *The Policy-making Process* (Englewood Cliffs, N.J.: Prentice-Hall, 1968).

tives. His decisions are basically remedial in nature, and he proceeds in small steps, never moving too far from the given status quo. In this way, the policy-maker comes to terms with his complex environment.

Cyert and March's strategy-maker, although working in the business firm, operates in much the same fashion. Again, his world is complex and he must find the means to cope with it. Cyert and March suggest that he does so in a number of ways. He consciously seeks to avoid uncertainty, sometimes solving pressing problems instead of developing long-run strategies, other times "negotiating" with the environment (for example, establishing cartels). Furthermore, because the organization is controlled by a coalition of disparate interests, the strategy-maker must make his decisions so as to reduce conflicts. He does this by attending to conflicting goals sequentially, ignoring the inconsistencies:

> Just as the political organization is likely to "go left" and "go right" by first doing one and then the other, the business firm is likely to resolve conflicting pressures to "smooth production" and "satisfy customers" by first doing one and then the other.[10]

Four major characteristics distinguish the adaptive mode of strategy-making:

1. *Clear goals do not exist in the adaptive organization; strategy-making reflects a division of power among members of a complex coalition.* The adaptive organization is caught in a complex web of political forces. Unions, managers, owners, lobby groups, government agencies, and so on, each with their own needs, seek to influence decisions. There is no one central source of power, no one simple goal. The goal system of the organization is characterized by bargaining among these groups, with each winning some issues and losing others. Hence, the organization attends to a whole array of goals sequentially, ignoring the inconsistencies among them. The organization cannot make decisions to "maximize" any one goal such as profit or growth; rather it must seek solutions to its problems that are good enough, that satisfy the constraints.

2. *In the adaptive mode, the strategy-making process is characterized by the "reactive" solution to existing problems rather than the "proactive" search for new opportunities.* The adaptive organization works in a difficult environment that imposes many problems and crises. Little time remains to search out opportunities. And even if there were time, the lack of clear goals in the organization would preclude a proactive approach:

  > . . . if [*the strategy-makers*] *cannot decide with any precision the state of affairs they want to achieve, they can at least specify the state of affairs from which they want to escape. They deal more confidently with what is wrong than with what in the future may or may not be right.*[11]

  Furthermore, the adaptive organization seeks conditions of certainty wherever possible, otherwise it seeks to reduce existing uncertainties. It establishes cartels to ensure markets, negotiates long-term purchasing arrangements to stabilize sources of supply, and so on.

3. *The adaptive organization makes its decisions in incremental, serial steps.* Because its environment is complex, the adaptive organization finds that feedback is a crucial ingredient in strategy-making. It cannot take large decisions for fear of venturing too far into the unknown. The strategy-maker focuses first on what is familiar, considering the convenient alternatives and the ones that differ only slightly from the status quo. Hence, the organization moves

---

[10] R. M. Cyert and J. G. March, *A Behavioral Theory of the Firm* (Englewood Cliffs, N. J.: Prentice-Hall, 1963), p. 118.

[11] Lindblom, op. cit., (1968), p. 25.

forward in incremental steps, laid end to end in serial fashion so that feedback can be received and the course adjusted as it moves along. As Lindblom notes, "... policy-making is typically a never-ending process of successive steps in which continual nibbling is a substitute for a good bite."[12]

4. *Disjointed decisions are characteristic of the adaptive organization.* Decisions cannot be easily interrelated in the adaptive mode. The demands on the organization are diverse, and no manager has the mental capacity to reconcile all of them. Sometimes it is simply easier and less expensive to make decisions in disjointed fashion so that each is treated independently and little attention is paid to problems of coordination. Strategy-making is fragmented, but at least the strategy-maker remains flexible, free to adapt to the needs of the moment.

Lindblom provides us with an apt summary of the adaptive mode:

Man has had to be devilishly inventive to cope with the staggering difficulties he faces. His analytical methods cannot be restricted to tidy scholarly procedures. The piecemealing, remedial incrementalist or satisficer may not look like an heroic figure. He is nevertheless a shrewd, resourceful problem-solver who is wrestling bravely with a universe that he is wise enough to know is too big for him.[13]

THE PLANNING MODE

In a recent book, Russell Ackoff isolates the three chief characteristics of the planning mode:

1. Planning is something we do in advance of taking action; that is, it is *anticipatory decision-making*....

2. Planning is required when the future state that we desire involves a set of interdependent decisions; that is, a *system of decisions*....

3. Planning is a process that is directed toward producing one or more future states which are desired and which are not expected to occur unless something is done.[14]

Formal planning demands rationality in the economist's sense of the term—the systematic attainment of goals stated in precise, quantitative terms. The key actor in the process is the analyst, who uses his scientific techniques to develop formal, comprehensive plans.

The literature of planning is vast, and is growing rapidly. Much of the early writing concerned "operational planning"—the projecting of various budgets based on the given strategies of the organization. More recently, attention has turned to the planning of organizational strategies themselves, the more significant and long-range concerns of senior managers. Two techniques have received particular attention —strategic planning in business and planning-programming-budgeting system (PPBS) in government.

George Steiner has written what up to this point is the definitive book on business planning, entitled *Top Management Planning.* The general prescriptive flavor of the planning literature is found throughout this book. For example, "plans can and should be to the fullest possible extent objective, factual, logical, and realistic in establishing objectives and devising means to attain them."[15] Steiner outlines a stepwise procedure for business planning which begins with three studies: (1) fundamental organizational socio-economic purpose, (2) values of top management, and (3) evaluation of external and internal

---

[12]Ibid., p. 25.
[13]Ibid., p. 27.
[14]R. L. Ackoff, *A Concept of Corporate Planning* (New York: Wiley Interscience, 1970), pp. 2–5.
[15]G. A. Steiner, *Top Management Planning* (New York: Macmillan, 1969), p. 20.

opportunities and problems, and company strengths and weaknesses. Strategic plans are then devised, and these lead to the formulation of medium-range programs and short-range plans. In Steiner's opinion, comprehensive planning is important because it simulates the future, applies the systems approach, prevents piecemeal decision-making, provides a common decision-making framework throughout the company, and so on.

In PPBS, the focus is on the budget rather than the general plan (although a budget is, of course, one type of plan). The steps in the process are, by now, well known—the determination of overall governmental goals and objectives, the generation of program proposals to achieve these, the evaluation of these proposals in terms of costs and benefits, the choice of a group of proposals that will satisfy the objectives while not overextending the resources, and the translation of these into five-year and one-year budgets for implementation.

We can delineate three essential features of the planning mode:

1. *In the planning mode, the analyst plays a major role in strategy-making*. The analyst or planner works alongside the manager, and assumes major responsibility for much of the strategy-making process. His role is to apply the techniques of management science and policy analysis to the design of long-range strategies. A U.S. Senator notes the reasons for this:

    I am convinced that we never will get the kind of policy planning we need if we expect the top-level officers to participate actively in the planning process. They simply do not have the time, and in any event they rarely have the outlook or the talents of the good planner. They cannot explore issues deeply and systematically. They cannot argue the advantages and disadvantages at length in the kind of give-and-take essential if one is to reach a solid understanding with others on points of agreement and disagreement.[16]

2. *The planning mode focuses on systematic analysis, particularly in the assessment of the costs and benefits of competing proposals*. Formal planning involves both the active search for new opportunities and the solution of existing problems. The process is always systematic and structured. As one business planner wrote recently:

    No doubt much of top-level management is unscientific. But by applying a systematic, structured approach to these problems, we have a better basis for analyzing them. We may identify more specifically the challenges and needs in the situation and see how they are interrelated.[17]

Formal planning follows a stepwise procedure in which particular attention is paid to the cost-benefit evaluation of proposals, where the planning methodology is best developed. The planner tests proposals for feasibility, determines their efficiency (or economic value), and relates them to each other. The planner deals best with conditions known to the management scientist as "risk"—where the uncertainty can be expressed in statistical terms. Conditions of certainty require no planning; those of pure uncertainty cannot be subjected to analysis.

3. *The planning mode is characterized above all by the integration of decisions and strategies*. Ackoff notes that "the principal complexity in planning derives from the interrelatedness of decisions rather than from the decisions themselves."[18] But this inter-

---

[16] Quoted in R. N. Anthony, *Planning and Control Systems: A Framework for Analysis* (Boston: Harvard Graduate School of Business Administration, 1965), pp. 46–47.

[17] M. F. Cantley, "A Long-range Planning Case Study," *OR Quarterly* (20, 1969), pp. 7–20.

[18] R. L. Ackoff, op. cit., p. 3.

relatedness is the key element in planning. An organization plans in the belief that decisions made together in one systematic process will be less likely to conflict and more likely to complement each other than if they were made independently. For example, planning can ensure that the decision to acquire a new firm complements (or at least does not conflict with) the decision to expand the product line of an existing division. Thus, strategic planning is a process whereby an organization's strategy is designed essentially at one point in time in a comprehensive process (all major decisions made are interrelated). Because of this, planning forces the organization to think of global strategies and to develop an explicit sense of strategic direction.

To conclude, the planning mode is oriented to systematic, comprehensive analysis and is used in the belief that formal analysis can provide an understanding of the environment sufficient to influence it.

The upper part of Table 1 presents in summary form the characteristics of the three modes of strategy-making, while Figure 1 depicts these three modes in graphic form. The first figure shows the taking of bold steps consistent with the entrepreneur's general vision of direction. In the second figure, we see a purely adaptive organization taking incremental steps in reaction to environmental forces, while the third figure indicates a precise plan with a specific, unalterable path to one clear end point.

THE DETERMINATION OF MODE

What conditions drive an organization to favor one mode of strategy-making over the others? We may delineate a number of characteristics of the organization itself, such as its size and the nature of its leadership, and features of its environment, such as competition and stability. These are discussed below and are summarized in the lower portion of Table 1.

The *entrepreneurial* mode requires that strategy-making authority rest with one powerful individual. The environment must be yielding, the organization oriented toward growth, the strategy able to shift boldly at the whim of the entrepreneur. Clearly, these conditions are most typical of organizations that are small and/or young. Their sunk costs are low and they have little to lose by acting boldly. Young organizations in particular have set few precedents for themselves and have made few commitments. The way is open for them to bunch a number of key decisions at an early stage and take them in entrepreneurial fashion. This behavior may also be characteristic of the organization in trouble—it has little to lose by acting boldly, indeed this may be its only hope. In a study of the Montreal radio industry, one student concluded that the less successful stations were predisposed to adopt an entrepreneurial approach in order to catch up and displace the leader (whose behavior was primarily adaptive).

To satisfy the condition of centralized power, the organization must be either a business firm (often with the owner as chief executive), or an institutional or governmental body with a powerful leader who has a strong mandate. The entrepreneurial mode is often found with charismatic leadership. Charles de Gaulle could have been characterized as an entrepreneur at the head of government.

Use of the *adaptive* mode suggests that the organization faces a complex, rapidly changing environment and a divided coalition of influencer forces. Goals cannot be agreed upon unless they are in "motherhood" form and non-operational (they cannot be quantified). Here we have a clear description of the large established organization with great sunk costs and many controlling groups holding each other in check. This is typical of most universities, of many large hospitals, of a surprising number of large corporations, and of many governments, especially those in

Table 1 Characteristics and Conditions of the Three Modes

Characteristic	Entrepreneurial Mode	Adaptive Mode	Planning Mode
Motive for Decisions	Proactive	Reactive	Proactive & Reactive
Goals of Organization	Growth	Indeterminate	Efficiency & Growth
Evaluation of Proposals	Judgmental	Judgmental	Analytical
Choices made by	Entrepreneur	Bargaining	Management
Decision Horizon	Long Term	Short Term	Long Term
Preferred Environment	Uncertainty	Certainty	Risk
Decision Linkages	Loosely Coupled	Disjointed	Integrated
Flexibility of Mode	Flexible	Adaptive	Constrained
Size of Moves	Bold Decisions	Incremental Steps	Global Strategies
Vision of Direction	General	None	Specific
Condition for Use			
Source of Power	Entrepreneur	Divided	Management
Objectives of Organization	Operational	Non-Operational	Operational
Organizational Environment	Yielding	Complex, Dynamic	Predictable, Stable
Status of Organization	Young, Small or Strong Leadership	Established	Large

Figure 1 Paths of the three modes.

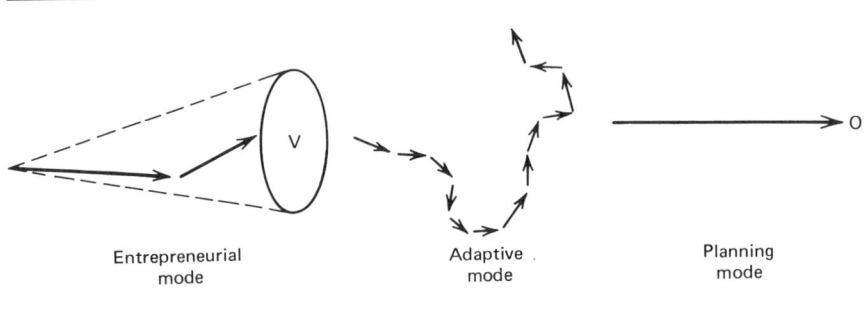

minority positions or composed of coalitions of divergent groups. Indeed, the American system of government has been expressly designed to create conditions of divided power, and it is, therefore, not surprising that Charles Lindblom, the chief proponent of the adaptive approach, is a student of the U. S. public policy-making process.

In order to rely on the *planning* mode, an organization must be large enough to afford the costs of formal analysis, it must have goals that are operational, and it must face an environment that is reasonably predictable and stable. (This last point inevitably raises the comment that planning is most necessary when the environment is difficult to understand. This may be true, but the costs of analyzing a complex environment may be prohibitive and the results may be discouraging. As one Latin American chief executive commented: "Planning is great. But how can you plan—let alone plan long-term—if you don't know what kind of government you'll have next year?"[19])

The above conditions suggest that formal comprehensive planning will generally be found in business firms of reasonable size that do not face severe and unpredictable competition and in government agencies that have clear, apolitical mandates. NASA of the 1960s is a prime example of extended use of the planning mode in government. Its goal was precise and operational, its funding predictable, its mission essentially apolitical in execution. The communist form of government with its five-year plan is another good example. The power system is hierarchical, goals can be made operational, the home environment can be controlled and made more or less stable and predictable (at least as long as the crops are good).

MIXING THE MODES

What is the relationship between our three abstractions and strategy-making reality? Clearly, few organizations can rely on a pure mode. More likely, an organization will find some combination of the three that reflects its own needs. Management students at McGill University have examined a number of business and public organizations according to these three modes, and they have uncovered a variety of ways in which organizations mix these modes. I shall discuss four combinations below, citing examples from these studies to illustrate each.

Combination 1: Mixing The Pure Modes

As we have seen, the literature tends to delineate three modes which are quite distinct in their char-

---

[19]Quoted by H. Stieglitz, *The Chief Executive and His Job* (New York: National Industrial Conference Board, Personnel Policy Study Number 214, 1969), pp. 46–47.

acteristics. This trichotomy provides a convenient starting point for analysis; however, we cannot preclude the existence of other modes that mix their characteristics. Indeed, studies have revealed various combinations of the modes. We have, for example, found a number of adaptive entrepreneurs. One owned a car dealership. Reluctant to delegate authority but unable to achieve further growth without doing so, he was content to hold power absolutely, like the entrepreneur, but to avoid risk and move in incremental steps, like the adaptive strategy-maker.

We can find the two other combinations of the pure modes as well. In entrepreneurial planning, the organization takes bold, decisive steps in terms of a systematic plan for growth, while in adaptive planning the organization reaches a specific goal through a flexible path. Herbert Simon describes an example of adaptive planning found in nature:

> We watch an ant make his laborious way across a wind- and wave-molded beach. He moves ahead, angles to the right to ease his climb up a steep dunelet, detours around a pebble, stops for a moment to exchange information with a compatriot. Thus he makes his weaving, halting way back to his home. . . . [His path] has an underlying sense of direction, of aiming toward a goal. . . . He has a general sense of where home lies, but he cannot foresee all the obstacles between. He must adapt his course repeatedly to the difficulties he encounters. . . .[20]

Combination 2: Mixing Modes By Function

Within single organizations, we have found different modes in different functional areas. One group of students carefully studied all departments of a large downtown hotel, and found evidence of all three modes. Where operations were largely routinized and predictable, as in housekeeping and the front office, the planning mode was used. In marketing, where there was room for imagination and bolder action, the hotel tended to act in an entrepreneurial fashion, while in the personnel department, which faced a complicated labor market, the mode was clearly adaptive.

Another group studied a modeling agency and found that in the area of fashion it was forced (as were all its competitors) to adapt to the dictates of the hautes couturieres of Paris, while it was free to be entrepreneurial or to plan in the areas of marketing and operations. Clearly, different parts of an organization can employ those modes which best fit their particular situations.

Combination 3: Mixing Modes Between Parent And Subunit

Neil Withers, a member of a group studying the Montreal International Airport (which comes under the purview of the Canadian Department of Transport), became interested in the relationship between a parent organization and its subunit (a division, a subsidiary, an agency, and so on). The question he addressed was: If the parent uses a particular mode, what limitations does that impose on the subunit (assuming, of course, that there is not enough decentralization to allow the subunit to operate independently)? Withers considers all nine possible combinations in which each could use one of the three modes, and he draws some interesting conclusions.

Figure 2 shows the use of the adaptive mode by both parent and subunit—a situation Withers refers to as "muddling through times two." In this case, the subunit merely follows the path of the parent, adapting to its incremental moves, and following a slightly more varied and lagged path. Withers concludes that the adaptive mode is, in fact, always an acceptable one for the subunit, no matter what the mode of the parent.

Withers believes "entrepreneurial duets"—whereby both parent and subunit employ the entrepreneurial mode—to be "the worst possible combination." The subunit is subjected not only to its own bold moves but to the unexpected bold

---

[20]H. A. Simon, *The Sciences of the Artificial* (Cambridge, Mass.: MIT Press, 1969), pp. 23–24.

Figure 2 Muddling through times two.

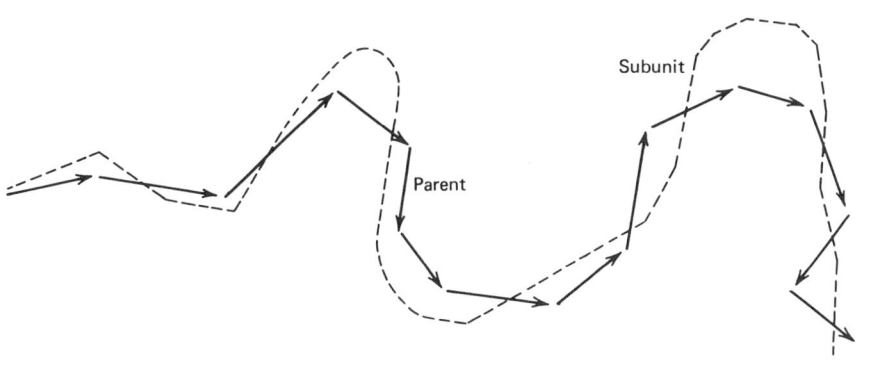

moves of the parent. The disruption may prove intolerable. One is led to conclude that no centralized organization is big enough for two entrepreneurs. Sooner or later one must make a bold, unexpected move that interferes with the other. (In contrast, another group described a decentralized social work agency where strategy-making was largely in the hands of the social workers. They were all entrepreneurs, acting independently to initiate original programs and seeking approval from the main office whose behavior was described as adaptive.)

Finally, Withers considers the conditions under which the subunit can plan. Figure 3 shows a situation where the subunit plans while the parent organization adapts. The subunit at time t_1 anticipates the trend of the parent's strategy and plans accordingly.

Up to time t_2, no difficulties are incurred, and the subunit continues to extrapolate. But soon the parent's direction begins to change, and the subunit finds itself in conflict with the parent. According to Withers, "The use of planning in this uncertainty may not yield sufficiently improved results over [adapting] to justify the cost of planning and the long-term commitment of resources." Withers concludes that subunit planning will work only if the parent plans and if the two planning centers are properly coordinated.

Combination 4: Mixing Modes By Stage Of Development

A number of writers have described the growth of organizations in terms of three or four basic stages—generally corresponding to a life cycle

Figure 3 Planning in an adaptive environment.

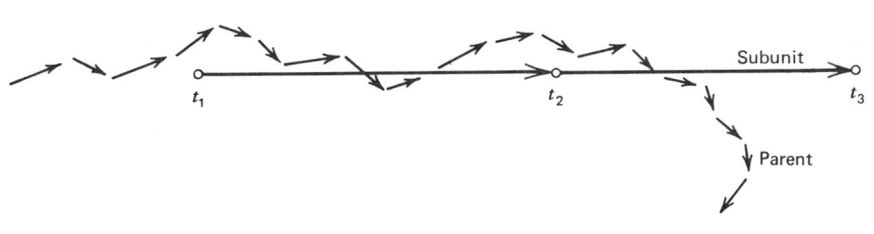

beginning with youth and ending with maturity. It appears that we can characterize the various stages by the mode of strategy-making employed.

Generally, the young organization is entrepreneurial—it has few committed resources, it stands to lose little and to gain much by taking bold steps, leadership tends to be charismatic, and there is much spirit associated with its mission. This is the period of expansion and growth. But each new strategic decision commits additional resources, and gradually the organization locks itself into specific strategies, bureaucratic structures, and demanding pressure groups. The adaptive mode sets in. For example, one group of students studied a Montreal hospital which began in a most entrepreneurial fashion, with dramatic innovations in design and operation. Some time later, when the hospital was established, the provincial government took over increasing control of its budgets and by the time of the study these students felt that the adaptive mode was most descriptive of this organization's strategy-making behavior.

The adaptive mode may signal the final stage of maturity, or the conditions may be such that an organization can attempt to regenerate itself through a new period of entrepreneurship. In fact, it appears that the way to turn around a large, adaptive organization requiring major change is to bring in an entrepreneurial leader. Only by consolidating power in the hands of one strong newcomer will it be possible to override the established factions and the entrenched attitudes.

Some organizations appear to develop cyclical patterns in which periods of entrepreneurship are alternated with periods of adaptiveness. They make a set of bold changes in order to grow, then settle down to a period of stability in which the changes are consolidated, later embark on a new period of growth, and so on. Perhaps in some cases these follow economic cycles—an entrepreneurial mode in an expanding economy, an adaptive mode during recession.

Some time ago, I interviewed the president of a hotel chain who traced his firm's strategy through to the third distinct cycle of change and consolidation. The first stage of growth, as a real estate firm, involved the purchase of a number of older downtown hotels as property investments. Later, realizing the potential of investments, the firm entered a period of consolidation in which the properties were developed into an efficient hotel chain. Having reached this point after some years, a second wave of entrepreneurial growth began. First the firm became public in order to obtain expansion capital and then it entered into a major expansion program involving primarily the construction of a chain of modern motor hotels. Toward the end of the program, the firm found that its financial resources were overextended, partly due to higher expansion costs than anticipated. Again growth was halted while the firm consolidated its new units, concentrating on making them efficient, and waiting until its financial reserves were sufficient to begin to grow again. About three years later, at the time of the interview, cycle three has just begun, this time with the emphasis on the construction of larger downtown hotels.

Such an approach to strategy-making may, in fact, be a sensible one. It proceeds on the assumption that it is better to keep the modes distinct, concentrating fully on one mode at a time rather than mixing them and having to reconcile the different styles of strategy-making.

Other organizations, as they mature, tend to use the planning mode—the development of new strategies by controlled, orderly change. As these organizations grow large, they commit more and more of their staff resources to planning. Indeed, this is the thesis of John Kenneth Galbraith who claims, in *The New Industrial State*, that large business firms are controlled by the planners (the "techno-structure") who use their techniques to enable the firms in turn to control their markets.

Our studies have not covered these large firms, but analyses of the strategy-making behaviors of a diverse array of smaller organizations—airlines, brokerage firms, universities, race tracks, cultural centers—suggest that virtually all start in the entrepreneurial mode, most later shift to an adaptive mode, and some move on to planning or back to entrepreneurship in their maturity.

IMPLICATIONS FOR STRATEGIC PLANNING

What can we conclude from this description of strategy-making? One point merits special emphasis. *Planning is not a panacea for the problems of strategy-making.* As obvious as this seems, there is little recognition of it in planning books or by planners. Instead, one finds a focus on abstract, simple models of the planning process that take no cognizance of the other two modes of strategy-making. Little wonder then that one finds so much frustration among formal planners. Rather than seeking panaceas, we should recognize that the mode used must fit the situation. An unpredictable environment suggests use of the adaptive mode just as the presence of a powerful leader may enable the organization to best achieve its goals through the entrepreneurial mode.

Some situations require no planning, others only limited planning. Often the planning mode can be used only when mixed with the others. Most important, planners must recognize the need for the manager to remain partially in the adaptive mode at all times. Crises and unexpected events are an important part of every strategy-maker's reality. Conventional planning requires operational goals which managers cannot always provide (the coalition may simply not agree on anything specific). Furthermore, it must be recognized that good planning is expensive, it often requires unrealistic stability in the environment, and, above all, it is the least flexible of the strategy-making modes. All this is not to conclude that planning is useless; rather, it suggests that the planner must become more realistic about the limitations of his science.

Often there is a need to redesign the formal planning process. Adaptive planning would differ from conventional planning in a number of important respects. The plans would be flexible so that the manager could adjust as the future unfolded itself. He would be able to time his moves accordingly—to begin construction on the new plant when interest rates fall, to reorganize the structure after certain executives retire. The plans would also provide for different options—alternate locations for a new plant depending on impending state legislation, different possible acquisition strategies depending on the success of recent acquisitions, and so on. In other words, like the path of the ant described earlier, strategic plans would specify end points and perhaps alternate routes, but they would also leave the manager with the flexibility necessary to react to his dynamic environment.

In addition, the planner could draw up a series of contingency plans to help the manager deal with any one of a number of possible events that could have a sudden, devastating effect on the organization. He could also be prepared to "plan in the real-time," that is, to apply his analytical techniques quickly for the manager who faces an unforeseen crisis. By preparing in this way, planners can more closely adapt themselves to the realities of strategy-making.

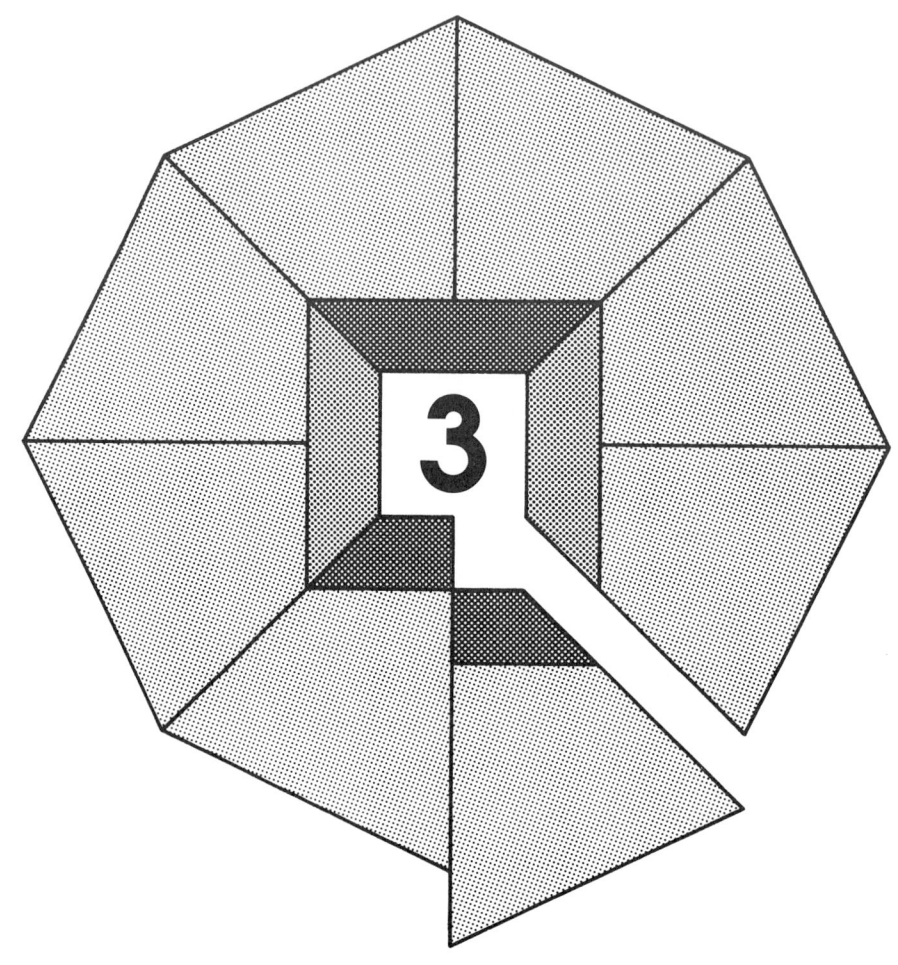

STRATEGY FORMULATION
relating environmental
forces to internal capabilities and values

This chapter continues the discussion of corporate strategy, The focus here is on the dynamic interplay among environmental forces, corporate capabilities, and personal values in the process of strategy formulation.

THE ASSESSMENT OF CAPABILITIES

The very obvious assumption underlying the discussion of environmental forces in Chapter 2 is that it is not enough for a firm merely to identify and analyze the nature and types of market opportunities that may present themselves. That process means very little if the firm cannot *capitalize* on its opportunities. In addition, the firm must be able to exploit a particular opportunity *better* than someone else. In order to resolve the first issue—whether the firm in fact can seize a new opportunity—it is necessary to conduct a resource or capability audit to determine what it is capable of doing strategically. In order to resolve the second issue—whether the firm can seize the market opportunity better than its competitors—it is necessary to analyze further the implications of the resource audit in terms of customer needs and the ability of competitors to satisfy those needs. With respect to the latter, the firm is attempting to establish a *competitive advantage* as exemplified by its ability to satisfy some customer need that is currently unfulfilled by competitors.

The Capability or Resource Audit

The basic goal of the resource audit is to generate an inventory of the firm's strengths and weaknesses which then can be used to assess the feasibility of exploiting any new product/market opportunities. The best generic approach to this problem, without reference to any particular market opportunity, is to delineate *areas* for analysis without trying to conclude beforehand what is "good" or "bad." After all, what may be a strength or a plus factor for entering one market may be a neutral or even a negative factor in another. For example, a firm that possesses an abundance of skills in close tolerance, precision manufacturing may have an obvious strength if it is considering diversification from watch manufacturing to production of precision control instruments, as Elgin did in the late 1950s. However, this same skill may be of no use at all if the firm is considering diversification into basic steel production. Consequently, the approach taken here is to delineate areas for analysis without making any value judgments concerning what may be a strength under the various categories. The important point is that each area must be assessed in relation to the product/market opportunity under consideration by a particular firm. The reading at the end of the chapter provides additional guidelines for judging the resources and capabilities of a firm. The areas of analysis appropriate for the internal resource audit are summarized in the following paragraphs.

Human resources. What are the dominant values of top management and other key personnel? What is the overall quality of personnel in the various areas? What are their special skills? Are there attitudinal problems?

Are there undesirable instances of interpersonal conflict? Are work group and intergroup relationships satisfactory? Do employees identify with and support the goals and objectives of the firm? In short, what are the firm's personnel problems and weaknesses? What are its strengths?

Financial resources. What is the overall financial situation with regard to liquidity, leverage, working capital, profitability, and growth? Does the firm have the ability to raise additional capital? Is the contemplated opportunity financially feasible? What are the firm's financial strengths and weaknesses?

Physical resources and production. What types of production processes are currently utilized? What is the overall condition of plant and equipment? Is plant capacity being fully utilized? What particular operating skills exist? Can the production requirements of the contemplated opportunity be in any way integrated into present processes or would they only exist "side by side" or in separate plants? What is the situation with regard to inventories, quality control, and scheduling? What are the production strengths and weaknesses?

Marketing. What are the channels of distribution utilized to implement the present strategy? What channels would be required to implement the contemplated strategy? What is the overall quality of sales personnel and managers? Are current promotional techniques effective? What are the basic skill requirements for sales and advertising? Does a market research program exist? What are the strengths and weaknesses of the marketing operation?

Research and development. Does the company emphasize basic or applied research? What are the research and development requirements associated with the present strategy? What are the requirements associated with the contemplated strategy? What are the particular technical orientations and skills of the present scientific personnel? What are the research and development strengths and weaknesses?

Organizational. What are the current structural arrangements? What modifications in structure must occur to accommodate any new strategy? Is the present structure flexible? Effective? Efficient? What are the structural strengths and weaknesses?

Present strategic posture. What are the present product mix, customer mix, geographic limits of the market(s) served, competitive emphasis, and objectives (performance criteria) of the firm? Does the potential opportunity represent a radical departure from the present posture? What would be the effects of a radical shift on company image, customer identification and loyalty, investor evaluations of the firm, employee identification, and overall firm-environment relationships? What is the overall outlook for the present strategy? What is the overall outlook for the contemplated strategy?

Environmental research capabilities. The most important assessment in this area relates to the financial and human resources currently devoted to external research. Is the firm "active" or "passive" in this area? Would the opportunity under consideration necessitate a shift in philosophy? Would it necessitate gaining a previously unexplored type of environmental knowledge? If exploited, would the idea require much more resources for market research, economic forecasting, and long-range planning than has been thus far necessary? Is the firm contemplating movement into a dynamic and unstable industry while having been in a relatively stable situation? In general, how different from the important factors in the present markets are those in the contemplated markets? Are our external research skills transferable to the new situation?

Establishing a Competitive Advantage

As indicated earlier, it is not enough for a firm simply to possess the resources to exploit an environmental opportunity or to respond to some new environmental constraint. Establishing that the firm *can* enter a contemplated market is only the first step toward success. The second step is to determine whether or not the firm can capitalize on the opportunity *better* than its potential (or existing) competitors. There are many ways in which a firm can establish a competitive advantage. Robert L. Katz has identifed the following ones:

1. Excellence in product design and/or performance (engineering ingenuity).
2. Low-cost, high-efficiency operating skill in manufacturing and/or in distribution.
3. Leadership in product innovation.
4. Efficiency in customer service.
5. Personal relationships with customers.
6. Efficiency in transportation and logistics.
7. Effectiveness in sales promotion.
8. Merchandising efficiency. High turnover of inventories and/or of capital.
9. Skillful trading in volatile price movement commodities.
10. Ability to influence legislation.
11. Highly efficient, low-cost facilities.
12. Ownership or control of low-cost or scarce raw materials.
13. Control of intermediate distribution or processing units.
14. Massive availability of capital.

15. Widespread customer acceptance of company brand name. Company reputation.
16. Product availability, convenience.[1]

The resource audit of a company should indicate the strengths *from which* a competitive advantage may be developed. It must be recognized, however, that mere possession of a particular strength does not guarantee its utility to the consumer. Therein lies the necessity to evaluate thoroughly the *needs* of the target consumers in relation to what the firm can provide. For example, prime location of manufacturing facilities much nearer to an industrial consumer than competitors can be a decided advantage for a firm, either in terms or providing more rapid deliveries and better service or providing a lower-price product because of lower transportation costs. However, if the customer does not *need* rapid delivery and if quality, not price, is the more important variable affecting the purchase decision, the firm has no "distinctive competence" and may have no competitive advantage at all. The key point is that possession of a strength is valuable only if that strength is important for filling a customer need and is not possessed by a competitor.

The following examples will illustrate how companies in a variety of industries have developed differential advantages over their competitors. First, a reputation for *excellence in product performance* seems to be an important factor in the plans of Japan's manufacturers of automobile parts to expand their operations to the United States. The shift to compact cars in the United States will obviously increase the demands for small-car parts, and the Japanese companies have long held an edge in both quality and price.[2] It should come as no surprise, then, that various states and municipalities are actively courting these companies in order to boost corporate tax revenues and alleviate unemployment problems.

Consider also the type of competitive advantage achieved by White Consolidated, a little-known producer of refrigerators, washers, dryers, and ranges. This company now stands third in the appliance industry with a market share of 25% compared to the 30% held by General Electric and Whirlpool's 27%. White Consolidated has achieved this position primarily because of its skill in developing *low-cost, highly efficient production processes* in an industry characterized by heavy price competition:

> White Consolidated has become an industry power thanks to a strategy that is disarmingly simple in concept, if not in execution. The company has merely elevated the doctrine of cost control to a corporate religion, one it pursues with messianic fervor, using an incredible array of cost-cutting techniques. At a time

---

[1] Robert L. Katz, *Cases and Concepts in Corporate Strategy* (Englewood Cliffs, N.J.: Prentice-Hall, 1970), p. 215.
[2] "Japan Auto Parts Makers Mount a U.S. Invasion," *Business Week*, April 23, 1979, p. 58.

when executives, economists, and policymakers are deeply concerned about the long-term leveling of productivity in the U.S., White Consolidated has achieved a drastic increase in the efficiency of plants, people, and equipment that were cast off in despair by much bigger corporations.[3]

The White Consolidated case also illustrates how a company is "reading the signs" that have emerged from a thorough environmental analysis:

> Of course, such consolidation of acquired appliance operations is likely to produce only short-term gains, and White is mindful of the need for long-term productivity improvements. Thus, even the company's research work is decidedly slanted in favor of production economies instead of marketing innovations. The company spent $8.2 million on appliance research and development last year, and nearly all of it went to make money-saving changes in existing products rather than to develop new ones.[4]

The Allen Group is a good example of a company that has developed a competitive advantage based on *leadership in product innovation*. Acting in response to increased engine-testing requirements coming from the federal government, the Allen Group set out to develop computerized processes for accomplishing such tests. Led by Chairman Walter B. Kissinger (younger brother of the former secretary of state), the company was successful in developing the most advanced engine-controls system in the industry.[5] Its reputation now seems fairly secure as a result of being a leader in product innovation.

Walt Disney Productions is, of course, an example of a company that has definitely secured a *reputation as the industry leader* in family entertainment in the United States. This reputation has enabled the company to expand geographically, as evidenced by its joint venture with the Tokyo-based Oriental Land Company to build Tokyo Disneyland—a $300 million project due to open in 1983.[6] Disney Productions will receive a percentage of the gross revenues in return for planning, designing, and overseeing all construction and operation of the park. This is Disney's first foreign project, although its reputation has certainly been worldwide for many years.

An illustration of how companies must gear their priorities to the needs of their customers is apparent in the U.S. farm equipment industry. The most successful farm equipment dealer is the one, in all likelihood, who is providing the *best parts and service* to farmers. Farmers are always very concerned about breakdowns in machinery because such breakdowns cost

---

[3] "White Consolidated's New Appliance Push," *Business Week*, May 7, 1979, p. 94.
[4] Ibid., p. 96.
[5] "Allen Group: Meeting the Demand for Sophisticated Auto Testing Gear," *Business Week*, May 21, 1979, p. 109.
[6] "Disneyland in Tokyo," *Business Week*, May 14, 1979, p. 38.

time and money! Consequently, providing reliable parts as well as fast service—much more important than price in most cases—will be the key to success for a dealer.

The Concept of Synergy

A useful concept to consider in the attempt to match external opportunities with internal capabilities and resources is that of *synergy*. Positive synergy is best described as the "2 + 2 = 5" effect, or alternatively, the "whole is greater than the sum of its parts." In the process of strategy formation or change, it refers to the degree of complementarity between *present* skills and resources and the *future* skills and resources that would be required by an alteration of strategy. The higher the degree of complementarity that exists between the present strategic posture and the contemplated posture, the greater the opportunity for realizing positive synergy. This somewhat elusive concept is best explained through the consideration of different types of synergy and how they relate to the process of strategy formation. *In each of the following cases, assume that a new product/market opportunity is being considered by an existing firm.*

First, maximum *production synergy* would be achieved if the production facilities, processes, and skills currently in operation also could be utilized to produce the contemplated product. This situation, given some existing excess capacity, obviously could result in decreased unit production costs because factory overhead would be spread over a greater volume. Also, neither quality nor efficiency should suffer, as worker skills would be completely transferable to the new production requirements. This "ideal" synergy would occur when one firm horizontally merged with another that manufactured the same or substantially similar products. In the case of internal growth, positive production synergy would occur to the extent that new products developed are compatible with existing skills and resources. On the other hand, there is little chance for production synergy if, for example, a writing instrument manufacturer diversifies into the production of copying machines and ceramics (as Scripto did in the late 1960s, with negative results).

Production synergy can occur if only some "common thread" between two operations can be found, regardless of the degree of market congruence insofar as end uses of the products are concerned. Chrysler's purchase of the Lone Star Boat Company illustrates this last point. Chrysler foresaw the application of its experience and skills in the mass production of automobiles to the mass production of boats. Thus experience and skill in assembly line techniques and administration provided a common thread in operations.

Second, maximum *marketing synergy* would be achieved if the current sales force, distribution channels, physical facilities, and promotional techniques also could be utilized to market the contemplated product addition. This type of synergy differs somewhat from the production case, since a high degree of synergy may be achieved here even if the products are physically different from one another. A very high degree of marketing synergy may exist for a work shoe manufacturer adding a work glove line, whereas substantially less production synergy would occur. This is because the work gloves may be distributed through the same channels, by the same sales force (no different skills required), and supported by substantially equivalent promotional techniques; on the other hand, although some aspects of the production process may be similar, such as stitching, the degree of overlap between facilities and skills requirements in production is not nearly so great as in the marketing sphere.

As marketplaces become more and more competitive, the existence of marketing synergy becomes more and more important. The Warner-Lambert Corporation places great emphasis on this factor in evaluating prospective acquisitions. This company, best known for Listerine and drugs, has become a major force in consumer packaged goods through an aggressive growth and merger strategy. In analyzing companies to be acquired, it focuses on those "whose products. . . fit snugly into Warner-Lambert's own distribution channels."[7] Warner-Lambert's latest acquisition is Entenmann's, a baker of premium-price products that previously served a limited geographical region along the east coast. Warner-Lambert plans to expand this product line on a national basis, using the:

> . . .distribution system that has long been in place for W.L.'s American Chicle Div., which makes and markets chewing gum and which in 1977 beat out Wrigley's for leadership of this $650 million market. "Our Chicle people are in and out of almost every supermarket in the country daily" says Hagan (Ward S. Hagan, Chairman of Warner-Lambert). "And Entenmann's is distributed within the same channels in which we operate—through route operators." He counts on W.L.'s relationships with the supermarkets to open the way for the retailers' ready acceptance of Entenmann's products.[8]

All acquisitions now made by Warner-Lambert must "fit" an existing distribution channel—and all but one made since 1961 have followed this pattern. The one exception is American Optical Corporation; this company has been Warner-Lambert's "most troubled subsidiary."[9]

Third, *research and development synergy* would be achieved if the technologies supporting the development of both the present and contemplated product lines are substantially similar. The potential in this area usually emanates either from similar research skills (e.g., basic versus applied, product versus process orientation, chemistry versus computer science) or from similar functional characteristics of the products.

---

[7]"Turning Warner-Lambert Into a Marketing Conglomerate," *Business Week*, March 5, 1979, p. 60.
[8]Ibid., p. 61.
[9]Ibid.

Fourth, *financial synergy* is the one major type of synergy that is virtually unrelated to the degree of similarity between present and contemplated strategic postures. This is because the skills and techniques of financial planning and control have a high degree of transferability across both industry and institutional lines. The *opportunity* for positive synergy in this area lies in the extent to which the firm can achieve a larger capital base for investment, increased borrowing power, and greater earnings growth through the speading of administrative overhead over a greater volume. Note that this type of synergy is frequently the *only* rationale for addition of some product lines and is the underlying reason for conglomerate growth and expansion. In essence, the conglomerate firm attempts to achieve a larger capital base and earnings growth than the sum of what could be achieved by its various product lines operating as completely separate companies.

The declining fortunes of many conglomerates in the 1960s indicates all too clearly that financial synergy alone is a tenuous base for expansion. Boise Cascade is a prime example of a company that set about becoming a conglomerate in the late 1960s, as ventures were made into recreational vehicles, real estate, utilities, and a variety of other unrelated industries. The company did well for a few years but was in "desperate shape" by 1972.[10] After a changeover in the presidency of the firm, Boise Cascade began to sell off several of these product lines in order to get back to their basic business of forest products (paper, wood products, office supplies, building materials). This strategy had resulted in record profits for the company by 1978—a dramatic piece of evidence to support the argument that companies should not spread themselves too thin!

Fifth, *general management synergy* occurs when the skills, experience, and knowledge of key managers are transferable from the present strategy to the contemplated one. Basically, knowledge requirements for *any* successful general manager are twofold: (1) general knowledge of the processes and techniques of administration (initially acquired in business school and sharpened through experience), and (2) technical knowledge about the manager's specific industry and firm (generally acquired only through on-the-job training and experience). The first type of knowledge, which is essentially a methodological base, is freely transferable to all types of industries and institutions. The second type, however, indicates that there is a definite learning period for managers moving from one firm to another. Moreover, the greater the dissimilarity between strategies of firms, the longer the learning period. A manager may have little trouble moving freely from Firm A to Firm B within the same industry. However, if the move is from Firm A in Industry A to Firm B in Industry B, the task is progressively more difficult. In general, the further a manager moves "from home" in terms of firm and industry characteristics, the longer the learning period. The extreme cases, of course, would be encountered when a general manager moves from one

---

[10]"Boise Cascade: Expansionism That Now Sticks Close to Home," *Business Week*, February 19, 1979, p. 55.

broad type of institution to another (e.g., from vice president of a business firm to hospital administrator).

In conclusion, the concept of synergy is useful *only* for assessing the potential complementarity of skills and resources when contemplating an alteration of strategy. One cannot conclude that potential positive synergy is directly correlated with future success, since many factors other than complementarity affect future revenues and costs. One may conclude, however, that the greater the potential for achieving positive synergy, the greater the *probability* for success, simply because eliminating duplicate functions, spreading overhead, and utilizing similar skills are directly related to unit cost reduction.

THE INFLUENCE OF PERSONAL VALUES ON STRATEGY

The iterative judgmental process of "matching" external opportunities and constraints with internal resources and capabilities usually results in the generation of alternative strategic postures for the firm. Up to this point, we have assumed a somewhat rational process and have not explicitly accounted for the influence of personal values on strategy. The role of *judgment* in strategic decision making has long been recognized, primarily because of three major factors:

1. All information related to the numerous external forces operating in any situation cannot possibly be gathered, assimilated, and evaluated.
2. The information that can be collected and evaluated is frequently imperfect.
3. The many variables related to strategic decisions cannot be "modeled" in the sense of establishing precise functional relationships that provide deterministic outputs or "correct" decisions.

The *personal values* of top managers are an integral component of strategic decisions. Moreover, such values should be reflected and satisfied by decisions on major issues such as corporate strategy.

Culturally Derived Values

A personal value can be viewed as one's "conception of the desirable." Eduard Spranger identified six major kinds of value orientations that are useful for distinguishing among types of people.

1. *Theoretical.* Dominant intellectual interest in an empirical and rational approach to systematic knowledge.
2. *Economic.* Orientation toward practical affairs, the production and consumption of goods, the uses and creations of wealth.
3. *Aesthetic.* Dominant interest in the artistic, in form, symmetry, and harmony.
4. *Social.* Primary value is the love of people and warmth of human relationships.

5. *Political.* Dominant orientation toward power, influence, and recognition.
6. *Religious.* Primary orientation toward unity and creation of satisfying and meaningful relationship to the universe.[11]

All these values may be viewed as "culturally derived." As noted by Guth and Taguiri, values are transmitted to a person "through his parents, teachers, and other significant persons in his environment who, in turn, acquired their values in similar fashion."[12] These culturally derived values are guiding principles for decision making in our everyday life. Because they are such an integral and active component of one's personality structure, it is logical to expect that such values also will be guiding principles in making decisions on organizational issues, such as strategy, for which no predetermined "correct" solution exists.

Since the success of any business firm is generally measured by economic criteria,[13] the tendency has been to impute dominant economic values or orientations to decision makers. Although little research has been done in this area, the results to date reveal enormous individual variations among the value structures of U.S. executives—some have dominant economic values, while others may be primarily oriented to the aesthetic, political, social, theoretical, or religious.[14] Granted these individual variations exist, what may be the nature of their respective influences on corporate strategy? Or, to put it another way, how might executives with diverse value structures differ in their general perceptions of the most desirable course of action for the firm?

Obviously, the executive with dominant economic values would tend to emphasize strategic opportunities that promise the greatest increases in growth and/or profitability of the firm. On the other hand, an executive with dominant aesthetic values would be more prone to eschew profitable opportunities that would require, for example, "cheapening" the design of a product and thus detracting from the firm's image as the quality producer in the industry. An executive with dominant social values may veto profitable opportunities that might threaten to upset interpersonal relationships within the organization, assuming, of course, that a reasonable return on investment is being earned with the present strategy. The individual with dominant social values also would be more favorable toward strategies that are "socially responsible" than other managers who are *primarily* con-

---

[11]William D. Guth and Renato Taguiri, "Personal Values and Corporate Strategy," *Harvard Business Review, 43* (5), September-October 1965, p. 124.
[12]Ibid., p. 125.
[13]This obviously remains true today and for the near future, although growing public dissatisfaction with profits as the primary criterion for business success may eventually result in "social performance" indicators. This movement in itself represents a shift in the personal values of the larger society and was discussed more fully in Chapter 2.
[14]Guth and Taguiri, "Personal Values and Corporate Strategy," pp. 126–127.

cerned with increasing the profitability of the firm. An individual with a dominant political or power orientation will tend to emphasize the opportunities that promise to increase the various indicators of the size of a firm, such as sales volume, total assets, or total employees. An executive with a primary orientation toward the theoretical may be more prone to emphasize long-range research and development activities at the expense of short-run economic returns. Finally, strategic opportunities likely will be evaluated by the highly religious person in terms of their moral implications for the "nature of man" vis á vis the Creator and the total universe. The highly religious person also might evaluate opportunities in terms of ethical criteria, which are generally thought to be beyond the rightful concern of business people—that is, the ethics that are more philosophical or religious in nature instead of those related to everyday business practice, such as fair trade or the independent determination of prices.

The general overview just presented would lead one to believe that some companies do *not* see "profit maximization" as their primary objective. For these kinds of companies profits are necessary, but *not sufficient*, for their continued existence. Consider the Reader's Digest Association, the $1 billion giant in magazine and book publishing, record distribution, and direct-mail marketing houses. This corporation has long been criticized for its conservative approach in the publishing world, including an unwillingness to change the "staid" format of *Reader's Digest*. The typical response from top executives of the company is that "profits are secondary to providing a good product at a reasonable price and making this a good place to work."[15] Their objective is to help customers "improve themselves mentally, materially, and spiritually."[16] Meanwhile, the *Reader's Digest* continues to flourish as the most widely read magazine in the world.

Another example of a highly successful company that emphasizes noneconomic values is Service Master. Once strictly a carpet cleaning business, the company now specializes in the cleaning of health care facilities and has over 70% of the contracts to manage hospital maintenance departments. Service Master is run, unabashedly, on Christian values, and its goals are listed in the folowing order: "to honor God in all we do, to help people develop, to pursue excellence, to grow profitably."[17]

Finally, it is interesting to consider how a company might disregard basic economic criteria when trying to decide on the basic direction or orientation of the business. For example, Uniroyal had expanded during the past decade to become a diversified producer of fire hoses, golf balls, and other products in addition to its basic tire operations. The company has had

---

[15] "Reader's Digest: Modernizing The Beat of a Different Drummer," *Business Week*, March 5, 1979, p. 98.
[16] Ibid.
[17] "Service Master: The Protestant Ethic Helps Clean Hospitals Better," *Business Week*, February 19, 1979, p. 58.

troubles, however, and has cut out approximately 20 different operations during the past 5 years.[18] *But* this retrenchment program has now ended, and Uniroyal has apparently not addressed its biggest economic problem: the U.S. tire business! This operation has been only marginally profitable, and the total tire industry is predicted to grow by only 2% annually during the next few years. Moreover, little relief is in sight because of longer-lasting radial tires and excess capacity in the industry. But Uniroyal is extremely reluctant to face this issue squarely, as evidenced by the comment of one senior executive that "to quit the tire business would be to cut the heart out of Uniroyal."[19] Furthermore, the president has stated that the tire operation is "...too big a piece of Uniroyal to walk away from. It's our backbone."[20] It will be interesting to watch this company for the next few years to see if its aesthetic values concerning what is "right for Uniroyal" can be adhered to in the face of economic adversity.

These examples indicate that, consciously or subconsciously, our culturally derived personal values may serve as criteria for choice among competing strategic alternatives, assuming, of course, that all the alternatives satisfy minimum economic criteria for the perpetuation of the firm. The following section discusses the manner in which our organizationally derived values may exert a similar influence.

Organizationally Derived Values

A second classification of values may be viewed as "organizationally derived." Within this general classification, it is possible to identify five major types.

1. *Production.* Dominant value is cost reduction, operating efficiency, commitment to schedules, work simplification, and certainty and stability of operations.
2. *Research and Development.* Primary orientation toward innovation, design ingenuity, "scientific challenge," discovery of new knowledge, and technical superiority of products over those of competitors.
3. *Marketing.* Dominant value is increased sales volume and market share.
4. *Financial.* Dominant value is profits, return on investment, efficient cash flows, safety of assets, orderly records.
5. *Personnel.* Greatest emphasis is on organizational stability and worker satisfaction and development.

These values tend to be associated with one's major role grouping within an organization. Thus different functional area personnel tend to have dif-

---

[18] "Uniroyal: Narrowing Choices as it Clings to the Tire Business," *Business Week*, June 11, 1979, p. 74.
[19] Ibid.
[20] Ibid.

ferent "conceptions of the desirable" for their firm with regard to product mix, customer designation, product characteristics and quality, priority of objectives, and the like. Specific market opportunities would be perceived differently by the various functional area personnel as a result of their differences in orientation. Each manager involved would apply different criteria to the same opportunities for the firm, consciously or not, and this would logically result in disagreements over the efficacy of the various decisions proposed. Examples of this divergence are discussed next.

Cases of Conflicting Values

The following examples illustrate cases where culturally and organizationally derived values have contributed to conflict and disagreement among top managers.

Consider first the case of a brewery located in the Midwest. It was founded in 1862 and soon established itself over a two-state area as the top producer of premium draught beer. This reputation was enhanced as further improvements in brewing techniques were developed and implemented. Then the brewing industry turned to packaged (canned and bottled) beer and found immediate consumer acceptance. By the middle 1960s, over 80% of national beer consumption was in canned and bottled beer. The brewery in question, however, continued to emphasize premium draught beer in the face of declining sales and despite numerous market surveys that indicated consumer preferences for packaged beer. A strategy session was called by the president and also included the vice presidents of sales, production, and finance. The subject was: What should be the future product/market scope (basic strategy) of the firm in light of the changing preference of beer consumers?

Three basic alternatives were advanced by the executives:

1. The sales vice president was in favor of switching to cans and concentrating on retail grocery outlets and packaged liquor stores. He pointed out that this change in basic strategy would reflect consumer preferences and offered the greatest potential for increasing sales volume in the local area. He presented detailed statistics to support his proposal, including information to show that national markets were beyond the firm's capabilities at the present time.
2. The production vice president (brewmaster) argued against the preceding alternative. He strongly held the conviction that "packaged beer taste as differently from draught beer as cabbage tastes from sauerkraut. Can or bottle it and it is no longer the real thing." He favored maintaining the firm's present strategy of producing and selling premium draught beer in the the two-state area.
3. The president felt that the firm should expand nationally with both canned and draught beer and that his personal skill in advertising would enable him to at least match the greater resources devoted to

advertising by the national brands. Selective exploitation of restricted market areas would be necessary until a greater capital base was established; the accumulation of such efforts over the years to come would result in the brewery's becoming truly national in scope.

An examination of the alternatives reveals the influence of three differing value orientations on perceptions of *the same basic set of market data*. The sales vice president exhibits a dominant economic orientation. Note his emphasis on the strategy that "offered the greatest potential for increasing sales volume." The production vice president's idea of maintaining the status quo appears to result from his concern over the aesthetic nature (quality and taste) of the product. Finally, the president's proposed strategy exhibits a tendency toward a political or power orientation. Note the emphasis on the firm's becoming "truly national in scope."

To illustrate how organizationally derived values may conflict, consider the fact that most top management decision-making groups are composed of functional area vice presidents. Paul R. Lawrence and Jay W. Lorsch provide rich examples of such potential conflict in their discussion of differentiation and integration in organizations.[21] In the following excerpt from their book, imagine that the sales manager and the research scientist are vice presidents of marketing and research and development, respectively, and that the integrator is the chief executive of the firm:

> In the plastics organization we might find a sales manager discussing a potential new product with a fundamental research scientist and an integrator. In this discussion the sales manager is concerned with the needs of the customer. What performance characteristics must a new product have to perform in the customer's machinery? How much can the customer afford to pay? How long can the material be stored without deteriorating? Further, our sales manager, while talking about these matters, may be thinking about more pressing current problems. Should he lower the price on an existing product? Did the material shipped to another customer meet his specifications? Is he going to meet this quarters's sales targets?
>
> In contrast, our fundamental scientist is concerned about a different order of problems. Will this new project provide a scientific challenge? To get the desired result, could he change the molecular structure of a known material without affecting its stability? What difficulties will he encounter in solving these problems? Will this be a more interesting project to work on than another he heard about last week? Will he receive some professional recognition if he is successful in solving the problem? Thus our sales manager and our fundamental scientist not only have quite different goal orientations, but they are thinking about different time dimensions—the sales manager about what's going on today and in the next few months; the scientist, how he will spend the next few years.[22]

---

[21]Paul R. Lawrence and Jay W. Lorsch, *Organization and Environment* (Homewood, Ill.: Richard D. Irwin, 1969).
[22]Ibid., pp. 134–135.

It is obvious from this example that the two individuals are applying different criteria in evaluating the feasibility of a new product proposal. The fact that many alternative strategies available to a given firm are economically sound permits the intrusion of these organizationally derived values, in addition to the fact that the "correct" decision solution at this level, however defined, is never known in advance. If a proposed alternative could satisfy *both* sets of criteria being employed in the example, obviously little disagreement would occur. However, when one considers that the problem is usually compounded by the presence of other functional specialities, at least production and finance, in evaluation of decisions affecting the total firm, the potential for considerable disagreement and conflict exists.

The Resolution of Conflicting Values

The preceding illustrations raise the issue of how to resolve conflicting values in the process of decision making. Although there is no easy answer to such conflict, several comments can be made. First, we must be *aware* of our own values and the manner in which they affect our decisions. Second, although one value orientation may be dominant in an individual, other values also are possessed by that same person. Thus it may be possible to appeal to these "lower-order" values in an attempt to effect some sort of compromise when disagreement occurs over future strategy or other decision issues. Third, we should be aware of the tendency to exaggerate value differences between ourselves and others. As shown by Guth and Taguiri's study, there is frequently a tendency to attribute inaccurately dominant value orientations to individuals based on our own stereotypes of their particular organizational roles.[23] For example, those researchers found that scientists and research personnel attributed higher economic and political value scores to a group of executives than the executives actually indicated for themselves. Similarly, the executives attributed higher theoretical values to the research personnel than the latter indicated for themselves. Thus, there may be more "common ground" for agreement than is apparent at first glance. Fourth, we should recognize that this type of conflict is healthy for the firm. The assessment of decision alternatives from several different value perspectives lends another dimension to the advantage of obtaining a "diversity of inputs" in decisions of major importance. Such advantage is usually couched in terms of obtaining a diversity of *technical* inputs from different functional areas of expertise. It seems that a diversity of *value* inputs would contribute greatly toward illumination of the more subtle elements of decisions—the extent to which the decision outcomes may be congruent with the value structures of those who will bear primary responsibility for decision implementation.

Finally, it is particularly important that the chief executive of a firm maintain a workable balance among the various types of values, those that

---

[23]Guth and Taguiri, "Personal Values and Corporate Strategy," pp. 130–131.

are culturally derived and those that emanate from organizational role groupings. As noted by Katz, there can be no "separate, permanent, 'general management' set of values and criteria."[24] To integrate effectively the various cultural and organizational orientations in a manner that will ensure enterprise success and personal commitment *simultaneously* remains the responsibility of the chief executive. It is mandatory that this individual carefully examine his or her own innate bias and compensate for it in the attempt to reconcile value conflicts among immediate subordinates.

SUMMARY

Continuing the presentation begun in the previous chapter, Chapter 3 discussed the dynamic interplay among environmental forces, corporate capabilities, and personal values in the formulation of strategic decisions by the firm. An outline of areas for analysis in an internal capability audit was presented, with more detailed guides for conducting the audit covered in the reading that follows this chapter. The various means by which firms can establish a competitive advantage were briefly discussed, with emphasis on the interrelation of a given firm's capabilities with those of competitors.

Various types of synergy were described as well as the means by which an organization can assess the extent to which its internal capabilities are sufficient to meet the challenges posed by a new product/market opportunity. The key areas of analysis with regard to determining synergistic potential were presented as production, marketing, research and development, financial, and general management synergy.

Finally, the role of personal values in the process of strategy formation was discussed in some detail. Emphasis was placed on distinguishing "culturally derived" and "organizationally derived" values when trying to assess underlying reasons for certain strategic moves.

This chapter concludes the discussion of overall strategy from a "formulative" perspective. Quite clearly, however, the process of strategy formulation cannot be completely separated from a discussion of its implementation and its effects on the various internal activities of the firm. Consequently, even though the following chapters concentrate primarily on the integrative aspects of functional area decision making within the firm, the effects of changes in product mix, customer mix, and the other components of overall strategy on those functional areas is discussed at appropriate points.

---

[24]Katz, *Cases and Concepts in Corporate Strategy*, p. 19.

HOW TO EVALUATE A FIRM

Robert B. Buchele

The sharp drops in earnings and even losses recently suffered by many so-called "growth" companies, whose stocks had been bid so high, have cast doubts upon the adequacy of the established methods which are used by investment specialists to evaluate companies.

Equally dramatic but less evident have been the serious declines of numerous companies shortly after having been rated as "excellently managed" by the best known of the evaluation systems using a list of factors covering numerous aspects of corporate management.

What has happened to render these evaluation systems so inadequate? What lessons can be learned by persons whose work requires them to do overall evaluations of companies—investors, acquisition specialists, consultants, long-range planners, and chief executives? Finally, what are the requirements for a system for evaluating firms that will function reliably under today's conditions?

After all, the decline of even blue chip companies is not a new phenomenon. To quote from an unpublished paper recently presented by Ora C. Roehl before a management conference at UCLA:

> The Brookings Institution sometime ago made a study of the 100 top businesses in the USA in the early 1900s, and they found that after 40 years only 36 were still among the leaders.
>
> We all look at the Dow-Jones Industrial Average practically every day and we know the companies that are a part of the Average today—from Allied Chemical, Aluminum Company of America, and American Can to U.S. Steel, Westinghouse, and Woolworth. But, as we go back in time a bit, we find names that once were important enough to be a part of the Average and which we have heard of, such as Hudson Motors, Famous Players-Lasky, and Baldwin Locomotive. It is not long, however, before we run into one-time business leaders whose names are strange to us, such as Central Leather, U.S. Cordage Company, Pacific Mail, American Cotton Oil Company, and one with a nostalgic sort of name, The Distilling and Cattle Feeding Company.[1]

What is new, however, is the current pace of such events. Stemming in part from the rise of industrial research expenditures from less than $200 million in 1930 to an estimated $12.4 billion in 1960,[2] the pace of industrial change has been accelerating for many years. It is now so rapid that firms can rise or fall more quickly than ever before.

Sophisticated technologies are spreading to many industries; in addition, as we shall see in this article, various management techniques contribute to the quickening pace of change. In consequence, the rapid rate of change now affects a great many American firms rather than just that minority known as "growth" companies.

PRESENT EVALUATION METHODS

Financial Analysis

This method typically consists of studying a "spread" of profit and loss figures, operating statements and balance sheet ratios for the past five or ten years. The underlying assumption is that the future performance of a company can be reliably projected from trends in these data. The reasoning is that these data represent the "proof of the pudding." If they're sound, the company as a whole, particularly its top management, must be sound, for a competent top management will keep a firm healthy.

Through the years this method has worked well because the basic assumption has been reasonably valid. Despite the fact that some blue chip companies have failed, it is still reasonably valid for the large firms who are thoroughly entrenched in their markets and who make substantial investments in executive development, in market development, and in any technology that promises to threaten one of their market positions.

However, the assumption is becoming less safe, especially in connection with medium-sized and small firms, as the pace of industrial change steadily accelerates. Thus, a firm whose financial record is unimpressive may be on the verge of a technological breakthrough that will send its profits rocketing ahead; conversely, a company that looks good in financial analyses may be doomed because it is being bypassed technologically or marketing-wise or because rigor mortis has taken over the executive offices.

In practice the financial analysis method is often supplemented by market research in the form of interviews with leading customers, by interviews with the firm's top executives, and by consultation with scientists capable of evaluating technological capabilities and trends. While these supplementary activities help, financial analysis still is neither adequately comprehensive nor adequately oriented to the future.

Thus, this type of market research can yield some insights into the effectiveness of past and present performance but is too superficial to tell much about the future. The interviews with top executives can be more misleading than informative simply because they are conducted by financial people inexperienced in management, marketing, or technology.[3] The use of scientists is a commendable step forward. However, it provides help in only one and possibly two of the many areas essential to a thorough evaluation.

Key Factor Ratings

Systems more comprehensive than the financial analysis method have been developed, mainly by consultants seeking to understand firms' overall strengths and weaknesses in order to be able to prescribe for them. Such systems typically involve ratings based on a series of key factors underlying the financial factors themselves. Little has been published about these systems because the consulting firms regard them as proprietary secrets. One system that has been published and, therefore, is well known is that developed by the American Institute of Management.[4] That this system is not adequately future-oriented is clearly proved by the fact that numerous companies have encountered deep trouble shortly after being rated "excellently managed" by the AIM.[5]

Professor Erwin Schell a decade ago set forth a comprehensive system with some future-oriented elements; however, he recently stated that his system should be revised to give greater emphasis to the future via more attention to the R & D function.[6]

As indicated in the outline for evaluation which accompanies this article, the evaluation of a firm, as it is at present and as it will be in the future, can be organized around a series of penetrating questions. Thorough study of the areas covered by these questions will yield a picture, oriented to the future, of the strengths and weaknesses of the firm under consideration and a reliable indication of its chances for success in the future.

There are, as the outline shows, four vital areas in a firm about which you should ask questions. They are: its product lines and basic competitive position; its R & D and operating departments; its financial position as revealed by analysis of the traditional financial data plus an

OUTLINE FOR EVALUATION OF A FIRM

I. PRODUCT LINES AND BASIC COMPETITIVE POSITION

A. PAST

What strengths and weakness in products (or services) have been dominant in this firm's history—design features, quality-reliability, prices, patents, proprietary position?

B. PRESENT

What share of its market(s) does the firm now hold, and how firmly? Is this share diversified or concentrated as to number of customers? In what phases of their life cycles are the present chief products and what is happening to prices and margins? How do customers and potential customers regard this firm's products? Are the various product lines compatible marketing-wise, engineering-wise, manufacturing-wise? If not, is each product line substantial enough to stand on its own feet?

C. FUTURE

Is the market(s) as a whole expanding or contracting, and at what rate? What is the trend in this firm's share of the market(s)? What competitive trends are developing in numbers of competitors, technology, marketing, pricing? What is its vulnerability to business cycle (or defense spending) changes? Is management capable of effectively integrating market research, R & D, and market development into a development program for a new product or products?

II. R & D AND OPERATING DEPARTMENT

A. R & D AND ENGINEERING

What is the nature and the depth of its R & D capability? Of engineering capability? What are engineering's main strengths and weaknesses re creativity, quality-reliability, simplicity? Is the R & D effort based on needs defined by market research, and is it an integral part of an effective new product development program? Are R & D efforts well planned, directed, and controlled? What return have R & D dollars paid in profitable new products? Have enough new products been produced? Have schedules been met?

B. MARKETING

Nature of the Marketing Capability—What channels of distribution are used? How much of the total marketing job (research, sales, service, advertising and promotion) is covered? Is this capability correctly tailored to match the nature and diversity of the firm's product lines? Is there a capability for exploiting new products and developing new

OUTLINE FOR EVALUATION OF A FIRM
(continued)

markets? Quality of the marketing capability—Is market research capable of providing the factual basis that will keep the firm, especially its new product development and R & D programs, truly customer-oriented? Is there a capability for doing broad economic studies and studies of particular industries that will help management set sound growth and/or diversification strategies?

C. MANUFACTURING

What is the nature of the manufacturing processes, the facilities and the skills—are they appropriate to today's competition? How flexible are they—will they be, or can they be made, appropriate to tomorrow's competition? What is the quality of the manufacturing management in terms of planning and controlling work schedule-wise, cost-wise, and quality-wise? Is there evidence of an industrial engineering capability that steadily improves products and methods?

III. FINANCIAL ANALYSIS AND FINANCIAL MANAGEMENT

A. FINANCIAL ANALYSIS

What main strengths and weaknesses of the firm emerge from analysis of the trends in the traditional financial data: earnings ratios (to sales, to tangible net worth, to working capital) and earnings-per-share; debt ratios (current and acid tests, to tangible net worth, to working capital, to inventory); inventory turnover; cash flow; and the capitalization structure? What do the trends in the basic financial facts indicate as to the firm's prospects for growth in sales volume and rate of earnings? Does "quality of earnings" warrant compounding of the earnings rate?

B. FINANCIAL MANAGEMENT

What is the quality of financial management? Is there a sound program for steadily increasing return on investment? Do the long-range financial plans indicate

B. TOP MANAGEMENT AND THE FUTURE

What are top management's chief characteristics? How adequate or inadequate is this type of management for coping with the challenges of the future? Will the present type and quality of top management continue? Will it deteriorate, will it improve, or will it change its basic character?

C. BOARD OF DIRECTORS

What influence and/or control does the Board of Directors exercise? What are the capabilities of its members? What are their motivations?

V. SUMMARY AND EVALUATION STRATEGY

What other factors can assume major importance in this particular situation? (Use a check list.) Of all the factors studied, which if any, is

Does manufacturing management effectively perform its part of the process of achieving new products?

D. SUMMARY ON R & D AND OPERATING DEPARTMENTS

Is this a complete, integrated, balanced operation; or have certain strong personalities emphasized some functions and neglected others? What is the quality of performance of key R & D and operating executives; do they understand the fundamental processes of management, namely planning, controlling organizing, staffing and directing? Are plans and controls in each department inadequate, adequate or over-developed into a "paperwork mill?" Is there throughout the departments a habit of steady progress in reducing overhead, lowering breakeven points and improving quality? Are all departments future-minded? Do they cooperate effectively in developing worthy new products geared to meet the customer's future needs?

that management understands the cost of capital and how to make money work hard? Have balance sheets and operating statements been realistically projected for a number of years into the future? Is there careful cash planning and strong controls that help the operating departments lower breakeven points? Are capital expenditures inadequate or excessive with respect to insuring future operating efficiency? Are capital investment decisions based on thorough calculations? Does management have the respect of the financial community? Is the firm knowledgeable and aggressive in tax administration?

IV. TOP MANAGEMENT

A. IDENTIFICATION OF TOP MANAGEMENT AND ITS RECORD

What person or group constitutes top management? Has present top management been responsible for profit-and-loss results of the past few years?

overriding in this particular situation? Which factors are of major importance by virtue of the fact that they govern other factors? What are the basic facts-of-life about the economics and competition of this industry now and over the next decade? In view of this firm's particular strengths and weaknesses, what are the odds that it will succeed, and at what level of success, in this industry? What are the prospects of its succeeding by diversifying out of its industry?

estimate of the quality of its financial management; its top management with emphasis not only upon its past record, but also on its adequacy to cope with the future.

When these data have been assembled and summarized, you are in a position to evaluate both the present situation and potential of the firm under study as an investment possibility or as a management problem.

The rest of this article will be devoted to a discussion of these factors one by one. First we shall pose the questions contained in the outline; then we shall discuss the techniques professional analysts use for obtaining such data and determining what it means.

PRODUCT LINES AND COMPETITION

The first things to investigate are a firm's product lines and its basic competitive position. This involves a study of its past, present, and future. Here are the lines your inquiry should take:

Past. What strengths and weaknesses in products (or services) have been dominant in this firm's history—design features, quality-reliability, prices, patents, proprietary position?

Present. What share of its market(s) does the firm now hold, and how firmly? Is this share diversified or concentrated as to number of customers? In what phases of their life cycles are the present chief products and what is happening to prices and margins? How do customers and potential customers regard this firm's products? Are the various product lines compatible marketing-wise, engineering-wise, manufacturing-wise? If not, is each product line substantial enough to stand on its own feet?

Future. Is the market(s) as a whole expanding or contracting, and at what rate? What is the trend in this firm's share of the market(s)? What competitive trends are developing in numbers of competitors, technology, marketing, pricing?

What is the vulnerability to business cycle (or defense spending) changes?

Is there the capability effectively to integrate market research, R & D and market development into a new products development program?

The past-present-future structure furnishes the material needed to determine whether the firm has presently or in-the-pipeline the type of products needed for success in the future.

A key technique here is to determine how much quantitative information the company executives have and, then, to spot-check the quality of that information by the evaluator's own research. The firm that has sound, pertinent market data usually has achieved the first step to success—a clear definition of the job to be done. Conversely, the firm that has only sparse, out-of-date, out-of-focus data and relies heavily on executives' opinions is usually a poor bet for the future. Unsupported opinions, no matter how strongly held or ably stated, can be misleading. Although top management often must rely on such opinions, failure to secure the data that are available is a serious weakness.

LIFE CYCLE CURVES FOR PRODUCTS MADE

Another device for focusing on the basic facts of life about a product line is the building of S, or life cycle curves. These curves plot sales and/or margins for a product against time. For a given firm such plots picture clearly the life expectancy of products. Composite plots can show the trends in life expectancies. Also, they can indicate developing gaps. When past data are joined to carefully projected estimates of the future, dangerous situations can be revealed. Thus, the firm that is currently highly profitable but has not provided for the future will show virtually all of its products at or near the period of peak profitability.[7]

The question of compatibility of product lines may seem too elementary for mention; however, major mistakes are made in this area, especially by firms headed by scientists. Seeing their own skill as the key one in business, scientists tend to underestimate the importance and difficulty of other management activities. In consequence, they often develop or acquire products that present marketing problems far beyond the financial or managerial capability of the firm.

One science-based and scientist-led company, after an acquisition binge, was attempting to market ten distinct product lines through one centralized marketing organization, all with a total of less than $18 million annual volume. None of the products could individually support a top-flight marketing organization; yet no two of them could be effectively marketed through the same people. The result was disaster.

Integration of market research, R & D and market development into an effective new product development program is one of the newer and more difficult arts of management. Such integration, which is the heart of profit planning, apparently accounted for much of the success of the Bell and Howell Company during the decade of the '50s.[8]

In vivid contrast to the coordinated profit planning of Bell and Howell is the case of the small glamor firm that "went public" in early 1961 for $1,000,000 and has since seen the price of its stock triple. The scientist-president and his associates have developed a dazzling array of technically ingenious new products; however, they have little data on the market for the products and have not yet started to build an organization for distributing and selling them.

R & D AND OPERATING DEPARTMENTS

Having probed a firm's product lines and competitive position, the second vital area for investigation is its R & D, marketing, and operating divisions. Good questions to guide your analysis are:

R & D and Engineering. What is the nature and the depth of the R & D capability? Of the engineering capability? What are the main strengths and weaknesses re creativity, quality-reliability, simplicity?

Is the R & D effort based on needs defined by market research, and is it an integral part of an effective new product development program? Are R & D efforts well planned, directed and controlled? What return have R & D dollars paid in profitable new products? Have enough new products been produced, and have schedules been met?

A truly basic change in American industry since the start of World War II has been that thousands of companies have R & D programs whereas earlier only a handful of firms did so. The figures cited earlier concerning the growth of R & D expenditures indicate that sophisticated technologies and rapidly changing products and markets characterize not only electronics and defense industries but also such diverse fields as food processing, photography, communications, pharmaceuticals, metallurgy, plastics, and equipments used in industrial automation processes. The consequence is that most firms beyond the "small business" category must have R & D programs; increasingly a firm must take on the characteristics of a "growth" firm in order to survive.

HOW TO EVALUATE A FIRM'S R & D

One of the newest of management activities, R & D management, is one of the hardest to evaluate. For lack of better technique, the vogue has been to assume that the volume of dollars spent on R & D is commensurate with results achieved. However, we now know that there has been great waste; also, there has been deception by firms "padding" their reported R & D expenditures to give the impression of being more R & D oriented than they really are.

A growing literature reports useful techniques for conceiving, planning, controlling and directing R & D programs and for evaluating R & D output.[9] The truth is being established that

R & D management is a capability different from and much rarer than the capability of performing straight engineering or scientific work.

The first task of the evaluator is to determine whether the selection of R & D programs is integrated with a sound overall long-range plan and is based on market research findings. The next task is to compare the nature and depth of the R & D capability with the job to be done. Can it cope with the firm's future needs in regard to maintaining and improving market position by an integrated new products program? The third job is to compare cost and output. Techniques for evaluating output include assessing the quantity and quality of patents produced, measurement of the contribution of R & D to increased (or maintained) sales volume and profit margins, and measurement of the contribution to lowered break-even points via improved materials and methods.

ARE ITS INNOVATIONS WELL TIMED?

An evaluator needs to understand the time cycle required for research, development and introduction to application; also, he must be able to relate this understanding to the basic facts about the market being served. Such an evaluator can tell when a firm is proceeding in the vanguard of the competition or when it is jumping on a bandwagon too late—as so many electronics firms did with respect to the transistor bandwagon.

MARKETING

Closely allied with R & D and product innovation are the marketing skills of the firm under analysis. Strengths and weaknesses in this area can be uncovered by digging into the following topics.

Nature of the Marketing Capability. What channels of distribution are used? How much of the total marketing job (research, sales, service, advertising, and promotion) is covered? Is this capability correctly tailored to match the nature and diversity of the firm's product lines?

Is there a capability for exploiting new products and for developing new markets?

Quality of the Marketing Capability. Is market research capable of providing the factual basis that will keep the firm, especially its new product development and R & D programs, truly customer-oriented? Is there a capability for doing broad economic studies and studies of particular industries that will help management set sound growth and/or diversification strategies?

The evaluator will already have learned much about market research capability in answering the product line questions posed earlier in this article. There it was indicated that the firm that knows the facts about trends in its market and technologies is well on the way to success in the future. This clearly places great responsibility on market research, a field still neglected or abused by many science-based firms, especially those in defense work.

To cope adequately with the challenges of the future requires more than market research in the old narrow concept; rather, it requires an ability at economic analysis of entire industries. Survival and growth in a rapidly changing economy sometimes demands more than a stream of new products; often it requires diversification into substantially different fields that offer greater growth and better profits for a given time period.

Diversification strategy is another subject that is currently being developed.[10] The aircraft industry today presents a case study in which certain firms are prospering because ten years ago they started to diversify while other firms are suffering badly because they failed to do so.

The accelerating rate of change in industry is a process that feeds on itself. Thus, sophisticated methods of market research and planning not only help a firm cope with rapid change but also foster more rapid change.

The evaluator must know enough about quantitative methods of research to be able to distinguish between valid use and abuse of market research. If not so equipped, he is at the mercy of the supersalesman with a smattering of scientific lore who can spin great tales about how a given firm has made a technological breakthrough that soon will have tremendous impact upon the market.

The evaluator must also be able to distinguish between creative market research and pedestrian fact-gathering that plods along a year too late to help management conquer the future. Only when market research secures fresh quantitative data on future markets can management integrate market development with product development.

MANUFACTURING

The next area to be studied is production. Questions to be asked include:

Manufacturing. What is the nature of the manufacturing processes, the facilities and the skills—are they appropriate to today's competition? How flexible are they—will they be or can they be made appropriate to tomorrow's competition?
What is the quality of the manufacturing management in terms of planning and controlling work schedule-wise, cost-wise, and quality-wise? Is there evidence of an industrial engineering capability that steadily improves products and methods? Does manufacturing management effectively perform its part of the process of achieving new products?

The answers to these questions call mainly for conventional type analysis which need not be commented upon here. This is not to say that there are not now, as always, new and better techniques being developed in the manufacturing field. Certainly an alert manufacturing management will use such progressive techniques as "value engineering" to simplify product designs and, thus, reduce costs; and it will use electronic data processing and other modern industrial engineering methods of controlling the work pace and other cost elements.

But, basically, manufacturing management still is, and long has been, evaluated on the basis of performance schedule-wise, cost- and quality-wise, and techniques for such evaluations are among the oldest and best-developed tools of management consultants and others concerned with industrial engineering.

The quickening pace of technological change does, however, require special attention to the ability of the engineering and manufacturing departments to cooperate effectively in bringing new products into production and in utilizing new processes. Also, it requires special caution with respect to firms with heavy investments in inflexible capital equipment because such investments might be susceptible to almost sudden obsolescence.

SUMMARY ON R & D AND OPERATIONS

To make the most of information acquired about a firm's operating departments and R & D, it is well at this point to pull all this sometimes diffuse information together into a sight summary that pulls the whole picture of operations into focus. Questions running along lines such as these help clarify it.

The Overall Picture. Is this a complete, integrated, balanced operation; or have certain strong personalities emphasized some functions and neglected others?
What is the quality of performance of key R & D and operating executives; do they understand the fundamental processes of management, namely planning, controlling, orga-

nizing, staffing, and directing? Are plans and controls in each department inadequate, adequate, or overdeveloped into a "paperwork mill"?

Is there throughout the departments a habit of steady progress in reducing overhead, lowering breakeven points and improving quality?

Are all departments future-minded; do they cooperate effectively in developing worthy new products geared to meet the customer's future needs?

Finance is the third area of a corporation which should be analyzed carefully in appraising its present and future development. In this connection, both the men handling a company's finances and the figures on the balance sheet should be studied. Beginning inquiries could be:

Financial Analysis. What main strengths and weaknesses of the firm emerge from analysis of the trends in the traditional financial data: earnings ratios (to sales, to tangible net worth, to working capital) and earnings-per-share; debt ratios (current and acid tests, to tangible net worth, to working capital, to inventory); inventory turnover; cash flow; and the capitalization structure?

What do the trends in the basic financial facts indicate as to the firm's prospects for growth in sales volume and rate of earnings? Does "quality of earnings" warrant compounding of the earnings rate?

Although this article has already pointed out limitations of financial analysis standing alone as a method of evaluating firms, its importance as one of the key elements of an evaluation should never be overlooked. Because financial analysis has been so important for so long, its techniques have been well developed. Therefore, it is not necessary to discuss them here.

One concept concerning "growth" companies, however, does require comment. The technique of evaluating a growth firm on the basis of an assumption that it will "plow back" its earnings and thereby achieve a compounded rate of increase in earnings per share is of questionable validity. By compounding earnings on a straight-line (or uninterrupted) basis, financial analysts arrive at estimates of future earnings that justify stock prices from 40 to 100 times present earnings per share.

NO FIRM PROGRESSES EVENLY

The concept of straight-line progress just doesn't square with the facts of life as observed by students of management. Especially in small and medium-sized companies, progress typically occurs in a sawtooth, rather than a straight-line pattern. This phenomenon is based partly on the experience of business cycles and partly on the fact that firms are affected by the strengths and limitations of the humans in key positions. There are stages in which the typical growing firm requires managerial talents greater than—or, possibly, only different from—those talents essential to its start.

At these critical periods the earnings per share may slow down or even turn into losses. Such events devastate the compounding process; if one compounds a more realistic 5-10 percent rate of growth per year, the result is far less sensational than is secured by compounding a 20-25 percent rate. It is exceedingly rare that a firm achieves the higher percentages for any sustained period; Litton Industries and IBM appear to be the exceptions that prove the rule. The reference to quality of earnings is meant to shed light on the sustainability of the rate of improvements in earnings. Here the evaluator must distinguish between continuous, sustainable improvement and isolated events (such as a single acquisition or securing an especially favorable contract) or cyclical events (a period of high profitability certain to be followed by a corresponding low).

THE MONEY MEN

Figures alone don't tell the complete financial story of a firm. Its money management must be rated and this involves an evaluation of both policies and men, not only those in the financial division but also the men in charge of planning and top management. You need to know their attitudes about:

Financial Management. Is there a sound program for steadily increasing return on investment? Do the long-range financial plans indicate that management understands the costs of capital and how to make money work hard? Have balance sheets and operating statements been realistically projected for a number of years into the future?

Is there careful cash planning and strong controls that help the operating departments lower breakeven points? Are capital expenditures inadequate, adequate, or excessive with respect to insuring future operating efficiency? Are capital investment decisions based on thorough calculations?

Does management have the respect of the financial community?

Is the firm knowledgeable and aggressive in tax administration?

While many financial departments function only as record keepers and rules-enforcers, some play a truly creative role. Financial management can today contribute as much or more to improvement in earnings per share as can any other part of management.[11] In fact, in recent years bold use of the newer forms of financing have in many cases contributed as much to the rapid rise of companies as have technological innovations. And, alas, bold but unwise financing has ruined many a promising young company.

The questions here are designed to help the evaluator discover whether or not the financial people are vigorously contributing in a number of ways to the steady improvement of earnings currently and in the long run.

RATING TOP MANAGEMENT

All study of management invariably and understandably leads to a searching examination of the top management men. Here there are pitfalls for the unwary. The analyst must first identify the true top management before he can examine their performance record. Things, in terms of who actually runs the show, are not always what they seem on the organization chart. So key topics are:

Top Management and Its Record. What person or group constitutes top management? Has present top management been responsible for profit-and-loss results of the past few years?

The problem is to determine the individual or group of individuals who contribute directly and regularly to those decisions that shape the basic nature of this business and significantly affect profit and loss results. This usually cannot be determined reliably by direct questions to persons in key positions; few men are objective about themselves on these matters.

WATCH THEM WORK

Rare is the top executive who will admit that he is a one-man rule type; rare is the vice president or department head who will admit that he is a highly paid errand boy. Accordingly, direct observation of management at work is needed. Some additional information can also be gained through examination of minutes of meetings and files of memos.

After top management has been identified, the evaluator must ask whether this management has had time to prove itself one way or the other. The criterion is whether or not major decisions and programs put forth by this top management have come to fruition. It is not simply a matter of looking at profit and loss figures for a few years. We all know that in certain situations factors other than top management capability (for example, an inherited product line that is unusually strong) can produce good profits for a number of years.

Next comes consideration of:

Top Management and the Future. What are top management's chief characteristics? How adequate or inadequate is this type of management for coping with the challenges of the future?

Will the present type and quality of top management continue, or will it deteriorate, will it improve, or will it change its basic character?

We must ask how and why top management has achieved the results that it has achieved so that we can judge how adequate it will be for meeting tomorrow's challenges. Exploring the how and why gets the evaluator into the subject of types of management and their effects on profitability—the thorniest area of contemporary management theory. Over the past twenty years a tremendous literature has accumulated on such subjects as participative leadership, autocratic vs. bureaucratic vs. democratic types of management, and related subjects.

Some writers have claimed or implied great virtues for participative-democratic methods; others have attacked such methods as wasteful and ineffective, wholly inappropriate in industrial life and have advocated "benevolent autocracy." The confusion recently reached a zenith with the almost simultaneous publication of conflicting views by eminent professors from the same university.[12]

Industrial psychologists and sociologists have provided valuable insights into management practices and their effects upon profitability. While a skilled social scientist could contribute importantly to the evaluation of a firm's top management, there is a more direct way of evaluating top management's capability for coping with future challenges.

The direct method is to determine how top management has in the past coped with the future. This technique is based on the idea that management is essentially the process of planning to achieve certain goals and, then, controlling activities so that the goals are actually attained. It is in the processes of planning and controlling that top management does its major decision-making. Since planning and controlling are the heart of the managerial process, it is in these activities that top management most fully reveals its vital characteristics.

The evaluator can probe deeply into the content of the firm's past and current long-range and short-range plans, into the methods by which the plans are formulated, and into the controls used to bring those plans to fruition. This technique gets away, to a considerable extent, from subjective judgments; it deals with such facts as what was planned, how it was planned and what actually happened.

Fortunately these activities can be studied without great difficulty and by persons who do not have formal training in the behavioral sciences. A simple yet highly informative procedure is to compare succeeding sets of old long-range plans with one another, with present plans and with actual events.

DO THEIR PLANS WORK?

First, a firm that is effectively tomorrow-minded will have long-range plans. These may not be neatly bound in a cover labeled "long-range plans"; however, they will exist either in minutes of meetings, in memos, in reports to stockholders or in other places. Second, the old plans will contain evidence as to whether top management truly has studied the future to determine and anticipate the nature of the opportunities and threats that will inevitably arise.

Third, the old plans will contain evidence of the nature and quality of the solutions developed for meeting the challenges of the future—how creative, aggressive and realistic management has been in initiative matters such as selecting R & D programs, establishing diversification strategy and program, developing new markets, planning the organizational changes needed to keep fit for new tasks, and effectively utilizing advanced techniques (e.g., operations research, automation, etc.) when feasible.

Special attention to initiative matters will indicate whether or not top management is creative and aggressive enough to keep up with an accelerating rate of change.

Fourth, comparison of succeeding sets of plans will indicate whether consistent progress has been made or top management is recklessly aggressive in that it undertakes unrealistic, ill-conceived, unachievable plans.

The same technique can be applied to short-range plans such as annual budgets, sales forecasts and special developmental programs of many types. This study will indicate whether or not forecasts are typically accurate, whether or not plans typically are successfully completed, whether or not new products are developed on schedule, and whether or not they are supported by marketing, finance, and management programs ready to go at the right time. Again, as in the case of long-range plans, the inquiry will reveal whether decision making is mature or immature. Has management made profitability a habit, or just a subject of wishful thinking?

A management that knows how to bring plans to fruition builds into every plan a set of controls designed to give early warning of problems and an indication that corrective action is needed. Examination of the controls and the ways in which they are used will indicate whether or not top management is on top of its problems or vice versa.

WHO MAKES THE PLANS?

Investigation of the methods by which plans are formulated and control is exercised will reveal a great deal about whether top management is autocratic, bureaucratic or democratic. This inquiry holds more than academic interest; the extent to which lower levels of management contribute to the formulation of plans and the extent to which they are held accountable for results will tell much about the firm's down-the-line strength.

EXECUTIVE TURNOVER

Also, these factors are particularly important indicators of whether top management will retain its vigor, will improve or will deteriorate. Thus, they indicate whether or not top management is making sincere efforts to recruit and develop middle management that will become a new and better generation of top management. Other insights into whether management is bringing in too little or too much new blood can be gained by examining age patterns and statistics on turnover in executive ranks, by reviewing formal executive development efforts and by interviews with some of the men.

YARDSTICK TO GAUGE GROWTH FACTORS

In summary, the technique of probing deeply into the firm's actual plans and controls and methods of planning and control can yield abundant evidence to indicate whether or not top management has the characteristics of a growth firm. Their characteristics have been set forth in a major study by Stanford Research Institute of the factors that usually distinguish growth from nongrowth firms. They are:

- Affinity for growth fields.
- Organized programs to seek and promote new opportunities.
- Proven competitive abilities in present lines of business.
- Courageous and energetic managements, willing to make carefully calculated risks.
- Luck.

Incidentally, this study found that high growth companies had twice the earning power of low growth companies, while maintaining four times the growth rate.[13]

THE BOARD OF DIRECTORS

Rounding out the top management of every corporation is an enigmatic, unpublicized group of men about whom a competent analyst should be most curious. They are the Board of Directors. Questions such as these should be asked about them: What influence and/or control does the Board of Directors exercise? What are the capabilities of its members? What are their motivations?

In the author's experience one of the most frequent and serious errors of small and medium-sized firms is failure to have and use effectively a strong Board of Directors. Too often the entrepreneurial types who start firms disdain help until they are in deep trouble.

Especially in firms headed by a scientist or a supersalesman, a strong and active Board can be invaluable in helping make up for the top executives' lack of rounded managerial training and experience. Except in a few unusual situations, a Board must be an "outside," or nonemployed Board to be strong.

DUMMIES OR POLICY MAKERS

To be active and helpful, an "outside" Board must have some motivation, either financial or the psychic motivation involved in being confronted with real problems and being able to contribute to their solution. Examination of files and minutes of Board meetings will reveal whether or not there is a good flow of information to the outside directors and a contribution by them to the solution of significant problems.

ADDING UP THE FACTS

With all the data in about the four vital areas of a firm, products and competition, operations and R & D, finance, and top management, the analyst ends his task by posing one more set of questions which might be called Summary and Evaluation Strategy. They should run something like this:

What other factors (use a checklist)[14] can assume major importance in this particular situation?

Of all the factors studied, which, if any, is overriding in this particular situation? Which factors are of major importance by virtue of the fact that they govern other factors?

What are the basic facts of life about the economics and competition of this industry now and over the next decade? In view of this firm's particular strengths and weaknesses, what are the odds that it will succeed and at what level of success, in this industry? What are the prospects of its succeeding by diversifying out of its industry?

DETERMINING OTHER VITAL FACTORS

There is a purpose behind every evaluation study. That purpose or the particular nature of the firm and its industry might place importance upon any of an almost infinite number of factors. Accordingly, the evaluator must thoughtfully run through a checklist containing such considerations as: personnel management practices (e.g., labor relations, profit-sharing, compensation levels), valuation questions (e.g., valuation of fixed or real assets or inventory or unique assets), geographical location as related to labor markets, taxes, cost of distribution, seasonality factors, in-process or impending litigation, or any matter footnoted in the financial reports so that the auditing firm is, in effect, warning of an unusual circumstance.

The purpose of a particular evaluation study often will determine which factor, if any, is overriding. Logically, the quality of top management should usually be the overriding factor. By definition a highly competent top management group can solve the other problems such as securing competent scientists and other personnel, developing new products, getting financing, etc. However, there may be an investment or acquisition situation in which the product line, for example, is the overriding factor because it is so obsolete that even the finest management could not effect a recovery within existing time and financial parameters.

MATCHING BUYER AND ACQUISITION

If the evaluation is being done to help decide the advisability of an acquisition, many additional considerations come into play. The problem is one of matching the acquiring and acquired firms; many firms have acquired grief rather than growth because they have neglected this point. At one extreme, acquisition of one healthy company by another may be unwise because the two are so different that the acquirer may mismanage the acquired company. At the other extreme, it may be wise for one unhealthy company to acquire another unhealthy one if the strengths of one remedy the weaknesses of the other, and vice versa.

THE CHARACTER OF THE COMPANY

The acquirer must precisely define his objectives in acquiring. Also, he must carefully consider the "character," or "climate," of the other firm in relation to his own. The subject of "company character" has not been well developed in management practice or literature.[15] Nevertheless, a consideration of the "character" of the two companies is highly relevant, and the outline presented in this article will help the evaluator consider some of the more obvious elements of "company character" such as the nature of its engineering and manufacturing skills, the type of distribution channels and marketing skills required, the type of managerial leadership practiced and top management's aggressiveness and the quality of its decisions in initiative matters.

In sum, the evaluation of a firm requires a clinical judgment of the highest order. The purposes of the evaluation study set the criteria for the judgment. Except in a few instances in which conditions are highly stable, the day is rapidly passing when simple financial analyses, or even financial analyses supplemented by a few interviews and judgments of scientists will suffice for evaluation of a firm.

REFERENCES

(The author, while retaining full responsibility for the content of this article, wishes to express thanks to Drs. Harold D. Koontz, William B. Wolf, J. F. Weston, and Mr. Ora B. Roehl for suggestions that have been most helpful. R. B. B.)

1. "Evaluating Your Company's Future," an unpublished paper presented at the Fourth Annual Management Conference, UCLA Executive Program Association, Los Angeles, October 20, 1960, p. 2.
2. Data from the National Science Foundation,

cited in: *Research Management*, Autumn, 1960, Volume III, No. 3, p. 129.

3. Lee Dake explains in detail a case in which a financial analyst and a management consultant arrived at opposite conclusions about a firm's prospects in "Are Analysts' Techniques Adequate for Growth Stocks?" *The Financial Analysts Journal*, Volume 16, No. 6, Nov.–Dec., 1960, pp. 45–49. Dake's thesis can be confirmed many times over in the present author's experience. Particularly distressing was the case where a persuasive but incompetent chief executive persuaded three investment firms to recommend his stock less than six months before declaration of losses exceeding the firm's tangible net worth!

4. The factors are: (a) Economic Function; (b) Corporate Structure; (c) Health of Earnings; (d) Services to Stockholders; (e) Research and Development; (f) Directorate Analysis; (g) Fiscal Policies; (h) Production Efficiency; (i) Sales Vigor; (j) Executive Evaluation. The factors and their use are explained in detail in a series of ten reports: *The Management Audit Series* (New York: The American Institute of Management, starting in 1953).

5. Most dramatic was the case of the Douglas Aircraft Company whose "excellently managed" rating for 1957-8-9 was followed by staggering losses in late '59 and '60. Among numerous other examples that can be cited are the 1957 ratings of Olin Mathiesen Chemical Co. and Allis-Chalmers Manufacturing Company, both of whom, soon after receiving "excellently managed" ratings, suffered serious declines that have been openly discussed in business magazines. For the ratings, see: *Manual of Excellent Managements* (New York: The American Institute of Management, 1957). For accounts of the travails of these firms see *Business Week*, April 9, 1960, p. 79, and April 15, 1961, pp. 147–149.

6. "Industrial Administration Through the Eyes of an Investment Company," *Appraising Managerial Assets—Policies, Practices and Organization*, General Management Series #151 (New York: American Management Association, 1950). The new emphasis is suggested in a postscript to a reprint published in 1960 by the Keystone Custodian Funds, Inc. (Boston, Mass.: 1960, p. 13). Professor Schell suggested increased emphasis on tax administration, too. The original factors were: (a) Breadth and variety of viewpoint in administration; (b) Vigor and versatility in operating management; (c) Clarity and definiteness of long-term objectives; (d) Vigilance in matters of organization; (e) Dependence upon far-reaching plans; (f) Maintenance of integrated controls; (g) Upkeep in harmony with an advancing art; (h) Improvement as a normal expectancy; (i) Creativeness through high morale; (j) Effectiveness of managerial attitudes; (k) Resources for consistently distinguished leadership in a specific industry.

7. For an illustration and discussion of use of life-cycle curves, see C. Wilson Randle, "Selecting the Research Program. A Top Management Function," *California Management Review*, Volume II, No. 2 (Winter, 1960), pp. 10–11.

8. The Bell and Howell methods are described in two articles: "How to Coordinate Executives," *Business Week*, September 12, 1953, p. 130 ff., and "How to Plan Profits Five Years Ahead," *Nation's Business*, October 1955, p. 38.

9. An invaluable review of this literature up to early 1957 is given in: Albert H. Rubenstein, "Looking Around: Guide to R & D," *Harvard Business Review*, Volume 35, No. 3, May–June, 1957, p. 133 ff. Among the most pertinent articles since Rubenstein's review are: Ora C. Roehl, "The Investment Analyst's Evaluation of Industrial Research Capabilities," *Research Management*, Volume III, No. 3, Autumn, 1960, p. 127 ff.; Maurice Nelles, "Changing the World Changers," a paper presented at the Ninth Annual Management Conference, The Graduate School of Business Administration, University of Chicago, March 1, 1961; C. Wilson Randle, "Problems of R & D Management," *Harvard Business Review*, Volume 37, No. 1, January–February 1959, p. 128 ff.; James B. Quinn, "How to Evaluate Research Output," *Harvard Business Review*, Volume 38, No. 2, March–April 1960, pp. 69 ff.; and "Long-Range Planning of Industrial Research," *Harvard Business Review*, Volume 39, No. 4, July–August 1961, pp. 88 ff.

10. H. Igor Ansoff, "Strategies for Diversification," *Harvard Business Review*, September–October, 1957.

11. For an exposition of this thought as applied to large firms, see: "The New Power of the Financial Executive," *Fortune*, Volume LXV, No. 1, January 1962, p. 81 ff. See also the new text by J. Fred Weston, *Managerial Finance* (New York: Holt, Rinehart & Winston, 1962).

12. Rensis Likert, reporting on a decade of social science research into patterns of management, makes a case for participative management in *New Patterns of Management* (New York: McGraw-Hill Publishing Company, 1961). George Odiorne, reporting on studies of successful managements, warns strongly against the views of social scientists and makes a case for the more traditional, somewhat autocratic, business leader in *How Managers Make Things Happen* (New York: Prentice-Hall, Inc., 1961). Both authors are professors at the University of Michigan.

13. *Environmental Change and Corporate Strategy* (Menlo Park, California: Stanford Research Institute, 1960), p. 8. A more recent report on this continuing research project is given by Robert B. Young, "Keys to Corporate Growth," *Harvard Business Review*, Volume 39, No. 6, Nov.-Dec., 1961, pp. 51-62. Young concludes: "In short, the odds for corporate growth are highest when the top executives of a firm treat their future planning as a practical decision making challenge requiring personal participation, and direct their planning efforts toward the origins of opportunity itself. Such an approach can make the difference between having constantly to adapt to day to day crises and enjoying profitable future growth."

14. For one such checklist, see: Robert G. Sproul, Jr., "Sizing Up New Acquisitions," *Management Review*, XLIX, No. 1, Feb. 1960, pp. 80-82.

15. A new textbook brings together for the first time the few and scattered writings on the subject of "company character." See William B. Wolf's *The Management of Personnel* (San Francisco: Wadsworth Publishing Company, Inc., 1961), pp. 8-43.

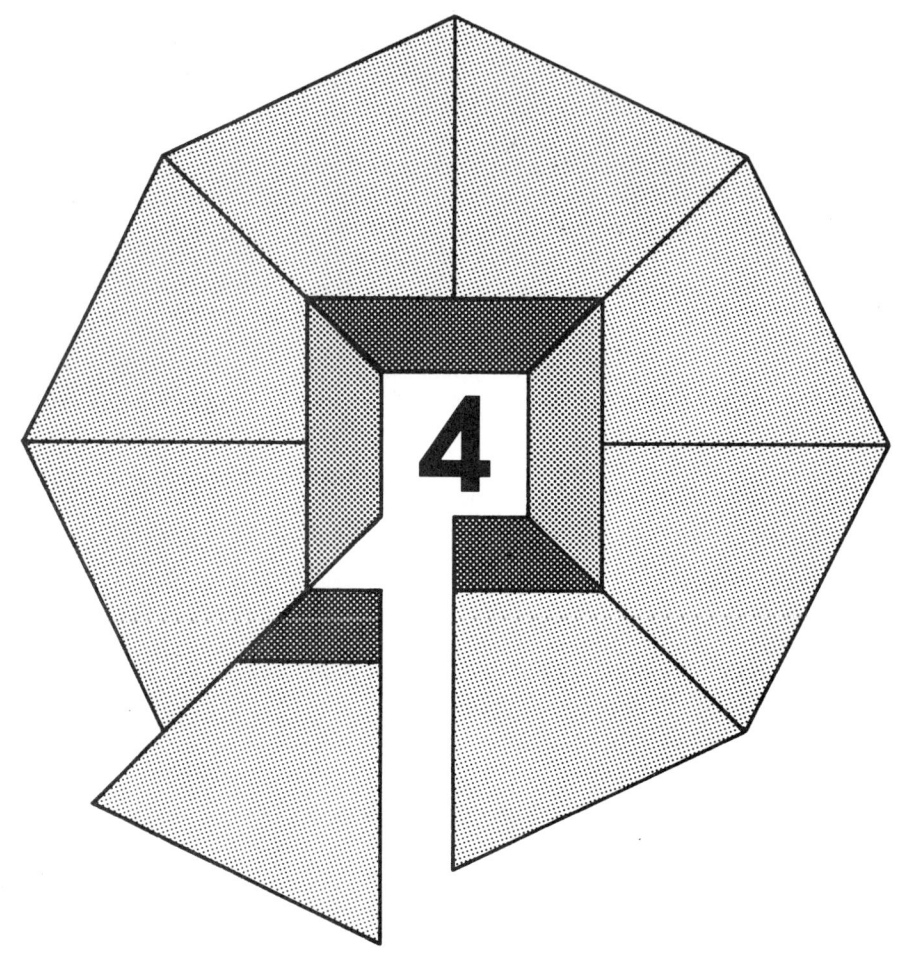

FINANCIAL ANALYSIS
process and techniques

This chapter is divided into three major sections. The first section deals with the role of financial analysis in policy cases. The second presents a brief discussion of break-even analysis, it uses, and its limitations. The final section discusses the C_3 finance decision variables from a top or general management viewpoint, as is done with marketing variables in Chapter 5 and production/operations variables in Chapter 6. This is followed by a list of the C_4 finance decision variables. Throughout the chapter, emphasis is placed on the functional interdependence of certain finance decisions and relationships.

FINANCIAL ANALYSIS IN BUSINESS POLICY CASES

This section demonstrates how financial analysis can be useful in the three major phases of case study: analysis of the situation, problem identification, and development of plans of action to eliminate the problems. In many ways, financial analysis is analogous to a doctor's initial assessment of a patient's health in terms of body temperature, pulse rate, and blood pressure. These indicators are used by the doctor to determine treatment needed to cure the patient or to identify additional tests needed for further diagnosis. The student should be warned that this type of analysis identifies symptoms, not problems. These symptoms may then point to the root cause(s) of the problem(s) in a situation. With this in mind, the student can use his or her knowledge of how the indicator (symptom) is arrived at to help trace down the root cause(s) of the problem(s). Although financial analysis cuts across traditional functional boundaries, there is a wide variety of problems that this type of analysis will not reveal. But the relative ease with which it can be carried out and the number of strategic and/or functional area problems it can identify make financial analysis an excellent starting point for analyzing case studies.

Analysis of the Situation

An analysis of the situation is the first general step in the problem-solving process. This stage involves the collection of facts that are relevant for an assessment of the firm's external effectiveness, internal efficiency, and major strengths and weaknesses. Information gathered here also should relate to the consideration of difficulties that exist in various areas of the firm.

It is hard to indicate the precise information that should be gathered in each and every case. This is partially because of the situational nature of case analysis and also because all the desired information is frequently unavailable. Consequently, the following discussion delineates the *maximum* amount of information that should be gathered to assess the firm's basic financial position.

Evidence of Financial Objectives

The student should attempt to determine the profitability, growth, and survival objectives of the firm. These objectives may or may not be explicitly stated in the case. A target return on investment or a growth rate in earnings per share are examples.

Basic Financial Statements

At the outset, the student should have the historical income statements and balance sheets at hand. These two basic statements provide the data necessary for most of the financial analyses discussed here. The student should be aware of several precautions concerning the use of these statements in financial analysis. The balance sheet figures refer to one instance in time, while the income statement figures refer to events *over a period of time*. Therefore the income statement figures are best compared to the historical average of the balance sheet figures when such comparisons are needed.[1] While conducting the financial analysis, the student also should be aware of seasonality, window dressing,[2] and adjustments described in footnotes to either of these statements.

These financial statements only present information that lends itself to quantification in terms of dollars. This can be both an advantage and a disadvantage. The primary advantage is that dollars provide a common denominator and enable us to add up the cost aggregates of a variety of assets. But these statements contain little direct information about the people responsible for operating the firm. Except in aggregate terms, these data reveal little about things such as the quality of planning, efficiency of scheduling, and communications difficulties, or about the success of the company being highly contingent on the talents of one person.

Financial analysis can start by comparing the financial statements over time if a series of statements are available. The changes that occurred in individual categories are calculated from year to year and over the years. The percentage change should be calculated along with the absolute amount. Examination of this information could reveal trends that have developed. Such trends in one category would be compared to trends in related items. For example, a year-to-year increase in sales of 12% accompanied by a year-to-year increase of 17% in cost of goods sold indicates a need for further investigation.

Another approach to analyzing financial statements is to convert them into what is called common-size statements. The proportion a single category represents of the total statement is calculated (i.e., everything is converted to percentages). In the case of the balance sheet, the total statement (100%) is represented by the total assets (or liabilities). Each item on the balance sheet is made a percentage by dividing by the total assets. For the income statement, net sales represent the total statement (100%). Because the percentage totals of the individual categories always total 100%, these state-

---

[1]This raises the question of whether one should use a simple average or a weighted average. From a practical standpoint, it probably will depend on the amount and type of information the student has with regard to the balance sheet data.

[2]Companies have been known to take deliberate steps to "clean up" their balance sheets. For instance, loans may be paid off just before the end of a year, which increases the current ratio, and then money is borrowed again early in the next year.

ments are termed "common size." In this form, the student can easily see what proportion each category represents of the total, and comparisons over the years could alert the student to areas requiring more analysis. Comparisons could also be made with industry data, if available, to become aware of major differences.

Evidence of External Effectiveness

At this stage, the major financial indicators of the external effectiveness of the firm can be computed for subsequent analysis of their meaning and significance. The most important indicators are usually in ratio form and are discussed next. The student should be cognizant of the components that make up the ratio, since this will help him or her to backtrack and identify the root cause of the problem, if one of these symptoms indicates there is one. A summary of these and other financial ratios is provided in Figure 4-1.

Profitability indicators. Evidence of the firm's profitability should be analyzed to determine the extent to which objectives are being accomplished and to illuminate the current well-being of the firm. There are two types of profitability ratios: (1) those showing profitability in relation to sales, and (2) those showing profitability in relation to investment. Gross profit margin (sales minus cost of goods sold divided by sales) and net profit margin (net profit after taxes divided by sales) are examples of the first type. Rate of return on common stock equity (net profit after taxes minus preferred stock dividend divided by net worth minus par value of preferred stock) and return on assets (net profit after taxes divided by total tangible assets) are examples of the second type. Incidentally, return on assets is also the product of the net profit margin (net profit after taxes divided by sales) and the turnover ratio (sales divided by total tangible assets), which might be useful in later stages of the analysis. Ultimately, these ratios indicate how effectively the firm is being managed. It should be recognized, however, that the ratios themselves do not provide direct answers as to why a firm is or is not profitable.

Liquidity indicators. Computation of liquidity ratios enables determination of the firm's ability (1) to react to unforeseen opportunities in the environment, and (2) to meet its maturing financial obligations. Two common indicators of liquidity are the current ratio (current assets divided by current liabilities) and the acid test or quick ratio (current assets minus inventories divided by current liabilities). The fact that inventories are the least liquid of current assets, and are also the assets on which losses are most likely to occur in the event of liquidation makes the acid test extremely important.

Leverage indicators. These ratios indicate the firm's basic position with respect to creditors and its propensity to assume risk. With respect to the

Figure 4-1 Summary of financial ratio analysis.

Profitability ratios

 Gross profit margin $\qquad \dfrac{\text{Sales-cost of goods sold}}{\text{Sales}}$

 Net profit margin $\qquad \dfrac{\text{Net profit after taxes}}{\text{Sales}}$

 Rate of return or common stock equity $\qquad \dfrac{\text{Net profit after tax—preferred stock dividend}}{\text{Net worth—par value of preferred stock}}$

 Return on assets $\qquad \dfrac{\text{Net profit after taxes}}{\text{Total tangible assets}}$
  or
  net profit margin × turnover ratio
  (i.e., sales ÷ total tangible assets)

 Return on capital (equity) $\qquad \dfrac{\text{Net profit after taxes}}{\text{Net worth}}$

 Earnings per share (common stock) $\qquad \dfrac{\text{Net profit after taxes—preferred dividends}}{\text{Number shares common stock outstanding}}$

Liquidity ratios

 Current $\qquad \dfrac{\text{Current assets}}{\text{Current liabilities}}$

 Acid test (or quick ratio) $\qquad \dfrac{\text{Current assets—inventories}}{\text{Current liabilities}}$

 Cash $\qquad \dfrac{\text{Cash and equivalent}}{\text{Current liabilities}}$

 Inventory to net working capital $\qquad \dfrac{\text{Inventory}}{\text{Current assets—current liabilities}}$

Leverage ratios

 Debt $\qquad \dfrac{\text{Total debt}}{\text{Total assets}}$

 Debt to equity Total debt $\qquad \dfrac{\text{Total debt}}{\text{Net worth}}$

 Long-term debt $\qquad \dfrac{\text{Long-term debt}}{\text{Net worth}}$

Figure 4-1 (continued)

Assets to equity	$\dfrac{\text{Total assets}}{\text{Net worth}}$
Fixed charge coverage, such as bond interest, lease payments (number of times interest earned) Before tax	$\dfrac{\text{Earnings before interest and taxes}}{\text{Fixed charges}}$
After tax	$\dfrac{\text{Net profit after taxes + fixed charges}}{\text{Fixed charges}}$

Activity ratios

Inventory turnover	$\dfrac{\text{Sales}}{\text{Inventory}}$
Fixed assets turnover	$\dfrac{\text{Sales}}{\text{Fixed assets}}$
Total assets turnover	$\dfrac{\text{Sales}}{\text{Total assets}}$
Average collection period	$\dfrac{\text{Accounts receivable} \times 365}{\text{Annual credit sales}}$
Accounts receivable turnover	$\dfrac{\text{Credit sales}}{\text{Accounts receivable}}$
Operating asset turnover	$\dfrac{\text{Sales}}{\text{Operating assets}}$

Other ratios

Dividend (current) yield on common stock	$\dfrac{\text{Annual dividends per share}}{\text{Current market price per share}}$
Earnings yield on common stock	$\dfrac{\text{Earnings per share of common}}{\text{Market price per share}}$
Price-earnings ratio	$\dfrac{\text{Market price per share}}{\text{Earnings per share}}$
Pay-out ratio	$\dfrac{\text{Annual dividends}}{\text{Annual earnings}}$
Cash flow per share	$\dfrac{\text{Net profit after taxes + depreciation}}{\text{Number of shares common outstanding}}$

former, decisions as to the use of leverage (the extent to which financing is provided by creditors instead of by owners) greatly affect future borrowing power. Furthermore, they always involve a trade-off between higher expected returns and increased risk. In keeping with these considerations, the debt ratio (total debt divided by total assets) measures the extent to which borrowed funds are utilized and hence the probable reactions of creditors to future requests for funds. The times-interest-earned ratio (profit before taxes plus interest charges divided by interest charges) and the fixed charge coverage ratio (gross income divided by fixed charges) measure the risk of debt by concentrating on the ability of the firm to meet its fixed charges. Long-term debt divided by total capitalization (long-term debt plus net worth) tells the relative importance of long-term debt in the capital structure.

Overall ability to obtain funds. Some of the ratios noted give an indication of the firm's ability to acquire funds, but additional information on creditor relations, amount of working capital on hand, and utilization of retained earnings will further illuminate the firm's basic financial position in this regard.

Evidence of Internal Efficiency

Basic indicators of the efficiency with which management has employed its resources may be obtained by calculating the following: inventory turnover ratio (sales divided by inventory), fixed assets turnover ratio (sales divided by fixed assets), average collection period (accounts receivable times 365 divided by annual credit sales), and aging of accounts—both receivables and payables.

Further Analysis of Financial Indicators

Once the various ratios have been calculated, the meanings of these ratios must be ascertained. For instance, what does a current ratio of 1.75 mean? Or an inventory turnover ratio of 6? To give the data greater significance, two further analyses can be performed. First, compare a present ratio with past and expected future ratios for the same company—that is, develop trends. Second, compare ratios of one firm with those of similar firms or with industry averages at the same point in time. Avoid using rules of thumb indiscriminately for all industries.

In trend analysis, first examine the composition of the change and determine if there has been an improvement or a deterioration in the financial condition and performance of the firm over a period of time. Do not simply look at one ratio and draw unwarranted conclusions! It is necessary to look at related ratios and possibly at the raw data before a proper interpretation can be made.

A major difficulty in making this type of comparison is the change in the dollar-measuring criterion. Over a period of time there are changes in the value of the dollar, changes in price levels and, because assets are stated as unexpired historical dollar costs, this causes particular difficulty with ratios calculated from such amounts.

Comparison with industry averages does not imply that all firms in the industry should be the same, but one should be suspicious of deviations and find out if they are justified. A particular firm may have encountered unreasonably good or bad fortune that was not shared by the industry. Comparison of a firm and industry ratio over time also may indicate whether the deviation is caused by an internal or an external condition.

There are several sources for obtaining comparison ratios and/or financial data. These include *Modern Industry* (Dun & Bradstreet); *Statement Studies* (R. Morris Associates); Moody's *Manual of Investments*; *Corporation Records* (Standard and Poor); and quarterly data on manufacturing companies, published by the Federal Trade Commission and the Securities and Exchange Commission. Also, some trade associations and public accountants publish ratios for specific industries. Figures 4-2, 4-3 and 4-4 present lists of selected Dun & Bradstreet financial ratios by various lines of business for odd-numbered years from 1969 to 1977.

These two analyses—trends and industry comparisons—give indications as to whether or not the firm is improving or deteriorating over the years and what its position is relative to other firms in the same industry. They also permit a comparison of financial objectives with actual results over a period of time and in relation to performance of competitors.

Break-even analysis is another tool that may be useful during financial analysis. This subject is reviewed in the last section of this chapter.

DIAGNOSIS OF PROBLEMS

The information gathered in the analysis-of-situation phase provides a fairly complete assessement of the firm's financial strengths and weaknesses. This information, in conjunction with data on other aspects of the external and internal situation (e.g., organization, marketing, production), provides the base from which problem identification and analysis can begin. For instance, why is the firm's profit margin on sales 2% below the industry average? Is it because prices are too low or because costs are too high? What marketing information in the case indicates that prices may be too low? In this case, a particular financial indicator of external effectiveness ultimately may lead to diagnosis of a problem in the firm's marketing strategy. On the other hand, information may exist to show that costs are too high because of an inefficient plant layout. Here, the profit margin indicator would have led to problem diagnosis in the area of programming the physical resources necessary to implement the master production plan.

Similarly, the student can use the other financial indicators to work back through the many factors that have a bearing on a particular problem. Thus, a low fixed asset turnover relative to other firms in the industry may indicate that the firm is not producing at a high enough percentage of ca-

Figure 4-2 Selected Dun & Bradstreet financial ratios of selected manufacturing businesses.

Line of Business	Year	Current Assets to Current Debt (Times)	Net Profit on Net Sales (Percent)	Net Profit to Tangible Net Worth (Percent)	Net Sales to Tangible Worth (Times)	Collection Period (Days)	Net Sales to Inventory (Times)	Fixed Asset to Tangible Net Worth (Percent)	Total Debt to Tangible Net Worth (Percent)	Inventory to Net Working Capital (Percent)
Agricultural chemicals	69	1.86	1.45	5.30	2.78	57	6.6	43.8	123.3	76.5
	71	2.06	2.08	7.11	2.84	57	8.5	41.7	139.4	59.8
	73	1.98	3.65	16.15	3.39	50	9.9	36.2	100.4	55.1
	75	2.21	6.60	21.59	3.83	38	7.4	31.6	97.3	87.0
	77	2.00	4.10	12.65	3.03	52	8.7	37.6	84.3	81.7
Airplane parts and accessories	69	2.16	3.04	9.06	2.92	59	5.2	53.6	72.4	86.6
	71	2.47	1.63	3.60	2.24	58	4.9	57.5	107.2	82.0
	73	2.24	3.94	12.70	2.81	52	4.7	50.1	120.6	88.2
	75	2.63	4.57	13.98	2.93	49	4.3	37.1	86.9	81.1
	77	2.14	4.23	9.07	2.99	54	5.1	45.2	93.6	75.3
Bakery products	69	1.88	2.54	8.70	4.08	22	28.9	80.8	49.6	57.9
	71	2.07	1.77	6.58	4.18	21	27.5	79.5	55.8	51.5
	73	1.90	1.37	6.45	4.25	26	22.7	74.9	77.7	62.5
	75	2.22	2.95	14.20	4.99	24	23.8	70.3	64.5	52.3
	77	1.98	2.24	11.53	5.27	25	29.0	87.2	103.1	57.3
Book publishing and printing	69	2.52	4.70	8.04	2.13	61	4.4	34.8	52.3	72.0
	71	2.59	4.71	8.15	1.94	68	4.1	36.0	57.8	65.6
	73	2.49	4.76	10.14	1.98	64	4.2	35.4	83.1	62.5
	75	2.92	5.24	11.30	2.25	64	4.7	31.7	74.8	65.1
	77	2.59	4.83	10.43	2.16	58	4.4	33.8	63.9	59.7
Bottled and canned soft drinks	69	1.70	3.91	11.94	3.20	21	17.0	83.9	83.9	83.5
	71	2.25	4.46	12.01	2.97	21	16.3	70.6	49.1	62.0
	73	2.32	3.71	11.57	3.27	22	15.3	71.2	55.4	61.0
	75	2.10	6.46	19.05	3.61	17	19.5	72.5	48.1	54.4
	77	2.58	6.48	19.40	3.26	24	14.7	66.4	97.8	62.3
Broad woven fabrics, cotton	69	3.10	2.42	4.88	1.92	56	5.1	57.0	45.9	69.0
	71	3.65	2.75	5.70	1.96	54	5.8	53.8	60.7	62.8
	73	3.32	3.37	8.18	2.38	57	6.3	52.8	85.2	61.6
	75	3.31	1.79	4.49	2.69	58	6.5	53.9	67.2	71.7
	77	2.83	2.39	7.87	3.24	53	6.7	57.0	62.9	68.8

Industry	Year									
Canned and preserved fruits, vegetables and sea foods	69	1.56	1.93	5.79	3.17	24	4.5	50.2	119.7	181.9
	71	2.03	2.66	7.64	3.20	26	4.4	56.0	106.0	124.3
	73	1.93	2.77	11.83	4.11	25	5.2	66.1	118.6	121.0
	75	1.75	2.50	9.18	3.81	25	4.1	58.2	145.3	150.9
	77	1.85	2.66	10.13	4.61	25	4.9	66.0	126.6	121.2
Communication equipment	69	2.44	3.78	10.34	2.70	61	5.0	37.2	64.3	75.0
	71	2.77	1.99	4.56	2.37	73	4.9	45.2	76.3	69.7
	73	2.44	4.48	11.95	3.07	68	4.5	45.2	121.0	76.3
	75	2.87	4.45	13.20	2.91	61	4.7	36.3	94.5	65.6
	77	2.38	5.47	13.69	2.66	68	4.4	39.5	100.0	75.8
Confectionary and related products	69	2.60	2.17	7.52	3.24	20	7.9	44.0	70.2	84.2
	71	2.55	1.46	5.25	3.48	21	7.6	53.6	65.1	85.1
	73	2.52	3.13	6.65	3.55	22	6.4	52.9	55.9	84.9
	75	2.41	3.24	13.41	4.15	16	8.7	43.9	67.2	79.4
	77	2.67	2.59	12.00	4.23	21	7.3	37.6	58.7	98.9
Construction and mining: handling machinery and equipment	69	2.60	4.02	10.32	2.30	55	4.6	34.9	67.2	80.5
	71	2.96	2.74	7.00	2.36	58	3.8	33.9	85.2	78.9
	73	2.46	3.70	11.72	3.13	55	4.4	36.2	111.0	83.2
	75	2.54	4.82	13.04	2.84	60	3.1	46.9	100.2	90.6
	77	2.56	4.49	12.90	2.95	52	4.2	38.9	100.0	87.2
Converted paper and paper board products	69	2.45	3.01	9.36	2.90	42	6.8	63.1	81.4	88.9
	71	2.94	2.20	7.46	2.95	41	7.5	54.9	72.6	71.3
	73	2.82	2.92	11.35	3.21	46	6.9	46.8	72.9	76.1
	75	2.97	3.25	11.47	3.24	44	6.6	49.2	86.1	65.6
	77	2.83	4.04	10.20	3.76	44	7.6	67.9	92.8	76.0
Cutlery, hand tools and general hardware	69	3.35	4.12	10.05	2.43	45	4.6	40.0	46.7	79.3
	71	3.87	4.27	8.42	2.27	46	4.4	37.3	71.9	73.2
	73	3.19	4.64	11.62	2.57	49	5.0	36.2	70.3	77.8
	75	3.19	3.86	10.19	2.28	45	4.2	38.5	72.0	81.3
	77	2.88	4.75	13.64	2.97	49	5.5	36.3	76.0	68.9
Dairy products	69	1.54	1.30	7.02	5.49	24	31.5	62.7	73.4	62.8
	71	1.60	1.39	8.71	6.02	26	28.0	63.4	81.7	59.9
	73	1.52	1.21	7.26	6.15	28	23.8	72.3	97.5	82.0
	75	1.40	1.59	12.54	8.03	27	24.8	69.4	110.1	99.4
	77	1.63	1.70	13.07	7.39	24	20.1	69.3	116.0	92.9
Drugs	69	2.24	4.76	12.95	2.12	55	6.0	40.1	54.9	78.9
	71	2.90	5.53	11.02	1.97	56	5.6	49.0	68.2	65.8
	73	2.75	6.05	13.40	2.13	59	5.2	44.6	71.8	68.8
	75	2.46	6.15	14.37	2.19	59	4.4	44.6	77.0	81.2
	77	2.67	6.70	15.67	2.80	50	5.5	60.0	103.8	72.2

Figure 4-2 (continued)

Line of Business	Year	Current Assets to Current Debt (Times)	Net Profit on Net Sales (Percent)	Net Profit to Tangible Net Worth (Percent)	Net Sales to Tangible Net Worth (Times)	Collection Period (Days)	Net Sales to Inventory (Times)	Fixed Asset to Tangible Net Worth (Percent)	Total Debt to Tangible Net Worth (Percent)	Inventory to Net Working Capital (Percent)
Electric lighting and wiring equipment	69	2.85	2.82	9.22	2.78	47	5.0	38.0	76.6	77.7
	71	3.07	2.21	8.47	2.71	45	5.1	48.4	55.6	74.8
	73	3.05	4.08	11.78	2.61	48	5.2	42.2	63.8	79.9
	75	4.06	2.79	8.61	2.54	43	4.5	33.4	57.4	72.9
	77	2.66	4.08	11.92	3.06	51	4.8	39.3	72.6	75.1
Electrical industrial apparatus	69	2.56	2.91	7.71	2.71	54	4.6	46.8	83.5	83.9
	71	2.85	2.01	6.08	2.72	60	4.7	42.8	84.1	70.9
	73	2.51	4.47	11.89	3.15	64	5.0	42.2	90.3	78.0
	75	2.59	3.68	9.59	3.00	57	4.3	41.6	101.5	75.2
	77	2.67	4.85	13.81	2.76	58	4.2	37.4	87.8	80.8
Electronic components and accessories	69	2.36	3.05	8.46	3.03	55	4.7	40.8	97.4	83.1
	71	2.55	1.83	5.04	2.45	59	4.6	55.1	86.7	79.3
	73	2.32	4.13	14.28	2.93	63	4.7	53.0	94.5	78.4
	75	2.79	3.48	9.87	2.74	56	4.9	42.7	83.7	71.5
	77	2.59	5.72	15.47	2.86	58	5.7	46.5	92.5	71.8
Engineering, laboratory, and scientific instruments	69	2.96	4.08	9.76	2.20	75	3.7	37.7	76.1	69.0
	71	3.41	3.10	5.76	1.96	66	3.9	35.4	74.8	63.9
	73	3.21	3.83	11.54	2.48	71	4.0	34.9	95.9	74.3
	75	3.39	3.75	8.73	2.33	72	3.5	35.0	77.6	71.1
	77	2.76	7.10	15.31	2.71	67	5.3	36.5	94.5	64.2
Fabricated structural metal products	69	2.69	2.23	7.40	3.13	54	6.1	38.6	93.0	73.6
	71	2.30	2.55	7.79	3.04	51	6.0	40.1	87.5	74.4
	73	2.30	3.03	11.38	3.51	51	6.6	42.0	94.2	75.3
	75	2.55	4.23	14.39	3.46	46	6.2	39.3	95.0	71.7
	77	2.23	4.22	13.73	3.61	49	6.6	45.7	110.4	67.8
Farm machinery equipment	69	2.79	2.42	8.95	2.45	43	3.9	38.4	77.2	85.7
	71	2.64	2.49	7.69	2.75	46	3.7	38.4	86.9	95.1
	73	2.49	3.60	13.87	3.16	43	4.0	35.8	94.3	97.7
	75	2.12	3.59	14.66	3.81	37	3.9	32.0	128.5	117.9
	77	2.35	3.01	10.83	3.27	46	3.8	37.8	164.3	100.6

Industry	Year										
Footwear	69	2.41	2.04	8.89	4.26	51	5.5	25.0	107.9	91.7
	71	2.68	1.73	7.38	3.78	51	5.6	23.7	108.4	83.8
	73	2.34	1.66	6.36	4.02	59	5.3	27.9	122.0	93.3
	75	2.70	3.12	8.83	3.73	49	5.7	17.3	87.9	85.7
	77	2.43	1.89	7.73	5.35	58	5.7	27.2	101.7	84.9
General building contractors	69	1.45	1.23	9.66	8.45	*	*	25.7	206.3	*
	71	1.54	1.53	12.73	8.99	*	*	24.8	202.8	*
	73	1.42	1.07	10.79	8.81	*	*	24.7	195.0	*
	75	1.43	1.18	11.30	7.32	*	*	22.9	234.0	*
	77	1.63	1.87	11.26	8.20	*	*	24.6	136.8	*
General industrial machinery and equipment	69	2.49	3.75	10.49	2.76	55	4.9	41.8	72.7	87.9
	71	3.02	2.13	6.08	2.41	54	5.0	42.1	74.9	72.3
	73	2.52	3.84	11.95	2.86	58	4.6	43.8	92.2	81.2
	75	2.61	5.16	13.63	2.91	48	4.2	39.1	86.2	81.5
	77	2.71	4.71	13.90	3.16	55	5.9	44.6	90.0	72.2
Heavy construction (except highway and street)	69	1.87	2.67	9.77	3.74	*	*	60.0	88.2	*
	71	1.90	2.09	8.61	4.12	*	*	52.0	101.7	*
	73	1.77	2.27	9.50	3.69	*	*	53.2	100.1	*
	75	1.89	2.69	10.60	3.85	*	*	53.8	104.0	*
	77	1.83	4.47	12.52	3.31	*	*	54.1	118.6	*
Household appliances	69	2.37	3.16	9.89	2.98	43	4.6	34.7	77.8	91.4
	71	2.65	3.31	10.29	3.23	48	4.9	36.1	97.4	86.3
	73	2.47	3.74	12.52	3.18	52	4.3	38.9	95.4	90.6
	75	3.03	3.92	10.43	2.90	60	4.5	34.4	68.5	75.0
	77	2.35	5.40	12.29	3.19	49	5.0	46.3	96.4	83.0
Industrial chemicals	69	1.93	4.35	9.68	2.07	51	7.1	62.8	57.6	88.3
	71	2.70	3.67	7.69	2.12	57	6.2	73.6	75.5	76.4
	73	2.45	5.25	12.34	2.21	61	7.7	79.6	98.7	69.0
	75	2.11	4.96	15.63	3.74	43	9.6	62.2	111.7	67.2
	77	2.42	5.77	13.40	2.68	54	7.6	68.1	86.2	72.8
Iron and steel foundries	69	2.42	2.87	7.53	2.62	46	11.0	59.2	57.1	68.5
	71	2.89	2.60	6.35	2.27	40	11.0	57.7	55.2	53.2
	73	2.53	3.56	8.95	2.59	51	8.8	63.2	59.9	64.7
	75	2.39	6.16	16.11	3.04	43	11.9	58.7	65.4	56.3
	77	2.87	4.69	14.52	2.87	42	12.4	64.1	74.2	46.0
Malt liquors	69	2.07	3.74	9.53	2.65	16	18.8	67.9	44.7	54.9
	71	2.12	1.91	6.83	2.61	14	16.4	75.6	59.5	59.1
	73	2.33	2.44	8.21	2.80	16	13.7	80.1	56.7	68.5
	75	1.66	3.23	9.46	3.28	12	14.0	85.8	71.7	106.9
	77	1.90	3.46	11.29	3.42	15	12.5	88.1	58.6	83.2

Figure 4-2 (continued)

Line of Business	Year	Current Assets to Current Debt (Times)	Net Profit on Net Sales (Percent)	Net Profit to Tangible Net Worth (Percent)	Net Sales to Tangible Worth (Times)	Collection Period (Days)	Net Sales to Inventory (Times)	Fixed Asset to Tangible Net Worth (Percent)	Total Debt to Tangible Net Worth (Percent)	Inventory to Net Working Capital (Percent)
Meat packing plants	69	2.06	0.91	8.50	9.33	15	30.5	58.4	71.2	68.3
	71	2.11	0.87	10.14	9.74	14	33.1	63.5	91.9	68.5
	73	1.97	0.64	9.85	11.68	14	28.5	65.2	96.7	88.2
	75	2.57	1.09	13.29	10.61	15	30.7	56.4	87.3	64.5
	77	2.35	1.12	8.28	10.29	14	28.1	65.7	94.6	62.5
Men's and boys' trousers	69	1.83	1.64	7.37	5.07	61	4.9	7.2	168.7	93.3
	71	2.07	1.32	9.20	4.78	54	5.6	9.1	135.3	78.9
	73	2.15	1.37	6.91	4.44	48	6.8	9.3	111.3	72.6
	75	2.29	1.20	5.23	5.31	61	7.1	10.2	80.9	67.9
	77	2.17	2.20	9.02	6.30	42	7.0	26.8	99.2	88.7
Metal stampings	69	2.32	2.63	7.03	3.07	36	8.6	50.0	76.4	75.7
	71	2.51	2.26	5.53	2.84	39	7.7	54.2	81.0	77.1
	73	2.11	2.82	10.91	3.48	43	7.8	54.0	99.0	93.2
	75	2.53	3.97	10.89	3.28	39	8.1	52.6	88.5	68.4
	77	2.14	3.97	11.61	3.69	40	9.0	62.1	98.5	76.3
Millwork	69	2.60	2.06	7.78	4.01	46	6.8	40.3	98.8	74.0
	71	2.65	2.47	7.53	3.73	42	6.9	38.3	91.9	67.4
	73	2.38	2.82	12.27	3.82	37	6.3	39.9	104.2	87.5
	75	2.69	2.20	6.58	3.62	39	6.4	35.0	80.0	83.6
	77	2.34	2.41	10.44	4.57	46	5.7	37.6	120.1	79.7
Motor vehicle parts and accessories	60	2.70	3.99	12.35	2.80	42	6.2	43.4	78.5	82.7
	71	2.79	3.29	8.81	2.59	45	5.3	46.0	83.9	78.0
	73	2.45	4.03	12.91	3.04	46	5.2	50.5	82.8	89.0
	75	2.93	3.51	9.82	3.07	45	5.2	46.6	85.0	79.3
	77	2.62	4.57	14.54	3.72	46	6.1	52.7	87.6	74.2
Nonferrous foundries	69	2.30	2.98	7.72	3.07	40	12.5	46.4	65.8	54.7
	71	2.87	2.17	4.61	2.36	39	13.9	45.0	53.2	45.8
	73	2.44	4.49	11.94	3.37	46	9.7	48.1	83.5	66.3
	75	2.91	4.47	11.78	3.11	43	8.6	43.6	55.8	57.5
	77	2.29	4.24	13.78	3.35	45	8.4	61.0	87.6	65.8

Industry	Year								
Office and store fixtures	69	2.08	3.07	10.80	3.91	59	8.6	32.7	123.0	65.7
	71	2.27	2.44	8.35	3.79	54	6.8	35.8	125.3	64.8
	73	2.17	2.85	9.35	3.53	57	6.7	33.6	130.3	89.5
	75	2.94	2.03	8.60	3.21	52	8.4	31.8	93.0	63.5
	77	2.71	3.47	8.84	3.91	46	10.1	35.4	101.2	49.3
Paints, varnishes, lacquers and enamels	69	3.14	2.48	7.32	2.85	41	6.6	34.3	64.4	71.3
	71	3.04	2.26	7.00	3.13	42	6.6	40.3	66.3	70.5
	73	2.93	2.61	8.49	3.18	42	6.3	36.6	70.2	76.4
	75	2.98	2.71	9.05	3.26	37	6.1	29.6	78.1	71.6
	77	2.77	2.61	8.63	3.73	42	6.7	37.1	82.3	76.5
Paper board containers and boxes	69	2.43	3.36	9.37	3.00	38	11.6	45.8	83.4	61.9
	71	2.55	2.60	6.72	3.06	34	8.5	67.2	70.4	74.5
	73	2.43	3.57	11.21	3.37	36	7.8	59.7	89.1	78.3
	75	3.52	3.26	7.88	3.23	31	7.8	45.3	75.0	53.5
	77	2.83	2.66	12.41	3.47	37	8.1	57.6	80.3	67.9
Passenger car, truck, and bus bodies	69	2.12	1.82	7.32	4.12	48	6.4	38.6	100.3	83.0
	71	2.63	1.85	8.29	3.54	49	6.6	41.8	90.1	80.3
	73	1.89	2.59	8.91	4.16	46	4.8	38.7	111.8	125.9
	75	2.57	2.37	11.00	3.63	34	4.7	33.6	75.7	90.0
	77	2.27	3.41	11.76	4.35	40	4.9	42.6	114.3	90.5
Petroleum refineries	69	1.14	3.76	6.84	1.78	30	13.0	41.1	23.6	117.8
	71	1.72	4.87	8.73	1.91	49	10.5	101.5	69.1	76.8
	73	1.70	7.03	14.37	2.08	59	12.1	99.2	66.0	66.7
	75	1.38	4.19	15.10	3.60	40	13.3	96.9	132.6	84.0
	77	1.32	5.97	14.65	2.36	47	12.7	114.0	114.6	77.8
Plastics, materials, and synthetics	69	1.88	2.75	8.30	2.63	53	8.0	61.0	60.0	79.0
	71	2.25	2.60	7.64	2.84	55	7.7	57.1	61.2	70.6
	73	2.24	3.80	11.89	2.83	57	7.9	67.7	96.4	72.4
	75	2.32	2.80	7.81	2.83	55	7.8	57.0	96.6	66.4
	77	2.02	3.42	11.96	3.58	51	8.1	79.7	90.5	73.3
Plumbing, heating, and air conditioning	69	1.74	1.71	11.79	6.07	*	*	21.8	114.3	*
	71	1.91	1.30	9.03	6.63	*	*	24.5	142.5	*
	73	1.71	1.29	9.16	6.12	*	*	21.7	171.4	*
	75	1.76	1.51	10.61	6.92	*	*	18.8	182.0	*
	77	1.86	2.22	13.08	5.44	*	*	32.2	120.1	*
Soap, detergents, perfumes, and cosmetics	69	2.27	3.95	12.36	3.22	54	7.8	33.4	57.5	70.9
	71	2.66	3.83	12.74	2.88	51	7.6	29.1	62.3	59.2
	73	2.37	4.04	11.61	3.16	52	7.1	38.7	68.9	65.7
	75	2.40	4.40	17.92	4.03	40	8.3	35.3	98.3	64.3
	77	2.32	3.52	13.21	4.06	50	9.5	39.9	93.7	65.3

115

Figure 4-2 (continued)

Line of Business	Year	Current Assets to Current Debt (Times)	Net Profit on Net Sales (Percent)	Net Profit to Tangible Net Worth (Percent)	Net Sales to Tangible Worth (Times)	Collection Period (Days)	Net Sales to Inventory (Times)	Fixed Asset to Tangible Net Worth (Percent)	Total Debt to Tangible Net Worth (Percent)	Inventory to Net Working Capital (Percent)
Special industry machinery	69	2.62	3.78	8.86	2.37	66	4.3	38.3	81.6	82.5
	71	3.16	2.08	4.35	2.03	59	4.7	35.2	62.0	68.2
	73	2.59	3.69	9.89	2.50	61	4.5	36.3	89.7	80.7
	75	2.53	3.82	11.15	2.85	61	4.3	35.6	80.5	80.0
	77	2.38	3.82	9.62	2.48	62	4.3	36.0	88.9	84.7
Toys, amusements, and sporting goods	69	1.97	2.55	9.22	3.87	55	5.0	38.3	129.9	116.5
	71	2.37	2.52	8.68	3.43	59	4.9	27.1	111.8	86.8
	73	2.40	3.89	11.90	3.17	56	4.6	39.4	107.4	85.7
	75	2.82	3.27	9.75	3.03	58	4.8	38.6	103.7	80.7
	77	2.32	3.15	13.03	3.77	62	5.5	41.1	130.4	87.1
Women's, misses', and juniors' dresses	69	1.58	1.17	10.60	9.30	49	13.4	7.4	179.6	83.3
	71	1.67	1.16	10.42	7.75	51	11.8	7.1	151.5	77.2
	73	1.73	1.19	8.27	6.77	53	8.9	10.8	168.1	86.4
	75	2.06	.50	2.63	5.83	51	9.9	8.2	135.5	71.9
	77	1.87	1.38	8.43	6.48	49	9.2	14.5	164.4	83.5
Wooden and upholstered household furniture	69	3.02	3.30	9.99	2.90	42	6.4	33.4	55.7	75.7
	71	2.88	2.69	9.57	3.13	47	7.1	35.2	60.2	71.3
	73	2.92	3.18	11.32	3.17	44	6.2	39.2	69.4	82.7
	75	3.11	1.74	5.49	2.79	46	5.2	37.2	85.4	79.7
	77	2.88	2.36	7.91	3.20	46	6.9	32.9	86.7	73.6
Work clothing, men's and boys'	69	2.86	2.23	6.80	3.14	46	3.8	15.4	89.8	82.1
	71	2.68	2.63	8.48	3.25	55	4.2	19.5	99.1	89.3
	73	3.19	2.60	8.44	3.29	53	4.6	17.2	89.1	84.9
	75	3.12	3.37	12.54	3.14	42	4.3	16.6	67.4	76.3
	77	2.12	3.32	12.55	5.97	41	4.9	36.2	124.0	69.6

NOTE: Median values taken from *Dun's Reviews*.
*Data not available or not applicable.

SOURCE: Reprinted with the special permission of *Dun's Review*, November 1970, 1972, 1974, 1978 and December 1976. Copyright © 1970, 1972, 1974, 1976, 1978, Dun and Bradstreet Publications Corporation.

pacity. This, in turn, indicates that the firm either made too large an investment in fixed assets or that sales for some reason have not met previous expectations. If the former is the case, the problem possibly may be traced further to an outdated, completely intuitive process of capital budgeting. If sales have not achieved forecasted levels, the problem may be traced either to unforeseeable environmental changes or to some problem in market planning or implementation such as market definition, pricing, or the distribution system.

These examples suggest the nature and use of most financial information in a business policy case as a starting point for problem identification. Financial data can indicate only symptoms of problems, leading to consideration of more basic factors that better serve to explain why financial growth, profit, liquidity, or efficiency are below industry averages or objectives for the firm. Financial difficulties never, upon identification, constitute an end to the problem-solving process.

In connection with the process of problem identification, the student should be familiar with the interrelationships of the financial data and ratios discussed earlier. An understanding of two different kinds of interrelationships is important here. The first is how internal efficiency and external effectiveness indicators interact to determine the profitability of the firm's assets. A basic tool for gaining an appreciation of this interaction is the Du Pont system of financial control shown in Figure 4-5. This system provides a ready-made schematic whereby interactive effects of basic financial ratios may be traced and understood. The second is an appreciation of the implications of shifts in the various ratios and their effects on other ratios. For example, a low fixed charge coverage ratio in conjunction with a high debt ratio may indicate a substantial weakness in the firm from a creditor's perspective. An increase in gross income may raise the fixed charge coverage ratio significantly, however, and therefore offset the disadvantages of a high debt ratio to some extent. The ability to perceive interrelationships between the ratios is a prerequisite for understanding the total financial position, present and projected, of a firm.

Finally, the student should have a basic understanding of the implications of each basic financial indicator in and of itself. For example, just how significant is a high debt ratio to creditors? What other factors may offset this deficiency? Or, to use another example, what are the implications of a low fixed asset turnover for new capital proposals, both present line oriented and new product oriented?

DEVELOPMENT OF PLANS OF ACTION

The use of financial analysis in the development of recommended plans of action may be approached from two basic perspectives. First, the student must ascertain the financial feasibility of all recommendations, expressed in terms of (1) the effects of plans developed on the basic indicators of financial effectiveness, efficiency, and objectives; (2) the availability of short- or

Figure 4-3 Selected Dun & Bradstreet financial ratios of selected wholesale businesses.

Line of Business	Year	Current Assets to Current Debt (Times)	Net Profit on Net Sales (Percent)	Net Profit to Tangible Net Worth (Percent)	Net Sales to Tangible Worth (Times)	Collection Period (Days)	Net Sales to Inventory (Times)	Fixed Asset to Tangible Net Worth (Percent)	Total Debt to Tangible Net Worth (Percent)	Inventory to Net Working Capital (Percent)
Chemicals and allied products	69	1.95	1.62	8.36	6.07	44	12.1	25.6	167.8	66.6
	71	2.05	1.16	8.15	6.18	45	11.3	33.3	198.1	76.5
	73	1.91	1.78	14.70	5.53	47	11.3	30.8	162.1	75.8
	75	1.99	3.35	16.60	5.94	36	11.5	29.4	89.7	75.7
	77	2.24	3.38	14.39	4.74	45	11.4	27.0	107.5	65.8
Clothing and furnishings, men's and boys'	69	2.66	1.17	4.68	5.18	46	5.6	5.7	93.1	81.4
	71	2.50	1.15	6.91	5.07	45	5.6	6.4	91.9	90.2
	73	2.52	1.06	4.39	4.51	41	5.6	6.4	93.3	83.2
	75	2.28	1.35	8.04	4.92	39	5.5	7.1	112.5	96.1
	77	2.36	2.05	11.55	4.98	36	5.0	8.4	103.4	72.8
Dairy products	69	1.73	1.03	9.47	6.83	29	30.5	39.1	122.3	50.0
	71	1.91	1.09	8.46	6.85	27	31.3	45.3	134.0	48.8
	73	1.86	1.65	12.15	6.84	31	23.0	39.0	144.2	55.6
	75	1.65	1.70	11.52	6.44	32	22.7	28.8	137.0	52.7
	77	1.51	1.42	12.74	9.68	25	39.3	39.6	182.6	40.4
Electrical appliances, TV and radio sets	69	1.86	1.29	7.98	6.15	42	6.0	8.0	168.9	123.4
	71	1.91	1.22	7.69	6.12	42	5.9	7.5	171.5	117.7
	73	1.76	1.58	10.70	6.42	41	6.1	8.2	159.8	126.3
	75	1.86	1.10	5.92	5.84	41	6.3	9.0	142.0	105.6
	77	1.99	1.97	9.38	4.89	40	5.6	11.4	110.9	103.5
Electronic parts and equipment	69	2.32	2.35	8.72	4.90	42	4.2	11.8	135.8	106.7
	71	2.34	1.77	7.03	3.86	45	4.3	14.7	113.7	98.2
	73	2.17	2.24	10.52	4.64	43	4.5	15.5	150.9	108.5
	75	2.26	1.55	9.71	5.84	44	4.5	14.4	206.7	107.1
	77	2.22	3.00	13.81	5.22	41	5.5	17.9	144.4	100.1

Furniture and home furnishings	69	2.12	1.50	7.93	5.08	44	7.1	10.5	156.4	83.0
	71	2.35	1.43	7.02	4.23	48	6.3	11.8	113.1	85.8
	73	2.19	1.67	8.48	4.74	43	6.2	13.8	97.9	91.7
	75	2.71	1.61	7.58	4.97	41	6.3	10.5	114.5	79.7
	77	2.13	1.67	9.97	5.87	42	6.8	11.2	164.2	79.6
Groceries, general line	69	2.07	0.58	6.81	10.72	13	11.2	24.7	138.2	119.6
	71	2.08	0.59	7.89	11.91	12	12.3	24.2	142.9	122.8
	73	1.91	0.69	8.84	12.76	12	12.5	39.3	148.4	141.0
	75	2.80	0.83	10.26	12.94	11	13.2	28.2	138.7	114.8
	77	1.96	0.80	8.57	10.58	15	13.3	30.4	140.0	113.3
Hardware	69	2.89	1.48	4.85	3.27	44	4.5	13.8	83.9	93.4
	71	2.89	1.39	4.94	3.61	43	4.5	15.0	79.5	93.5
	73	2.69	1.75	7.48	4.00	42	5.2	12.6	98.5	96.5
	75	2.87	1.77	7.37	3.84	38	4.9	12.7	99.2	94.3
	77	2.72	2.25	8.78	4.22	40	5.0	13.3	88.3	87.9
Lumber and construction materials	69	2.47	1.80	8.42	5.42	44	7.6	24.0	118.5	89.9
	71	2.26	1.62	9.82	5.29	47	7.7	23.2	132.6	83.1
	73	2.35	2.03	13.87	5.79	44	8.5	22.2	118.8	77.8
	75	2.55	1.34	7.97	5.23	41	7.7	17.3	102.9	77.4
	77	2.07	2.26	10.21	5.32	41	7.2	23.3	127.8	85.3
Petroleum and petroleum products	69	2.12	2.00	8.63	4.15	33	17.5	50.0	66.8	54.7
	71	2.14	1.62	9.44	5.17	29	18.9	50.7	71.5	62.2
	73	2.06	1.98	10.12	5.22	29	24.2	48.7	72.4	56.9
	75	1.80	1.73	12.49	6.25	23	18.0	44.0	87.7	80.1
	77	1.85	0.90	6.09	7.62	26	26.2	64.4	121.6	67.1
Tobacco and tobacco products	69	1.87	0.46	6.25	12.72	17	17.7	13.8	118.5	100.2
	71	1.99	0.62	9.55	14.18	15	18.4	14.2	104.7	94.3
	73	2.02	0.67	8.47	13.92	16	17.6	14.2	102.2	99.5
	75	2.55	0.93	11.85	12.00	16	16.0	14.7	106.4	91.3
	77	2.33	0.64	8.18	11.76	14	16.0	14.5	112.2	88.9

NOTE: Median values taken from *Dun's Reviews*.

SOURCE: Reprinted with the special permission of *Dun's Review*, October 1970, 1972, 1974, 1976, 1978. Copyright © 1970, 1972, 1974, 1976, 1978, Dun & Bradstreet Publications Corporation.

Figure 4-4 Selected Dun & Bradstreet financial ratios of selected retail businesses.

Line of Business	Year	Current Assets to Current Debt	Net Profit on Net Sales	Net Profit to Tangible Net Worth	Net Sales to Tangible Worth	Collection Period	Net Sales to Inventory	Fixed Asset to Tangible Net Worth	Total Debt to Tangible Net Worth	Inventory to Net Working Capital
		(Times)	(Percent)	(Percent)	(Times)	(Days)	(Times)	(Percent)	(Percent)	(Percent)
Auto and home supply stores	69	2.58	2.12	8.54	3.93	*	6.1	23.6	85.9	90.1
	71	2.23	2.39	10.71	3.76	*	6.5	18.5	127.0	85.3
	73	2.01	2.83	9.09	3.60	*	5.5	22.0	99.6	96.9
	75	1.98	1.54	7.04	4.01	*	5.7	29.4	93.0	89.7
	77	2.24	1.58	7.29	3.84	*	4.5	32.8	124.7	93.3
Department stores	69	2.76	2.12	6.46	3.15	*	5.5	24.7	75.7	76.9
	71	2.89	1.55	5.42	3.13	*	5.6	26.0	82.0	76.9
	73	2.82	1.89	5.65	3.32	*	5.3	33.9	91.8	81.4
	75	2.81	1.61	5.47	3.64	*	5.7	33.0	88.9	80.2
	77	3.06	2.12	8.18	4.03	*	5.5	27.3	96.7	77.8
Discount stores	69	1.82	2.00	13.19	6.30	*	5.2	27.9	131.6	153.7
	71	1.88	1.49	9.97	6.28	*	5.2	28.9	120.1	146.1
	73	2.02	1.35	9.10	6.13	*	5.0	32.1	147.9	146.7
	75	2.18	1.42	9.04	5.84	*	5.3	30.9	123.1	130.9
	77	2.21	1.26	11.22	7.03	*	5.2	35.5	122.2	135.3
Family clothing stores	69	3.20	2.61	8.38	3.11	*	4.3	11.4	72.7	82.5
	71	3.18	2.85	8.28	3.53	*	4.8	12.3	88.8	79.7
	73	3.16	1.99	8.55	3.24	*	4.4	12.7	107.5	85.2
	75	3.41	2.06	6.24	3.01	*	4.6	11.3	77.3	76.8
	77	3.86	3.27	8.26	2.59	*	3.7	16.4	100.0	78.0
Furniture stores	69	2.87	2.13	6.32	2.58	109	5.0	10.3	104.2	59.4
	71	2.67	2.11	6.02	2.67	104	4.7	11.4	85.9	68.7
	73	2.51	2.37	7.73	2.76	96	4.5	10.7	102.0	75.6
	75	2.82	2.00	5.66	2.94	83	4.5	12.0	111.8	69.5
	77	3.70	2.80	6.50	2.59	76	4.6	12.7	102.2	67.1

Grocery stores	69	1.69	1.06	10.34	9.72	*	16.1	66.7	96.0	135.2
	71	1.73	1.00	10.48	10.26	*	17.1	66.5	97.5	141.3
	73	1.76	.89	9.61	11.27	*	15.5	71.8	127.2	134.2
	75	1.63	.94	12.78	12.80	*	16.1	77.2	117.3	155.9
	77	1.70	1.12	12.35	12.25	*	16.7	76.5	124.8	147.5
Household appliance stores	69	2.20	1.56	8.26	10.10	34	5.6	13.1	128.5	100.3
	71	1.95	1.54	8.54	4.74	37	5.1	15.3	137.2	100.5
	73	1.87	1.67	10.62	4.91	30	5.2	18.4	206.9	111.9
	75	2.00	1.20	7.26	5.34	26	4.7	19.7	150.7	108.8
	77	2.49	3.66	11.21	4.01	30	4.9	15.8	111.9	100.0
Jewelry stores	69	2.91	3.81	3.13	2.11	*	2.9	9.0	90.8	77.8
	71	3.16	2.66	5.73	2.05	*	3.0	10.6	73.6	77.1
	73	3.38	2.80	7.17	2.12	*	2.8	7.0	85.8	80.5
	75	3.46	3.79	7.46	1.87	*	3.0	8.0	81.8	80.3
	77	3.37	4.60	8.52	1.95	*	2.4	10.0	75.9	91.8
Radio and television stores	69	—	—	—	—	—	—	—	—	—
	71	—	—	—	—	—	—	—	—	—
	73	2.19	2.00	11.87	5.32	*	5.0	17.3	84.0	113.4
	75	2.28	1.48	10.17	4.79	*	4.8	22.7	143.3	126.1
	77	2.20	3.26	13.20	3.64	*	5.0	19.8	102.5	128.8
Shoe stores	69	3.48	3.06	9.05	3.18	*	3.9	13.0	81.9	102.3
	71	3.20	1.67	5.24	3.30	*	3.8	12.5	82.4	103.7
	73	2.95	1.65	5.45	3.23	*	3.8	13.8	108.2	106.7
	75	2.69	1.34	4.45	3.45	*	3.7	13.2	106.7	104.1
	77	4.05	3.54	8.90	2.50	*	3.7	12.6	46.9	95.4
Women's ready-to-wear stores	69	2.50	2.18	8.73	3.78	*	6.1	14.7	125.8	78.3
	71	2.57	1.81	6.68	3.95	*	6.6	18.6	104.0	76.7
	73	2.65	2.05	8.92	3.82	*	6.7	18.3	98.5	73.0
	75	2.68	1.82	6.68	3.89	*	7.1	29.4	109.4	72.5
	77	2.63	2.13	6.82	3.83	*	6.1	20.8	103.7	72.8

NOTE: Median values taken from *Dun's Reviews*.
*Data not available or not applicable.

SOURCE: Reprinted with the special permission of *Dun's Review*, September 1970, 1972, 1974, 1976, 1978. Copyright © 1970, 1972, 1974, 1976, 1978, Dun & Bradstreet Publications Corporation.

Figure 4-5 DuPont system of financial control.

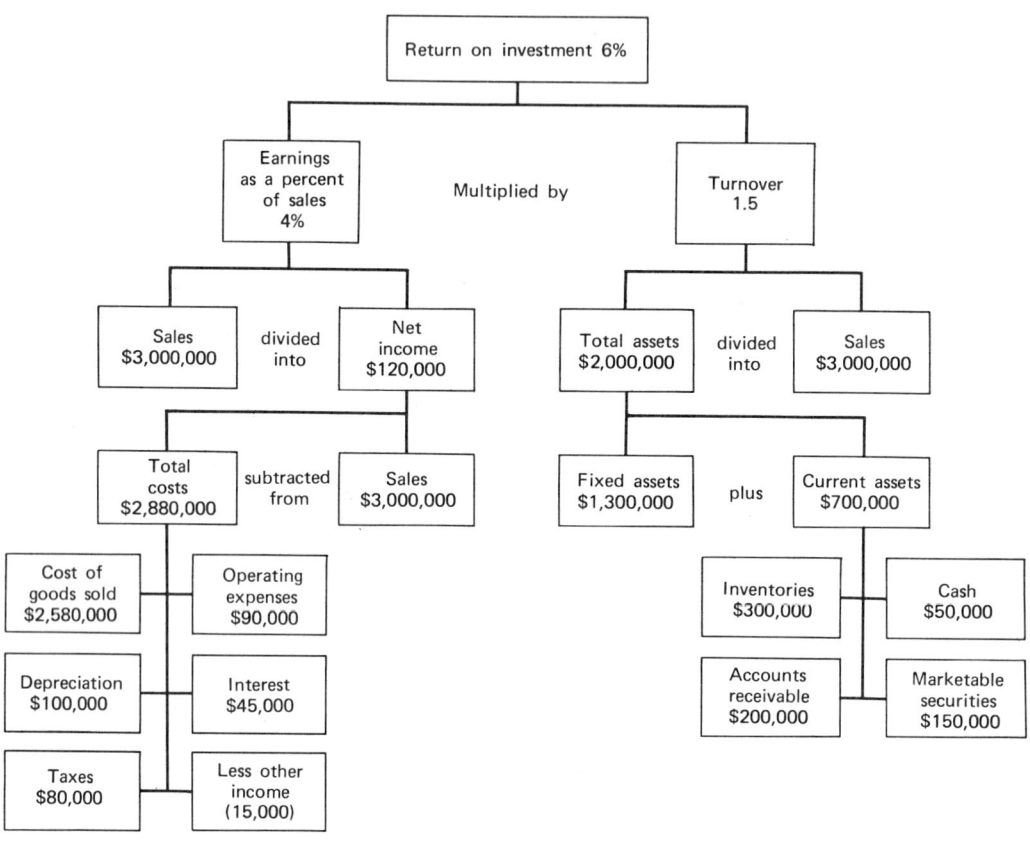

SOURCE: *Essentials of Managerial Finance, 2nd ed.*, by J. Fred Weston and Eugene F. Brigham. Copyright © 1968, 1971 by Holt, Rinehart and Winston, Publishers. Reprinted by permission of The Dryden Press.

long-term financing, either internally or externally, to implement the recommendations; and (3) the risk-taking propensity of top management. Second, the student must be prepared to compare alternative courses of action in terms of feasibility and risk; this requires a basic understanding of capital investment theory.

With respect to the first line of inquiry, information developed in the analysis-of-situation phase is once again of primary importance. Its use is significantly different, however, from what was previously discussed in the problem identification phase. In the present phase, the ratios and other indicators must be projected for their future implications as to the financial position of the firm if a given recommendation is implemented. For example, if a recommendation is made to enter a new product market, what would be the effect of the new sales forecast for the firm as a whole on a currently unsatisfactory turnover of fixed assets? Is a heavy investment in fixed assets required to achieve the new sales forecast? If so, how much lead time would be required before sales increased enough in the new product line to offset the short-run inefficiency indicated by an even lower turnover of fixed assets? What will be the impact on creditor relations? How can creditors and stockholders be convinced "to be patient?" These and other similar implications for the financial standing of the firm must be explored to determine the merits of each recommendation. However, it is not always necessary to formulate detailed projections of sales and investment requirements. It is more appropriate in a policy case to assess the recommendations in terms of their general implications for the future financial position of the firm.

The student also must be able to prove that adequate resources exist to finance the recommended plans. How will the new plans be financed? What seem to be the trade-offs between external and internal financing? How might the trade-offs be calculated? One should be able to recognize the specific calculations that may be necessary and the trade-offs that actually exist among alternative modes of financing. The major implication of this reasoning is that any recommendation involving deployment of a high volume of financial resources must be qualified by the recognition that alternative modes of financing carry alternative implications for the firm's basic financial structure.

Finally, with respect to feasibility, the student must take into account top management's psychological propensity to assume financial risk. This is a basic aspect of feasibility that is often ignored, but one that is vital in gaining acceptance of proposals.

As noted, the second major use of financial analysis in developing plans of action requires a familiarity with the techniques of comparison of alternative proposals. The question arises, however, as to what extent the student should be required to rank alternative investment proposals in terms of the appropriate discounted cash flow technique. The literature existing in capital investment theory will have been explored in previous finance courses. It seems, however, that detailed evaluation of investment proposals (usually a C_4 variable) through the application of the net present value method, internal rate of return method, or profitability index methods is outside the scope of a business policy course. The student should understand how the cost-of-capital (supply-of-funds) schedule interacts with projected revenue streams (investment opportunities open to the firm) to determine the optimum capital budget under conditions of uncertainty. This understanding then can be expressed in terms of a qualification of recommendations concerning capital investment until appropriate computations are completed by financial analysts within the firm. The foregoing refers only to the financial feasibility of investment proposals. Implications of the proposals for the

BREAK-EVEN ANALYSIS

present and future strategy, organization, and other matters should have been explored to justify the existence of the recommendations in the first place.

This section reviews some of the definitions, mathematical relationships, uses, and limitations of a basic management tool called break-even analysis. This type of analysis is usually displayed on a break-even chart or graph that shows the relationships among profits, fixed costs, variable costs, and volume in a compact and visual form. Figure 4-6 presents a typical break-even chart; the horizontal axis is volume in units and the vertical axis is in dollars.

One of the first inputs the student must develop is the total cost line. Usually, it is assumed that total cost can be broken into two linear components, fixed and variable costs. Fixed costs are considered to be constant as volume of output changes. Some typical examples of such costs are depreciation on plant and equipment, rentals, interest charges on debt, property taxes, occupancy cost (such as heat and lights), general office expenses, and salaries of supervisory, research, and executive staffs.

Variable costs are assumed to vary directly with the volume produced. The usual components of variable costs include direct labor, direct material, sales commissions, and supplies. One of the problems involved in classifying a cost into one of these categories is the time horizon to which you are referring. Some may argue that all costs are variable, or at least not fixed, in the long run, while others say that in the very short run, all costs are fixed. The conflict is partially resolved when the time period or horizon to be covered by the break-even analysis is determined; this is usually 1 year.

Figure 4-6 Typical break-even chart.

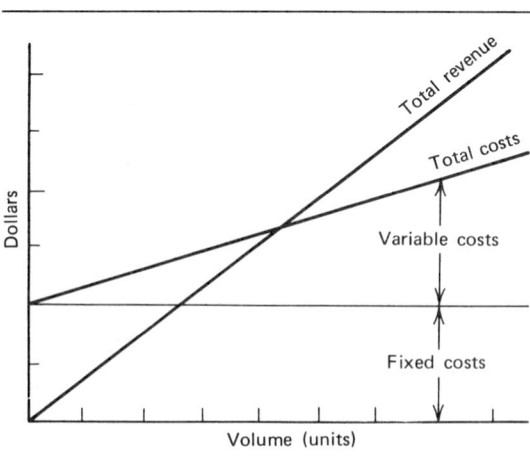

It may be difficult to classify each cost into either the fixed or variable category over the entire volume range. The semivariable cost has both a fixed and a variable component. Examples of this type of cost are indirect labor, maintenance and clerical costs.

There are several ways to approximate this cost-volume relationship other than just having the components given in a situation. One way is to locate two points on the break-even chart. The student needs to know the total costs at two different volumes, preferably with some "spread" between them. The straight line that connects these points defines the total cost function. Another method is to plot the historical cost-volume points on the graph and fit a straight line through the resulting scatter diagram. In either case, the fixed cost is where the total cost line intercepts the vertical axis, and the slope of the line is the variable cost per unit.

There are some difficulties involved in using these approaches. First they concentrate on past relationships. By doing this, one implicitly assumes that the conditions that prevailed in the past are still operating, and that may not be the case. Factors other than volume or cost also may have been operating. Then there are the dangers present in any regression analysis—extrapolating data beyond their boundaries and having too few observations.

The other primary input to break-even analysis is the total revenue line. It is assumed that revenue is derived solely from sales made at a constant price per unit. Incidentally, it also is assumed that production volume for the year is the same as sales volume—that is, no net change in inventory.

The point at which these two lines cross is called the break-even point. Some say that because of the impreciseness of the inputs (total cost and total revenue), it might be better labeled a "break-even region." Mathematically, the break-even point is where total costs equals total revenue. From this we can easily find an expression for break-even volume. At break-even point:

$$TC = TR \tag{1}$$

where
$TC = F + VN$
$TR = SN$
F = fixed cost
N = volume of output in units
V = variable cost per unit
S = selling price per unit

Substituting, we get
$F + VN = SN$
$VN - SN = F$
$N(S - V) = F$
$$N = F/(S - V) \tag{2}$$

Thus we have a fairly simple equation for break-even volume. Using the same notation, we can arrive at an expression for profit.

$$\text{Profit } (P) = TR - TC \tag{3}$$

Substituting the same expressions, equation 3 becomes

$$P = SN - (F + VN)$$
$$P = SN - VN - F$$
$$P = N(S - V) - F \quad (4)$$

Notice that in both equations 2 and 4 the term $(S - V)$ appears. This is called the contribution per unit; that is, this is the amount that covers fixed costs and later profit each time an additional unit is sold. Letting C represent contribution, equations 2 and 4 become

$$N = \frac{F}{C} \quad (5)$$
$$P = NC - F \quad (6)$$

respectively.

A brief example might clarify the situation. The Phinque Company has an annual fixed cost of $100,000. The variable cost per unit is $.50 and the product sells for $1. The break-even chart and break-even point for this situation is shown if Figure 4-7 but, if you have run out of graph paper, you can rely on equation 2.

$$N = \frac{\$100,000}{\$1 - \$.50} = 200,000 \text{ units}$$

If you want to find the profit at a particular volume, such as 250,000 units, use equation 4.

$$P = 250,000 \, (\$.50 - \$1) - \$100,000$$
$$P = \$125,000 - \$100,000$$
$$= \$25,000$$

Break-even analysis can be used in a variety of ways. One of the more obvious uses is to examine the sensitivity of the break-even point and profit to changes in four factors: selling price, variable costs, fixed costs, and volume. For instance, the greater the ratio of price to variable cost per unit, the greater the absolute sensitivity of profits to volume. By examining Equation 2, you can see the cost-price-volume relationship explicitly. If you decrease direct labor by adding an automatic piece of equipment, you may increase fixed costs. How are profits and break-even volume affected? Equations 2 and 4 or the break-even chart can be used to answer this type of question easily.

Analysis of the cost-price-volume structure may lead you to some less obvious conclusions. For example, where there is a great cost variability with volume, cost reduction efforts can be fruitful. On the other hand, if a large percentage of the total cost is fixed, it would be best for a company to focus on sales promotion because, with high fixed costs, the best way to change profits is through increased volume.

Figure 4-7 Break-even chart—Phinque Company.

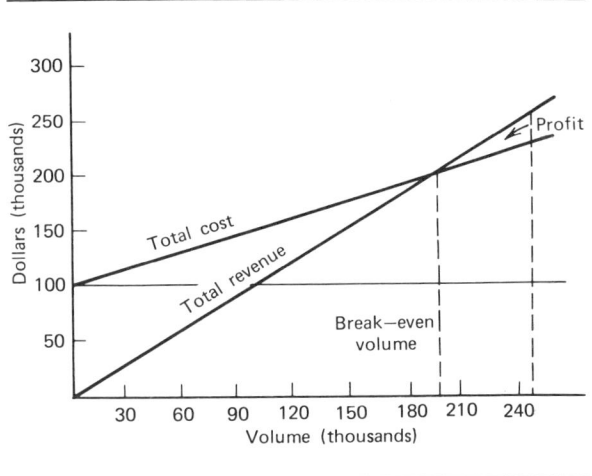

Given the approximate break-even point, management can compare fluctuations in expected future volume with this point to ascertain stability of profits. This type of information is important to the financial manager in determining the ability of the firm to cover its debt obligations. If there are plans to acquire assets that will increase fixed costs, this knowledge becomes important.

Break-even analysis may be used to evaluate proposals for the expansion or contraction of the firm's operations. For example, the abandonment of, or addition to, a company's facilities can have a far-reaching effect on its financial equilibrium, and break-even analysis can provide management with a fairly accurate estimate of this change. Break-even analysis may be beneficial when examining technological changes, new product decisions, a modernization or automation program, or whenever a horizontal or vertical merger is contemplated. For example, when faced with a decision as to whether or not to purchase another company, one line of analysis is to look at the composite break-even chart. It may reveal that the fixed charges are so high that the break-even point is raised dangerously high and, consequently, this purchase would not be desirable.

Another use for break-even analysis is in plant location analysis. The economic effects of changing production volumes on the operating costs and profits that exist in alternative plant sites can be analyzed using break-even analysis. In this case, one assumes that sales revenue is not affected by the location decision. Break-even analysis allows the manager to consider the relative economic feasibility of alternative sites at different operating volumes. The manager must then decide what the future operating volume will be before a decision can be reached.

Unfortunately, there are several limitations to break-even analysis. These are usually associated with the assumptions that are made. For instance, it is assumed that the selling price and variable cost per unit are constant over the entire volume range. Thus the end results are linear relationships. The additional assumption is made that each factor is independent of the others. As one learns in economics, however, volume may influence the market price. Also, costs may increase as full capacity is approached because of the use of marginal labor or costly overtime help. Setup costs and learning prevent labor costs from following a straight line. Quantity discounts make material costs nonlinear.

One way to get around these problems is to develop relationships between total sales and volume and between total cost and volume. This would lead to nonlinear relationships that would correspond more closely to reality but would also make analysis a bit more complicated.

Break-even analysis is best suited for a one-product firm. If it is assumed that the product mix does not change, break-even analysis can be used for multiple products. When the product mix changes, one is faced with the problem of allocating expenses that are common to all product lines. Also, the horizontal axis of the break-even chart must be expressed in some aggregate measure.

Informational inputs for break-even analysis are usually based on historical relationships. However, it is the future that is usually of interest, and these historical relationships may not be stable over time. The short time horizon used in break-even analysis is a limitation for long-range planning. The benefits of certain expenditures, such as capital expenditures and research and development outlays, are not likely to be realized during the period of time encompassed by most break-even analyses.

Break-even analysis implicitly assumes that changes in the four factors are not accompanied by changes in the amount of capital used. If a decrease in variable cost arises (e.g., because of the purchase of a new machine), the effect on return on investment is not given by break-even analysis.

Finally, as in financial analysis, break-even analysis does not take intangible factors, such as the reactions of customers and employees and the reactions of competitors, into account. But even with all of these and other limitations break-even analysis is still a valuable management tool.

FINANCE FUNCTION

A brief description of the finance function in a firm is offered here, followed by a discussion of the functionally dependent (C_3) decision variables and their determinants. A listing of functionally independent (C_4) decision variables concludes the section.

The manager of the finance function has three major concerns.

1. Determining the total amount of funds to be used by an enterprise.
2. Determining what specific assets the firm should acquire or allocating the funds among various assets in an efficient manner.

3. Determining how the needed funds should be financed or obtaining the best mix of financing with relation to the overall valuation of the firm.

According to Van Horne, these concerns manifest themselves in the form of three major decisions.

1. *Investment Decision.* Deals with capital budgeting, reallocation of capital, management of existing assets, and mergers and acquisitions.
2. *Financial Decision.* Involves the determination of the best financing mix or capital structure for the firm.
3. *Dividend Decision.* Concerns the percentage of the firm's earnings paid to stockholders in cash dividends.[3]

The financing decision and a portion of the investment decision are considered C_2 decisions within our framework. This was discussed in Chapter 1 and will not be dealt with further.

Some determinants of a particular decision variable may in turn depend on other C_3 variables or their determinants. This leads to the realization that in order to approach optimum finance decisions, one must make or solve these decisions simultaneously. This aspect of finance decisions is beyond our present scope, but the student should be aware of this situation.

FINANCE DECISION VARIABLES

The following finance decision variables and their determinants are described in this section of the chapter:

Level of working capital = f(uncertainty of cash receipts and disbursements, borrowing capacity, management's utility preference for cash, efficiency of cash management, volume of credit sales, seasonality of sales, credit policies, C_1 and C_2 variables).

Level of dividend payment = f(dividend payment history, the stability of earnings, rate of growth and profit levels, desire for control, liquidity position, ability to borrow, debt contract restrictions, tax position of stockholders, legal constraints, C_1 and C_2 variables).

Level of Working Capital

This decision variable is concerned with the determination of the level of working capital (short-term assets minus short-term liabilities) a firm should maintain. Current assets are usually in the form of (1) cash and marketable securities, (2) accounts receivable, and (3) inventories. Current liabilities are primarily accounts payable.

---

[3] J.C. Van Horne, *Financial Management and Policy*, 2d ed. (Englewood Cliffs, N.J.: Prentice Hall, 1971), Chapter 1.

Management of working capital is significant for several reasons. First, there is typically a direct relationship between growth in sales and the level of accounts receivable, inventories, and possibly cash balances. Second, current assets often represent more than one-half of the total assets of many firms and thus deserve efficient management. Finally, the small firm cannot rely on capital markets as heavily as the larger firms can and therefore must make greater use of trade credit and short-term bank loans—both of which increase current liabilities, which affects net working capital.

Because the last component of working capital, inventories, and its determinants are described in Chapters 5 and 6, the determinants of only the first two components are discussed here.

Determinants. The determinants of the level of cash and marketable securities, hereafter referred to as cash, are discussed first, followed by an exploration of the determinants of the level of accounts receivable.

The uncertainty with regard to cash receipts and disbursements is a primary determinant of cash level. One approach is to use a cash flow forecast to examine the factors such as sales revenues, average collection period of accounts receivable, production schedules, maturity structure of debt, and other expenses that affect the magnitude and timing of cash flows. The possible deviation of these flows from their forecasted values is also important in deciding on the level of cash. For instance, if the magnitude of the actual cash flow is uncertain (i.e., there is a potentially large variance or dispersion of its distribution), a higher level of working capital or cushion would be needed than if the magnitude of the cash flow is known with relative certainty.

The firm's borrowing capacity to meet emergency needs is another influence on the amount of cash. If a firm has a readily accessible source of funds to carry it through a tight liquidity situation, the level of working capital could be reduced.

Another determinant is the utility preferences of management with respect to the risk of cash insolvency. A risk-averse management obviously would prefer a higher level of cash than a less risk-averse management. This may lead to a loss of income as a result of idle funds, but the risk-averse management is willing to suffer that loss for the security of cash. This type of preference was demonstrated by the actions of Sewell Avery, president of Montgomery Ward, after World War II. Avery felt the United States would face a depression soon after the war ended. Based on this analysis, the company built up a tremendous cash reserve ($360 million), while its chief competitor, Sears, expanded rapidly. It is only recently that Montgomery Ward has been able to overcome this mistake and compete effectively with Sears.

A final determinant of the level of cash is the efficiency with which cash is managed. This has to do with reducing the time between when a customer pays a bill and when it becomes usable funds for the firm. As this time is reduced, the level of cash can be lowered. Programs such as concentrated banking and lockbox systems are attempts to achieve this objective. For example, the C.I.T. Finance Corporation has established a cash management system consisting of a banking network with central, regional, and local depository banks, lockboxes, and a computerized financial information system. According to Alfred DeSalvo, treasurer and vice president of C.I.T.:

> Our system is not cumbersome or expensive. More important it works. Indeed, it works so well that the company can borrow from $25 million to $100 million a day for its 925 branches and subsidiaries and at the same time maintain unused cash at an extremely low level. In fact, C.I.T., which uses about $1 billion in short-term funds to run its business, usually concludes a working day with no cash in its banks above the compensating balances needed to maintain credit lines. The remainder of the company's short-term money is at work or en route to work.[4]

The accounts receivable level is determined by the volume of credit sales, seasonality of sales, and the firm's credit policies. This is an area where the interaction between the marketing and finance functions is quite apparent. Sales personnel do not want to be hindered by a lot of red tape about credit ratings and the like or to confront a potential customer with embarrassing questions concerning credit worthiness. What might be considered stringent credit terms by the salesperson may eliminate some potential customers and, therefore, sales revenue. Also, annoying or abrasive collection policies may cost the firm some of its existing customers. On the other hand, the finance people feel that it is their function to convert credit sales dollars into usable funds for the firm as quickly and reliably as possible. A popular way to do this is through the use of discounts and discount periods. Of course, an overriding concern is that of bad-debt losses.

In theory, the firm should reduce its quality standards for accounts accepted as long as the profitability of sales generated exceeds the added cost of the receivables.[5] In practice, factors such as the industry's characteristic terms of sale and credit, the firm's financial position, and even the condition of the national economy will affect the level of accounts receivable. For example, if the other companies in the industry give their customers the terms "2/10, net 30," a given firm would implicitly consider these to be *minimum* terms. The firm may choose to give its customers better terms as a means of attracting or keeping customers.

In recent years a factor that has been dormant has begun to influence credit policies: short-term interest rates. Consider the following example:

> The first glimmer of a slowdown in payments typically appears when companies forgo the cash discounts of one-half of 1% to 2½% that many suppliers offer in

---

[4]Alfred DeSalvo, "Cash Management Converts Dollars into Working Assets," *Harvard Business Review, 53* (3), May-June 1972, p. 93.
[5]Van Horne, *Financial Management and Policy*, p. 442.

return for paying bills early. American Standard Inc., the $1.8 billion manufacturer of industrial equipment and building products, has examined the trade-off between the value of cash discounts to the debtor and alternate uses of the cash. Treasurer Richard H. Francis says the company found that as interest rates rise, fewer discounts are worth taking, and he issued guidelines to the company's divisions detailing "at which level of interest rates it makes sense to take the discount and at what level it does not." For example, Francis says that a couple of months ago, when short-term rates were 8%, a cash discount of 9.1% looked good. Today, with the prime at 10.75%, he says that American Standard would have delayed paying such a bill until its due date and invested the cash elsewhere.[6]

Level of Dividend Payment

Management must first determine whether or not to pay a dividend to stockholders and, if so, at what level. The difference between earnings and dividends is retained earnings. Thus a conflict can arise: should a firm retain its earnings to finance its growth, return these earnings to the equity investors, or do both to some degree? This decision takes on importance because it affects the valuation of the firm by present and potential investors, which can, in turn, affect the firm's cost of capital. There are two basic viewpoints on this issue. The first is that the stability of dividends is important and, therefore, that the dividend payment level has its rightful claim on the firm's earnings. The second is that investors would prefer the firm to retain and reinvest the earnings, as long as the return on the reinvested earnings exceeds the rate of return that the investor could obtain on other investments of comparable risk. In other words, the firm should reinvest its earnings in opportunities available to it until funds are exhausted or a minimum return is not obtained. The remainder or residual of earnings then could be dispersed as dividends. The latter viewpoint implies that dividends are irrelevant and that the investor shows no preference for dividends over capital gains.

Note that the determinants of dividend policy are oriented more toward external influences on the firm, with little direct influence from the other functional areas.

Determinants. The determinants of dividend policy include dividend payment history, stability of earnings, rate of growth and profit levels, desire for control, liquidity position, ability to borrow, debt contract restrictions, tax position of stockholders, and legal constraints.

Maintenance of a stable or target dividend is important for several reasons. First, dividends have informational content. They can convey management's view of the firm's future earnings to the investor. Investors may consider a decrease in the dividend payments level as an announcement of a change in the expected future profitability of the firm. This may lead to a reaction in the form of a change in the price of the stock. The following ex-

---

[6]"Companies Start to Pay Bills Late," *Business Week*, November 20, 1978, p. 139.

cerpt from a 1979 issue of a business publication provides some evidence of the importance of dividend stability.

> Du Pont, GM, Koppers, and others have recently decided to husband some of their cash by reining in the growth of their dividend payout. "We paid out 73% of earnings in dividends in 1973," says Prendergast. "We now pay out only 45%." In failing to take similar action, managements are "cannibalizing their companies," says analyst Glove.
>
> Hundreds of companies are unwilling to lower their dividend payout for fear that disgruntled shareholders will dump their stocks, making it harder to sell new equity. Indeed, when GM trimmed its yearend special dividend last Nov. 6, its stock price skittered $6 to $54 per share, where it has remained.[7]

Some investors live on dividends; for them, dividend stability is a very desirable characteristic. Institutional investors can invest only in firms included on a legal list. One qualification to be placed on this list is dividend stability.

In 1974 the Consolidated Edison Company found itself with a liquidity problem. Part of top management's solution was to omit, for the first time in 89 years, its quarterly dividend, with the following reactions.

> The waves that those decisions generated are battering the stocks and driving down the bond ratings of most other power companies. This week, too, they were pounding the Con Edison management at one of the most boisterous annual meetings on record. There, management faced irate stockholders protesting the loss of their dividends and angry customers furious about steep increases in Con Ed rates.
>
> Most Wall Streeters and power companies think that Con Ed Chairman Charles F. Luce had no idea of the furor his decision would produce. Says one analyst: "Luce is a power man, not an investment man. He just didn't realize that big utilities don't cut their dividends." Others, like Cook, believe that Con Ed and some other urban power companies that are under fierce cost pressures must face up to a wholly different future. Says one: "Con Ed lost the institutions long ago, but its dividend allowed it to count on the little old lady in tennis shoes. Now it has lost her, too. And lost her for a lot of other utilities."[8]

Closely related to the stability of dividends is the stability of earnings. A firm that has relatively stable earnings is more likely to pay out a higher percentage in dividends. Conversely, a firm with less stable earnings would pay out a lower percentage to avoid endangering the stability of dividends during periods of low earnings.

On January 31, 1978, U.S. Steel reported an 89% slide in fourth-quarter earnings and a cut in its dividend to $.40 from $.55. Prior to that announcement, financial analysts had been optimistic, but here was one reaction.

---

[7] "The Profit Illusion," *Business Week*, March 19, 1979, p. 111.
[8] "Con Edison: Archetype of an Ailing Utility," *Business Week*, May 25, 1974, p. 102.

Says one analyst who had been recommending most of the steel stocks before the U.S. Steel fourth quarter was announced: "On the day U.S. Steel cut its dividend, I removed my recommendation from the whole group."[9]

The rate of growth and profitability affects the number of investment opportunities available to the firm. A company in a growth industry, such as computers or electronics, would have more investment opportunities available to it than would a company in a mature industry, such as coal or steel, with fewer investment opportunities. The former firm would be more willing to use its earnings to finance these investments. The latter firm would be more prone to pay out a greater portion of its earnings in dividends.

A related issue is the timing of investment opportunities. A company may retain earnings for use on a project in the future, but it might be better off if it paid out these earnings in dividends and financed the project using external sources when the time came.

Some managements prefer not to dilute control of a firm by raising capital through the issuance of new stock. Therefore the firm is financed primarily through retained earnings, leaving little or no funds for dividends. This philosophy could work in reverse if "outsiders" seeking control could convince stockholders that the company was not maximizing shareholder wealth (or some other objectives) and that they, the outsiders, could do a better job. Thus a company that fears it may be acquired by such tactics may establish a high dividend to appease stockholders.

Because payment of dividends is a drain on cash, the liquidity position of the firm may act as a constraint. If a firm has the flexibility to borrow funds on short notice, this constraint can be offset somewhat. Typically, the age and size of a company will determine the access it has to capital markets. A well-established firm is more likely to have a higher dividend pay-out rate than a new or small firm. This argument correlates well with the preceding "mature industry" discussion.

The effect of several determinants, dividend payment history, liquidity position, and ability to borrow is illustrated in the following examples. Western Union traditionally has paid a quarterly dividend of $.35. The company reported an annual deficit to the Internal Revenue Service but was able to report a net profit to the stockholders because of a combination of accounting devices. Because the company did not generate enough earnings to pay its traditional dividends, part of the cash came from borrowed funds. Utility companies are finding themselves in a similar situation.

> The lack of profit not only shrinks the amount of internally generated cash flow available for new construction but also jeopardizes the utilities' ability to service current debt. Utility companies' coverage ratio—the number of times earnings cover interest expense—has taken a frightening tumble, from 5.3 in 1965 to 2.8

---

[9]"Shattered Hopes for Steel Stocks," *Business Week*, March 6, 1978, p. 103.

today. Earnings of industrial companies, meanwhile, are sufficient to cover interest charges 8 times. Wall Street also worries that some utility dividends are imperiled. The average utility now pays out about 75% of its reported earnings in dividends, and plenty actually borrow money to do it.[10]

The composition of a firm's stockholders, in terms of their personal income tax brackets, can influence dividend policy. Stockholders in higher tax brackets would prefer capital gains instead of dividends, while stockholders in lower tax brackets generally prefer the opposite. The closeness with which a company is held and the ability of a firm to discern stockholder preference will determine the strength of such an influence in the dividend decision. If a company has a wide diversity of stockholders with regard to income, the impact of this determinant will be minimal. For example, General Motors has well over 1 million stockholders. In this case, it would be difficult to assess the preferences of all stockholders on this issue. The reasoning of the Chairman and Executive Officer of the Crane Company when it acquired the Medusa Corporation in 1979 is an interesting twist on this determinant.

> "We try to give our shareholders a hedge against inflation," says Thomas Mellon Evans, chairman and chief executive of $1.2 billion Crane Co. "It would take them many years to put together an investment in a natural resource company with their dividends. So we try to give them that in their investment." On March 27, Evans provided his shareholders with just such a hedge by wrapping up the acquisition of Medusa Corp. Medusa, a cement, aggregate, and construction service business, fits Evans' bill perfectly. Its value is "in the ground," and its reserves are likely to appreciate with inflation. Its plants are modern, making their value substantially more than the historical cost reflected on Medusa's books. And Evans was able to acquire the company, he notes, "without diluting Crane's stock."[11]

The last two determinants are somewhat related in that both are constraints on dividend payments. The first deals with contractual constraints that may be written into debt contracts. For instance, payment of dividends may be made contingent on the amount of net working capital. The second constraint includes legal rules such as state statutes and court decisions concerning corporation dividends. Typical rules include the net profits rule, which says dividends can be paid only from past and present earnings; the capital impairment rule, which protects shareholders and creditors by forbidding payment of dividends from capital; and the insolvency rule, which prohibits a firm from paying dividends while insolvent.

---

[10] "Why There Will Be A Money Crunch," *Business Week*, May 28, 1979, p. 114.
[11] "Crane: Its Acquisition of Medusa Will Give Shareholder's a Hedge," *Business Week*, April 9, 1979, p. 116.

FUNCTIONALLY INDEPENDENT FINANCE VARIABLES

A number of finance decisions are usually not significantly influenced by factors in other segments of the organization.

1. Call features of debt instruments.
2. Conversion features of debt instruments.
3. Maturity and yield trade-off.
4. Method of project proposal evaluation.
5. Priority of payment of debt instruments.
6. Redemption features of debt instruments.
7. Rights of preferred stockholders.
8. Rights of lenders when payments are missed.
9. Risk yield trade-off in financial investments.
10. Security offered with debt instruments.
11. Time to maturity of debt instruments.

In accordance with the framework developed in Chapter 1, these C_4 decision variables do not usually require detailed knowledge on the part of the general manager, so they are not emphasized here.

SUMMARY

The first section of this chapter concentrated on the use of financial analysis in the three phases of case analysis: analysis of the situation, problem identification, and development of plans of action to eliminate the problems. Because financial ratios were used to perform much of the financial analysis, this section included a review of selected ratios and an explanation of how these ratios act as symptoms that can aid in identifying problem areas. It also showed how alternative courses of action may be evaluated through the use of this type of financial analysis.

The next section contained a brief discussion of break-even analysis and its uses and limitations for policy cases.

After a brief review of the finance function, the final section discussed two functionally dependent decision variables—level of working capital and level of dividend payment—together with the factors that influence each variable. The section concluded with a listing of functionally independent finance decision variables.

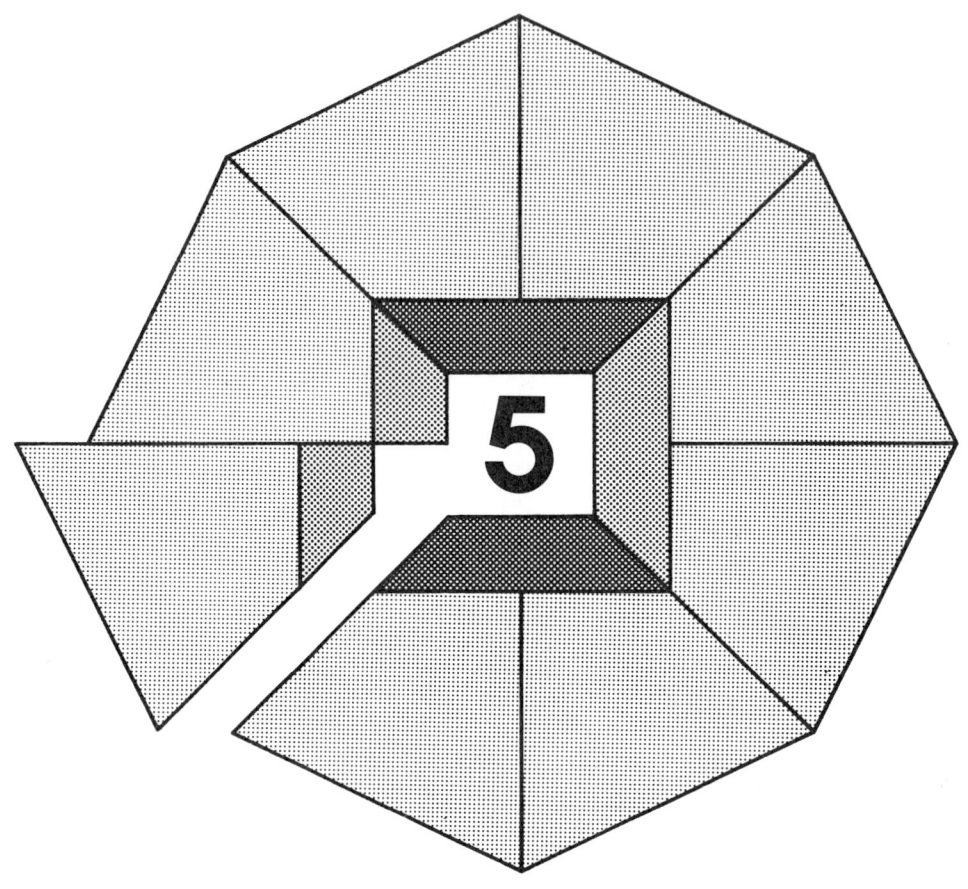

MARKETING
the interdependent nature of decision making

There is no universal agreement as to what marketing is. It can be described as: (1) a group of related business activities—including product development, pricing, personal selling, advertising, physical distribution, and marketing research; (2) a structure of institutions including manufacturing, wholesaling, and retailing; (3) an economic process dealing with the exchange or transfer of ownership of products; (4) social behavior, because it involves interaction between buyers and sellers as well as adaptive and formative behavior by marketing institutions to meet changing consumer lifestyles and demands and to influence their buying behavior; (5) a macroprocess involving a view of marketing as an institution (pervasive behavior) in a society; (6) a microprocess performed by the firm or the consumer; and (7) a management process involving the planning, organizing, and controlling of marketing activities.[1]

These viewpoints are all legitimate and justifiable. Marketing is a multidimensional endeavor, as illustrated in Figure 5-1. As shown, marketing as a field of study encompasses:

1. The core elements of marketing functions, marketing institutions, and the environment in which institutions perform functions.
2. Themes of analysis and integration that can be used in marketing planning.
3. A basic or general approach that is integrative in nature.
4. Tools of analysis to aid in marketing analysis, planning, implementation, and control.

A discussion of these four dimensions of the field follows.

A MULTIDIMENSIONAL VIEW OF MARKETING

Marketing's Core Elements

The core elements of marketing are the:

1. Set of marketing *functions* that has to be performed to bridge market "gaps" and "separations."
2. Set of marketing *institutions* that evolve to perform these marketing functions.
3. *Environment* in which marketing is performed. It encompasses the same elements of the business environment as discussed in earlier chapters.

Figure 5-2 relates the concepts of market gaps, functions, and institutions.

---

[1] Marketing Staff of the Ohio State University, "A Statement of Marketing Philosophy," *Journal of Marketing*, 29, January 1965, pp. 43–44.

Figure 5-1 A multidimensional view of marketing.

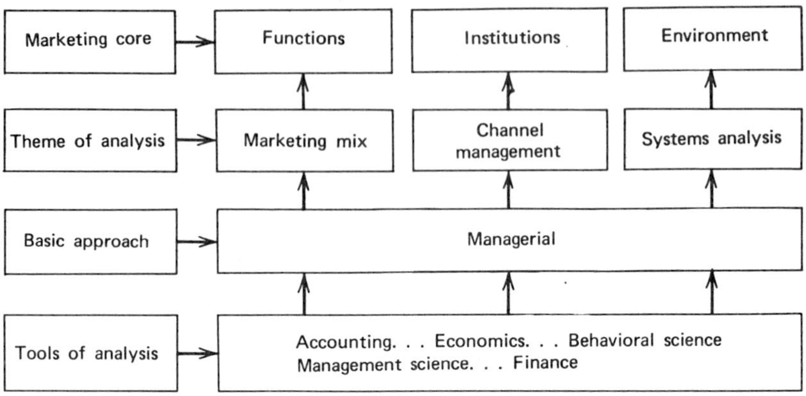

Marketing core →	Functions	Institutions		Environment
Theme of analysis →	Marketing mix	Channel management		Systems analysis
Basic approach →	Managerial			
Tools of analysis →	Accounting... Economics... Behavioral science Management science... Finance			

SOURCE: Adel I. El-Ansary, "Marketing: A Model's Approach to Subject Identification," in Adel I. El-Ansary (ed.), New *Essays in Marketing Education*, paper number 6, Division of Research, College of Business Administration, Louisiana State University, Baton Rouge, Louisiana, 1972, p. 7a.

Themes of Analysis and Integration

The themes of integration that can be used in developing a coherent marketing plan include:

1. The *marketing mix*, which integrates marketing functions. Marketing functions are mixed in different kinds and proportions by marketers to reach different market segments.
2. *Channel management*, which integrates marketing institutions into superorganizations managed and controlled to facilitate the flow of goods and services from producers to consumers.
3. *Systems analysis*, which integrates marketing management into the broader environment. The environment provides marketing management inputs, dictates constraints in the design of marketing programs, and assimilates marketing outputs.

A Basic Approach to Marketing

As indicated earlier, one can view marketing differently depending on his or her vantage point and the dimension of concern. Because of the general management nature of strategy formulation and implementation, we should adopt an holistic view of marketing in this text. Thus marketing management can be described as:

the analysis, planning, implementation, and control of programs designed to bring about desired exchanges with target markets for the purpose of achieving organizational objectives. It relies heavily on designing the organization's offering in terms of the market's needs and desires and using ef-

Figure 5-2 Marketing gaps, functions, and institutions.

Gaps or separation	Ownership	Space		Time		Information or perceptual		Posession (values)	
Functions	Buying and Selling	Assemblies Dispersion	Transportation	Ware—housing	Risk Management	Promotion	Market Research	Credit (Financing)	Pricing
Institutions (participants):									
Consumers	X		X	X				X	
Manufacturers	X	X	X	X	X	X	X	X	X
Wholesaling	X	X	X	X	X	X	X	X	X
Retailing	X	X	X	X	X	X	X	X	X
Specialized									
Warehousing		X	X	X					
Transportation			X	X					
Credit								X	
Marketing research							X		
Advertising						X			

Gaps flow from Producer → Consumer.

SOURCE: Adel I. El-Ansary, "Marketing: A Model's Approach to Subject Identification," in Adel I. El-Ansary (ed.), *New Essays in Marketing Education*, paper number 6, Division of Research, College of Business Administration, Louisiana State University, Baton Rouge, Louisiana, 1972, p. 7a.

fective pricing, communication, and distribution to inform, motivate, and service the market.[2]

This definition is general in nature in order to account for the broad and pervasive nature of marketing.[3] For example, marketing functions are performed to promote and enhance not only the image of products and services but also:

1. *Organizations.* The church, police department, NASA.
2. *Persons.* Political candidates, celebrities.
3. *Places.* Tourism in states and nations, museums.
4. *Social Causes.* Family planning, defensive driving, and antismoking.

---

[2] Philip Kotler, *Marketing Management: Analysis, Planning, and Control*, 4th ed. (Englewood Cliffs, N.J.: Prentice-Hall, 1980), p. 22.
[3] Philip Kotler and Sidney Levy, "Broadening the Concept of Marketing," *Journal of Marketing*, *33*, January 1969, pp. 10–15.

Therefore, in case analyses involving strategy for nonbusiness and nonprofit organizations, the analyst should also look for strategic marketing problems. Indeed, one may ascribe the failure of some organizations to a top management view of the organization as a government agency or a philanthropic concern without considering it as a marketing institution as well.

One is encouraged to examine strategic marketing programs that pertain to the organization's product or service offering to its direct customers and to make sure that the organization has developed marketing programs designed to relate to *all* of its publics.[4] An example of this would be the advertisement of a firm's attempt to abate environmental pollution, contribute to urban renewal efforts, or train the hard-core unemployed. Another example of such a marketing campaign would be that of a nonprofit, family planning organization that must (1) promote the family planning concept to potential users of birth control methods; (2) relate to private foundations providing financial and technical assistance; (3) relate to a hostile church or minority community concerned with religious premises or race genocide; and (4) interact with a hostile medical society and community concerned with the ramifications of the organization's success in the promotion of socialized medicine.[5]

Tools of Analysis for Marketing

Managerial economics, behavioral science, management science, accounting, and finance are tools used to aid marketing management in the planning, decision making, control, and assessment of marketing performance. Table 5-1 outlines these essential tools and illustrates their uses in marketing management.

MARKETING MANAGEMENT: ENVIRONMENT AND CHALLENGES

In a marketing-oriented organization, marketing begins and ends with consumer needs; satisfying these needs is the key to successful marketing. Therefore it becomes necessary for marketing management to determine the nature of demand. Table 5-2 outlines the different possible demand states and marketing action to deal with each state.

One of the major challenges to marketing management is to *balance* consumer need satisfaction with other considerations, including:

1. The overall objectives of the firm as related to sales volume, growth, and the like.
2. Shrinking world resources of raw materials, capital, and energy.

---

[4] Philip Kotler, "A Generic Concept of Marketing," *Journal of Marketing*, 36, April 1972, pp. 46–54.
[5] Adel El-Ansary and Oscar E. Kramer, Jr. "Social Marketing: The Family Planning Experience," *Journal of Marketing*, 37, July 1973, pp. 1-7.

Table 5-1 Marketing Tools of Analysis

Tools	Uses
Managerial economics	Sales forecasting
	Pricing decisions
	Optimization of the allocation of the marketing mix
	Competitive and market analysis
Behavioral science	Consumer behavior analysis
	Executive behavior analysis
Management Science	Multivariate statistics for marketing research
1. Statistics	Linear programming for allocation of advertising budgets
2. Operations research	
3. Mathematics	Queueing models for customer service facilities
Accounting	Sales volume analysis by product, customer type, territory, etc.
	Marketing cost analysis by function, customer type, territory, etc.
Finance	Return on investment
	Cash flow by product and brand
	Payback on promotional budgets

Table 5-2 Corporate Tasks Relating to the Consumer

Demand State	Corporate Task	Formal Name	Example
I. Negative demand	Disabuse demand	Conversional marketing	Dental work
II. No demand	Create demand	Stimulation marketing	Unfamiliar product
III. Latent demand	Develop demand	Developmental marketing	Low-tar, high-flavor cigarettes
IV. Faltering demand	Revitalize demand	Remarketing	Furs, hotels, autos
V. Irregular demand	Synchronize demand	Synchromarketing	Boats, hotels
VI. Full demand	Maintain demand	Maintenance marketing	Most products one time or another
VII. Overfull demand	Reduce demand	Demarketing	Supply shortages
VIII. Unwholesome demand	Destroy demand	Countermarketing	Energy, cigarettes

SOURCE: Reprinted from Philip Kotler, "The Major Tasks of Marketing Management," *Journal of Marketing*, October 1973, p. 43, published by the American Marketing Association.

3. Environmental protection considerations, including the impact of products in use (e.g., automobiles) and after use (e.g., disposables) on the quality of the environment.
4. Consumer safety, protection, and welfare regulations and ethical considerations. The following are illustrative examples:
   (a) Should a cigarette manufacturer conduct research and development on marijuana cigarettes in anticipation of its legalization or should it be restrained by consumer health and welfare considerations?
   (b) Should a food processor extend nutritional labeling to cover a broad range of possible information needed by consumers with special health problems or needs despite the additional cost involved?
   (c) Should a supermarket chain institute a unit pricing program in all its stores and educate the consumers about its use despite the huge expenditures involved?
   (d) How can a manufacturer of cereals or toys promote its products without advertising to children?
   (e) How can a manufacturer of deodorants and perfumes promote to consumers without the use of sex appeal or puffery that borders on false claims?
   (f) Should a manufacturer of tires or an insurance company avoid the use of fear appeals to promote their products?

In short, marketing management is faced with the challenging task of creatively responding to consumer demand. Managers must balance the need satisfaction of consumers with (1) other corporate objectives, and (2) considerations of shrinking world resources, environmental protection, and consumer safety.

MARKETING MANAGEMENT: STRATEGY AND TASKS

Marketing management requires the selection of a marketing strategy position and the development and implementation of marketing plans, organization, and controls. A discussion of these follow.

Alternative Marketing Strategy Positions

Figure 5-3 illustrates alternative marketing strategy positions and explains each briefly. Table 5-3 provides examples of firms occupying alternative strategy positions.

Marketing Planning

The development of marketing plans is a key task to successful marketing. Marketing plans are extensive and detailed in nature. A topic outline for a product line marketing plan for a home furnishing products company is presented in the appendix to this chapter. This example demonstrates the

Figure 5-3 Alternative marketing strategy positions.

SOURCE: David W. Cravens, "Marketing Strategy Positioning," *Business Horizons*, Vol. 18 (December 1975), pp. 53-55. Copyright © 1975 by the Foundation for the School of Business at Indiana University. Reprinted by permission.

Balancing Strategy. The organization focuses on existing products.
Market Retention Strategy. The organization's product line is under consideration for possible modifications or the market expanding.
Market Development Strategy. A commitment to new markets or new products.
Growth Strategy. Large scale market development. The organizations make a substantial commitment to enter new markets with new products.
New Venture Strategy. A totally new undertaking by the organization.

multitude of planning variables, the need for detailed information, and the interrelationships between marketing and financial decisions. Marketing plans entail the preparation of elaborate budgets and financial measures of the success of marketing efforts, including profitability, cash flow, and payback considerations. (See Chapter 4 for a more elaborate discussion of financial analysis in business policy courses.)

Table 5-3 Firms Occupying Alternative Strategy Positions

Balancing strategy
Strategy position occupied by railroads, electric utilities and various other mature industries
Holiday Inn's provision of motel services to its existing markets

Market retention strategy
Annual model changes of appliance manufacturers aimed at retaining market share
Introduction by Kentucky Fried Chicken of ribs to their food line
Modification of styles and models by automobile manufacturers

Market development strategy
Procter & Gamble's development of "Pringles" potato chips
Efforts of public transportation firms to lure people away from use of the automobile through modification of services
Movement of the large aluminum companies into automobile and beverage can markets for their products

Growth strategy
Offering (at a fee) first run movies on T.V. private channels in hotels and motels
Texas Instruments' move into consumer electronic calculator markets
Design and marketing of a low premium $1 million umbrella personal liability insurance policy for individuals

New venture strategy
Polaroid's introduction of the original Land camera
Xerox's pioneering development and marketing of copying equipment
Initial publication and marketing of *Playgirl* magazine

SOURCE: David W. Cravens, "Marketing Strategy Positioning," *Business Horizons*, Vol. 18 (December 1975), p. 57. Copyright © 1975 by the Foundation for the School of Business at Indiana University. Reprinted by permission.

The Profit Impact of Marketing Strategy (PIMS) project of the Marketing Science Institute examined the relationships of market share to key financial and operating ratios. One of the key findings of PIMS was the strong positive correlation between market share and return on investment, as shown in Figure 5-4. Other findings regarding the relationship of market share and financial and operating ratios are shown in Table 5-4.

In general, PIMS findings point to the fact that return on investment and cash flow as measures of performance are largely determined by:[6]

1. Attractiveness of market environment.
   (a) Long run (4 to 10 years ahead) industry growth rate.
   (b) Short run (up to 3 years ahead) industry growth rate.
   (c) Stage in the product life cycle.

---

[6]Derek F. Abell and John S. Hammond, *Strategic Marketing Planning* (Englewood Cliffs, N.J.: Prentice-Hall, 1979), p. 276.

2. Strength of competitive position.
   (a) Market share.
   (b) Relative market share.
   (c) Relative product quality.
   (d) Relative breadth of product line.
3. "Effectiveness" of use of investment.
   (a) Investment intensity (total investment/sales; also total investment/value added).
   (b) Fixed capital intensity (fixed capital/sales).
   (c) Vertical integration (value added/sales).
   (d) Percent capacity utilized.
4. Discretionary budget allocations.
   (a) Marketing expenses/sales.
   (b) Research and development expense/sales.
   (c) New product expense/sales.
5. Current changes in market position.
   (a) Change in market share.

Figure 5-4 Market share and return on investment.

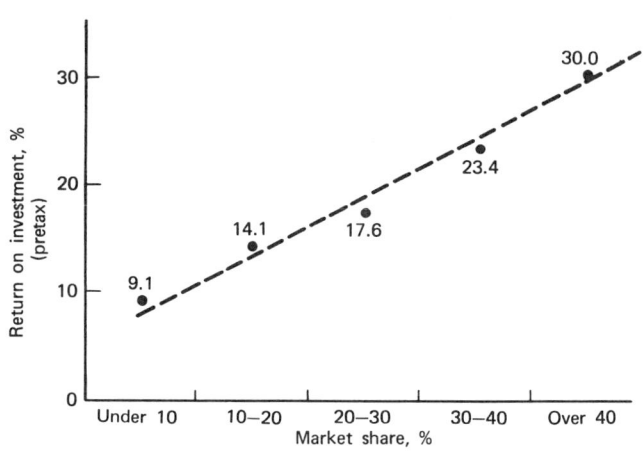

SOURCE: Reprinted by permission of the *Harvard Business Review*. Exhibit from "Market Share—A Key to Profitability" by Robert D. Buzzell, Bradley T. Gale, and Ralph G. M. Sultan (January-February 1975). Copyright © 1975 by the President and Fellows of Harvard College; all rights reserved.

Table 5-4 Relationships of Market Share to Key Financial and Operating Ratios

Financial/Operating Ratios, %	Under 10%	10 to 20%	20 to 30%	30 to 40%	Over 40%
Capital structure:					
Investment/sales	68.66	67.74	61.08	64.66	63.98
Receivables/sales	15.52	14.08	13.96	15.18	14.48
Inventory/sales	9.30	8.97	8.68	8.68	8.16
Operating results:					
Pretax profit sales	−0.16	3.42	4.84	7.60	13.16
Purchases/sales	45.4	39.9	39.4	32.6	33.0
Manufacturing/sales	29.64	32.61	32.11	32.95	31.76
Marketing/sales	10.60	9.88	9.06	10.45	8.57
R&D/sales	2.60	2.40	2.83	3.18	3.55
Capacity utilization	74.7	77.1	78.1	75.4	78.0
Product quality: % superior minus % inferior	14.5	20.4	20.4	20.1	43.0
Relative price[a]	2.72	2.73	2.65	2.66	2.39
Number of businesses	(156)	(179)	(105)	(67)	(87)

SOURCE: Reprinted by permission of the *Harvard Business Review*. Exhibit from "Market Share—A Key to Profitability" by Robert O. Buzzell, Bradley T. Gale, and Ralph G. M. Sultan (January–February 1975). Copyright © 1975 by the President and Fellows of Harvard College; all rights reserved.

[a]Average value on 5 point scale: 5 = 10% or more lower than leading competitors' average; 3 = within 3% of competition; 1 = 10% or more higher than competition.

Because of the critical relationship of market share and performance, marketing planners should carefully examine and select among the alternative strategies to increase market share. As described by Kotler, key *growth* strategies include:[7]

A. Market penetration (increasing use of present products in present markets)
    1. Increasing the unit of purchase
        (a) Increasing the unit of purchase
        (b) Increasing the rate of product obsolescence
        (c) Advertising other uses
        (d) Giving price incentives for increased use
    2. Attracting competitors' customers
        (a) Establishing sharper brand differentiation
        (b) Increasing promotional effort

---

[7]Based on Kotler, *Marketing Management*, 4th ed., 1980, pp. 71–75 and 273–275 and as listed in the 2nd edition, 1972, p. 237.

3. Attracting nonusers
   (a) Inducing trial use through sampling, price inducements, and so on
   (b) Pricing up or down
   (c) Advertising new uses
B. Market development (selling present products in new markets)
   1. Opening additional geographical markets
      (a) Regional expansion
      (b) National expansion
      (c) International expansion
   2. Attracting other market segments
      (a) Developing product versions to appeal to other segments
      (b) Entering other channels of distribution
      (c) Advertising in other media
C. Product development (developing new products for present markets)
   1. Developing new product features
      (a) Adapt (to other ideas, developments)
      (b) Modify (change color, motion, sound, odor, form, shape)
      (c) Magnify (stronger, longer, thicker, extra value)
      (d) Minify (smaller, shorter, lighter)
      (e) Substitute (other ingredients, process, power)
      (f) Rearrange (other patterns, layout, sequence, components)
      (g) Reverse (inside out)
      (h) Combine (blend, alloy, assortment, ensemble; combine units, purposes, appeals, ideas)
   2. Developing quality variations
   3. Developing additional models and sizes (product proliferation)

Marketing Organization

The task of organizing for marketing is an integral part of the determination of overall corporate structure. Alternative organization structures are discussed in detail in Chapter 7.

Marketing Controls

Increasing competition, a changing and turbulent environment, and the tendency for performance to deviate from plans all dictate the need for continuous monitoring of the organization's products, markets, profits, competition, government, and other elements of the environment, as well as its own reorganizational capabilities. The types (levels) of marketing control are outlined in Table 5-5.

As shown in Table 5-5, the marketing audit is the basic tool for strategic marketing control. An example of a marketing audit is presented in Table 5-6. A useful supplement to the marketing audit is a close examination of reasons for failure of marketing ventures. An overview of reasons why ventures fail is presented in Table 5-7. It summarizes the results of six major studies and therefore reflects critical variables worthy of close scrutiny by management.

Table 5-5 Types of Marketing Control

Type of Control	Prime Responsibility	Purpose of Control	Approaches
I. Annual-plan control	Top management Middle management	To examine whether the planned results are being achieved	Sales analysis Market share analysis Sales-to-expense ratios Financial analysis Attitude tracking

II. Profitability control	Marketing controller	To examine where the company is making and losing money	Profitability by:
			  product
			  territory
			  customer group
			  trade channel
			  order size

III. Efficiency control	Line and staff management
	
	Marketing controller
		To evaluate and improve the spending efficiency and impact of marketing expenditures	Efficiency of
			  sales force
			  advertising
			  sales promotion
			  distribution

IV. Strategic control	Top management Marketing auditor	To examine whether the company is pursuing its best opportunities with respect to markets, products, and channels	Marketing-effectiveness rating instrument Marketing audit

SOURCE: Philip Kotler, *Marketing Management*, 4th edition, copyright © 1980, p. 629. Reprinted by permission of Prentice-Hall, Inc., Englewood Cliffs, New Jersey.

Table 5-6 Components of A Marketing Audit

The Marketing Environment Audit

I. Macro-Environment

Economic-Demographic
1. What does the company expect in the way of inflation, material shortages, unemployment, and credit availability in the short run, intermediate run, and long run?
2. What effect will forecasted trends in the size, age distribution, and regional distribution of population have on the business?

Technology
1. What major changes are occurring in product technology? In process technology?
2. What are the major generic substitutes that might replace this product?

Political-Legal
1. What laws are being proposed that may affect marketing strategy and tactics?
2. What federal, state, and local agency actions should be watched? What is happening in the areas of pollution control, equal employment opportunity, product safety, advertising, price control, etc., that is relevant to marketing planning?

Social-Cultural
1. What attitudes is the public taking toward business and toward products such as those produced by the company?
2. What changes are occurring in consumer life styles and values that have a bearing on the company's target markets and marketing methods?

II. Task Environment

Markets
1. What is happening to market size, growth, geographical distribution, and profits?
2. What are the major market segments? What are their expected rates of growth? Which are high opportunity and low opportunity segments?

Customers
1. How do current customers and prospects rate the company and its competitors, particularly with respect to reputation, product quality, service, sales force, and price?
2. How do different classes of customers make their buying decisions?
3. What are the evolving needs and satisfactions being sought by the buyers in this market?

Competitors
1. Who are the major competitors? What are the objectives and strategy of each major competitor? What are their strengths and weaknesses? What are the sizes and trends in market shares?
2. What trends can be foreseen in future competition and substitutes for this product?

Table 5-6 (continued)

Distribution and Dealers
1. What are the main trade channels bringing products to customers?
2. What are the efficiency levels and growth potentials of the different trade channels?

Suppliers
1. What is the outlook for the availability of different key resources used in production?
2. What trends are occurring among suppliers in their pattern of selling?

Facilitators
1. What is the outlook for the cost and availability of transportation services?
2. What is the outlook for the cost and availability of warehousing facilities?
3. What is the outlook for the cost and availability of financial resources?
4. How effectively is the advertising agency performing? What trends are occurring in advertising agency services?

Marketing Strategy Audit

Marketing Objectives
1. Are the corporate objectives clearly stated and do they lead logically to the marketing objectives?
2. Are the marketing objectives stated in a clear form to guide marketing planning and subsequent performance measurement?
3. Are the marketing objectives appropriate, given the company's competitive position, resources, and opportunities? Is the appropriate strategic objective to build, hold, harvest, or terminate this business?

Strategy
1. What is the core marketing strategy for achieving the objectives? Is it a sound marketing strategy?
2. Are enough resources (or too much resources) budgeted to accomplish the marketing objectives?
3. Are the marketing resources allocated optimally to prime market segments, territories, and products of the organization?
4. Are the marketing resources allocated optimally to the major elements of the marketing mix, i.e., product quality, service, sales force, advertising, promotion, and distribution?

Marketing Organization Audit

Formal Structure
1. Is there a high-level marketing officer with adequate authority and responsibility over those company activities that affect the customer's satisfaction?
2. Are the marketing responsibilities optimally structured along functional product, end user, and territorial lines?

Table 5-6 (continued)

Functional Efficiency
1. Are there good communication and working relations between marketing and sales?
2. Is the product management system working effectively? Are the product managers able to plan profits or only sales volume?
3. Are there any groups in marketing that need more training, motivation, supervision, or evaluation?

Interface Efficiency
1. Are there any problems between marketing and manufacturing that need attention?
2. What about marketing and R & D?
3. What about marketing and financial management?
4. What about marketing and purchasing?

Marketing Systems Audit

Marketing Information System
1. Is the marketing intelligence system producing accurate, sufficient, and timely information about developments in the marketplace?
2. Is marketing research being adequately used by company decision makers?

Marketing Planning System
1. Is the marketing planning system well-conceived and effective?
2. Is sales forecasting and market potential measurement soundly carried out?
3. Are sales quotas set on a proper basis?

Marketing Control System
1. Are the control procedures (monthly, quarterly, etc.) adequate to insure that the annual plan objectives are being achieved?
2. Is provision made to analyze periodically the profitability of different products, markets, territories, and channels of distribution?
3. Is provision made to examine and validate periodically various marketing costs?

New Product Development System
1. Is the company well-organized to gather, generate, and screen new product ideas?
2. Does the company do adequate concept research and business analysis before investing heavily in a new idea?
3. Does the company carry out adequate product and market testing before launching a new product?

Marketing Productivity Audit

Profitability Analysis
1. What is the profitability of the company's different products, served markets, territories, and channels of distribution?
2. Should the company enter, expand, contract, or withdraw from any business segments and what would be the short- and long-run profit consequences?

Table 5-6 (continued)

Cost-Effectiveness Analysis
1. Do any marketing activities seem to have excessive costs? Are these costs valid? Can cost-reducing steps be taken?

Marketing Function Audit

Products
1. What are the product line objectives? Are these objectives sound? Is the current product line meeting these objectives?
2. Are there particular products that should be phased out?
3. Are there new products that are worth adding?
4. Are any products able to benefit from quality, feature, or style improvements?

Price
1. What are the pricing objectives, policies, strategies, and procedures? To what extent are prices set on sound cost, demand, and competitive criteria?
2. Do the customers see the company's prices as being in line or out of line with the perceived value of its offer?
3. Does the company use price promotions effectively?

Distribution
1. What are the distribution objectives and strategies?
2. Is there adequate market coverage and service?
3. Should the company consider changing its degree of reliance on distributors, sales reps, and direct selling?

Sales Force
1. What are the organization's sales force objectives?
2. Is the sales force large enough to accomplish the company's objectives?
3. Is the sales force organized along the proper principle(s) of specialization (territory, market, product)?
4. Does the sales force show high morale, ability, and effort? Are they sufficiently trained and incentivized?
5. Are the procedures adequate for setting quotas and evaluating performances?
6. How is the company's sales force perceived in relation to competitors' sales forces?

Advertising, Promotion, and Publicity
1. What are the organization's advertising objectives? Are they sound?
2. Is the right amount being spent on advertising? How is the budget determined?
3. Are the ad themes and copy effective? What do customers and the public think about the advertising?
4. Are the advertising media well chosen?
5. Is sales promotion used effectively?
6. Is there a well-conceived publicity program?

SOURCE: Philip Kotler, *Marketing Management*, 4th edition, copyright © 1980, pp. 652-655. Reprinted by permission of Prentice-Hall, Inc., Englewood Cliffs, New Jersey.

Table 5-7 Classification Scheme of Reasons Why Ventures Fail

Management Organization and Capabilities	Execution of the Marketing Mix	External Environment: the Consumer and Competition
Inadequate market analysis	Deficiency in product	Lack of consumer involvement or need
Higher cost than anticipated	Weakness in marketing efforts: poor promotion, insufficient advertising spending, weak level of distribution	Consumer loyalty
Poor timing of decision to market		Severe competition
Failure to think through development goals		Dangers in frontal assault
Overparticipation by top management	Insignificant/product differentiation	
"Pat" organizational thinking	Poor product positioning	
Loose administrative practices	Confusing tactics and strategy	
Lack of formal evaluation and screening	Faulty communication	
Wrong market for company, failure to define one's business adequately	Unbalancing the marketing mix	
Underestimating involved parties	Imperfect fit, e.g., of sales force	
Inflexibility in planning and execution	Greedy pricing	
Overoptimism		
Premature abandoning of research		
Ignoring feedback		
Lack of marketing know-how		
Limited management attention		
Factory thinking		

SOURCE: From Burton H. Marcus and Edward M. Tauber, *Marketing Analysis and Decision Making*, Table 1.4, p. 25. Copyright © 1979 by Burton H. Marcus and Edward M. Tauber. Reprinted by permission of the publisher, Little, Brown, and Company.

Another strategic control tool is gap analysis. Figure 5-5 summarizes the different types of gaps and their attendant remedial strategic alternatives to be evaluated by management.

Figure 5-5 Summary of gaps and attendant remedial strategies.

1. Natural changes in the size of IMP
2. New uses or new user segments
3. Innovative product differentiations
4. Add new product lines
} Industry market potential (IMP)

5. Fill out existing product lines
6. Create new product line elements
} Product line gap

7. Expand distribution coverage
8. Expand distribution intensity
9. Expand distribution exposure
} Distribution gaps

10. Stimulate nonusers
11. Stimulate light users
12. Increase amount used on each use occasion
} Usage gaps

13. Penetrate substitute's positions
14. Penetrate direct competitor's position(s)
} Competitive gaps

15. Defend firm's present position } Firm sales

SOURCE: John A. Weber, *Growth Opportunities Analysis* (Reston, Va.: Reston Publishing Co., 1976), p. 184. Reprinted with permission of Reston Publishing Co., Reston, Virginia.

MARKETING DECISION VARIABLES

Chapter 1 established a distinction between C_1, C_2, C_3, and C_4 decision variables. C_1 and C_2 variables are the decisions that provide the strategic and coordinative constraints on the marketing function of the firm. The C_3 variables are the marketing decisions that depend heavily on other functional area inputs as well as on marketing inputs. A summary of the C_3 marketing variables and their determinants must be presented before the detailed discussion of them can be initiated. This is expressed in terms of functional equations where, for example, the dependent variable "product research and development" is a function of production technology, financial strength, marketing feasibility, and C_1 (strategic) variables. It should be clear, however, that the dependence and independence expressed in these functional equations is only relative. For example, financial strength is expressed as an independent variable that partially determines the nature and direction of product research and development (Equation 1) and marketing research (Equation 2). From a financial perspective, however, financial strength becomes a variable dependent on product research and development and marketing research. The marketing decision variables to be discussed in this chapter are:

1. *Product research and development* = f (financial strength, marketing feasibility, production technology, C_1 and C_2 variables).

2. *Marketing research and information systems* = f (financial strength, production equipment and facilities, financial and accounting information needs, C_1 and C_2 variables).
3. *Distribution channel structure* = f (nature of the market, product characteristics, availability of middlemen and other channel specialists, financial requirements, firm's market position, C_1 and C_2 variables).
4. *Price* = f (cost structure, product quality, stage of product life cycle, target market share, functional discounts, quantity discounts, return on investment objective, C_1 and C_2 variables).
5. *Discounts: type and structure* = f (production planning, financial arrangements and cash flows, expectations of channel intermediaries, C_1 and C_2 variables).
6. *Promotion* = f (production capacity and planning, financial strength, channel intermediaries capacity, C_1 and C_2 variables).
7. *Credit* = f (channel intermediaries requirements, cash flow requirements, C_1 and C_2 variables).
8. *Physical distribution warehouse location* = f (plant location, transportation modes, customer location, customer geographic distribution [concentration], service level requirements, C_1 and C_2 variables).
9. *Inventory levels* = f (demand forecast, customer service level, warehouse and plant location, financial strength, production capacity and production planning and scheduling, C_1 and C_2 variables).

Each of these marketing decision variables is now discussed more fully.

Product Research and Development

Most firms adopt growth goals at different rates. These goals usually are dictated by heavily competitive environments in which a firm that does not plan for growth, in all probability, will not survive. In addition, stockholders generally expect firms to grow, and the personal aspirations of many executives for prestige and power generally promote expansion plans, as well.

Growth may require the addition of new product lines and a redefinition of the nature of the corporate business. For example, Avon added ceramics, costume jewelry, and needlepoint kits to its door-to-door selling of cosmetics and also entered into the marketing of family fashions by direct mail and plastic housewares through a "party plan."

Product development strategy is one of the major growth strategies as evidenced by the following remark.

One of the fastest-growing budgets in this generation has been the nation's research and development budget. In 1928, R & D expenditures totaled less than $100 million. By 1953, it had grown fifty times larger, to $5 billion, and by 1976,

R & D stood at over $37 billion, or almost 2.3 percent of gross national product (GNP).[8]

The reasons for the heavy emphasis on internal product research and development are numerous. They include the antitrust implications of growth through acquisitions and mergers, the desirability of developing new products, and the need to acquire firsthand experience of the problems of R & D.

Determinants. As indicated earlier, investment in product research and development is a function of the financial strength of the firm, of marketing feasibility, and of the availability of production technology and skills. When an individual company lacks the necessary financial strength, it may join forces with one or more other firms to pursue a joint-development strategy.

The availability of production technology and skills is also necessary for successful implementation of product R & D results. Mass production and marketing are not possible without production resources, including capacity and skills. One of the major requirements for product R & D is the pool of engineering, marketing, and finance personnel. Certain coordination and communication problems arise because of their different orientations.[9] Management has to devote attention to their solution.

Beyond the point of research and development completion, a product is usually market tested and then introduced if market tests indicate market potential and profit opportunities. Two key observations are of paramount importance at this juncture. First, marketing strategy changes are necessary as the product life cycle changes. Figure 5-6 illustrates the life cycle and Table 5-8 outlines the strategy adjustments necessary at each stage. Second, it is not necessarily true that marketing decisions are the controlling decisions throughout the life cycle of a product. For example, research and development decisions may predominate at the introduction stage, production decisions at the growth stage, marketing decisions at the maturity stage, and financial decisions at the decline stage. One can readily see that at the growth stage, the concern is one of keeping up with the rapidly expanding demand and minimizing stock-out conditions. At the maturity stage, promotion becomes a vital factor in order to sustain sales volume. As the decline and saturation stages are reached, the concern becomes one of maintaining vigilant control over return on investment and cost reduction procedures.[10]

---

[8]Philip Kotler, *Marketing Management: Analysis, Planning, and Control* 4th edition, 1980, pp. 113–114.
[9]David Luck and Theodore Nowak, "Product Management-Vision Unfulfilled," *Harvard Business Review*, *43*, May–June 1965, pp. 143–157.
[10]Theodore Levitt, "Exploit the Product Life Cycle," *Harvard Business Review*, *43* (6), November–December 1965, pp. 81–94.

Figure 5-6 Dynamic competitive strategy and the market life cycle.

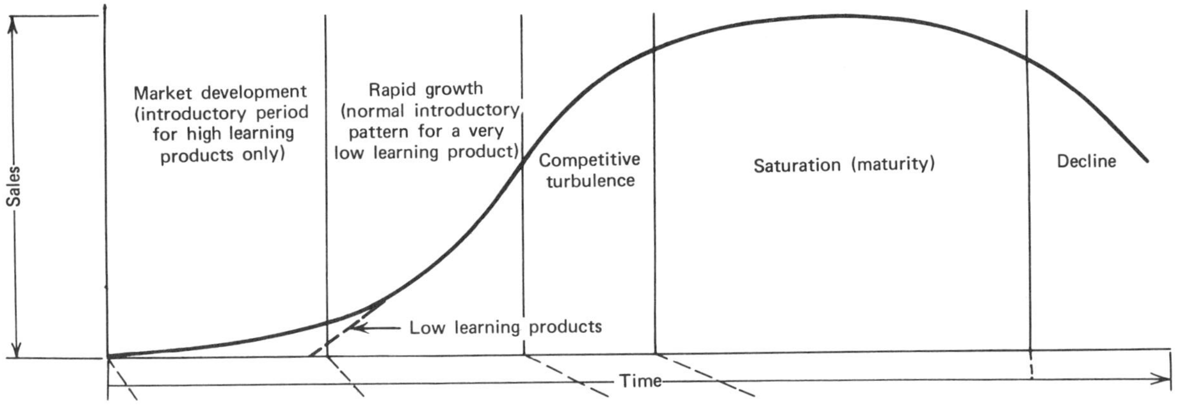

SOURCE: Reproduced from Chester R. Wasson, *Dynamic Competitive Strategy and Product Life Cycles*, 3rd Edition, pp. 256–257, Austin Press, Austin, Texas, 1978. By permission of the copyright owner.

Marketing Research and Information Systems

Traditionally, marketing research had a project or problem orientation; however, the contemporary perspective emphasizes information systems geared to the continuous collection and analysis of environmental data.

The marketing information system consists of four component subsystems for gathering, processing, and utilizing data collected from the organization's macro environment:

1. *Internal Accounting.* This subsystem supplies management with information on current operations and performance. For example, it provides sales volume and cost data by product salespeople, customer groups, and geographic region.
2. *Marketing Intelligence.* This subsystem includes data collected from secondary and primary sources concerning the environment. For example, management may need information about competitors' plans to introduce new products, shifts in consumer life-styles, current work on technological innovations, and federal government intentions regarding price controls.
3. *Marketing Analysis.* This subsystem is project oriented. Its task is to gather, evaluate, and report information needed by marketing executives for decision making regarding *specific projects* or problems. These project-oriented studies may include sales forecasts, evaluation of advertising effectiveness, consumer attitude surveys, and brand preference studies.

Table 5-8 Marketing Strategy Adjustments for Stages of Product Life Cycle.

Marketing Strategy Component	Market Development (Introduction)	Growth	Competitive Turbulence	Saturation (Maturity)	Decline
Strategy Objective	Minimize learning requirements, locate and remedy offering defects quickly, develop widespread awareness of benefits, and gain trial by early adopters	To establish a strong brand market and distribution niche as quickly as possible	To maintain and strengthen the market niche achieved through dealer and consumer loyalty	To defend brand position against competing brands and product category against other potential products, through constant attention to product improvement opportunities and fresh promotional and distribution approaches	To milk the offering dry of all possible profit
Outlook for Competition	None is likely to be attracted in the early, unprofitable stages	Early entrance of numerous aggressive emulators	Price and distribution squeezes on the industry, shaking out the weaker entrants	Competition stabilized. Few or no new entrants. Market shares relatively stable except when a brand gains substantial added perceived value through product improvement or price repositioning	Similar competition declining and dropping out because of decrease in consumer interest
Product Design Objective	Limited number of models with physical product and offering designs both focused on minimizing learning requirements. Designs cost- and use-engineered to appeal to most receptive segment. Utmost attention to quality control and quick elimination of market-revealed defects in design	Modular design to facilitate flexible addition of variants to appeal to every new segment and new use-system as fast as discovered	Intensified attention to product improvement, tightening up of line to eliminate unnecessary specialties with little market appeal	A constant alert for market pyramiding opportunities through either bold cost- and price-penetration of new markets or major product changes. Introduction of flanker products. Constant attention to possibilities for product improvement and cost cutting. Reexamination of necessity of design compromises	Constant pruning of line to eliminate any items not returning a direct profit
Pricing Objective	To impose the minimum of value perception learning and to match the value reference perception of the most receptive segments. High trade discounts and sampling advisable	A price line for every taste, from low-end to premium models. Customary trade discounts. Aggressive promotional pricing, with prices cut as fast as costs decline due to accumulated production experience. Intensification of sampling	Increased attention to market-broadening and promotional pricing opportunities	Price repositioning whenever demand pattern and competitors' strategies permit. Defensive pricing to preserve product category franchise. Search for incremental pricing opportunities, including private label contracts, to boost volume and gain an experience advantage	Maintenance of profit level pricing with complete disregard of any effect on market share

Promotional Guidelines Communications objectives	(a) Create widespread awareness and understanding of offering benefits (b) Gain trial by early adopters	Create and strengthen brand preference among trade and final users. Stimulate general trial	Maintain consumer franchise and strengthen dealer ties	Maintain consumer and trade loyalty, with strong emphasis on dealers and distributors. Promotion of greater use frequency	Phase out, keeping just enough to maintain profitable distribution
Most valuable media mix	In order of value: Publicity Personal sales Mass communications	Mass media Personal sales Sales promotions, including sampling Publicity	Mass media Dealer promotions. Personal selling to dealers. Sales promotions. Publicity	Mass media Dealer-oriented promotions	Cut down all media to the bone—use no sales promotions of any kind
Distribution Policy	Exclusive or selective, with distributor margins high enough to justify heavy promotional spending	Intensive and extensive, with dealer margins just high enough to keep them interested. Close attention to rapid resupply of distributor stocks and heavy inventories at all levels	Intensive and extensive, and a strong emphasis on keeping dealer well supplied, but with minimum inventory cost to him	Intensive and extensive, with strong emphasis on keeping dealer well supplied, but at minimum inventory cost to him	Phase out outlets as they become marginal
Intelligence Focus	To identify actual developing use-systems and to uncover any product weaknesses	Detailed attention to brand position, to gaps in model and market coverage, and to opportunities for market segmentation	Close attention to product improvement needs, to market-broadening chances, and to possible fresh promotion themes	Close analysis of competitors' strategies. Regular monitoring of trends in use patterns and possible product improvements. Sharp alert for potential new technological and new interproduct competition or other signs of beginning product decline	Information helping to identify the point at which the product should be phased out

Note: Strictly speaking, this is the cycle of the category market, and only a high learning introduction passes through all phases indicated above. The term *product life cycle* is sometimes applied indiscriminately to both brand cycles and category cycles. Most new brands are only emulative of other products already on the market, have a much shorter life cycle than the product category, and must follow a strategy similar to any low-learning product.

Reproduced from Chester R. Wasson, DYNAMIC COMPETITIVE STRATEGY AND PRODUCT LIFE CYCLES, 3rd Edition, pp. 256–257, Austin Press, Austin, Texas, 1978. By permission of the copyright owner.

4. *Marketing Management-Science.* This subsystem task involves the application of sources such as queuing models, brand-switching models, sales territory design models, and statistical tools to complex marketing problems and operations. The intent of this subsystem is to optimize marketing operations.

Determinants. Marketing information systems require significant financial investment for development and maintenance. Therefore their development hinges on the financial strength of the firm.

The marketing research conducted by Samsonite for their "Travel Bureau Line" is illustrative of the functional dependence and cooperation necessary for a successful outcome. The project involved 3 years of high-level teamwork and cost several hundred thousand dollars. The group that worked on product and marketing research included the marketing vice president and the heads of the merchandising, cost analysis, research, product planning, design, and engineering departments.

Often the availability of production and marketing capacity is conducive to research on the feasibility of market expansion for existing products or additional products. Normally, undertaking research for new markets and/or products requires at least some assurance of availability of production capacity when needed. The role of marketing research and its relationship to the overall process of strategy formation was discussed more fully in Chapter 2.

As indicated earlier, the internal accounting system is one of the components of the marketing information system. Naturally, the internal accounting system also serves financial and fiscal information needs. Therefore these needs are important determinants of the marketing information system.

Distribution Channel Structure

Many variables can influence the determination of the firm's channels of distribution. From a top management perspective, however, the channel decisions will be constrained by product, customer, and geographic concentration policies and by competitive emphasis. More specifically, they are greatly influenced by the product mix, the markets and market segments concentrated on, the company's primary markets, and the basis on which it has chosen to compete. Thus major changes in the channels of distribution will come as a result of a change in one of these strategic variables.

Determinants. Some of the most important determinants, or constraints, that must be considered when channel decisions are made include:

1. *Customer Characteristics.* Including the number, geographical dispersion, purchasing patterns, and susceptibility to different selling methods.
2. *Product Characteristics.* Including perishability, bulk, degree of product standardization, service requirements, and unit value.

3. *Middleman Characteristics.* Including the strengths and weaknesses of the intermediaries handling the tasks.
4. *Competitive Characteristics.* Especially the channels that competitors use.
5. *Company Characteristics.* Including size, financial strength, product mix, and past channel experience.
6. *Environmental Characteristics.* Including economic conditions and legal regulations and restrictions.[11]

It readily can be seen that some of the important determinants of channels already have been defined by product policy, customer policy, competitive emphasis, and geographic limits. The decision on these commitments have, in turn, defined the environment within which the firm operates. In examining the determinants and functions, it is evident that production supplies the multifunctional aspect of the variable. Perishability, bulk, and service requirements are, in most cases and to some degree, capable of being influenced by production.

The John Deere case is illustrative of the multifunctional, interdependent nature of channel decisions. When it introduced its new consumer and heavy industrial product lines, the company did not expect all of the current dealers handling its agricultural products to carry the new products as well. Handling the new industrial lines might require redesigning service areas, expanding inventories and parts departments, and adding more personnel. In addition, urban dealers would be more likely to handle the new lines because of their proximity to potential customers.

Financial considerations represent an important determinant of distribution channels. Different channels require varying amounts of capital from the manufacturer. If the manufacturer elects to distribute directly to retailers, this would involve the performance of wholesaling functions that require greater capital investment by the manufacturer. Financial strength enables a manufacturer to control its entire distribution system vertically. For example, Schwinn Bicycles delivers its products to distributors and dealers on consignment. The title to the product transfers directly from Schwinn to the consumer. Because Schwinn's financial liability is great as it finances all inventories in the distribution channel, it achieves territorial, price, and service controls over its distributors and dealers.

Ideally, the manufacturer should consider the "opportunity cost" of investing capital in performing marketing functions versus using the capital in the manufacturing process. If a greater return on investment can be generated by deploying capital in manufacturing, then wholesalers should be used for distribution.[12]

---

[11] Kotler, *Marketing Management*, 4th ed., 1980, pp. 430–433.
[12] Ibid., pp. 437–438.

Price

The most common pricing approaches include cost-, demand-, and competition-oriented approaches. The favoring of one of these approaches over another depends partly on the specific price objectives of the firm, as discussed next. It also should be noted that under the conditions of raw material and product shortages that prevailed in the early 1970s, more and more pricing decisions became market or value oriented instead of cost oriented.

Determinants. Regardless of the specific approach, there are certain components of the price over which the marketer has no control, particularly the fixed and variable costs of production.[13] These costs are a function of product design and various other product characteristics, including quality, material, size, and shape. Such costs determine the minimum price that must be charged if the firm is to recover production, marketing, and other costs. For example, when the Archer-Daniels-Midland Corporation decided to invest in a new technology for producing sugar, sugar prices had to remain above a certain level in order for the technology to be cost effective. Thus the company was caught when prices fell below the break-even level for this technology. Management was left with excess capacity and fixed costs that had to be covered out of pocket.[14]

Allowances and deals, distributors' and retailers' markups, and discount structure are additional factors that must be considered before the final price of the product can be determined. They are only a portion of the total cost of the product and are determined within the boundaries of the cost floor, which is set by production and by the pricing policy developed by top management, as discussed in Chapter 1. The pricing policy must be in the form of well-defined pricing objectives. One study of 20 of the largest corporations in the United States found that their most typical pricing objectives are to: (1) achieve a target return on investment; (2) stabilize price and margin; (3) realize a target market share; and (4) prevent or meet competition.[15] Other pricing objectives include market penetration, market skimming, generating early cash flows, and product line promotion such as the use of one product as a loss leader.

It should be noted that pricing objectives may change, depending on the product life cycle. The price objective at the introductory stage might be to skim the market. Later, at the growth stage, the objective could change to market penetration. For example, when it was first introduced, the Polaroid SX-70 was selling for $179. Less than a year after its introduction, the

---

[13]Taxes, buildings and equipment depreciation, power, heat and light, material and labor are a few of these costs.

[14]"When Competition Against Sugar Turned Sour," *Business Week*, November 15, 1976, pp. 136–140.

[15]Robert F. Lanzillotti, "Pricing Objectives in Large Companies," *American Economic Review*, *48*, December 1958, pp. 921–940.

SX-70 was selling for as low as $129 at some major discount mass merchandising chains.

Given these considerations, a company's decisions on allowances and deals, distributor and retailer markups, and discount structure must be made in light of (1) the cost to produce the product, and (2) the selling price necessary to achieve either a target return, a stable price and margin, or a price that meets or prevents competition. It should be clear, then, that decisions on the price variables of the marketing department must be made within the limits set by production costs and the pricing objectives set by top management. These limits define an amount that can be "spent" on allowances and deals, distributor and retailer markups, and discount structure.

Under conditions of rising costs and tough competition some companies pull detail pricing responsibility from the field and move it up in the corporate organization—sometimes all the way up to the chief executive officer. Some companies even bring specialists in production, finance, and marketing research together to examine pricing decisions.

Discounts: Type and Structure

Different types of discounts exist in different industries. However, the pervasive types include quantity, cash, trade, seasonal, and geographic discounts.

Determinants. Quantity discounts are partially determined by production planning which, in turn, determines inventory levels. A manufacturer may find it advantageous to make larger production runs, since the setup cost may exceed the cost of carrying the inventory. Also, manufacturers may grant quantity discounts to avoid inventory carrying costs that exceed the discount granted.

Cash discounts are used to accelerate the incoming cash flow. Normally, there is a cost involved in financing sales and carrying receivables. Also, dollars tied up in receivables cannot be used in production or inventories.

Trade discounts are generally determined by the expectations of the channel members involved in product distribution. Seasonal discounts generally are utilized to help even out production times. They enable the manufacturer to produce for the whole year and simultaneously move inventories forward in the channel. The seasonal discount compensates the channel members for their inventory carrying costs for the extended period.

Geographic discounts allow the supplier to even out customer location differences by varying the list price on the basis of geographic proximity of customers to points of distribution.

Promotion

Promotion involves a mix of personal selling, advertising, sales promotion, and public relations or publicity.

Personal selling involves a mix of tasks ranging from prospecting, communicating, selling, servicing, information gathering to allocating in times of shortages.[16] The emphasis on personal selling depends on the company strategy. For example, furniture manufacturers use a push strategy, relying on their sales force to sell to furniture dealers. Meanwhile, the majority of food processors use a pull strategy whereby massive consumer advertising is used to get consumers to request the brand at retail outlets.

The importance of advertising lies in the fact that it is an extremely effective way to present information to potential buyers. It can be persuasive to some extent and can also reinforce or even create buyer preference for company products. Although some models have been developed that attempt to measure the effects of advertising on sales and thus help to determine advertising expenditures, firms have, for the most part, relied on simple rules such as a percentage of sales or a fixed amount the company can afford.

In addition to determining the amount of money to be allocated to advertising, decisions also involve the following considerations.

1. What message and mode of presentation should be used?
2. What media should be used?
3. How should the advertising be phased during the year?[17]

Sales promotion can be described as a variety of tools directed at different people, from the manufacturer's own sales force to the final consumer and including all the resellers in between. Samples, coupons, money refund offers directed at consumers; free goods, merchandise allowances, and dealer-listed promotions directed at the trade; and bonuses, sales force contests, and sales meetings directed at the firm's own sales force are all examples.

Publicity is the activity of "securing editorial space, as divorced from paid space, in all media read, viewed, or heard by a company's customers and prospects, for the specific purpose of assisting in the meeting of sales goals."[18] Publicity can have far-reaching effects in terms of media coverage at relatively little cost to the company. Because of this, many firms have placed greater emphasis on this component of the promotion mix in the form of public relations agents. These agents can tailor public relations releases to fit the various target markets and customers.

Marketing management has to allocate the promotion budget among personal selling, advertising, and sales promotion. Factors influencing this allocation decision include: (1) the stage of consumers on the sales cycle (i.e.,

---

[16]Kotler, op. cit., pp. 467–477.
[17]Kotler, op. cit., p. 35.
[18]George Black, *Planned Industrial Publicity* (Chicago: Putnam, 1952), p. 3. Cited in Arthur M. Merims, "Marketing's Stepchild: Product Publicity," *Harvard Business Review*, 50 (6), November–December 1972, p. 107.

awareness, interest, desire, and action); (2) the stage of the product life cycle; and (3) the strategic choice of push or pull strategies.

Determinants. The decisions concerning promotional objectives and budgets are limited by certain strategic variables. First, resource allocation decisions by top management may be the essential constraining factor on promotion decisions. How top management has chosen to allocate promotion funds will affect the choice of media which, in turn, may affect the message and mode of presentation. In addition, a smaller budget may call for only one advertising campaign where a relatively larger budget, all other factors the same, may call for a number of campaigns throughout the year, placed monthly or weekly. Also, production capacity and the capacity of channel intermediaries to handle varying levels of sales volume influence promotional objectives and budgets. For example, when Proctor & Gamble introduced Pringles Potato Chips, it eased Pringles into national distribution and backed the effort with an extensive advertising campaign. By the middle of 1978, Procter & Gamble had spent $50 million in advertising Pringles and had invested heavily in two chip-processing plants in Tennessee and North Carolina to meet anticipated demand.[19]

The message and mode of presentation and, to some extent, the choice of media are also a function of the product, the specific characteristics of the potential buyers of the product, and the geographic location of the potential customers. The message content also may be a function of the company's basis for competition. For example, if a competitive advantage is quality, this factor should be stressed in advertisements.

Credit

It is debatable whether credit is a finance or a marketing function, which should clearly indicate the functional interdependence of credit decisions.[20]

Determinants. Regardless of whether credit is a marketing or a finance function, credit extension is governed by return on investment and cash flow criteria. For example, if credit to consumers is used to promote sales volume, the return on investment for credit extended should be equal to or exceed the return on investment in alternative marketing program components such as promotion. Furthermore, the period for which credit is extended is determined on the basis of anticipated cash inflows. Cash inflows from accounts receivable, arising from the extension of credit, are needed to finance cash outflows for accounts payable.

The price of the product, the buying power of the customers, and expectations of the distributors and the retailers who handle the product influ-

---

[19] "A Stubborn Proctor-Gamble Still Likes Pringles," *Business Week*, June 19, 1978, p. 30.
[20] Robert Bartels, "Credit as a Marketing Function," *Journal of Marketing*, *28*, July 1964, pp. 59–61.

168 MARKETING

ence credit type and policy. For example, high-priced items and low consumer buying power necessitate installment credit.

Physical Distribution and Inventory Levels

Both the location of the physical distribution warehouse and the variable dealing with inventory levels are in the domain of logistics. Logistics involves the integration of the functions of materials management and physical distribution under the auspices of one manager. These functions include:

1. Plant and warehouse location.
2. Transportation of inputs and outputs.
3. Purchasing.
4. Material handling.
5. Warehousing of inputs and outputs.
6. Inventory levels for inputs and outputs.
7. Order processing.

Some would add production planning and scheduling to this list.

Figure 5-7 illustrates the integration of material management and physical distribution into logistics. This type of organization typifies some large corporations such as Pillsbury and Xerox. Prior to adopting the logistics organization, these companies had materials management under the jurisdiction of production because it dealt with inputs necessary for production. By the same token, physical distribution was under the jurisdiction of the marketing manager. Transportation and traffic management for both inputs and outputs were under the jurisdiction of production.

Figure 5-7 Alternative orientations of integrated distribution management.

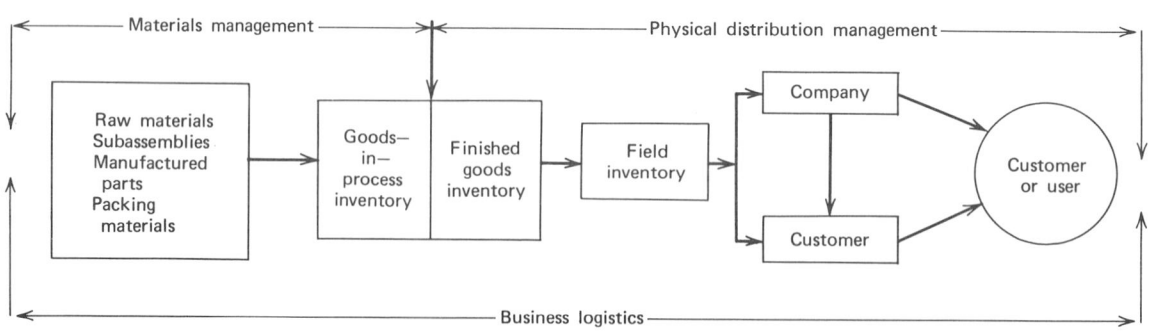

SOURCE: B. J. LaLonde, "Integrated Distribution Management—The American Perspective," *Long Range Planning*, December 1969, Pergamon Press Ltd.

The integration was necessary to provide for *coordination* among these functions and to provide for the optimal utilization of resources. For example, the logistics manager may decide to use the space in the warehouse designated for raw material to accommodate temporarily the extra finished goods inventory that is beyond the capacity of the finished goods warehouses.

Determinants. Figure 5-8 clearly demonstrates the nature of the conflict that can arise between the functional areas when logistics functions are diffused and no effort is undertaken to coordinate them. For example, if the location of the physical distribution warehouse were determined exclusively by plant location factors, this might result in higher total distribution cost because of customer location and geographic concentration, available transportation modes, and service level requirements. Second, if inventory levels were determined by financial considerations alone, the financial manager could reduce inventory levels in order to cut part of the cost of carrying inventory. However, this might result in (1) higher production costs because of shorter production runs, and (2) lost sales because of shorter production

Figure 5-8 Traditional organization for physical distribution.

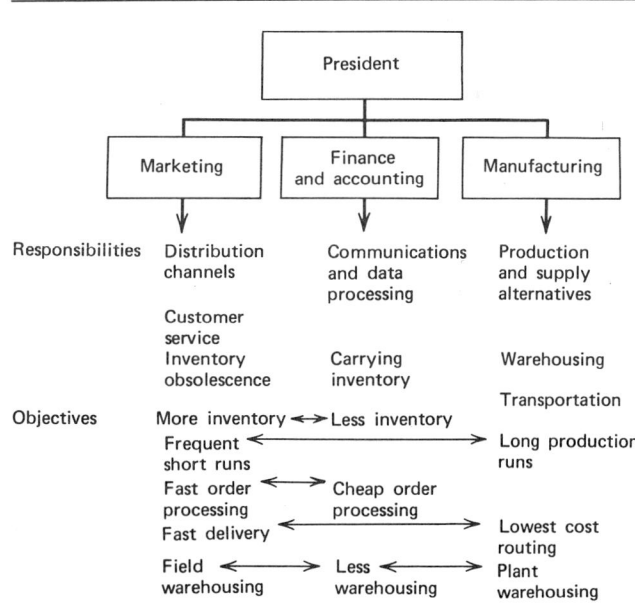

SOURCE: John F. Stolle, "How to Manage Physical Distribution," *Harvard Business Review*, 45,4 (July-August 1967): 95.

runs and stock-out conditions. The production cost increases and the cost of lost sales may exceed savings from carrying lower inventory levels. Therefore, in determining inventory levels, the trade-offs between the costs involved in inventory carrying, production, and stock-outs must be recognized. It is evident that inventory levels are affected by financial and production capacity, production planning and scheduling, demand forecast, desired customer service level (i.e., the period elapsed between placement of order and receipt of goods), and warehouse and plant locations.

It is evident from the organization of this textbook that it adopts the traditional organizational view of handling physical distribution as a marketing function and materials management as a production function. This emphasis is appropriate for two reasons. First, the majority of firms still operate in this way; the logistics organization is certainly not a panacea for all firms. Second, the main objective of adopting the logistics concept in organizations is to provide for coordination in decision making for these functionally interdependent decisions. The spirit of the logistics concept is that of the systems approach, where effects on the total system are considered when decisions pertaining to one part are being made.[21] The system's view requires coordination in decision making that can be achieved without altering the organization structure.

Given this traditional orientation, all functionally interdependent decisions pertaining to materials management are treated in Chapter 6.

FUNCTIONALLY INDEPENDENT MARKETING VARIABLES

Class 4 functionally independent marketing variables are not of major concern to the strategic and general management orientation of this textbook, as noted in Chapter 1. Therefore they will not be discussed in detail here. Instead, the following is a list of some of the more significant C_4 marketing variables.

1. Brand names and branding decisions.
2. Marketing budget allocation.
3. Promotion budget allocation.
4. Selection of sales promotional activities.
    (a) Displays.
    (b) Shows.
    (c) Exhibitions.
    (d) Demonstrations.
5. Personal selling.
    (a) Allocation of sales territories.
    (b) Personal selling operational management.
        (1) Compensation of sales personnel.

---

[21]Lee Adler, "Systems Approach to Marketing," *Harvard Business Review*, *45*, (4), May–June 1967, pp. 105–118.

(2) Supervision of sales personnel.
   (3) Motivation of sales personnel.
    (c) Evaluation of sales personnel.
6. Advertising decisions.
    (a) Selection of advertising types.
        (1) Product and institutional.
        (2) National and local.
    (b) Selection of media.
    (c) Evaluation of advertising programs.
    (d) Selection of message.
    (e) Timing of advertising effort.
    (f) Selection of advertising agency.
    (g) Adjusting the advertising agency.
7. Specific channel decisions.
    (a) Selection of specific channel intermediaries.
    (b) Determination of middlemen margins.
    (c) Evaluation and termination of channel intermediaries.
8. Specific credit decisions.

SUMMARY This chapter has examined marketing from a general management perspective. Since C_1 and C_2 variables were discussed in previous chapters, this chapter was devoted to a discussion of C_3 multifunctional marketing decision variables. These included product research and development, marketing research and information systems, distribution channel structure, price, discount type and structure, promotion, credit, physical distribution and inventory levels.

The article following the appendix by George S. Day titled "A Strategic Perspective on Product Planning" emphasizes the role of new products and markets versus established ones and the choice of areas of new products to be pursued. The process of setting objectives for new and established products is discussed in detail in the article.

Appendix: TOPIC OUTLINE FOR PRODUCT LINE MARKETING PLAN

I. PRODUCT POLICY STATEMENT

State briefly but explicitly the price range, quality level, distribution policy and brand strategy being used to reach the line's intended consumer markets.

II. MARKETING BACKGROUND

1. *Definition of Consumer Markets*

   Describe the consumer markets in which each product line has been sold.

   a. Characteristics of Significant Consumer Groups

      Show population and per capita purchases by:
      - Intended use of purchase (own use, gift, etc.)
      - Family status and size
      - Family income
      - Geographic region
      - Other significant consumer characteristics

   b. Known or Assumed Consumer Preferences and Buying Habits
      - Product feature preferences
      - Shopping habits
      - Motivations for purchases (rank by importance)
        - Product features
        - Brand awareness
        - Price
        - Advertising
        - Promotion
        - Packaging
        - Display
        - Sales assistance
        - Other

   c. Significant Consumer Market Trends: Size, Characteristics and Buying Habits
      - Recent trends
      - Expected changes

SOURCE: The Conference Board. *The Short Term Marketing Plan*. Report Number 565, 1972, pp. 27-32.

Appendix (continued)

2. *Market Size and Sales Statistics*
   a. Market Trends (past 5 years)
      - Industry sales
      - Product type sales
      - Price index
   b. Distribution Trends
      - Industry sales by type of outlet (i.e., retail, premium and institutional, and further by major types of outlets within each broad area, i.e., department store, chain store, specialty store, etc.)
      - Product type sales by type of outlet
      - Product type sales by method of distribution (direct or wholesale)
   c. Product Line Sales Trends
      - Sales dollars
      - Sales dollars by type of outlet
      - Share of total market
      - Share of product type market
      - Share of key outlet distribution
      - Sales dollars by method of distribution
      - Price index

3. *Product Line Profit and Cost History* (*5 years*)
   a. Profit History
      - Net profit dollars
      - Net profit as percent of sales
      - Return on investment
   b. Manufacturing Cost History
      - Gross profit dollars
      - Gross profit as percent of sales
   c. Marketing Cost History (5 years)
      Show how marketing money has been spent and with what results
      - Advertising cost
        —Dollars by type, i.e., national, cooperative, and trade
        —Percent of sales
        —Share of advertising vs. share of market
      - Promotion, display and fixturing cost
        —Dollars
        —Percent of sales
        —Fixture placements vs. potential

Appendix (continued)
- Distribution cost (includes distributor discount, transportation, warehousing, inventory carrying costs, and the cost of distributor selling aids)
  —Dollars
  —Percent of sales
  —Distribution coverage vs. potential
  - kind of accounts
  - number of accounts
  - sales potential of accounts
- Field selling costs
  —Dollars
  —Percent of sales
  —Direct account coverage vs. potential

4. *Competitive Comparison*

   Highlight significant differences between this company and its competition.
   - Product line composition and acceptance
   - Distribution methods and coverage
   - Field selling methods
   - Consumer marketing programs

5. *Conclusions*

   Summarize the major problems and opportunities requiring action based on analysis of background information. Consider:
   - Consumer and trade market penetration
   - Distribution coverage
   - Product line needs
   - Price revisions
   - Cost reductions
   - New market and product opportunities

III. PRIMARY MARKETING AND PROFIT OBJECTIVES

   1. *Marketing Objectives*
      - Sales dollars
      - Market share by major type of outlet
   2. *Profit Objectives*
      - Gross profit dollars
      - Gross profit as percent of sales
      - Net profit dollars
      - Net profit as percent of sales
      - Return on investment

Appendix (continued)

Note external qualifying assumptions such as business cycle trends, industry trends, changes in size and characteristics of consumer market segments, distribution trends, competitive activity, price levels, import quotas, and factory capacity.

IV. OVERALL MARKETING STRATEGY

State the strategic direction to be followed in order to achieve primary product line marketing and profit objectives.
1. *Consumer and Trade Market Emphasis*
2. *Trademark and Product Feature Emphasis*
3. *Marketing Mix Emphasis*
4. *Functional Objectives*

Establish the contribution needed from each functional area in order to implement the overall strategy and to achieve primary objectives.

    a. Field Selling
- Distribution objectives expressed in number, size, quality, and type of wholesale, retail, premium and institutional accounts needed to meet sales volume objectives.

    b. Product Development
- New product objectives expressed in numbers, types, introductory dates, sales volume and profit contributions from new products.

    c. Advertising
- Identify markets to be reached
- Communication objectives (nature of message and retention level sought by consumers and trade customers)
- Trade participation objectives in cooperative advertising programs

    d. Promotion and Fixturing
- Sales objectives for major promotions
- Fixture placement and sales volume objectives

    e. Merchandising
- Objectives for the number and type of new merchandising programs and for trade participation in the company's programmed merchandising.

    f. Business Operation
- Customer delivery service objectives
- Inventory turnover objectives
- Product line composition and size objectives
- Pricing objectives

Appendix (continued)

V. PRO FORMA FINANCIAL STATEMENTS AND BUDGETS
  1. *Marketing Budgets*
     - Field selling expense
     - Advertising expense
       —national
       —cooperative
       —trade
     - Promotion expense
       —consumer
       —trade
     - Fixturing and display expense
     - Product development expense
     - Market research expense
     - Distribution expense
     - Administrative and allocated expense
  2. *Pro Forma Financial Statements*
     a. Annual Profit and Loss Statement (expense detail as shown above)
        - Next year pro forma by quarter
        - Current year budget by quarter
        - Last year actual by quarter
     b. Annual Revision of Five-Year Pro Forma Profit and Loss Statement (expense detail for broad categories)

VI. ACTION PLANS
  1. *Product Line Plans*
     a. New Product Objectives
     b. New Product Positioning vs. Identified Product Needs of Consumers
     c. New Product Specifications
        - Style, weight, size, finish, etc.
        - Manufacturing cost
        - Selling price
     d. New Product Budgets
        - Exploration and screening
        - Development
        - Market introduction
     e. New Product Event Schedule
        - Design releases
        - Designs complete
        - Market tests complete

Appendix (continued)
- Production releases
- Advertising planned and scheduled
- Selling aids complete
- Distribution achieved
- Commencement of consumer advertising, promotion, and selling.
   f. Planned Deletions and Accompanying Phase-Out Programs
2. *Advertising Plans*
   a. National Advertising (by individual campaign)
      - Definition of consumers and their buying motivations
      - Message theme and objectives
      - Reach and frequency objectives
      - Budgets
      - Preparation and execution schedules
      - Creative plans
      - Media plans
   b. Cooperative Advertising Programs
      - Trade participation objectives
      - Budget
      - Relationships to other marketing programs
      - Preparation and execution schedule
   c. Trade Advertising (by individual campaign)
      - Message and audience objectives
      - Budgets
      - Preparation and execution schedules
      - Creative plans
      - Media plans
   d. Trademark Changes
3. *Sales Promotion and Display Plans*
   a. Consumer and Trade Promotion Objectives
   b. General Description of Promotion Programs, Budgets and Calendar
   c. Fixturing Programs and Budgets
4. *Major Packaging Plans*
5. *Trade Selling Plans*
   a. Description of Significant Changes in Distribution Policy
      - Approved outlets
      - Distribution methods
   b. Distribution Coverage Objectives
   c. Account Coverage Objectives

Appendix (continued)
- d. Selling Expense Budgets
- e. Specific New Account Targets
- f. Special Trade Merchandising Programs and Calendar
- g. Field Selling Programs and Calendar
- h. New Services for Trade Customers
  - Delivery service
  - Inventory backup
  - Selling support, or the like
- i. Sales Quotas for Each Salesman by Product Line

6. *Special Market Research Projects*

   Include a general description of each project, its objectives, budget and timetable.

7. *Pricing Recommendations*

8. *Special Cost Reduction Programs*

   Include a general description of each program, its expected dollar savings, and an assignment of responsibilities.

A STRATEGIC PERSPECTIVE ON PRODUCT PLANNING

George S. Day

INTRODUCTION

The past decade has seen growing recognition that the product planning function within diversified companies of all sizes involves trade offs among competing opportunities and strategies. During this period the combination of more complex markets, shorter product life cycles and social, legal and governmental trends put a premium on minimizing the degree of risk in the product mix. More recently, managers have had to cope with severe resource constraints, stemming partly from weaknesses in the capital markets and a general cash shortage, and the triple traumas of the energy crisis, materials shortages and inflation.

Some of the manifestations of the new climate for product planning are skepticism toward the value of full product lines, unwillingness to accept the risks of completely new products, an emphasis on profit growth rather than volume growth and active product elimination and divestment programs.[1] Yet managements cannot afford to turn their backs on all opportunities for change and attempt to survive simply by doing a better job with the established products and services. Eventually all product categories become saturated or threatened by substitutes and diversification becomes essential to survival. Consumer goods companies are especially feeling this pressure as the productivity of line extensions or product adaptations directed at narrow market segments declines. Also the likelihood of regulatory actions directed at products, such as aerosols and cyclamates, points up the risks of having a closely grouped product line.[2] More than ever, long-run corporate health is going to depend on the ability of product planners to juggle those conflicting pressures of diversification and consolidation.

The pervasive nature of the resource allocation problem in product planning is the focus of this article. The emphasis is on the basic issues of the role of new and established products and markets and the choice of areas of new product development to pursue. The first issue is addressed in the context of the product portfolio, which describes the mixture of products that generate cash and in which the company can invest cash. A detailed examination of the product portfolio begins with its component parts, the product life cycle and the notion of market dominance, and then turns to the implications for strategic planning and resource allocation.

Once the role of new products has been established, the issue of where to look is addressed with an explicit statement of a search strategy. This statement defines the characteristics of desirable opportunities in terms that are meaningful to product planners.

STRATEGIC PLANNING AND PRODUCT PLANNING

There are as many concepts of strategy as writers on the subject.[3] Several of the more useful definitions for our immediate purposes are:

• Decisions today which affect the future (not future decisions)

SOURCE: Reprinted from *Journal of Contemporary Business*, Spring 1975, pp. 1-34, with permission of the *Journal of Contemporary Business*, copyright © 1975.

- Major questions of resource allocation that determine a company's long-run results
- The calculated means by which the firm deploys its resources—i.e., personnel, machines and money—to accomplish its purpose under the most advantageous circumstances
- A competitive edge that allows a company to serve the customers better than its competitors
- The broad principles by which a company hopes to secure an advantage over competitors, an attractiveness to buyers and a full exploitation of company resources.

Following these definitions, the desired output of the strategic planning process is a long-run plan "that will produce an attractive growth rate and a high rate of return on investment by achieving a market position so advantageous that competitors can retaliate only over an extended time period at a prohibitive cost."[4]

Most strategic planning processes and the resulting plans show a distinct family resemblance, although the specifics obviously vary greatly. These specifics usually include[5]: (1) a statement of the mission of the strategic business unit (SBU),[6] (2) the desired future position the SBU and the corporation wants to attain, comprising measurable profitability, sales, market share, efficiency and flexibility objectives, (3) the key environmental assumptions and the opportunities and threats, (4) a statement of the strengths, weaknesses and problems of the SBU and its major competitors, (5) the strategic gap between the desired and forecasted position of the SBU, (6) actions to be taken to close the gap—the strategy and (7) the required resources and where they can be obtained, including financial resources such as net cash flow, the equity base and debt capacity and management capabilities. These are the main elements of the planning process that are relevant to product planning, leaving aside the issues of detailed implementation plans, contingency plans, which state in advance what modifications will be made if key environmental or competitor assumptions turn out to be false, and the monitoring procedures.

What is lacking in the planning process just described is a systematic procedure for generating and choosing strategic alternatives. One of the greatest weaknesses of current strategic plans is the lack of viable strategy alternatives which present very different approachs and outcomes. Too frequently top management sees only one strategy which the SBU has decided is best in terms of its own and the managers' personal needs and objectives. This ignores the interdependency among products (the portfolio aspect)[7] and the possibility that what is best for each SBU is not necessarily best for the entire company.[8] In recognition of this problem, the planning process shown in Figure 1 incorporates an analysis of the product portfolio. The remainder of this paper is devoted to the uses and limitations of the product portfolio and the implications for developing strategy alternates that optimize the long-run position of the firm.

THE COMPONENTS OF THE PRODUCT PORTFOLIO

Market share and stage in the product life cycle have long been regarded as important determinants of profitability. The contribution of the product portfolio concept is that it permits the planner to consider these two measures simultaneously in evaluating the products of an entire company or a division or SBU.

The Value of Market Share Dominance

The belief in the benefits of a dominant market share is rooted deeply in the experience of executives. It is reinforced by the facts of life in most markets:

- The market leader is usually the most profitable
- During economic downturns, customers are likely to concentrate their purchases in suppliers with large shares, and distributors and retailers will try to cut inventories by eliminating the marginal supplier

Figure 1 Highlighting product planning activities in the strategic planning process.

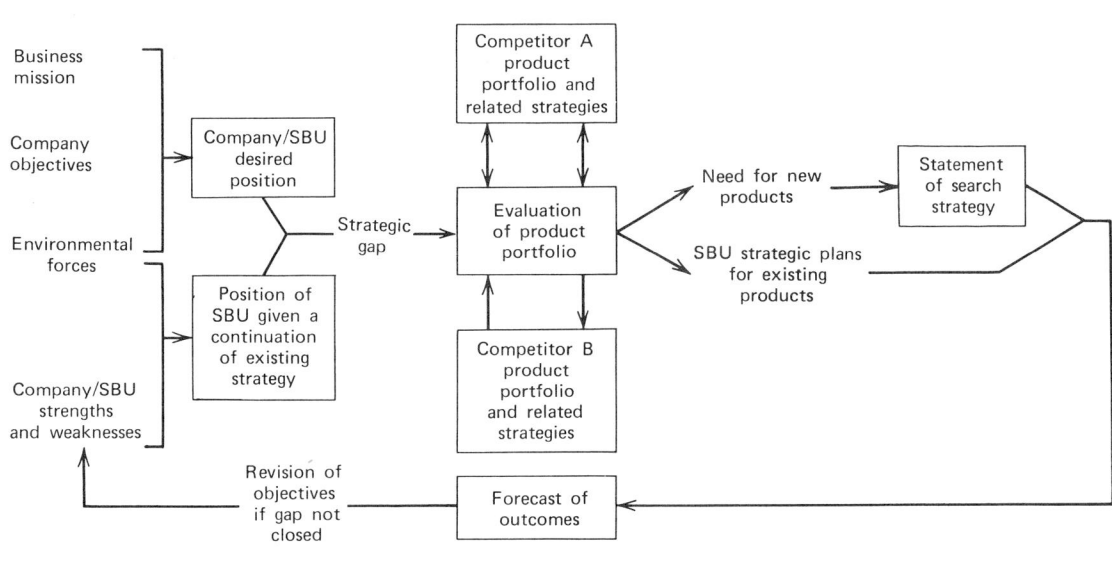

- During periods of economic growth, there is often a bandwagon effect with a large share presenting a positive image to customers and retailers.[9]

Of course, market domination has its own pitfalls, beyond antitrust problems, "... monopolists flounder on their own complacency rather than on public opposition. Market domination produces tremendous internal resistance against any innovation and makes adaptation to change dangerously difficult. Also, it usually means that the enterprise has too many of its eggs in one basket and is too vulnerable to economic fluctuations."[10] The leader is also highly vulnerable to competitive actions, especially in the pricing area, since the leader establishes the basic industry price from which smaller competitors can discount.

The clearest evidence of the value of market share comes from a study of The Profit Impact of Market Strategies (PIMS) of 620 separate businesses by the Marketing Science Institute which, in turn, draws on earlier work by General Electric. Early results indicated that market share, investment intensity (ratio of total investment to sales) and product quality were the most important determinants of pretax return on investment, among a total of 37 distinct factors incorporated into the profit model.[11] On average it was found that a difference of 10 points in market share was accompanied by a difference of about 5 points in pretax ROI. As share declined from more than 40 percent to less than 10 percent, the average pretax ROI dropped from 30 percent to 9.1 percent.

The PIMS study also provided some interesting insights into the reasons for the link between market share and profitability.[12] The results point to economies of scale and, especially, the opportunities for vertical integration as the most important explanations. Thus high-share businesses (more than 40 percent) tend to have low ratios of purchases to sales because they make rather than buy and own their distribution facilities. The ratio of purchases to sales increases from 33 percent for high-share businesses to 45 percent for low-share (less than 10 percent) businesses. But because of economies of scale in manufacturing and purchasing there is no significant relationship between manufacturing expenses or the ratio of sales to investment and the market share. To some degree these results also support the market power argument of economists; market leaders evidently are able to bargain more effectively (either through the exercise of reciprocity or greater technical marketing skills) and obtain higher prices than their competition (but largely because they produce and sell higher-quality goods and services). The fact that market leaders spend a significantly higher percentage of their sales on R & D suggests that they pursue a conscious strategy of product leadership.

Experience curve analysis. The importance of economies of scale in the relationship of market share and profitability is verified by the experience curve concept. Research, largely reported by the Boston Consulting Group, has found that in a wide range of businesses (including plastics, semiconductors, gas ranges and life insurance policies), the total unit costs, in constant dollars, decline by a constant percentage (usually 20 to 30 percent) with each doubling of accumulated units of output or experience.[13] Since the experience effect applies to all value added, it subsumes economies of scale and specialization effects along with the well-known learning curve which applies only to direct labor costs.

An experience curve, when plotted on a log-log scale as in Figure 2, appears as a straight line. The locations of the competitors on this curve are determined approximately by their respective accumulated experience, for which relative market share is a good surrogate (this may not be true if some competitors recently have entered the market by buying experience through licenses or acquisitions). Then it follows that the competitor with the greatest accumulated experience will have the lowest relative costs and, if prices are similar between competitors, also will have the greatest profits. Of course, companies that fail to reduce costs along the product category experience curve and who are not dominant will be at an even greater competitive disadvantage.

Figure 2 shows a price prevailing at one point in time. Over the long run, prices also will decline at roughly the same rate as costs decline. The major exception to this rule occurs during the introduction and growth state of the life cycle, when the innovator and/or dominant competitor, is tempted to maintain prices at a high level to recoup the development costs. The high price umbrella usually achieves this immediate end because unit profits are high. The drawback is the incentive to higher cost competitors to enter the market and attempt to increase their market shares. In effect, the dominant competitor is trading future market share for current profits. This may be sensible if the early leader: (1) has a number of attractive new product opportunities requiring cash, (2) there are potential competitors whose basic business position will enable them eventually to enter the product category regardless of the pricing strategy[14] or (3) significant barriers to entry can be erected.

Product Life Cycle

That products pass through various stages between life and death (introduction → growth → maturity → decline) is hard to deny. Equally accepted is the notion that a company should have

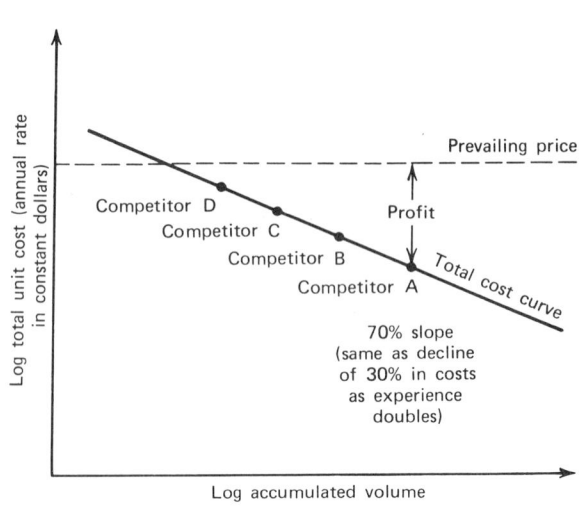

Figure 2 Cost experience curve showing relative profit levels of competitors.

a mix of products with representation in each of these stages.

Thus the concept of a product life cycle would appear to be an essential tool for understanding product strategies.[15] Indeed this is true, but only *if* the position of the product and the duration of the cycle can be determined. This caveat should be kept in mind when considering the following summary of the important aspects of the product life cycle:

- Volume and profit growth attract competition during the early *growth* (or takeoff) stage of the life cycle. The product market is even more attractive if the innovator lacks the capacity to satisfy demand. However, these competitors may contribute to the growth of sales by their market development expenditures and product improvements.
- Purchase patterns and distribution channels are still fluid during the rapid *growth* stage. For this reason, market shares can be increased at relatively low cost over short periods of time by capturing a disproportionate share of incremental sales (especially where these sales come from new users rather than heavier usage by existing users).
- As a product reaches *maturity* there is evidence of saturation, finer distinctions in benefits surrounding the product and appeals to special segments.
- There is often an industry shake-out to signal the *end* of the rapid growth stage. The trigger might be an excessive number of competitors who have to resort to price cutting to survive; a dominant producer who seeks to regain share; or a large competitor buying into the market (and all these effects will be accentuated by an economic slow down). The result is a period of consolidation during which marginal competitors either drop out, merge with other small competitors or sell out to larger competitors.
- During the *maturity* stage, market-share relationships tend to stabilize; distribution patterns have been established and are difficult to change. This, in turn, contributes to inertia in purchasing relationships and selling oriented toward maintaining relationships. Any substantial increase in share of market will require a reduction in a competitor's capacity utilization which will be resisted vigorously. As a result, gains in share are both time-consuming and costly. This is not necessarily the case if the attempt to gain shares is spearheaded by a significant improvement in product value or performance which the competitor cannot easily match. A case in point is the growth in private labels, or distributor-controlled labels, in both food and general merchandising categories.
- As substitutes appear and/or sales begin to decline, the core product behaves like a commodity and is subject to intense and continuing price pressure. The result is further competitors dropping out of the market, since only those with extensive accumulated experience and cost-cutting capability are able to generate reasonable profits and ROI's.
- The *decline* stage can be forestalled by vigorous promotion (plus, a new creative platform) and product improvement designed to generate more frequent usage or new users and applications.[16] Of course, if these extensions are sufficiently different, a new product life cycle is launched.

Measurement and Interpretation Problems

The concepts underlying the product portfolio are much easier to articulate than to implement.

What is the product-market?

The crux of the problem is well stated by Moran:

> In our complex service society there are no more product classes—not in any meaningful sense, only as a figment of file clerk imagination. There are only use classes—users which are more central to some products and peripheral to others—on a vast overlapping continuum. To some degree, in some circumstances almost anything can be a partial substitute for almost anything else. An eight-cent stamp substitutes to some extent for an airline ticket.[17]

Where does this leave the manager who relies on share of some (possibly ill-defined) market as a guide to performance evaluation and resource allocation. First he or she must recognize that most markets do not have neat boundaries. For example, patterns of substitution in industrial markets often look like continuua, i.e., zinc, brass, aluminum and engineered plastics such as nylon and polycarbonates can be arrayed rather uniformly along dimensions of price and performance. A related complication, more pertinent to consumer product markets, is the possibility of segment differences in perceptions of product substitutability. For example, there is a timid, risk-averse segment that uses a different product for each kind of surface cleaning (i.e., surface detergents, scouring powders, floor cleaners, bleaches, lavatory cleaners and general-purpose wall cleaners). At the other extreme is the segment that uses detergent for every cleaning problem. Thirdly, product/markets may have to be defined in terms of distribution patterns. Thus, tire companies treat the OEM and replacement tire markets as separate and distinct, even though the products going through these two channels are perfect substitutes so far as the end customer is concerned.

Perhaps the most important consideration is the time frame. A long-run view, reflecting strategic planning concerns, invariably will reveal a larger product-market to account for: (1) changes in technology, price relationships and availability which may remove or reduce cost and performance limitations, e.g., the boundaries between minicomputers, programmable computers and time-sharing systems in many use situations are becoming very fuzzy; (2) the time required by present and prospective buyers to react to these changes, which includes modifying behavior patterns, production systems, etc. and (3) considerable switching among products over long periods of time to satisfy desires for variety and change, as is encountered in consumer goods with snacks, for example.

Despite these complexities, the boundaries of product markets usually are established by four-digit Standard Industrial Classification (SIC) categories and/or expert judgment. The limitations of the SIC are well known[18] but often do not outweigh the benefits of data availability in a convenient form that can be broken down further to geographic markets. In short, the measure is attractive on tactical grounds (for sales force, promotional budget, etc., allocation) but potentially misleading for strategic planning purposes.

What is market dominance? A measure of market share, per se, is not a good indicator of the extent to which a firm dominates a market. The value of a 30 percent share is very different in a market where the next largest competitor has 40 percent than in one where the next largest has only 20 percent. Two alternative measures which incorporate information on the structure of the competition are:

- Company share ÷ share of largest competitor
- Company share ÷ share of largest three largest competitors.

The former measure is more consistent with the implications of the experience curve, while the latter is perhaps better suited to highly concentrated markets (where the four-firm concentration ratio is greater than 80 percent, for example). Regardless of which measure is used it is often the case that the dominant firm has to be at least 1.5 times as large as the next biggest competitor in order to ensure profitability. When there are two large firms of roughly equal shares, especially in a growth business such as nuclear power generators, the competition is likely to be severe. In this instance, both General Electric and Westinghouse have about 40 percent shares and don't expect to be profitable on new installations until after 1977. Conversely, when the two largest firms have small shares, say less than 5 percent, neither measure of market dominance is meaningful.

Evidence of market share dominance, no matter how it is measured, will not be equally meaningful in all product markets. Results from the PIMS study[19] suggest that importance of market share is influenced most strongly by the frequency of purchases.

While the full reasons for this difference in profitability are obscure they probably relate to differences in unit costs and prior buyer experience with the available alternatives which, in turn, determine willingness to reduce risk by buying the market leader and/or paying a premium price. Also, the frequently purchased category is dominated by consumer goods where there is considerable proliferation of brand names through spin offs, flankers, fighting brands, etc. in highly segmented markets. Each of these brands, no matter how small, shares production facilities and will have low production and distribution costs, although they may be treated as separate businesses.[20] It is hardly surprising that the experience curve concept is difficult to apply to consumer goods. Most of the successful applications have been with infrequently purchased industrial products; relatively undifferentiated, with high value added compared to raw material costs and fairly stable rates of capacity utilization.

A further caveat regarding the experience curve concerns the extent to which costs ultimately can be reduced. The experience curve clearly does not happen according to some immutable law; it requires careful management and some degree of long-run product stability (and, ideally, standardization). These conditions cannot be taken for granted and will be threatened directly by the customer demand for product change and competitive efforts to segment the market. In effect, product innovation and cost efficiency are not compatible in the long-run.[21]

A related question concerns the relevance of the experience curve to a new competitor in an established market. It is doubtful that a new entrant with reasonable access to the relevant technology would incur the same level of initial costs as the developers of the market.

What is the stage in the product life cycle?

It is not sufficient to simply know the current rate of growth of the product category. The strategic implications of the product life cycle often hinge on forecasting changes in the growth rate and, in particular, on establishing the end of the growth and maturity stages.

The first step in utilizing the life cycle is to ensure that the product class is identified properly. This may require a distinction between a broad product type (cigarettes) and a more specific product form (plain filter cigarettes). Secondly, the graph of product (type or form) sales needs to be adjusted for factors that might obscure the underlying life cycle, i.e., price changes, economic fluctuations and population changes. The third and most difficult step is to forecast when the product will move from one stage to another. The specific problems are beyond the scope of this article. However, the range of possibilities is illustrated by these various leading indicators of the "top-out" point.[22]

- Evidence of saturation; declining proportion of new trier versus replacement sales
- Declining prices and profits
- Increased product life
- Industry over capacity
- Appearance of new replacement product or technology
- Changes in export/import ratio
- Decline in elasticity of advertising and promotion, coupled with increasing price elasticity
- Changes in consumer preferences

These measures generally will indicate only the *timing* of the top-out point, and each is suffi-

Return on Investment

Share market	Infrequently purchased (<once/mon)	Frequently purchased (>once/mon)
Under 10%	6.9%	12.4%
10–19	14.4	13.7
20–29	17.8	17.4
30–39	24.3	23.1
Over 40	34.6	22.9

ciently imprecise that it is strongly advisable to use as many as possible in combination. Forecasts of the product sales *level* to be achieved at the top-out point may be obtained by astute incorporation of the leading indicators into: (1) technological forecasts, (2) similar product analysis (where sales patterns of products with analogous characteristics are used to estimate the sales pattern of the new product) or (3) epidemiological models whose parameters include initial sales rates and market saturation levels estimated with marketing research methods.[23]

ANALYZING THE PRODUCT PORTFOLIO

The product life cycle highlights the desirability of a variety of products/services with different present and prospective growth rates. However, this is not a sufficient condition for a well balanced portfolio of products that will ensure profitable long-run growth. Two other factors are market share position and the need to balance cash flows within the corporation. Some products should *generate* cash (and provide acceptable reported profits) and others should *use* cash to support growth; otherwise, the company will build up unproductive cash reserves or go bankrupt.[24] These issues are clarified by jointly considering share position and market growth rate, as in the matrix of Figure 3. The conceptualization used here is largely attributable to the Boston Consulting Group.[25]

It must be stressed that the growth-share matrix discussed here is simply one way of conceptualizing the product portfolio. It has been useful as a device for synthesizing the analyses and judgments of the earlier steps in the planning process, especially in facilitating an approach to strategic decision making that considers the firm to be a whole that is more than the sum of its separate parts. For these purposes, the arbitrary classifications of products in the growth-share matrix are adequate to differentiate the strategy possibilities.[26]

Product Portfolio Strategies

Each of the four basic categories in the growth-share matrix implies a set of strategy alternatives that generally are applicable to the portfolio entries in that category.[27]

Stars. Products that are market leaders, but also growing fast, will have substantial reported profits but need a lot of cash to finance the rate of growth. The appropriate strategies are designed primarily to protect the existing share level by reinvesting earnings in the form of price reductions, product improvement, better market coverage, production efficiency increases, etc. Particular attention must be given to obtaining a large share of the new users or new applications that are the source of growth in the market. Management may elect, instead, to maximize short-run profits and cash flow at the expense of long-run market share. This is highly risky because it usually is predicated on a continuing stream of product innovations and deprives the company of a cash cow which may be needed in the future.

Cash cows. The combination of a slow market growth and market dominance usually spells substantial net cash flows. The amount of cash generated is far in excess of the amount required to maintain share. All strategies should be directed toward maintaining market dominance—including investments in technological leadership. Pricing decisions should be made cautiously with an eye to maintaining price leadership. Pressure to overinvest through product proliferation and market expansion should be resisted unless prospects for expanding primary demand are unusually attractive. Instead, excess cash should be used to support research activities and growth areas elsewhere in the company.

Dogs. Since there usually can be only one market leader and because most markets are mature,

Figure 3 Describing the product portfolio in the market share growth matrix. (Arrows indicate principal cash flows.)

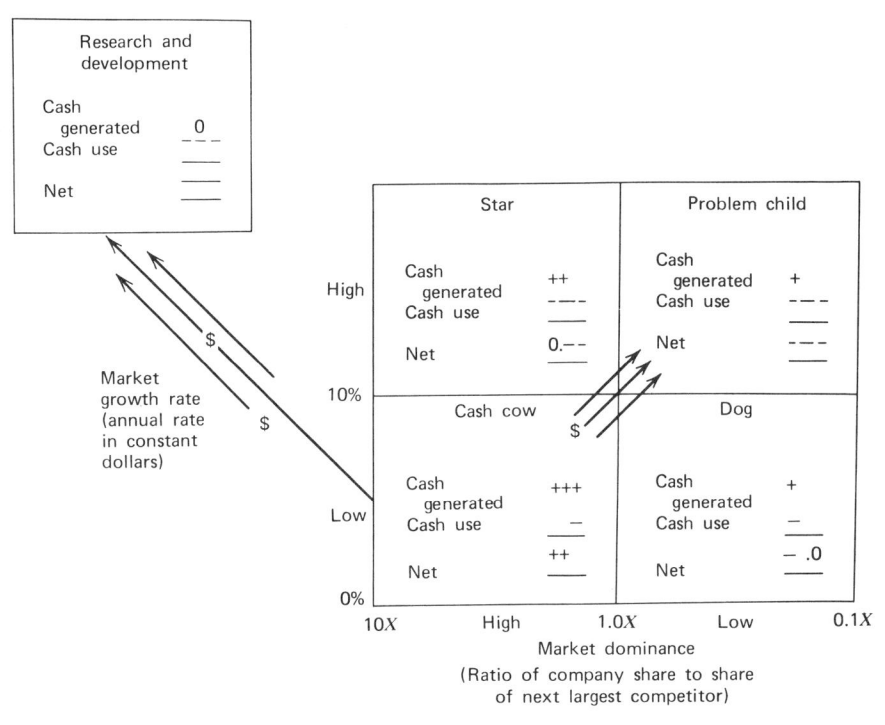

the greatest number of products fall in this category.[28] Such products are usually at a cost disadvantage and have few opportunities for growth at a reasonable cost. Their markets are not growing, so there is little new business to compete for, and market share gains will be resisted strenuously by the dominant competition.

The product remains in the portfolio because it shows (or promises) a modest book profit. This accounting result is misleading because most of the cash flow must be reinvested to maintain competitive position and finance inflation.[29] Another characteristic of a dog is that individual investment projects (especially those designed to reduce production costs) show a high ROI. However, the competitive situation is such that these returns cannot be realised in surplus cash flow that can be used to fund more promising projects. In addition there are the potential hidden costs of unproductive demands on management time (and consequent missed opportunities) and low personnel morale because of a lack of achievement.

The pejorative label of dog becomes increasingly appropriate the closer the product is to the lower-right corner of the growth/share matrix.[30] The need for positive action becomes correspondingly urgent. The search for action alternatives should begin with attempts to alleviate the problem without divesting. If these possibilities are unproductive, attention then can shift to finding ways of making the product to be divested as attractive as possible; then to liquidation and, finally if need be, to abandonment:

- Corrective action. Naturally all reasonable cost-cutting possibilities should be examined, but, as noted above, these are not likely to be productive in the long-run. A related alternative is to find a market segment that can be dominated. The attractiveness of this alternative will depend on the extent to which the segment can be protected from competition—perhaps because of technology or distribution requirements.[31] What must be avoided is the natural tendency of operating managers to arbitrarily redefine their markets in order to improve their share position and thus change the classification of the product when, in fact, the economics of the business are unchanged. This is highly probable when the product-market boundaries are ambiguous.
- Harvest. This is a conscious cutback of all support costs to the minimum level to maximize the product's profitability over a foreseeable lifetime, which is usually short. This cutback could include reducing advertising and sales effort, increasing delivery time, increasing the acceptable order size and eliminating all staff support activities such as marketing research.
- Value added. Opportunities may exist for reparceling a product or business that is to be divested. This may involve dividing the assets into smaller units or participating in forming a "kennel of dogs" in which the weak products of several companies are combined into a healthy package. This latter alternative is especially attractive when the market is very fractionated.
- Liquidation. This is the most prevalent solution usually involving a sale as a going concern but, perhaps, including a licensing agreement. If the business/product is to be sold as a unit, the problem is to maximize the selling price—a joint function of the prospective buyers need for the acquisition (which will depend on search strategy) and their overhead rate. For example, a small company may find the product attractive and be able to make money because of low overhead.
- Abandonment. The possibilities here include giveaways and bankruptcy.

Problem children. The combination of rapid growth rate and poor profit margins creates an enormous demand for cash. If the cash is not forthcoming, the product will become a dog as growth inevitably slows. The basic strategy options are fairly clear-cut; either invest heavily to get a disproportionate share of the new sales or buy existing share by acquiring competitors and thus move the product toward the star category or get out of the business using some of the methods just described.

Consideration also should be given to a market segmentation strategy, but only if a defensible niche can be identified and resources are available to gain dominance. This strategy is even more attractive if the segment can provide an entrée and experience base from which to push for dominance of the whole market.

Further Strategic Implications

While the product portfolio is helpful in suggesting strategies for specific products, it is equally useful for portraying the overall health of a multiproduct company. The issue is the extent to which the portfolio departs from the balanced display of Figure 4, both for the present and in 3 to 5 years.

Among the indicators of overall health are size and vulnerability of the cash cows (and the prospects for the stars, if any) and the number of problem children and dogs. Particular attention must be paid to those products with large cash appetites. Unless the company has abundant cash flow, it cannot afford to sponsor many such products at one time. If resources (including debt capacity) are spread too thin, the company simply will wind up with too many marginal products

Figure 4 A balanced product portfolio.

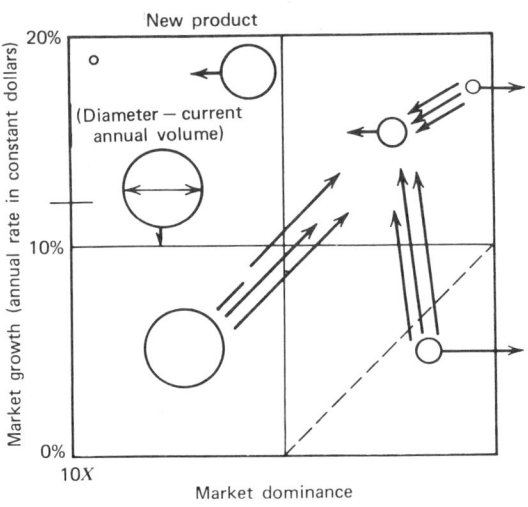

Figure 5 Market industry versus company growth rates. (Illustrative diversified company—diameters are proportional to current annual sales volume.)

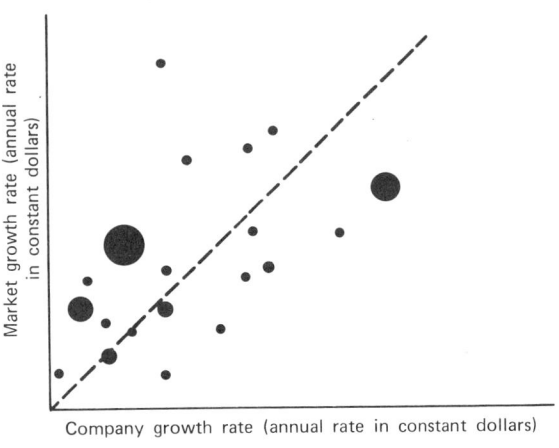

and suffer a reduced capacity to finance promising new product entries or acquisitions in the future. Some indication of this type of resource misallocation can be obtained from a comparison of the growth rates of the product class and the company's entrant (as illustrated in Figure 5). Ideally, nothing should be in the upper sector where market growth exceeds company growth—unless the product is being harvested.

Competitive analysis. Product portfolios should be constructed for each of the major competitors. Assuming competitive management follows the logic just described, they eventually will realize that they can't do everything. The key question is which problem children will be supported aggressively and which will be eliminated. The answer obviously will be difficult to obtain, but has an important bearing on the approach the company takes to its own problem children.

Of course, a competitive position analysis has many additional dimensions which must be explored in depth before specific competitive actions and reactions within each product category can be forecast.[32] This analysis, coupled with an understanding of competitive portfolios, becomes the basis for any fundamental strategy employing the military concept of concentration which essentially means to concentrate strength against weakness.[33]

Dangers in the pursuit of market share. Tilles has suggested a number of criteria for evaluating strategy alternatives.[34] The product portfolio is a useful concept for addressing the first three: (1) environmental consistency, (2) internal consistency and (3) adequacy of resources. A fourth criteria considers whether the degree of risk is acceptable, given the overall level of risk in the portfolio.

The experience of a number of companies, such as G.E. and RCA, in the main-frame computer business, points to the particular risks inherent in the pursuit of market share. An analysis of these "pyrrhic victories"[35] suggests that greatest risks can be avoided if the following questions can be answered affirmatively: (1) Are company financial resources adequate? (2) If the fight is stopped short for some reason, will the corporation's position be competitively viable? and (3) Will government regulations permit the corporation to follow the strategy it has chosen? The last question includes antitrust policies which now virtually preclude acquisitions made by large companies in related fields[36] and regulatory policies designed to proliferate competition, as in the airline industry.

Organizational implications. Although this discussion has focused on the financial and market position aspects of the product portfolio, the implications encompass the deployment of all corporate resources—tangible assets as well as crucial intangibles of management skills and time.

One policy that clearly must be avoided is to apply uniform performance objectives to all products, or SBU's, as is frequently attempted in highly decentralized profit-center management approaches. The use of flexible standards, tailored to the realities of the business, logically should lead to the recognition that different kinds of businesses require very different management styles. For example, stars and problem children demand an entrepreneurial orientation, while cash cows emphasize skills in fine tuning marketing tactics and ensuring effective allocation of resources. The nature of specialist support also will differ; e.g., R & D support being important for growth products and financial personnel becoming increasingly important as growth slows.[37] Finally, since good managers, regardless of their styles are always in short supply, the portfolio notion suggests that they not be expended in potentially futile efforts to turn dogs into profitable performers. Instead they should be deployed into situations where the likelihood of achievement and, hence, of reinforcement, is high.

Other methods of portraying the portfolio. The growth-share matrix is far from a complete synthesis of the underlying analyses and judgments as to the position of the firm in each of its product-markets. The main problem of the matrix concerns the growth rate dimension. While this is an extremely useful measure in that it can have direct implications for cash flows, it is only one of many possible determinants of the attractiveness of the market. A list of other possible factors is summarized in Table 1. (Not all these factors will be relevant to all markets.) The importance of each factor depends on the company's capabilities, but careful consideration will help to identify unusual threats, such as impending government regulations, that might significantly reduce future attractiveness. Similarly, market share may not provide a comprehensive indication of the company's position in each market; as in the case of a leader in a market that is rapidly fragmenting.

The qualitative aspects of overall attractiveness and position also can be incorporated into a

Table 1 Factors Determining Market and Industry Attractiveness

Market	• Size (present and potential) • Growth/stage in life cycle • Diversity of user segments • Foreign opportunities • Cyclicality
Competition	• Concentration ratio • Capacity utilization • Structural changes (e.g., entries and exits) • Position changes • Vertical threats/opportunities • Sensitivity of shares and market size to price, service, etc. • Extent of "captive" business
Profitability	• Level and trend of leaders • Contribution rates • Changes/threats on key leverage factors (e.g., scale economies and pricing) • Barriers to entry
Technology	• Maturity/volatility • Complexity • Patent protection • Product/process opportunities
Other	• Social/environmental • Government/political • Unions • Human factors

matrix which portrays the product portfolio. This matrix does not have the immediate cash flow implication of the growth-share matrix, thus, it should be used as a complementary, rather than a replacement approach.

NEW PRODUCT PLANNING

A product portfolio analysis identifies the need for new products or new markets and the probable level of available resources but does not indicate where to look. This presents management with a number of difficult questions:

- What degree of relationship to the present business is necessary and desirable?
- What are the possibilities for internal development versus acquisition?
- When is an innovation preferred to an imitation and vice versa?
- What are the characteristics of desirable new products?

These and innumerable other questions have to be answered before personnel in the product planning, corporate development or other responsible functions can pursue their tasks efficiently. In short, top management must decide how much growth is desired and feasible, the contribution of new versus established products and the broad direction as to how the growth will be achieved.

What is needed is a strategy statement that specifies those areas where development is to proceed and identifies (perhaps by exclusion) those areas that are off-limits. As Crawford notes, "the idea of putting definitive restrictions on new product activity is not novel, but use of it, especially sophisticated use, is still not widespread."[38] The major criticisms of a comprehensive statement of new product development strategy are that it will inhibit or restrict creativity and that ideas with great potential will be rejected. Experience suggests that clear guidance improves creativity by focusing energy on those areas where the payoff is likely to be greatest. Also, experience shows that significant breakthroughs outside the bounds of the product development strategy statement can be accommodated readily in an on-going project evaluation and screening process.

The New Product Development Strategy Statement

The essential elements of this statement are the specification of the product-market scope, the basic strategies to be used for growing within that scope and the characteristics of desirable alternatives. These elements guide the search for new product ideas, acquisitions, licenses, etc., and form the basis for a formal screening procedure.

Product-market scope. This is an attempt to answer the basic question, "what business(es) do we want to be in" and is a specific manifestation of the mission of the SBU or company. There is no ready-made formula for developing the definition of the future business. One approach is to learn from definitions that have been useful in guiding successful strategies. For exam-

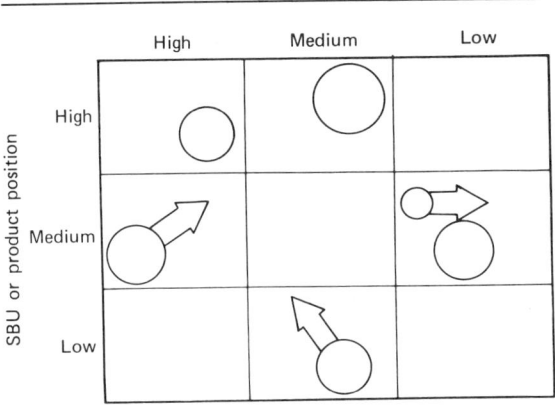

Industry or market attractiveness. [Arrow represents forecast of change in position. Diameter (of circles) is proportional to share of company sales contributed by product.]

ple, the General Electric Housewares SBU defines their present (circa 1973) business as "providing consumers with functional aids to increase the enjoyment or psychic fulfillment of selected life-styles"—specifically those dealing with preparation of food, care of the person, care of personal surroundings and planning assistance. In the future their business will expand to include recreation, enhancement of security and convenient care of the home.

This statement of the future business satisfied one important criteria: that it be linked to the present product-market scope by a clearly definable common thread. In the case of G.E. Housewares, the common thread is with generic needs being satisfied (or problems being solved, as the case may be). Ansoff argues that the linkage also can be with product characteristics, distribution capability or underlying technology—as long as the firm has distinctive competency in these areas.[39]

Other criteria for appraising the usefulness of a description of the future business opportunities are: (1) specificity—if the definition of product-market scope is too general, it won't have an impact on the organization (e.g., consider the vagueness of being in the business of supplying products with a plug on the end); (2) flexibility—the definition should be adapted constantly to recognize changing environmental conditions (e.g., Gerber no longer can say that babies are their only business), (3) attainability—can be undertaken within the firm's resources and competencies and (4) competitive advantage—it always is preferable to protect and build on these strengths and competencies that are not possessed as fully by the competition.[40]

Basic strategies for growth. At the broad level of a new product development strategy, the basic issues are the *growth vector*, or the direction the firm is moving within the chosen product-market scope, and the emphasis on *innovation* versus *imitation*.

There are almost an infinite number of possibilities for growth vectors. The basic alternatives are summarized in Figure 6.[41] There is no intention here to suggest that these strategies are mutually exclusive; indeed, various combinations can be pursued simultaneously in order to close the strategic gaps identified in the overall planning process. Furthermore, most of the strategies can be pursued either by internal development or acquisition and coupled with vertical diversification (either forward toward a business that is a customer or backward toward a business that is a supplier).

The choice of growth vector will be influenced by all the factors discussed earlier as part of the overall corporate planning process. Underlying any choice is, by necessity, an appraisal of the risks compared with the payoffs. The essence of past experience is that growth vectors within the existing market (or, at least, closely related markets) are much more likely to be successful than ventures into new markets.[42] Therefore, diversification is the riskiest vector to follow—especially if it is attempted by means of internal development. The attractiveness of acquisitions for diversification is the chance to reduce the risks of failure by buying a known entity with (reasonably) predictable performance.

An equally crucial basic strategy choice is the degree of emphasis on innovation versus imitation. The risks of being an innovator are well known so few, if any, diversified corporations can afford to be innovators in each product-market. There are compelling advantages to being first in the market if barriers to entry (because of patent protections, capital requirements, control over distribution, etc.) can be erected, the product is difficult to copy or improve on and the introductory period is short. The imitator, by contrast, is always put at a cost disadvantage by a successful innovator and must be prepared to invest heavily to build a strong market position. While profits over the life of the product may be lower for an imitator, the risks are much lower

Figure 6 Growth vector alternatives.

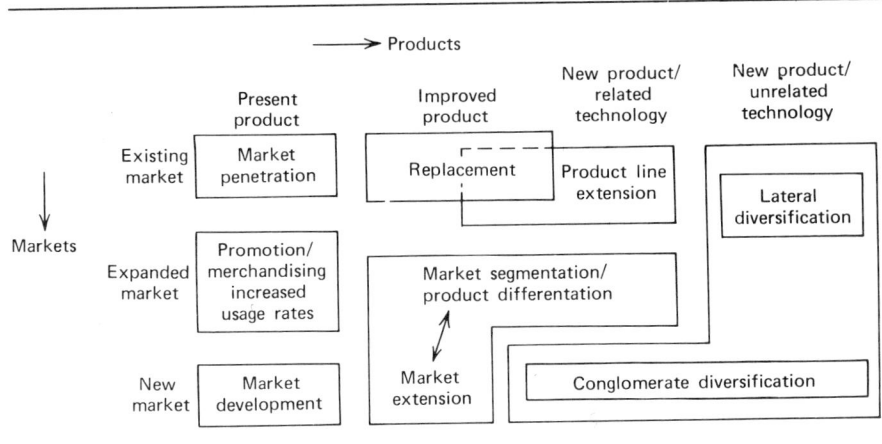

because the innovator has provided a full-scale market test which can be monitored to determine the probable growth in future sales. Also, the innovator may provide significant opportunities by not serving all segments or, more likely, by not implementing the introduction properly.

The conscious decision to lead or follow pervades all aspects of the firm. Some of the important differences that result can be seen from the various strategic orientations to high technology markets discussed by Ansoff and Steward:

- First to market . . . based on strong R & D, technical leadership and risk taking
- Follow the leader . . . based on strong development resources and the ability to act quickly as the market starts its growth phase
- Applications engineering . . . based on product modifications to fit the needs of particular customers in mature markets
- Me-too . . . based on superior manufacturing efficiency and cost control.[43]

Characteristics of desirable alternatives.
Three fundamental questions have to be asked of each new product or service being sought or considered: (1) How will a strong competitive advantage be obtained? The possibilities range from superiority in underlying technology or product quality, to patent protection, to marketing requirements. Another dimension of this question is the specification of markets or competitors to be avoided on the grounds that these situations would blunt the pursuit of a competitive advantage. (2) What is the potential for synergy? This asks about joint effects, or "the mutually reinforcing impact a product-market entry has on a firm's efficiency and effectiveness."[44] Synergy can be sought for defensive reasons, in order to supply a competence that the firm lacks or to spread the risks of a highly cyclical industry, as has motivated a number of mergers in the machine tool industry. Alternatively, synergy can utilize an existing competence such as a distribution system (notable examples here are Gillette and Coca Cola), a production capability, promotional skills, etc. In addition, "financial reinforcement may occur either because of the relative pattern of funds generation and demand . . . or because the combination is more attractive to the financial community than the pieces would be separately."[45] (3) What specific operating re-

sults are required? The possibilities here usually are expressed in terms of threshold or minimum desirable levels:

- Rate of market growth
- Payback period (despite its deficiencies it is a reflection of the risk level)
- Minimum sales level (This is a function of fixed costs and scale of operations: the danger is that a product with good long-run potential will be rejected because of modest short-run sales possibilities.)
- Profit levels, cash flow and return on assets. (Each of these financial requirements must be developed in light of the firm's product portfolio.)

SUMMARY

Too often product planning is conducted as though each established product or service, and new product opportunity being sought or evaluated were independent of the other products of the firm. The implication is that corporate performance is the sum of the contributions of individual profit centers or product strategies.[46]

This article emphasizes the need to consider the interdependencies of products as parts of a portfolio described by market share dominance and market growth rate before overall corporate performance can be optimized. Only then can decisions as to resource allocation, growth and financial objectives and specific strategies be developed for established products and the need for new products identified.

There is little doubt that the future will see increasing acceptance of a broad systems approach to overall corporate strategy, in general, and to product planning, in particular. There are already a number of successful practitioners to emulate (who have gained a competitive edge that cannot be ignored).[47] More importantly, as the business environment becomes increasingly resource-constrained there may be no other choice for most firms.

FOOTNOTES

1. "The Squeeze on Product Mix," *Business Week* (5 January 1974), pp. 50-55, "Toward Higher Margins and Less Variety," *Business Week* (14 September 1974), pp. 98-99; E. B. Weiss, "We'll See Fewer New Products in 1975—Culprit Is Shortage of Capital, Resources," *Advertising Age* (2 December 1974); "Corrective Surgery," *Newsweek* (27 January 1975), p. 50; and Jack Springer, "1975: Bad Year for New Products; Good Year for Segmentation," *Advertising Age* (10 February 1975), pp. 30-39.

2. Barry R. Linsky, "Which Way to Move with New Products," *Advertising Age* (22 July 1974), pp. 45-46.

3. George A. Steiner, *Top Management Planning* (London: Macmillan, 1969); H. Igor Ansoff, *Corporate Strategy* (New York: McGraw-Hill, 1965).

4. David T. Kollat, Roger D. Blackwell and James F. Robeson, *Strategic Marketing* (New York: Holt, Rinehart and Winston, 1972), p. 12.

5. This description of the planning process has been adapted from Kollat, et al., *Strategic Marketing*; Louis V. Gerstner, "The Practice of Business: Can Strategic Planning Pay Off?" *Business Horizons* (December 1972); Herschner Cross, "New Directions in Corporate Planning," An address to Operations Research Society of America (Milwaukee, Wisconsin: 10 May 1973).

6. The identification of "strategic business units" is a critical first step in any analysis of corporate strategy. Various definitions have been used. Their flavor is captured by the following guidelines for defining a business: (1) no more than 60 percent of the expenses should represent arbitrary allocations of joint costs, (2) no more than 60 percent of the sales should be made to a vertically integrated (downstream) subsidiary and (3) the served market should be homogeneous; i.e., segments are treated as distinct if they represent markedly different shares, competitors and growth rates.

7. E. Eugene Carter and Kalman J. Cohen, "Portfolio Aspects of Strategic Planning," *Journal of Business Policy*, 2 (1972), pp. 8-30.

8. C. H. Springer, "Strategic Managment in General Electric," *Operations Research* (November-December 1973), pp. 1177-1182.

9. Bernard Catry and Michel Chevalier, "Market Share Strategy and the Product Life Cycle," *Journal of Marketing*, 38 (October 1974), pp. 29-34.

10. Peter F. Drucker, *Management: Tasks, Responsibilities, Practices* (New York: Harper and Row, 1973), p. 106.

11. Sidney Schoeffler, Robert D. Buzzell and Donald F. Heany, "Impact of Strategic Planning on Profit Performance," *Harvard Business Review* (March-April 1974), pp. 137-145.

12. Robert D. Buzzell, Bradley T. Gale and Ralph G. M. Sultan, "Market Share, Profitability and Business Strategy," unpublished working paper, (Marketing Science Institute, August 1974).

13. For more extended treatments and a variety of examples, see Patrick Conley, "Experience Curves as a Planning Tool," *IEEE Transactions* (June 1970; *Perspectives on Experience* (Boston: Boston Consulting Group, 1970); and "Selling Business a Theory of Economics," *Business Week* (8 September 1974).

14. "An example of this situation was DuPont's production of cyclohexane. DuPont was the first producer of the product but the manufacture of cyclohexane is so integrated with the operations of an oil refinery that oil refiners have an inherent cost advantage over companies, such as DuPont, without an oil refinery." Robert B. Stobaugh and Philip L. Townsend, "Price Forecasting and Strategic Planning: The Case of Petrochemicals," *Journal of Marketing Research*, 12 (February 1975), pp. 19-29.

15. Theodore Levitt, "Exploit the Product Life Cycle," *Harvard Business Review* (November-December 1965), pp. 81-94.

16. Harry W. McMahan, "Like Sinatra, Old Products Can, Too, Get a New Lease on Life," *Advertising Age* (25 November 1974), p. 32.

17. Harry T. Moran, "Why New Products Fail," *Journal of Advertising Research* (April 1973).

18. See Douglas Needham, *Economic Analysis and Industrial Structure* (New York: Holt, Rinehart and Winston); Sanford Rose, "Bigness Is a Numbers Game," *Fortune* (November 1969).

19. Buzzell, Gale and Sultan, "Market Share, Profitability."

20. An extreme example is Unilever in the UK with 20 detergent brands all sharing joint costs to some degree.

21. William J. Abernathy and Kenneth Wayne, "Limit of the Learning Curve," *Harvard Business Review*, 52 (September-October 1974), pp. 109-119.

22. Aubrey Wilson, "Industrial Marketing Research in Britain," *Journal of Marketing Research*, 6 (February 1969), pp. 15-28.

23. John C. Chambers, Satinder K. Mullick and Donald D. Smith, *An Executives' Guide to Forecasting* (New York: John Wiley and Sons, 1974); Frank M. Bass, "A New Product Growth Model for Consumer Durables," *Management Science*, 15 (January 1969), pp. 215-227.

24. Of course the cash flow pattern also may be altered by changing debt and/or dividend policies. (For most companies, the likelihood of new equity funding is limited). Limits on growth are imposed when the additional business ventures to be supported have too high a business risk for the potential reward and/or the increase in debt has too high a (financial) risk for the potential rewards.

25. Among the publications of the Boston Consulting Group that describe the portfolio are: Perspectives on Experience (1970) and the following pamphlets authored by Bruce D. Henderson in the general perspectives series; "The Product Portfolio" (1970); "The Experience Curve Reviewed: The Growth Share Matrix or the Product Portfolio" (1973); and "Cash Traps" (1972).

26. A similar matrix reportedly is used by the Mead Corporation; see John Thackray, "The Mod Matrix of Mead," *Management Today* (January 1972), pp. 50-53, 112. This application has been criticized on the grounds of oversimplification, narrow applicability and the unwarranted emphasis on investment versus new investment. Indeed the growth-share matrix is regarded by Thackray as primarily a device for achieving social control.

27. William E. Cox, Jr., "Product Portfolio Strategy: An Analysis of the Boston Consulting Group Approach to Marketing Strategies," *Proceedings of the American Marketing Association*, 1974.

28. It is also typical that the weighted ratio of average market share versus the largest competitor is greater than 1.0. This reflects the contribution of the cash cows to both sales and profits. It also accounts for the familiar pattern whereby 20 percent of the products account for 80 percent of the dollar margin (a phenomena generally described as Pareto's Law).

29. The Boston Consulting Group defines such products as cash traps when the required reinvestment, including increased working capital, exceeds

reported profit plus increase in permanent debt capacity: Bruce D. Henderson, "Cash Traps," *Perspectives*, Number 102 (Boston Consulting Group, 1972).

30. The label may be meaningless if the product is part of a product line, an integral component of a system or where most of the sales are internal.

31. It should be noted that full line/full service competitors may be vulnerable to this strategy if there are customer segments which do not need all the services, etc. Thus, Digital Equipment Corp. has prospered in competition with IBM by simply selling basic hardware and depending on others to do the applications programming. By contrast, IBM provides, for a price, a great deal of service backup and software for customers who are not self-sufficient. "A Minicomputer Tempest," *Business Week*, (27 January 1975), pp. 79-80.

32. Dimensions such as product and pricing policy, geographic and distributor strength, delivery patterns, penetration by account size and probable reaction to our company initiatives need to be considered. See C. David Fogg, "Planning Gains in Market Share," *Journal of Marketing*, 38 (July 1974), pp. 30-38.

33. This concept is developed by Harper Boyd, "Strategy Concepts" unpublished manuscript, 1974, and is based on B. H. Liddel Hart, *Strategy: The Indirect Approach* (London: Faber and Faber, 1951).

34. Seymour Tilles, "How to Evaluate Corporate Strategy," *Harvard Business Review*, 41 (July-August 1963).

35. William E. Fruhan, "Pyrrhic Victories in Fights for Market Share," *Harvard Business Review*, 50 (September-October 1972).

36. "Is John Sherman's Antitrust Obsolete?" *Business Week* (23 March 1974).

37. Stephen Dietz, "Get More Out of Your Brand Management," *Harvard Business Review* (July-August 1973).

38. C. Merle Crawford, "Strategies for New Product Development: Guidelines for a Critical Company Problem," *Business Horizons* (December 1972), pp. 49-58.

39. H. Igor Ansoff, *Corporate Strategy*.

40. Kenneth Simmonds, "Removing the Chains from Product Policy," *Journal of Management Studies* (February 1968).

41. This strategy matrix was influenced strongly by the work of David T. Kollat, Roger D. Blackwell and James F. Robeson, *Strategic Marketing* (New York: Holt, Rinehart and Winston, 1972), pp. 21-23 which, in turn, was adapted from Samuel C. Johnson and Conrad Jones, "How to Organize for New Products," *Harvard Business Review*, 35 (May-June 1957), pp. 49-62.

42. According to the experience of A. T. Kearney, Inc., the chances of success are a direct function of how far from home the new venture is aimed. Specifically, the likelihood of success for an improved product into the present market is assessed as 0.75, declines to 0.50 for a new product with unrelated technology into the present market and to 0.25 for an existing product into a new market. The odds of success for external diversification are as low as 0.05. These numbers are mainly provocative because of the difficulties of defining what constitutes a failure (is it a product that failed in test or after national introduction, for example). See "Analyzing New Product Risk," *Marketing for Sales Executives* (The Research Institute of America, January 1974).

43. H. Igor Ansoff and John Steward, "Strategies for a Technology-Based Business," *Harvard Business Review*, 45 (November-December 1967), pp. 71-83.

44. Kollat, Blackwell and Robeson, *Strategic Marketing*, p. 24.

45. Seymour Tilles, "Making Strategy Explicit," in H. Igor Ansoff (ed.) *Business Strategy* (London: Penguin Books, 1969), p. 203.

46. Bruce D. Henderson, "Intuitive Strategy," *Perspectives*, No. 96 (The Boston Consulting Group, 1972).

47. See "Selling Business a Theory of Economics," *Business Week* (8 September 1973), "G. E.'s New Strategy for Faster Growth," *Business Week* (8 July 1972), "First Quarter and Stockholders Meeting Report (Texas Instruments, Inc., 8 April 1973); "The Winning Strategy at Sperry Rand," *Business Week* (24 February 1973), "How American Standard Cured Its Conglomeritis," *Business Week* (28 September 1974); "G. E. Revamps Strategy: Growth through Efficiency," *Advertising Age* (3 June 1974).

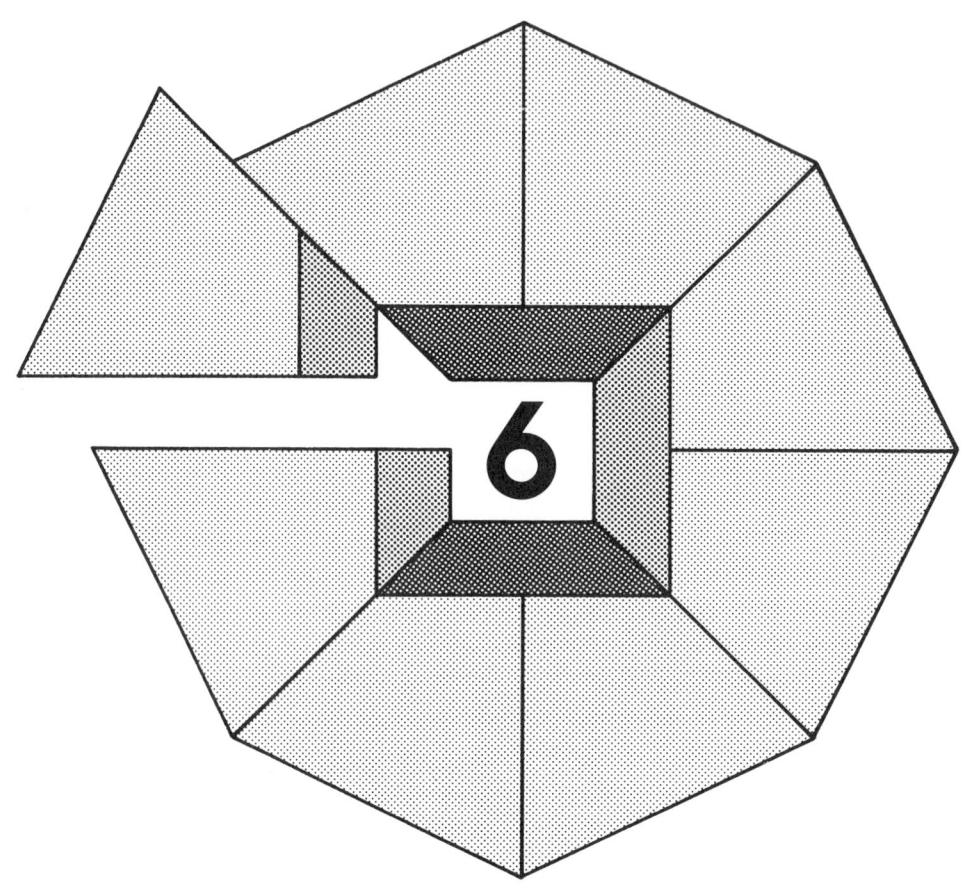

PRODUCTION/OPERATIONS
a multifunctional view

This chapter views the production/operations area from the perspective of top or general management. Therefore it focuses on the production/operations decision variables that depend heavily on inputs from other functional areas of the firm such as marketing and finance. This emphasis on interdependency is in keeping with the important coordinative aspect of top management and is consistent with the focus of a policy course.

"Production/operations" is a relatively new term associated with the expanded application of the principles and techniques traditionally associated with the functional area of production. Production/operations has broadened the scope of production from primarily manufacturing situations to any organized undertaking—private or public, profit or nonprofit. This function involves the transformation of a set of inputs to predetermined outputs in accordance with the objectives of the organization. Table 6-1 gives some examples of the inputs, transformations, and outputs that occur in various types of organizations. Production/operations management encompasses the design, implementation, operation, and control of systems made up of workers, materials, capital equipment, information, and money to accomplish some set of objectives.

Because the primary goals of this chapter are to identify and describe how inputs from the other functional areas may be determinants in production/operations decisions, a preliminary overview of such inputs is desirable. The following list is not exhaustive, and not all of these factors are used in the following discussion, but they should aid the student when he or she must decide on the determinants of production/operations decisions in the particular situation being analyzed.

Inputs from marketing include:
1. Size of potential market.
2. Volume of production to meet anticipated market needs.

Table 6-1 Inputs, transformations, and outputs for various types of organizations

System	Inputs	Transformation Process	Output
Factory	Raw materials and supplies	Change shape or form by fabrication and assembly	Completed product
Hospital	Patients	Health care (examinations, tests, operations, etc.)	Discharged patient
Department store	Customers	Fill customers' need, receive payment	Customers with purchase, less cash
College or university	High school graduates	Impart knowledge and skills	Educated individual

3. Desired finished goods inventory.
4. Pertinent data on sales orders, such as quantity, location, and timing.
5. New products or processes.
6. Customer quality requirements.
7. Packaging needs.
8. Customer feedback on products.
9. Special characteristics to be stressed in marketing program.

Inputs from finance include:
1. Budgetary information (allocations).
2. Investment analysis (current information about constraints and advice).
3. Provision of money for improvements.
4. Provision of information covering general condition of firm (accounting).

The following production/operations decision areas (C_3 decision variables) are described in this chapter along with their determinants:

1. Plant location and capacity = f (long-range forecast of the size and location of the market or supply of inputs, capital structure, environmental conditions, state of existing operations and logistics system, production technology, C_1 and C_2 variables).
2. Facilities layout = f (medium- and long-range forecast of demand and stability of product line, production technology, physical facilities constraints, safety considerations, C_1 and C_2 variables).
3. Planning of aggregate output = f (short-range forecast of demand, finished goods inventory levels, cash flow, employment policy, plant capacity, state of production/operations system at the time of the decision, C_1 and C_2 variables).
4. Raw materials and work-in-process inventory levels = f (forecast of demand, cash flow, supplier reliability, C_1 and C_2 variables).
5. Process planning and job design = f (demand forecasts, product engineering, production technology, labor force, design stability, C_1 and C_2 variables).

TYPES OF PRODUCTION/OPERATIONS SYSTEMS

The determinants of some of the decision variables described next are influenced by the type of production/operations system being examined. Two basic production/operations systems exist—continuous and intermittent. These classifications represent the ends of a continuum that is based on the flow of materials or services through a system. In a continuous production/operations system, a predetermined sequence of operations is followed that is relatively static over a period of time. A primary example of this is an assembly line such as those used in the automobile industry. On the other hand, in an intermittent flow system, each order (input) may require that a different set of operations be performed—as in a manufacturing job shop or in a hospital. Table 6-2 illustrates some general distinctions between these two basic types of systems.

The following discussion deals with the ways in which each type of system can influence the determinants of a production/operations decision. By knowing the characteristics of the two basic types, the student can get an idea of where the particular system being analyzed falls on the continuum. The student should then be in a position to decide how the set of decision determinants must be altered to accommodate the system under study.

PRODUCTION/OPERATIONS DECISION VARIABLES

This section describes each C_3 production/operations decision variable and tells how each component in its set of determinants can influence that decision variable.

Plant Location and Capacity

This decision involves location and determination of the size of an operating facility or facilities so that the objectives of the organization are optimized. Although it is usually an infrequent decision, it is vitally important because the organization probably will have to operate in the selected environment for some time in the future. It is also a dynamic decision because what seems to be a good location at one point in time may not be one later because of changes that occur.

From an economic standpoint, the decision may be based on an objective such as maximizing long-run return on investment. (Long-run return on investment $(R) = (SR - TC)/TA$ where SR = long-run sales revenue, TC = long-run total cost, and TA = total assets employed.) This incorporates many of the quantifiable factors but ignores many intangible costs and benefits that could override an economic analysis. Ultimately, the selected objectives for this decision would depend on factors such as management

Table 6-2 Basic characteristics of continuous and intermittent systems

Basic Characteristics	Types of Production Operations System	
	Continuous	Intermittent
Unit cost of product or service	Lower	Higher
Work-in-process inventories	Smaller	Larger
Lead time	Shorter	Longer
Investment	Higher	Lower
Type of facilities	Special purpose	General purpose
Material handling equipment	Fixed path	Variable path
Scheduling and control efforts	Less	Greater
Product line	Standardized	Flexible
Training efforts	Less	Greater

values and the particulars of the situation being analyzed. For example, economic analysis may indicate the best location to be near a small town but, because of the type of industry involved, the ire of the townspeople is aroused. Thus management may decide that this intangible factor surpasses the economic advantages and will locate elsewhere.

Some typical reasons why the decision on plant location may arise are:

1. New venture or business.
2. Change in either the level or geographic location of key resources.
3. Costs such as raw materials, services, and labor may increase because of price or depletion of that resource.
4. Opportunity cost of an existing site.
5. Legal constraints such as regulation of pollution.
6. Community or union relations.
7. Fire or other catastrophe.
8. Prestige.

Some alternatives available when making this decision include:

1. Adding capacity at present location or subcontracting.
2. Adding needed capacity at one or more new locations.
3. Selling off the plant at existing location(s) and relocating all needed capacity at one or more new locations.
4. Not expanding and allowing growth to go to competitors.

Determinants. As mentioned previously, the determinants of this decision are long-range forecasts of the size and location of the market, capital structure, environmental conditions, state of existing production/operations and logistics system, production technology, and C_1 and C_2 variables. The nature of the influence exerted by each of these determinants is now discussed.

A long-range forecast[1] of the size and location of the market is necessary because of the magnitude of both one-time and continuing costs dictated by the decision about location. If the forecast or planning horizon is too short, suboptimization occurs because most organizations cannot afford to react to short-term fluctuations in the location and size of the market or supply of inputs by continually changing the size or location of their facilities.

For organizations that are ultimate consumer- or service-oriented (restaurants, banks, department stores, theaters, etc.), location greatly affects revenue; consequently, the location decision takes on more of a marketing flavor. For other firms (warehouses, processors and manufacturers, etc.),

---

[1]The time span covered by a long-range forecast is dependent on the type of industry. For instance, a short-range forecast in the lumber industry may be 2 to 4 years; however, this would be considered a long-range forecast in some segments of the electronics industry.

location does not greatly influence revenue. Therefore initial and operating costs and total assets employed play an important role in this decision. For instance, location of the production facility relative to the market does affect transportation costs and possibly service level. Depending on the product and the industry, these costs could be critical competitive factors. Similar arguments also could be made for the supply side of the organization.

An example of a change in location because of supply problems is the coal industry. In the eastern United States, recoverable coal supplies contain too much sulfur to meet the standards set by the federal Clean Air Act, which took effect in July 1975. In the western United States, the sulfur content of the coal is lower, and it is easier for coal companies to acquire long-term leases. These and other reasons related to the supply of coal have forced the industry to move west.

> The debate is more than academic, for the industry is already trekking West, like an eager prospector in Gold Rush days. Western coal, most of it strip-mined, now accounts for more than 10% of the 600-million tons of coal the U.S. produces annually, up from 5% in 1966. In Wyoming, for instance, coal production has jumped from three-million tons in 1968 to 14-million tons last year and may reach 40-million tons by 1980 and 100-million tons by 2000. Meanwhile, production in West Virginia has fallen from 145-million tons in 1968 to 115-million tons last year and may drop further. In all, says a study made by the Atomic Energy commission, Western stripmined coal will provide 55% of the 1.8 billion tons of coal produced in the U.S. by 1985.[2]

The size or capacity decision could be affected by the flexibility the organization wants and can afford. A company may feel that it would be more economical to build a plant with a capacity 25% greater than the long-range forecast instead of having to expand at a later date. Inflationary building costs could be the rationale for such a decision. Of course, the company must support this idle space for some time and face the risk of the idle capacity never being needed.

In 1978 AMAX, Inc., a U.S. mining company, and Mitsui Co., a Japanese trading company, took a huge gamble. They invested $1 billion to make their fledgling aluminum producer, Alumax, Inc., a pacesetter in the industry. Alumax added capacity at a time when competitors were holding back.

> By Alumax's calculations, U.S. demand for aluminum will exceed domestic primary capacity this year by some 400,000 tons, and the gap could widen to nearly 1 million tons in four years. To some extent, the apparent shortage can be met by increased imports, intensified recycling efforts, and changes in the mix of aluminum end products. Still, most aluminum producers foresee an accelerating need for additional primary production. "Unless the industry starts adding capacity

---

[2]"The Coal Industry's Controversial Move West," *Business Week*, May 11, 1974, p. 134.

very soon," says John E. Blomquist, executive vice-president of Reynolds Metals Co., "there is no question that the metal will be in tight supply." But Reynolds is not adding any capacity now because profits are not yet high enough.

The situation is even worse in Japan. Because the islands are densely populated, land is at a premium. The cost of the 6,000 acres that Alumax will use for its South Carolina plant could be 10 times as high if the facility were in Japan. Moreover, pollution controls are even more stringent in Japan than they are in the U.S. And without any basic resources in fuel, Japan's generating costs for the energy-intensive aluminum business are staggering. As a result, Japan's shortfall in aluminum by 1980 could be as high as 800,000 tons, according to U.S. Bureau of Mines estimates.[3]

The existing and desired capital structure of the organization is the second determinant. In the case of expansion, will the capital structure support an increase in this type of asset? The question is especially pertinent if the firm is seeking external funds to finance this effort. As capacity is increased, there is usually an increase in working capital requirements because items such as inventories (i.e., raw material, work in process, transit, and finished goods) and accounts receivable increase along with the obvious investment in the additional facilities, such as bricks, mortar, and equipment.

A variety of environmental conditions directly or indirectly affect the location and capacity decision. In many cases, these circumstances take precedence over economic factors. The availability, wage rate, and productivity of the labor supply can directly influence costs. Labor attitudes and traditions also can affect costs indirectly. This would be particularly true for a foreign location. Often the attractiveness of a low hourly wage in a foreign country is greatly diminished when lower productivity is considered.

The textile industry was originally located in the southeastern United States to take advantage of the raw material and labor supply. The labor picture has now changed, as illustrated by the predicament in which Burlington Industries found itself:

Like other textile makers, Burlington is especially troubled by increased competition for labor from higher-wage industries in its primary operating area in the Southeast. Textile companies pay an average $3 an hour, compared with $4 for all manufacturing. Charles A. McLendon, a Burlington executive vice-president, cites an example in Fayetteville, N.C. There, he says, Burlington was once the major employer, but it now competes for workers with Dupont, Rohm & Haas, and Black & Decker.

"We've got a tough labor problem," Chairman Myers concedes. In some communities where Burlington has mills, the unemployment rate is down to 1%, and that, Myers says, is "awfully close to being the unemployables." The pinch is particularly painful in the Piedmont section of Virginia and the Carolinas. "For every worker we've got, we have another job we'd like to fill," says Lewis S.

---

[3]"Alumax Turning Aluminum Capacity Upside Down," *Business Week*, March 6, 1978, pp. 73–74.

Morris, chairman and president of Cone Mills. Worse yet, textile companies are also having trouble keeping their workers. Burlington's turnover rate is about 65% annually, five points better than the industry average. The rate tends to be highest in the lowest-skilled jobs.[4]

Are service facilities such as heat, electricity, water, rail, truck, and air freight available at capacities required and at what rates? The following is an example of how the cost of a primary utility influences the location decision in the fertilizer industry.

Mexican producers are able to undercut U.S. ammonia prices because they pay only 25¢ per thousand cu. ft. (mcf) for the natural gas they use to make their ammonia, U.S. sources say. And for the Russians, there is a "negative value," or no cost at all, for their raw material. By comparison, U.S. producers are paying up to $2.55 per mcf for their natural gas, and prices could double by the early 1980s if Congress decides to release control over interstate natural gas prices, as now expected.

The differences in the relative economics already are staggering. In California, ammonia now lists for $161.50 a ton, says James H. Lindley, president of Valley Nitrogen Producers Inc., a cooperative of 5,000 California growers that has closed two of its four ammonia plants there despite inherent tax advantages to its members from keeping them open. It now takes $102 worth of natural gas and $30 worth of power to produce that ton of ammonia, according to Lindley. By comparison, ammonia entering the U.S. from Mexico is selling for $83.50 a ton.[5]

Recreation facilities, housing, schools and churches, climate, and natural phenomena are examples of social and cultural factors to be considered. The political environment in terms of tax rates, zoning, and traditional relationships with business is another environmental determinant.

Xerox Corporation recently acquired a 104-acre site in Greenwich, Connecticut, for its corporate headquarters. Greenwich is an affluent community located near New York City. The residents were outraged at the prospect of having a corporation headquarters located in their community and fought zoning changes.[6] Another example where the environment could influence the location decision is the new state constitution passed by Louisiana.

Last month, a new constitution was adopted aimed at straightening out some of the property tax problems. Far from doing so, it has left many businessmen uncertain and fearful of having to pay heavier taxes than before. "There isn't any question that the new constitution is more antibusiness in attitude than the present one, which is already substantially antibusiness," says Edward Steimel, executive director of the non-profit Public Affairs Research Council in Baton Rouge.

---

[4]"Giant Burlington Faces Trying Time for Textiles," *Business Week*, March 2, 1974, p. 49.
[5]"The Carnage Imports Are Bringing to Fertilizer," *Business Week*, October 9, 1978, p. 108.
[6]"The Battle of Greenwich," *Newsweek*, June 5, 1972, pp. 80–81.

> "It's certainly going to hurt us in attracting additional firms into Louisiana" says John G. Philips, Chairman of Louisiana Land & Exploration Co., a $60-million oil and gas producer with headquarters in New Orleans.[7]

Many states and cities use their tax structure or zoning policies to entice industry to locate there. Countries also compete in this market; look at Mexico, for example.

> The government aims both to spur the growth of the local steel and auto components industries and to use Mexico's cheap and abundant labor supply to enable the carmakers to export. Besides DINA'S $165 million worth of investments with foreign joint-venture partners, the enticements include import-duty exemptions on some components; fiscal incentives of up to 25% of income taxes to companies investing in production of diesel engines, trucks, and buses; and up to 20% grants for investments in plants that make auto parts. But the biggest carrot of all is simply Mexico's swelling domestic market and its export potential.[8]

The location and capacity of the existing facilities are important inputs to this decision because a new or expanded facility will affect the manner in which the outputs are obtained. This reallocation could increase or decrease costs and, therefore, influence the decision. A similar argument holds for the logistics system. Presumably, the logistics system is designed around the present set of facilities. When new or expanded facilities are placed in the system, costs or customer service may be affected.

The age and condition of the existing production/operations system is another influence on the location/capacity decision. The technological age of the system should be considered along with the chronological age. Even though processes and equipment are relatively young in years, advances in product or production technology could render them obsolete and influence the capacity decision in particular. National Can considered this factor in the implementation of their strategy.

> Building new, efficient facilities and improving old ones are the key elements in National Can's design. Considine will soon unroll the blueprints for a pair of new plants that will make the lighter cheaper two-piece can, a product introduced in the 1960s that now accounts for three-fourths of the market for beer and soft-drink cans. The sites for these operations will almost certainly be in the Sunbelt states where National Can has clustered its most recent expansion projects. When completed in 1980, these two plants will boost the company's canmaking capacity by 10% on top of a 15% expansion this year.
>
> Meanwhile, some of National Can's existing packaging plants will receive smaller, productivity-lifting investments, and the company's rapidly growing for-

---

[7] "The Louisiana Tax Swamp," *Business Week*, May 25, 1974, p. 85.
[8] "Auto Makers Flock to Surging Market," *Business Week*, July 2, 1979, p. 33.

eign business is marked for expansion funding. In all, National Can's capital budget will increase 12% this year to $55 million.[9]

In some cases, the production of the product or service may require special technology or services that are only available in certain geographical areas. An illustration of this determinant can be found in the aluminum industry.

> Aluminum's energy bill now accounts for 25% of production costs, and the tab is rising fast. "The cost of energy, even nuclear energy, for a new smelter is now about eights mills per kilowatt hour," says James S. Apostolina, president of Ormet Corp., the country's fifth largest aluminum producer. That is about four times the price of hydroelectric power in the Pacific Northwest, around which much of the country's aluminum industry is built. And availability of the huge quantities of new power is even more of a problem.[10]

New technological developments in the aluminum industry could alter the influence power availability has on their location decision. The Alcoa Smelting Process is a new process developed by the Aluminum Company of America that will require 30% less energy than Alcoa's newest and most efficient electrolytic cells.[11]

Another example is the National Cash Register (NCR) response to a basic technological change in its product line that led to a change in its production technology which, in turn, led to a change in location.

> NCR's biggest cost saving—and most traumatic change—has been in manufacturing. The switch to electronic production was well under way when Anderson arrived. Some 80 percent of NCR production had been in Dayton, where the average wage rate was $4.95 an hour. The United Automobile Workers had organized NCR and was pushing for equality with Detroit auto plant pay scales.
>
> Now only 30 percent of NCR's production is in Dayton, and wage rates at other plants range from $2.50 to $3. Both Oelman and Anderson stress that moving production out of Dayton was not a reaction to the UAW or the long 1971 strike by NCR workers. Rather, it was dictated by the transition from metalworking to electronic production, because large numbers of skilled machinists were replaced by lower-paid electronics assemblers.[12]

The soda ash industry provides still another example.

> Few industries can match the extent of the changes that have swept through the soda ash business in the past few years. As recently as 1974, there were six giant

---

[9]"National Can: Getting Back to the Business It Knows Best," *Business Week*, April 30, 1979, p. 92.
[10]"Aluminum Prosperity is Riddled with Troubles," *Business Week*, September 1, 1973, p. 54.
[11]"A Revolutionary Alcoa Process," *Business Week*, January 20, 1973, p. 92.
[12]"The Rebuilding Job at National Cash Register," *Business Week*, May 26, 1973, p. 86.

Solvay-process facilities producing 4 million tons of soda ash annually in the U.S. Today, only one is still operating—a 900,000-ton unit in Syracuse, N.Y., owned by Allied Chemical Corp.

The other plants have all been shut down because their owners either found them too costly to operate or could not make them meet pollution standards. Yet users of soda ash in both the glass and chemical industries, whose demands have been increasing at a rate of almost 5% per year, have barely been inconvenienced. Indeed, the U.S. may soon become a leading world supplier of soda ash. The reason: In tandem with their shutdown of synthetic manufacturing units, U.S. soda ash makers have been opening plants in the West that can make the chemical more cheaply from a natural source—trona....

The inherent economies of trona are such that Allied's Syracuse plant may have only another 5 or 10 years to go. And a similar fate may be in store for many European and Japanese plants that are not much younger than the old Solvay plants in the U.S. that have been closed.[13]

The situation faced by many companies in the coke industry shows how several of the determinants first described can affect the location/capacity decision.

The task of rebuilding adequate domestic coke-making capacity is awesome. Wilputte Corp., a subsidiary of Salem Corp., and Koppers Co., the nation's leading coke-oven builders, estimate that at least a third of all coke ovens in the U.S. are more than 25 years old and should be overhauled or replaced. "The industry will have to sustain a massive rebuilding effort for the next decade to stay abreast of its needs," predicts Koppers Vice-President Jack D. Rice. But the price tag on construction of a new coke plant with a capacity of about 1 million tons has leaped 40%, to about $180 million, in the last five years, says Koppers marketing manager Joseph A. van Ackeren. The American Iron & Steel Institute figures it could cost $6.4 billion for the coke industry to comply with just one new coke-oven emission standard—that controlling benzene emissions.

Even if the U.S. coke-making industry somehow manages to muster the money, it faces another obstacle to boosting its capacity. Virtually every coke plant today is located in an area where no additional pollutants may be added to the air. "So to add a new facility," explains Philip X. Masciantonio, U.S. Steel's director of environmental control, "You have to shut something down—which means that you end up with no new capacity."

One solution would be to build new plants in undeveloped areas. But at least for now, steelmen scoff at this idea, maintaining that it is economically unfeasible to locate a coke plant far from the steel mill that it is meant to serve.[14]

Facilities Layout

Facilities layout describes the arrangement of departments, machines, storage areas, and so forth, usually within the confines of some physical structure such as a factory, office, or hospital. The objective is to provide the most effective and efficient arrangement of physical facilities that, at the

---

[13]"When Natural is Cheaper Than Synthetic," *Business Week*, April 16, 1979, p. 132.
[14]"A Smoldering Crisis in Coke," *BusinessWeek*, November 20, 1978, p. 78.

same time, will provide adequate flexibility to cope with future changes in product design, processes, levels of sales volume, and product mix.

Similar to the continuum involving continuous and intermittent production/operations systems presented previously, there are two basic types of layouts—product and process. The product layout is an arrangement of work stations that has been set up specially to manufacture a particular product or group of highly similar products (i.e., a continuous system). Before this type of layout is selected, one should consider the following points.

1. The rate and duration of output volume must be large enough and stable enough to justify the time and cost of designing, setting up, and operating a special arrangement.
2. There must be complete prior knowledge of what is to be produced and how.
3. Material being transferred through the layout must be movable.
4. The product should be uniform and the components interchangeable.

By balancing or equalizing the work performed at each station, idle time is minimized—and that is the objective in designing a product layout.

The process or functional layout groups similar operations, equipment, personnel, or material in a common area to facilitate moving the work, to provide increased utilization of workers and equipment, and to provide increased flexibility and control. This type of layout is appropriate for intermittent-flow systems. When a product or service has insufficient volume or stability of design, the process layout is used because one could not economically justify devoting a separate set of facilities to that product or service. Usually, when determining the spatial relationship between these groups, the objective is to minimize material-handling costs.

The decision in an ongoing concern with an established layout usually does not center on determining the basic type of layout to use but on whether the savings and benefits derived from rearranging the existing type of layout can justify the cost of rearrangement.

Determinants. Medium-range[15] as well as long-range forecasts of demand and stability of product line, production technology, physical facilities constraints, safety considerations, and the C_1 (strategic) and C_2 (coordinative) variables are the determinants for this decision variable.

The primary determinant of the type of layout selected is medium- and long-range forecast of the level of demand and the stability of the product or product line. This forecast will give an indication of the degree of flexibility needed in a layout. If the maturity of the product or the competitiveness of the market suggests that the product or product line will change frequently in the future, it would be difficult economically to justify designing and implementing an entirely new layout every time a change occurred. In

---

[15] A medium-range forecast is defined as covering 1 to 3 years in the future.

this case, the layout would be used to estimate the size of inventories (raw materials, work-in-process, and finished goods) necessary; therefore the storage space requirements for these inventories could be provided for in the layout.

Many companies that are forced to use a process layout would like to take advantage of a product layout but cannot because of uncertainty of demand. Rowe Furniture Corporation has attempted to circumvent this problem. Warehouse dealers carry the same furniture as conventional retailers, but their heavier volume allows them to buy and sell more cheaply. Small independent dealers have retaliated by dropping the lines of manufacturers who sell to mass merchandisers.

> Rowe hopes to walk a middle ground. It supplies the warehouse showrooms with the lines they want, but Rowe determines styles, quality, and price ranges. Meantime, Rowe urges the independents to place sizeable orders for furniture well in advance of delivery, which is what the warehouse showrooms do. Big advance orders eliminate uncertainty and last-minute production changes, thus sweetening Rowe's profit margins.[16]

This reduction of uncertainty in production requirements allowed Rowe to alter its plant layout.

> Rowe Furniture is now adding capacity at both its framemaking and assembly facilities in Salem while doubling the capacity of its Poplar Bluffs (Mo.) assembly plant.
>
> Traditionally, upholstered furniture has been manufactured on a so-called roundtable, with five or six craftsmen combining their talents to turn out a single piece. Rowe has gone to an all-out assembly line approach, including such niceties as automatic stapling guns. On the line, each worker performs just one simple task.[17]

Production technology can influence the layout decision in terms of the ease of flexibility of the facilities, the likelihood of new or revised processes, and material handling techniques. The production of some goods requires heavy, relatively stationary facilities while others can use light-weight, general purpose facilities. Obviously, the cost of relocating a piece of heavy equipment such as the hydraulic press or a die casting machine is much greater than moving an engine lathe. In the former case, the layout would remain fairly stable; in the latter case, the arrangement would be flexible.

The probability that the transformation processes could be revised or replaced and, if so, how long before this change would occur also can influence whether a layout revision is justified. We previously discussed a change in the product line that could mean a change in production technology. An-

---

[16] "Rowe Furniture's Strategy for Profits," *Business Week*, November 18, 1972, p. 49.
[17] Ibid., p. 51.

other source of change could be the development of new processes and technology by research and development. Some industries, such as electronics, are characterized by these developments while in other industries, such as steel, the production technology is relatively stable. The essential point is that if the production technology is likely to change in the near future, flexibility is desired in the layout.

The material handling techniques that are available and required for an operations system can be a determinant of the layout decision. The size, weight, or configuration of the product could exclude some material handling techniques. The amount of flexibility desired in the system also could limit the choice of material handling techniques. In either case, the number of layout alternatives is reduced.

The physical constraints of the site, building, and grounds also can dictate or limit the layout alternatives. For example, the location of transportation facilities, such as railway sidings and highways, would determine where the shipping and receiving area should be located. Considerations such as building columns, foundations, noise control, ventilation, pollution, and high bay areas definitely serve as constraints as to where certain departments can be located. By the same token, safety regulations given by federal, state, and local regulations, union contracts, and the firm's insurance company serve as limitations in rearranging layouts. A prime example of federal legislation that influences the layout decision, as well as the next decision variable, is the Occupational Safety and Health Act (OSHA) of 1970.

Process Planning and Job Design

Process planning is the designation of the processes required to produce the product or provide the service and their sequence. This phase of designing a production/operations system is usually performed after what is to be made and how many have been determined. Job design consists of specifying two components—work content and work design. Work content defines what must be accomplished at a work station. Work design indicates what methods, procedures, and work area layouts are to be used to perform that work. A variety of techniques are available to help make both decisions, ranging from relatively simple and inexpensive charting techniques to detailed, costly computer analysis.

Determinants. Determinants for this decision variable include a forecast of both the level of demand and stability of design, product engineering, production technology, labor force, and C_1 and C_2 variables.

A forecast of the level of demand and stability of product design is a critical determinant of what processes and facilities should be selected. If the forecast projects high volume and stable design, the processes and facilities selected would differ from those selected if the forecast projects low volume and unstable design. In the former case, expensive, special-purpose facilities with greater speed and precision could be justified, whereas in the latter case, less expensive general-purpose facilities with flexibility would be better. Break-even analysis can be helpful in determining this changeover or critical volume.

This forecast also would determine the amount of job design effort that can be justified. Use of detailed, relatively expensive techniques such as micro-motion analysis would be advisable only for a product with a forecast of high demand and design stability. In the case of a low-volume product, only inexpensive methods such as charting or the judgment of the first-line supervisor can be justified.

The remaining three determinants—product engineering, production technology, and labor force—will be discussed together. The efforts put forth for process planning and job design will depend on the complexity of the production technology, and the skills possessed by the labor force. Obviously, more effort must be devoted to planning the processes involved in producing semiconductor memory chips, which require 4 weeks and 112 separate steps that must be performed in sequence[18] than for producing paper clips. Presumably, if the labor force the organization is drawing from possesses certain desired skills, the job design task will be easier than if only an unskilled labor force is available.

Here are some examples of how process planning and job design are affected by these three determinants. Automation has been used at Zenith Radio Corporation to hold down assembly costs of color televisions and, at the same time, maintain flexibility of its production facilities.

> Several TV makers who tried to automate their lines failed because of this fast rate of change. "Technology is changing so rapidly that by the time you've built an automated plant, it's obsolete," says George Konkol, senior vice-president and general manager of GTE Sylvania's Entertainment Products Group.[19]

By standardization and an assembly machine called an automatic sequencer, Zenith has overcome these problems.

> Zenith jealously guards the data on the productivity of its new assembly line, but observers figure that the automated machinery cuts by half the total labor involved in building a TV chassis. Output per worker, they estimate, is 20 to 30 times greater than before.[20]

This change in manufacturing processes had an interesting relationship with the marketing function. Previously, Zenith advertising had emphasized such things as "hand-wiring" and "hand craftsmanship," "the extra care that makes the quality difference." With the automated production techniques, a different tactic had to be initiated.

---

[18] G. Bylinsky, "How Intel Won Its Bet on Memory Chips," *Fortune*, November 1973, p. 143.
[19] "Bringing TV Assembly Back to the U.S.," *Business Week*, August 19, 1973, p. 41.
[20] Ibid.

Levi Strauss hopes to use automation to overcome a decrease in the availability of labor in the clothing industry, which has traditionally depended on low-wage labor.

> In the fragmented, low-profit apparel industry, which traditionally depends on low-wage labor, automation is normally considered an expensive burden, rather than a potential blessing. But next month, Levi Strauss & Co., the world's largest manufacturer of trousers, takes the first major step toward fully automating its assembly lines by mating an electro-optical control system to a sewing machine. By 1978, the company predicts that this unit, and other automation innovations will increase its productivity by 50 per cent and help double its sales to $10 billion.
>
> The $1,500 Servo-Sewer is one example of an impressive array that Levi Strauss believes will eventually increase worker productivity at a time when the company faces a decline in the availability of skill labor.[21]

Cluett Peabody, maker of Arrow and other shirt lines, uses automation as a cornerstone of its strategy.

> Reliance on technology has been a Cluett tradition, ever since the company developed its Sanforized process in the early 1930's to control shrinkage of cotton shirts. Since then, the company has not only purchased new machinery developed by others but, through its research department, has pioneered the development of automatic trimmers, stackers, pocket attachment machines, and collar-sewing machines. Cluett in 1974 even purchased a small machinery company to produce such equipment, and this year it is spending heavily to expand the application of its so-called Cluepicker, a device that picks up a single ply of fabric and positions it for sewing, a breakthrough the company insists is vital to automating apparel.
>
> In the last two years, the company has also spent about $4 million on Gerber cutters, which it now uses in 80% of it's Arrow shirt production. Such devotion to mechanization has helped Cluett reduce the time involved in making a shirt from 20 minutes in the 1930's to 12 minutes today. "If we have a single goal, it's keeping our quality but automating our manufacturing to reduce labor content so that we can continue to compete as a domestic manufacturer," declares Henry H. Henly Jr., president and chief executive at Cluett.[22]

Technological improvements have allowed Japan's fourth largest steelmaker to compete in foreign markets. These advances have also affected the production process.

> Typical of the cost-cutting benefits of technological sophistication are the new methods being employed at Kawasaki's big Mizushima Works. The Mizushima facility boasts some of the most sophisticated computerized and automated mills in Japan. For example, the work force needed to run one of its hot rolling mills

---

[21] "Levi Strauss Legs It Toward Automation," *Business Week*, July 21, 1973, p. 62.
[22] "Apparel's Last Stand," *Business Week*, May 14, 1979, p. 63.

numbers just 850, compared with the 2,000 employees required at conventional facilities of similar size in the U.S.[23]

Advances in production technology have also changed the way diesel engines are produced.

"The volume we expect to reach in engine production allows us to use high-technology machining systems and automatic transfer lines to reduce unit costs and guarantee better quality," says President Robert E. Gilmore.
At its newest plants in Mossville, Ill., for example, Caterpillar has fitted its drilling, boring, and grinding machines with adaptive control devices that automatically compensate for tool wear in order to maintain the dimensions of machined parts and with measuring devices that signal when a machined part does not meet specifications. Elsewhere at the same complex, computers keep track of work in process and direct the flow of components from six tiers of storage racks to assembly lines so that the parts arrive at the precise moment they are needed. And at the company's new foundry in Mapleton, Ill., robots prepare sand molds and do precise machining operations as well.[24]

Even in the service industries, technology has influenced process planning. MetPath, Inc. uses the industry's largest clinical testing laboratory to analyze blood and tissue samples. Their strategy is to take advantage of economics of scale by consolidating facilities. MetPath is growing at three times the industry's growth rate. Technology has helped them to maintain the pace.

MetPath is making such gains because its highly automated central lab has helped it undercut the prices of competitors, while its network of local collection and delivery offices allows it to deliver its service as fast as most local labs. The company opened its first major automated lab in 1970 in Hackensack, N. J., financing it with its first public offering of stock. Last July, that lab was replaced with what is easily the industry's largest. Built at a total cost of $25 million in Teterboro, N. J., the new facility contains $11 million worth of testing equipment, roughly 20 times the amount of equipment used by the average local testing lab, and it can analyze up to 30,000 samples a day, compared with about 500 a day for most local labs.[25]

Planning of Aggregate Output

The decisions made here include the aggregate or total work force, aggregate production level, and the aggregate inventory level over a planning horizon or future time periods. The problem arises when an organization faces

---

[23]"Kawasaki Steel: Using Technology as a Tool to Bolster Exports," *Business Week*, January 29, 1979, p. 120.
[24]"A Revved-Up Market for Diesel Engine Makers," *Business Week*, February 5, 1979, p. 77.
[25]"MetPath: Price-Cutting With a Super-Lab Creates New Growth," *Business Week*, February 26, 1979, p. 132.

seasonal or fluctuating demands. The organization has many alternatives available to it to meet this type of demand: overtime, idle time, hire or fire workers, carry inventory, incur back orders, or subcontract are typical options available. However, with the selection of any of these alternatives, penalty costs are incurred. The objective of aggregate output planning is to examine what trade-offs are available between these costs along with the forecast of demand and to make a decision that will minimize, or at least reduce, the sum of these penalty costs over the planning horizon. When facing a seasonal increase in demand, a typical trade-off might involve (1) working the existing force overtime and paying a 50% direct labor premium, (2) hiring additional personnel and paying to train them, (3) building inventory in the previous slow or slack period and paying inventory carrying charges, (4) incurring back orders or lost sales and their associated costs.

This decision area is also known as "production smoothing" because the decision maker can look ahead through the use of a forecast and, by anticipating the fluctuations in demand, make decisions in the present that will lead to a "smooth" production plan. Many techniques are available to aid the manager in this decision, from simple graphic representations to highly complex, mathematically optimal algorithms.

Determinants. As listed in the introduction to this chapter, the determinants for this decision variable are a short-range forecast of demand, finished goods inventory levels, cash flow, employment policy, plant capacity, state of production/operations system at the time of the decision, and C_1 and C_2 variables.

The two inputs from the marketing sector include a short-range forecast of demand and desired finished goods inventory levels. The short-range forecast usually covers the next year or the length of a seasonal cycle and is the primary input to this decision. The finished goods inventory level is the minimum level that the aggregate plan is constrained to maintain.

From a financial standpoint, flow of cash to implement the plan should be analyzed. If cash needs are critical in other areas of the organization, cash flow considerations could be a constraint. These might include payroll and inventory costs.

The two additional constraints on the plan include the organization's employment policy and the capacity of its facilities. If the company has an explicit or implicit policy of maintaining a stable work force, the alternative of changing its size is limited. This means that fluctuations in demand must be absorbed by some other means, such as inventory or overtime. A similar argument can be made for customer service policy. The capacity constraint is obvious and, if it is continually encountered, this points out a capacity problem.

A final determinant of this decision is the state or status of the production/operations system with regard to inventory, work force, and production level at the time the decision is made. The state of the system can increase or decrease the alternatives a decision maker has available. For example, if there is a large inventory as opposed to little or none, the decision maker's alternatives are increased.

The natural gas industry is faced with uneven demand. In the winter months, residential and commercial users increase the aggregate demand significantly. Industrial customers helped in the past to smooth this demand by switching to oil purchased on the spot market when the gas supplies were diverted to the residential and commercial customers. In recent years gas companies have lost this balancing factor because many of these industrial customers have shifted to year-round fuel oil suppliers. The gas companies are faced with coping with their aggregate planning problem in other ways.

> With demand for gas becoming increasingly unbalanced, the gas industry has been forced to add 2 trillion cu. ft. of underground gas storage since 1972, at a cost of more than $2 billion. "The cost of storage is a topic we yet have to face as an industry," says Dominic J. Monetta, director of planning at the Gas Research Institute in Chicago.
>
> In addition to storage, a utility that serves a largely residential load also requires facilities such as LNG plants, to liquefy gas in the summer, or SNG plants, which manufacture synthetic gas from petroleum liquids such as naphtha. Both are extremely expensive investments.[26]

Raw Materials and Work-in-Process Inventory Levels

The production/operations function is usually responsible for obtaining raw materials and maintaining them at sufficient levels to insure the smooth operation of the system. This also is true of work-in-process inventories. Inventories serve the primary purpose of decoupling stages of operations from each other. If inventories cost nothing, the inventory level decision would be easy, but this is not the case. Production/operations stands in the middle, with the sales people on one side demanding immediate deliveries or a wide variety of products and models and the finance people on the other side telling production/operations not to tie up financial resources in inventories. This decision variable involves the trade-off that must be made.

Determinants. The determinants of this decision variable include forecast of demand, cash flow, supplier reliability, and C_1 and C_2 variables.

The forecast of demand (in terms of a marketing forecast of a promised delivery) must be converted to raw materials, subassembly and assembly requirements. Adjustments must be made for time lags such as delivery times of materials and processing time in the production/operations system. What is ordered today could be used for finished goods to be delivered 4 to 6 months from now. An accurate forecast of demand is essential.

Because deviation from a forecast is inevitable, the producton/operations manager could be tempted to provide a "cushion" against these uncertainties by ordering a little extra and carrying more inventory. Unfortunately, the inventory must be paid for, either by paying the vendor for the raw materials or by paying wages to transform these raw materials, and this creates

---

[26]"The Gloom Behind the Natural-Gas 'Bubble'," *Business Week*, April 23, 1979, pp. 76, 78.

a drain on the cash flow. Furthermore, the finance function does not like to see the organization's money tied up in inventories that are earning little, if any, return. For this reason, cash flow considerations affect inventory levels.

A factor that affects cash flow is the cost of money. In late 1978 an economic recession was forecast during 1979. Here are some typical reactions.

> As the cost of money skyrockets and fears of recession next year grow more widespread, such corporations as Monogram Industries, Bendix, and General Telephone & Electronics are tightening the screws on inventories—urging managers to cut back and to hold off on adding more. The results of increased restraint show up in a survey made public on Nov. 29 by the 23,000-member National Association of Purchasing Management: Inventory liquidation occurred in November for the first time this year (except March, for which the NAPM blames bad weather). Further, E. F. Andrews, chairman of NAPM's business survey committee and vice-president of materials for Allegheny Ludlum Industries Inc., predicts that stocks in December will be still lower.
>
> "With the prime rate effectively at 14%—including 20% compensating balances—any dollar you tie up in inventory is a damn costly dollar," gripes Martin Stone, chairman of Monogram, a maker of electrical materials, fasteners, and sanitation equipment. A couple of months ago, Stone fired off a memo to division managers telling them that he fears a recession in 1979 and urging them to trim inventories. "If not," Stone said, "I want the reason in writing."[27]

Another determinant of raw materials inventory levels would be the reliability of the suppliers with regard to providing the proper quantity and quality of materials or services at the best price. Although a deficiency in either of these areas could suggest a change in suppliers, this may not be economically justifiable or feasible. Raw materials inventory levels would have to be adjusted upward to account for these circumstances; an increased buffer between supplier and user would be necessary so that changes in supplies are not felt immediately by the user. A similar argument could be presented concerning the user of the raw materials and work-in-process inventories. If the scheduling or information system of an organization is not adequate, additional raw materials and work-in-process inventories may have to be carried to take care of unanticipated demands being placed on them.

One approach to solving this type of problem is to integrate (expand) vertically. This was the case with Lukens Steel.

> While Lukens' modern steelmaking technology has many benefits, it also presents the company with one major risk. Because its electricmelt furnaces use mostly steel scrap as a raw material, Lukens is susceptible to the vagaries of the scrap market.
>
> But Carlson is taking steps to lessen the company's 90% dependence on scrap. Three years ago, for example, Lukens built a facility for converting cheaper low-

---

[27]"Clearing Off the Inventory Shelf," *Business Week*, December 11, 1978, p. 109.

grade scrap into higher-quality iron pellets, or "briquets," that can also be used in its furnaces. And the company now has a long-term supply contract with Fior de Venezuela, a producer of iron ore briquets in which Lukens has an 11% interest. Shipments from Fior began this summer. "This gives us an anchor to the windward as far as supplies are concerned," says Carlson.[28]

Speculative buying may be a reason to increase raw materials inventories, especially in the face of inflation. Burlington Industries' president Horace C. Jones faced problems of obtaining raw materials at the right price.

Meanwhile, Jones has other priorities, such as insuring that Burlington continues to get the 2-billion lb. of natural and synthetic fibers that its 35 divisions and 167 plants gobble up each year. Last year the value of its raw materials inventory jumped 55%, to $93-million. Says a competitor, with a touch of envy: "My guess is that the increase is a lot of cotton at about 41¢ per lb. Raw materials purchasing is one of the things they do well." At one point last year, cotton shot up to 95¢ and now sells at around 65¢ a lb. Asked if Burlington had bought cheap cotton in anticipation of a run-up price, Jones chuckles. "Let's just say we don't look upon the increase in our raw materials inventory as a minus," he says.[29]

Functionally Independent Production/Operations Decision Variables

The production/operations decision variables listed here are not greatly influenced by factors in other functional areas of an organization. Under particular circumstances, any one of these areas might be classified as a C_3 variable. For example, if the student is dealing with an intermittent production/operations system, a determinant of the scheduling system employed may be the delivery promises made by the sales force. Thus the scheduling system becomes a C_3 decision variable. In a continuous system, the scheduling system is not necessarily a C_3 decision variable. It is up to the student to decide if the conditions in the case being analyzed warrant moving a C_4 variable to a C_3 variable, or vice versa.

C_4 variables include the selection and control of:

1. The maintenance system.
2. Scheduling.
3. Quality.
4. Inventories.
5. Purchasing.

SUMMARY

This chapter began with a brief review of the production/operations area and the distinctions between continuous and intermittent systems. It touched on five C_3 decision variables that require or are influenced by in-

---

[28] "Lukens Steel: A Specialist Blankets a High-Margin Market," *Business Week*, December 11, 1978, p. 128.
[29] "Giant Burlington Faces Trying Times for Textiles," *Business Week*, March 2, 1974, p. 47.

puts from sources external and internal to the organization. These variables include plant location and capacity, facilities layout, process planning and job design, planning of aggregate output, and raw materials and work-in-process inventory levels. The chapter described the determinants of each of these decision variables and provided examples to illustrate how various factors have influenced particular decisions. It concluded with a list of functionally independent decision variables.

Whereas the present focus has been on the coordinative elements of the production/operations function, the following reading focuses on the "link" between corporate strategy and various production/operations decisions.

MANUFACTURING—MISSING LINK IN CORPORATE STRATEGY

Wickham Skinner

A company's manufacturing function typically is either a competitive weapon or a corporate millstone. It is seldom neutral. The connection between manufacturing and corporate success is rarely seen as more than the achievement of high efficiency and low costs. In fact, the connection is much more critical and much more sensitive. Few top managers are aware that what appear to be routine manufacturing decisions frequently come to limit the corporation's strategic options, binding it with facilities, equipment, personnel, and basic controls and policies to a non-competitive posture which may take years to turn around.

Research I have conducted during the past three years reveals that top management unknowingly delegates a surprisingly large portion of basic policy decisions to lower levels in the manufacturing area. Generally, this abdication of responsibility comes about more through a lack of concern than by intention. And it is partly the reason that many manufacturing policies and procedures developed at lower levels reflect assumptions about corporate strategy which are incorrect or misconstrued.

MILLSTONE EFFECT

When companies fail to recognize the relationship between manufacturing decisions and corporate strategy, they may become saddled with seriously noncompetitive production systems which are expensive and time-consuming to change. Here are several examples:

Company A entered the combination washer-dryer field after several competitors had failed to achieve successful entries into the field. Company A's executives believed their model would overcome the technical drawbacks which had hurt their competitors and held back the development of any substantial market. The manufacturing managers tooled the new unit on the usual conveyorized assembly line and giant stamping presses used for all company products.

When the washer-dryer failed in the market, the losses amounted to millions. The plant had been "efficient" in the sense that costs were low. But the tooling and production processes did not meet the demands of the marketplace.

Company B produced five kinds of electronic gear for five different groups of customers; the gear ranged from satellite controls to industrial controls and electronic components. In each market a different task was required of the production function. For instance, in the first market, extremely high reliability was demanded; in the second market, rapid introduction of a stream of new products was demanded; in the third market, low costs were of critical importance for competitive survival.

In spite of these highly diverse and contrasting tasks, production management elected to centralize manufacturing facilities in one plant in order to achieve "economies of scale." The result was a failure to achieve high reliability, economies of scale, or an ability to introduce new products quickly. What happened, in short, was that the demands placed on manufacturing by a competi-

---

SOURCE: Wickham Skinner, "Manufacturing—Missing Link in Corporate Strategy," *Harvard Business Review*. May—June, 1969.© 1969 by the President and Fellows of Harvard College; all rights reserved.

tive strategy were ignored by the production group in order to achieve economies of scale. This production group was obsessed with developing "a total system, fully computerized." The manufacturing program satisfied no single division, and the serious marketing problems which resulted choked company progress.

Company C produced plastic molding resins. A new plant under construction was to come on-stream in eight months, doubling production. In the meantime, the company had a much higher volume of orders than it could meet.

In a strategic sense, manufacturing's task was to maximize output to satisfy large, key customers. Yet the plant's production control system was set up—as it had been for years—to minimize costs. As a result, long runs were emphasized. While costs were low, many customers had to wait, and many key buyers were lost. Consequently, when the new plant came on-stream, it was forced to operate at a low volume.

The mistake of considering low costs and high efficiencies as the key manufacturing objective in each of these examples is typical of the oversimplified concept of "a good manufacturing operation." Such criteria frequently get companies into trouble, or at least do not aid in the development of manufacturing into a competitive weapon. Manufacturing affects corporate strategy, and corporate strategy affects manufacturing. Even in an apparently routine operating area such as a production scheduling system, strategic considerations should outweigh technical and conventional industrial engineering factors invoked in the name of "productivity."

Shortsighted Views

The fact is that manufacturing is seen by most top managers as requiring involved technical skills and a morass of petty daily decisions and details. It is seen by many young managers as the gateway to grubby routine, where days are filled with high pressure, packed with details, and limited to low-level decision making—all of which is out of the sight and minds of top-level executives. It is generally taught in graduate schools of business administration as a combination of industrial engineering (time study, plant layout, inventory theory, and so on) and quantitative analysis (linear programming, simulation, queuing theory, and the rest). In total, a manufacturing career is generally perceived as an all-consuming, technically oriented, hectic life that minimizes one's chances of ever reaching the top and maximizes the chances of being buried in minutiae.

In fact, these perceptions are not wholly inaccurate. It is the thesis of this article that the technically oriented concept of manufacturing is all too prevalent; and that it is largely responsible for the typically limited contribution manufacturing makes to a corporation's arsenal of competitive weapons, for manufacturing's failure to attract the top talent it needs and *should* have, and for its failure to attract more young managers with general management interests and broad abilities. In my opinion, manufacturing is generally perceived in the wrong way at the top, managed in the wrong way at the plant level, and taught in the wrong way in the business schools.

These are strong words, but change is needed, and I believe that only a more relevant concept of manufacturing can bring change. I see no sign whatsoever that we have found the means of solving the problems mentioned. The new, mathematically based "total systems" approaches to production management offer the promise of new and valuable concepts and techniques, but I doubt that these approaches will overcome the tendency of top management to remove itself from manufacturing. Ten years of development of quantitative techniques have left us each year with the promise of a "great new age" in production management that lies "just ahead." The promise never seems to be realized. Stories of computer and "total systems" fiascoes are available by the dozen; these failures are always expensive, and in almost every case management has delegated the work to experts.

I do not want to demean the promise—and, indeed, some present contributions—of the systems/computer approach. Two years ago I felt more sanguine about it. But, since then, close observation of the problems in U.S. industry has convinced me that the "answer" promised is inadequate. The approach cannot overcome the problems described until it does a far better job of linking manufacturing and corporate strategy. What is needed is some kind of integrative mechanism.

PATTERN OF FAILURE

An examination of top management perceptions of manufacturing has led me to some notions about basic causes of many production problems. In each of six industries I have studied, I have found top executives delegating excessive amounts of manufacturing policy to subordinates, avoiding involvement in most production matters, and failing to ask the right questions until their companies are in obvious trouble. This pattern seems to be due to a combination of two factors:

1. A sense of personal inadequacy, on the part of top executives, in managing production. (Often the feeling evolves from a tendency to regard the area as a technical or engineering specialty, or a mundane "nuts and bolts" segment of management.)
2. A lack of awareness among top executives that a production system inevitably involves trade-offs and compromises and so must be designed to perform a limited task well, with that task defined by corporate strategic objectives.

The first factor is, of course, dependent in part on the second, for the sense of inadequacy would not be felt if the strategic role of production were clearer. The second factor is the one we shall concentrate on in the remainder of this article.

Like a building, a vehicle, or a boat, a production system can be designed to do some things well, but always at the expense of other abilities. It appears to be the lack of recognition of these trade-offs and their effects on a corporation's ability to compete that leads top management to delegate often-critical decisions to lower, technically oriented staff levels, and to allow policy to be made through apparently unimportant operating decisions.

In the balance of this article I would like to:

- Sketch out the relationships between production operations and corporate strategy.
- Call attention to the existence of specific trade-offs in production system design.
- Comment on the inadequacy of computer specialists to deal with these trade-offs.
- Suggest a new way of looking at manufacturing which might enable the nontechnical manager to understand and manage the manufacturing area.

STRATEGIC IMPLICATIONS

Frequently the interrelationship between production operations and corporate strategy is not easily grasped. The notion is simple enough—namely, that a company's competitive strategy at a given time places particular demands on its manufacturing function, and, conversely, that the company's manufacturing posture and operations should be specifically designed to fulfill the task demanded by strategic plans. What is more elusive is the set of cause-and-effect factors which determine the linkage between strategy and production operations.

Strategy is a set of plans and policies by which a company aims to gain advantages over its competitors. Generally a strategy includes plans for products and the marketing of these products to a particular set of customers. The marketing plans usually include specific approaches and steps to be followed in identifying potential customers, determining why, where, and when they buy, and learning how they can best be reached and convinced to purchase. The company must have an advantage, a particular appeal, a special push or pull created by its products, channels of distribution, advertising, price, packaging, availability, warranties, or other factors.

Contrasting Demands

What is not always realized is that different marketing strategies and approaches to gaining a competitive advantage place different demands on the manufacturing arm of the company. For example, a furniture manufacturer's strategy for broad distribution of a limited, low-price line with wide consumer advertising might generally require:

- Decentralized finished-goods storage.
- Readily available merchandise.
- Rock-bottom costs.

The foregoing demands might in turn require:

- Relatively large lot sizes.
- Specialized facilities for woodworking and finishing.
- A large proportion of low- and medium-skilled workers in the work force.
- Concentration of manufacturing in a limited number of large-scale plants.

In contrast, a manufacturer of high-price, high-style furniture with more exclusive distribution would require an entirely different set of manufacturing policies. While higher prices and longer lead times would allow more leeway in the plant, this company would have to contend with the problems implicit in delivering high-quality furniture made of wood (which is a soft, dimensionally unstable material whose surface is expensive to finish and easy to damage), a high setup cost relative to running times in most wood-machining operations, and the need to make a large number of nonstandardized parts. While the first company must work with these problems too, they are more serious to the second company because its marketing strategy forces it to confront the problems head on. The latter's manufacturing policies will probably require:

- Many model and style changes.
- Production to order.
- Extremely reliable high quality.

These demands may in turn require:

- An organization that can get new models into production quickly.
- A production control group that can coordinate all activities so as to reduce lead times.
- Technically trained supervisors and technicians.

Consequently, the second company ought to have a strong manufacturing-methods engineering staff; simple, flexible tooling; and a well-trained, experienced work force.

In summary, the two manufacturers would need to develop very different policies, personnel, and operations if they were to be equally successful in carrying out their strategies.

Important Choices

In the example described, there are marked contrasts in the two companies. Actually, even small and subtle differences in corporate strategies should be reflected in manufacturing policies. However, my research shows that few companies do in fact carefully and explicitly tailor their production systems to perform the tasks which are vital to corporate success.

Instead of focusing first on strategy, then moving to define the manufacturing task, and next turning to systems design in manufacturing policy, managements tend to employ a concept of production which is much less effective. Most top executives and production managers look at their production systems with the notion of "total productivity" or the equivalent, "efficiency." They seek a kind of blending of low costs, high quality, and acceptable customer service. The view prevails that a plant with reasonably modern equipment, up-to-date methods and procedures, a cooperative work force, a computerized information system, and an enlightened management will be a good plant and will perform efficiently.

But what is "a good plant"? What is "efficient performance"? And what should the computer be programmed to do? Should it minimize lead times or minimize inventories? A company cannot do both. Should the computer minimize direct labor or indirect labor? Again, the company cannot do both. Should investment in equipment be minimized—or should outside purchasing be held to a minimum? One could go on with such choices.

The reader may reply: "What management wants is a combination of both ingredients that results in the lowest *total* cost." But that answer, too, is insufficient. The "lowest total cost" answer leaves out the dimensions of time and customer satisfaction, which must usually be considered too. Because cost *and* time *and* customers are all involved, we have to conclude that what is a "good" plant for Company A may be a poor or mediocre plant for its competitor, Company B, which is in the same industry but pursues a different strategy.

The purpose of manufacturing is to serve the company—to meet its needs for survival, profit, and growth. Manufacturing is part of the strategic concept that relates a company's strengths and resources to opportunities in the market. Each strategy creates a unique manufacturing task. Manufacturing management's ability to meet that task is the key measure of its success.

TRADE-OFFS IN DESIGN

It is curious that most top managements and production people do not state their yardsticks of success more precisely, and instead fall back on such measures as "efficiency," "low cost," and "productivity." My studies suggest that a key reason for this phenomenon is that very few executives realize the existence of trade-offs in designing and operating a production system.

Yet most managers will readily admit that there are compromises or trade-offs to be made in designing an airplane or truck. In the case of an airplane, trade-offs would involve such matters as cruising speed, take-off and landing distances, initial cost, maintenance, fuel consumption, passenger comfort, and cargo or passenger capacity. A given stage of technology defines limits as to what can be accomplished in these respects. For instance, no one today can design a 500-passenger plane that can land on a carrier and also break the sonic barrier.

Much of the same thing is true of manufacturing. The variables of cost, time, quality, technological constraints, and customer satisfaction place limits on what management can do, force compromises, and demand an explicit recognition of a multitude of trade-offs and choices. Yet everywhere I find plants which have inadvertently emphasized one yardstick at the expense of another, more important one. For example:

An electronics manufacturer with dissatisfied customers hired a computer expert and placed manufacturing under a successful engineering design chief to make it a "total system." A year later its computer was spewing out an inch-thick volume of daily information. "We know the location of every part in the plant on any given day," boasted the production manager and his computer systems chief.

Nevertheless, customers were more dissatisfied than ever. Product managers hotly complained that delivery promises were regularly missed—and in almost every case they first heard about failures from their customers. The problem centered on the fact that computer information runs were organized by part numbers and operations. They were designed to facilitate machine scheduling and to aid shop foremen; they were not organized around end products, which would have facilitated customer service.

How had this come about? Largely, it seemed clear, because the manufacturing managers had become absorbed in their own "systems approach"; the fascination of mechanized data handling had become an end in itself. As for top management, it had more or less abdicated responsibility. Because the company's growth and success had been based on engineering and because top management was R&D-oriented, policy-making executives saw production as a routine requiring a lower level of complexity and brainpower. Top management argued further that the company had production experts who were well paid and who should be able to do their jobs without bothering top-level people.

Recognizing Alternatives

To develop the notion of important trade-off decisions in manufacturing, let us consider Exhibit 1, which shows some examples.

In each decision area—plant and equipment, production planning and control, and so forth—top management needs to recognize the alternatives and become involved in the design of the production system. It needs to become involved to the extent that the alternative selected is appropriate to the manufacturing task determined by the corporate strategy.

Making such choices is, of course, an ongoing rather than a once-a-year or once-a-decade task; decisions have to be made constantly in these trade-off areas. Indeed, the real crux of the problem seems to be how to ensure that the continuing process of decision making is not isolated from competitive and strategic facts, when many of the trade-off decisions do not at first appear to bear on company strategy. As long as a technical point of view dominates manufacturing decisions, a degree of isolation from the realities of competition is inevitable. Unfortunately, as we shall see, the technical viewpoint is all too likely to prevail.

TECHNICAL DOMINANCE

The similarity between today's emphasis on the technical experts—the computer specialist and the engineering-oriented production technician—and yesterday's emphasis on the efficiency expert—time-study man and industrial engineer—is impossible to escape. For 50 years, U.S. management relied on efficiency experts trained in the techniques of Frederick W. Taylor. Industrial engineers were kings of the factory. Their early approaches and attitudes were often conducive to industrial warfare, strikes, sabotage, and militant unions, but that was not realized then. Also not realized was that their technical emphasis often produced an inward orientation toward cost that ignored the customer, and an engineering point of view that gloried in tools, equipment, and gadgets rather than in markets and service. Most important, the cult of industrial engineering tended to make top executives technically disqualified from involvement in manufacturing decisions.

Since the turn of the century, this efficiency-centered orientation has dogged U.S. manufacturing. It has created that image of "nuts and bolts," of greasy, dirty, detail jobs in manufacturing. It has dominated "production" courses in most graduate schools of business administration. It has alienated young men with broad management educations from manufacturing careers. It has "buffaloed" top managers.

Several months ago I was asked by a group of industrial engineers to offer an opinion as to why so few industrial engineers were moving up to the top of their companies. My answer was that perhaps a technical point of view cut them off from top management, just as the jargon and hocus-pocus of manufacturing often kept top management from understanding the factory. In their isolation, they could gain only a severely limited sense of market needs and of corporate competitive strategy.

Enter the Computer Expert

Today the industrial engineer is declining in importance in many companies. But a new technical expert, the computer specialist, is taking his place. I use the term "computer specialist" to refer to individuals who specialize in computer systems design and programming.

I do not deny, of course, that computer specialists have a very important job to do. I do ob-

Exhibit 1 Some important trade-off decisions in manufacturing—or "you can't have it both ways."

Decision area	Decision	Alternatives
PLANT AND EQUIPMENT	Span of process	Make or buy
	Plant size	One big plant or several smaller ones
	Plant location	Locate near markets or locate near materials
	Investment decisions	Invest mainly in buildings or equipment or inventories or research
	Choice of equipment	General-purpose or special-purpose equipment
	Kind of tooling	Temporary, minimum tooling or "production tooling"
PRODUCTION PLANNING AND CONTROL	Frequency of inventory taking	Few or many breaks in production for buffer stocks
	Inventory size	High inventory or a lower inventory
	Degree of inventory control	Control in great detail or in lesser detail
	What to control	Controls designed to minimize machine downtime or labor cost or time in process, or to maximize output of particular products or material usage
	Quality control	High reliability and quality or low costs
	Use of standards	Formal or informal or none at all
LABOR AND STAFFING	Job specialization	Highly specialized or not highly specialized
	Supervision	Technically trained first-line supervisors or nontechnically trained supervisors

Exhibit 1 (continued)

Decision area	Decision	Alternatives
	Wage system	Many job grades or few job grades; incentive wages or hourly wages
	Supervision	Close supervision or loose supervision
	Industrial engineers	Many or few such men
PRODUCT DESIGN/ ENGINEERING	Size of product line	Many customer specials or few specials or none at all
	Design stability	Frozen design or many engineering change orders
	Technological risk	Use of new processes unproved by competitors or follow-the-leader policy
	Engineering	Complete packaged design or design-as-you-go approach
	Use of manufacturing engineering	Few or many manufacturing engineers
ORGANIZATION AND MANAGEMENT	Kind of organization	Functional or product focus or geographical or other
	Executive use of time	High involvement in investment or production planning or cost control or quality control or other activities
	Degree of risk assumed	Decisions based on much or little information
	Use of staff	Large or small staff group
	Executive style	Much or little involvement in detail; authoritarian or nondirective style; much or little contact with organization

ject, however, to any notion that computer specialists have more of a top management view than was held by their predecessors, the industrial engineers. In my experience, the typical computer expert has been forced to master a complex and all-consuming technology, a fact which frequently makes him parochial rather than catholic in his views. Because he is so preoccupied with the detail of a total system, it is necessary for someone in top management to give him objectives and policy guidance. In his choice of trade-offs and compromises for his computer system, he needs to be instructed and not left to his own devices. Or, stated differently, he needs to see the entire corporation as a system, not just one corner of it—i.e., the manufacturing plant.

Too often this is not happening. The computer is a nightmare to many top managers because they have let it and its devotees get out of hand. They have let technical experts continue to dominate; the failure of top management truly to manage production goes on.

How *can* top management begin to manage manufacturing instead of turning it over to technicians who, through no fault of their own, are absorbed in their own arts and crafts? How can U.S. production management be helped to cope with the rising pressures of new markets, more rapid product changes, new technologies, larger and riskier equipment decisions, and the swarm of problems we face in industry today? Let us look at some answers.

BETTER DECISION MAKING

The answers I would like to suggest are not panaceas, nor are they intended to be comprehensive. Indeed, no one can answer all the questions and problems described with one nice formula or point of view. But surely we can improve on the notion that production systems need only be "productive and efficient." Top management can manage manufacturing if it will engage in the making of manufacturing policy, rather than considering it a kind of fifth, independent estate beyond the pale of control.

The place to start, I believe, is with the acceptance of a theory of manufacturing which begins with the concept that in any system design there are significant trade-offs (as shown in Exhibit 1) which must be explicitly decided on.

Determining Policy

Executives will also find it helpful to think of manufacturing policy determination as an orderly process or sequence of steps. Exhibit 2 is a schematic portrayal of such a process. It shows that manufacturing policy must stem from corporate strategy, and that the process of determining this policy is the means by which top management can actually manage production. Use of this process can end manufacturing isolation and tie top management and manufacturing together. The sequence is simple but vital:

It begins with an analysis of the competitive situation, on how rival companies are competing in terms of product, markets, policies, and channels of distribution. Management examines the number and kind of competitors and the opportunities open to its company.

Next comes a critical appraisal of the company's skills and resources and of its present facilities and approaches.

The third step is the formulation of company strategy: How is the company to compete successfully, combine its strengths with market opportunities, and define niches in the markets where it can gain advantages?

The fourth step is the point where many top executives cut off their thinking. It is important for them to define the implications or "so-what" effects of company strategy in terms of specific manufacturing tasks. For example, they should ask: "If we are to compete with an X product of Y price for Z customers using certain distribution channels and forms of advertising, what will be demanded of manufacturing in terms of costs, deliveries, lead times, quality levels, and reliability?" These demands should be precisely defined.

Exhibit 2 The process of manufacturing policy determination.

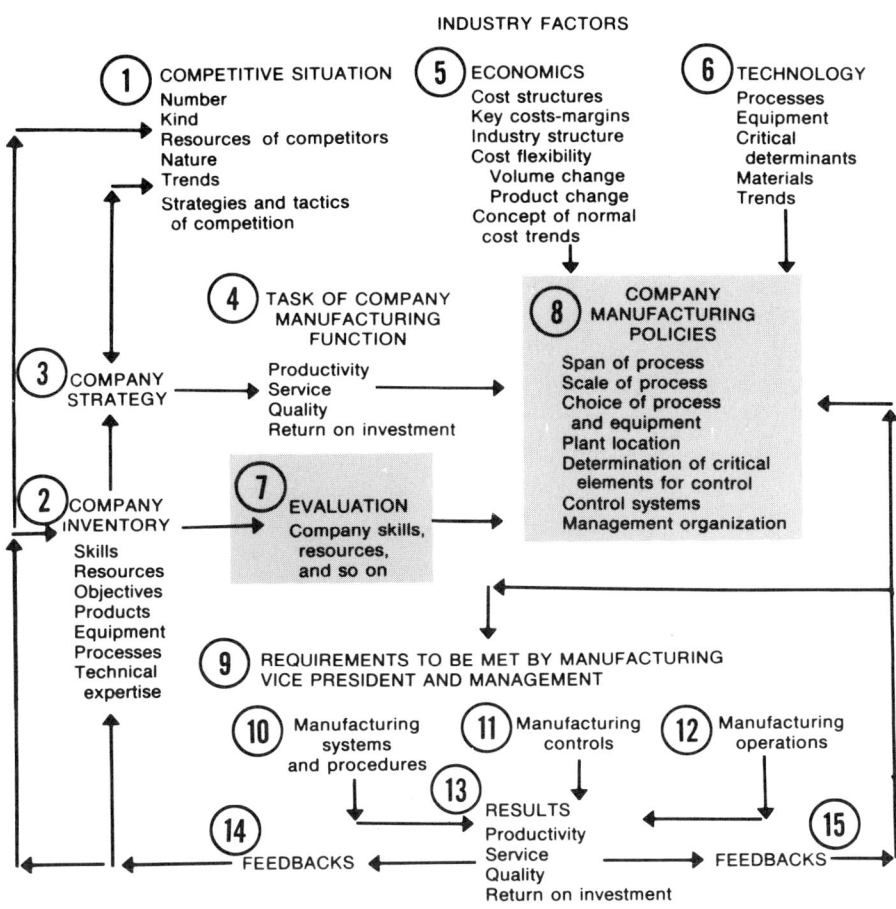

The fifth and sixth steps are to study the constraints or limitations imposed by the economics and the technology of the industry. These factors are generally common to all competitors. An explicit recognition of them is a prerequisite to a genuine understanding of the manufacturing problems and opportunities. These are facts that a nontechnical manager can develop, study, understand, and put to work. Exhibit 3 contains sample lists of topics for the manager to use in doing his homework.

The seventh and eight steps are the key ones for integrating and synthesizing all the prior ones into a broad manufacturing policy. The question for management is: "Given the facts of the economics and the technology of the industry, how do we set ourselves up to meet the specific manufacturing tasks posed by our particular competitive strategy?" Management must decide what it is going to make and what it will buy; how many plants to have, how big they should be, and where to place them; what processes and equipment to buy; what the key elements are which need to be controlled and how they can be controlled; and what kind of management organization would be most appropriate.

Next come the steps of working out programs of implementation, controls, performance measures, and review procedures (see Steps 9—15 in Exhibit 2).

Exhibit 3: Illustrative constraints or limitations which should be studied.

A. Economics of the industry

　Labor, burden, material, depreciation costs
　Flexibility of production to meet changes in volume
　Return on investment, prices, margins
　Number and location of plants
　Critical control variables
　Critical functions (e.g., maintenance, production, and personnel)
　Typical financial structures
　Typical costs and cost relationships
　Typical operating problems
　Barriers to entry
　Pricing practices
　"Maturity" of industry products, markets, production practices, and so on
　Importance of economies of scale
　Importance of integrated capacities of corporations
　Importance of having a certain balance of different types of equipment
　Ideal balances of equipment capacities
　Nature and type of production control
　Government influences

B. Technology of the industry

　Rate of technological change
　Scale of processes
　Span of processes
　Degree of mechanization
　Technological sophistication
　Time requirements for making changes

CONCLUSION

The process just described is, in my observation, quite different from the usual process of manufacturing management. Conventionally, manufacturing has been managed from the bottom up. The classical process of the age of mass production is to select an operation, break it down into its elements, analyze and improve each element, and put it back together. This approach was contributed years ago by Frederick W. Taylor and other industrial engineers who followed in his footsteps.

What I am suggesting is an entirely different approach, one adapted far better to the current era of more products, shorter runs, vastly accelerated product changes, and increased marketing competition. I am suggesting a kind of "top-down" manufacturing. This approach starts with the company and its competitive strategy; its goal is to define manufacturing policy. Its presumption is that only when basic manufacturing polices are defined can the technical experts, industrial and manufacturing engineers, labor relations specialists, and computer experts have the necessary guidance to do their work.

With its focus on corporate strategy and the manufacturing task, the top-down approach can give top management both its entrée to manufacturing and the concepts it needs to take the initiative and truly manage this function. When this is done, executives previously unfamiliar with manufacturing are likely to find it an exciting activity. The company will have an important addition to its arsenal of competitive weapons.

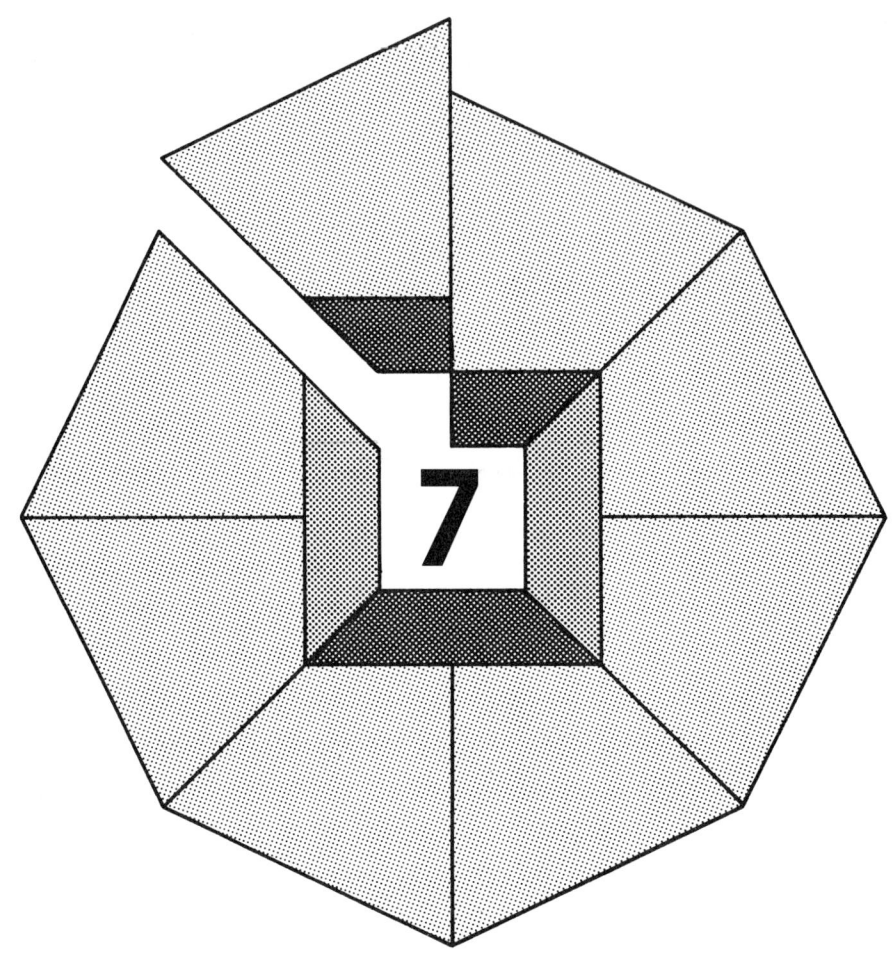

ORGANIZATIONAL STRUCTURE
a general management perspective

The first chapter of this book established a clear relationship between the strategy of the firm and the top management perspective necessary to develop that strategy. Policies must be designed to attain a balance between the opportunities and constraints of the corporate environment and the strengths and weaknesses of corporate resources. Because the organizational structure supplies the framework for operationalizing the strategic plan, the successful implementation of strategy requires that the chief executive officer shape the formal organizational structure of the firm to the peculiar needs of this strategy. Once the C_1 variables have been determined and the overall constraints on organizational activities defined, decisions involving C_2 variables, including the structural variables, can be formulated and implemented. Thus, in a very important sense, strategy and structure are *interdependent* variables. Decisions on organizational structure must be made in terms of the particular strategic posture developed for the firm, because implementation of strategy would be futile without an organizational structure designed to meet strategic needs and constraints.

A MULTIDIMENSIONAL VIEW OF ORGANIZATIONAL STRUCTURE

In his classic book *Strategy and Structure*, Alfred D. Chandler, Jr. offered a succinct definition of organizational structure:

Structure can be defined as the design of organization through which the enterprise is administered. The design whether formally or informally defined has two aspects. It includes, first, the lines of authority and communication between the different administrative offices and officers, and, second, the information and data that flow through these lines of communication and authority. Such lines and data are essential to assure the effective coordination, appraisal, and planning so necessary in carrying out the basic goals and policies and in knitting together the total resources of the enterprise.[1]

This definition recognizes both the formal and informal elements of organizational structure. An organizational structure cannot be portrayed solely by the formal organization chart described in procedural manuals. Individual and group behavior may substantially modify the formal structure of an organization. Indeed, the organization is:

a system of relationships involving two or more persons concerned with the satisfaction of needs or the achievement of objectives. Such relationships occur in a variety of patterns, determined by needs, convenience, status, sociability, and individual preference.[2]

Therefore, recognition of the people who make the structure work is important. Unless the formal organization satisfies their needs, informal organi-

---

[1]Alfred D. Chandler, Jr. *Strategy and Structure* (Cambridge, Mass.: The MIT Press, 1962), p. 16.
[2]David S. Brown, "Shaping the Organization to Fit People," *Management of Personnel Quarterly*, 5 (2), Summer 1966, p. 12.

zation(s) emerge. Furthermore, attempts to thwart the informal organization may impede the attainment of organizational objectives.

The formal structure, informal structure, and individual and group behavior in the organization are interrelated. Top management cannot and should not view each one separately. Suggestions by management thinkers and practitioners to view organizations as "varying composites" or "overlays" are appropriate in this regard. Albert Wickesberg suggests that the "varying composites" include: (1) command or formal structure action, (2) problem-solving structure, (3) communication structure, (4) social or informal structure, and (5) process structure (e.g., a special structure for planning and control).[3] The system of overlays suggested by Pfiffner and Sherwood includes (1) sociometric or special friendships structure, (2) functional or formal structure relating to operations, (3) decision-making structure, (4) power structure, and (5) communication structure.[4] Figure 7-1 provides an illustrative system of overlays prepared by Brown.

In short, top managment needs to design an organizational structure that incorporates (1) *technical-economic* considerations to perform communication, problem-solving, and decision-making tasks, (2) *human-social* considerations to accommodate the needs, values, and aspirations of individuals and human work groups in the organization, and (3) *change-dynamics* considerations to provide for organizational adaptation to a changing task environment. A discussion of organizational design follows.

ORGANIZATIONAL DESIGN

The first step in designing an organization structure is to identify the organization's task environment [i.e., that part of the environment seen by top management as relevant or potentially relevant to the mission (strategy) of the organization].[5] A list of environmental components is presented in Table 7-1.

The second step in the design process is for top management to determine the characteristics of the environment and assess its state. Duncan uses two dimensions to assess the state of the environment (i.e., the simple-complex dimension and the static-dynamic dimension). The result is a four-way classification of organizational environments presented in Table 7-2.

Once the organization's environment has been analyzed, top management faces the third step (i.e., determining the type of structure best suited for its environment and the particular decisions to be made). This approach to organizational design is termed the *contingency approach*. Simply, certain kinds of organization structures and formats are appropriate under

---

[3] Albert K. Wickesberg, *Management Organization* (New York: Appelton-Century Crofts, 1966), pp. 94–95.
[4] John J. Pfiffner and Frank P. Sherwood, *Administrative Organization* (Englewood Cliffs, N.J.: Prentice-Hall, 1960), pp. 16–27.
[5] Robert Duncan, "What is the Right Organization Structure?", *Organizational Dynamics*, Winter 1979, p. 62.

Figure 7-1 The System of overlays.

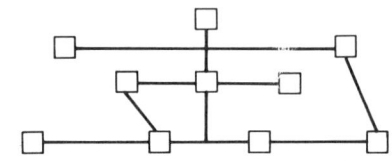

Special friendships: "I'll talk to my friend George in Purchasing, he'll know what to do."

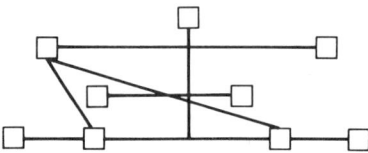

Functional overlay: Direct relationships between specialist assistants and operating departments. "You have to see personnel for approval to take that training course."

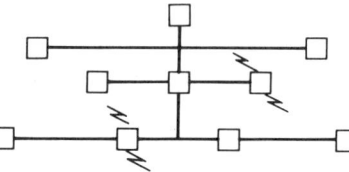

Power overlay: "Before you go further, you had better check that with Jack in Production Planning."

SOURCE: David S. Brown, "Shaping the Organization to Fit People," *Management & Personnel Quarterly*, Vol. 5, No. 2 (Summer 1966), p. 13. Reprinted by permission.

given sets of internal and external conditions.[6] An elaboration of the contingency approach will be intertwined with a discussion of the advantages and disadvantages of different organization structures later in this chapter. First, however, we will briefly examine several characteristics of formal organizations and some additional variables that must be considered when structuring organizational relationships.

Characteristics of Formal Organizations

Formal organization structures are characterized by a clearly defined set of activities, procedures, and communication processes. The overall structure of formal organizations is usually defined in terms of organization charts that show the hierarchical relationship of functions and positions. Job descriptions are frequently used to spell out the duties assigned to employees and managers. Formal relationships between positions are evident in the or-

---

[6]Herbert G. Hicks and C. Ray Gullett, *Organizations: Theory and Behavior* (New York: McGraw Hill, 1975), pp. 87–88.

Table 7-1 Environmental Components List

Internal Environment	External Environment
Organizational personnel component	Customer component
Educational and technological background and skills	Distributors of product or service
	Actual users of product or service
Previous technological and managerial skill	Suppliers component
	New materials suppliers
Individual member's involvement and commitment to attaining system's goals	Equipment suppliers
	Product parts suppliers
	Labor supply
Interpersonal behavior styles	Competitor component
Availability of manpower for utilization within the system	Competitors for suppliers
	Competitors for customers
Organizational functional and staff units component	Sociopolitical component
	Government regulatory control over the industry
Technological characteristics of organizational units	Public political attitude toward industry and its particular product
Interdependence of organizational units in carrying out their objectives	Relationship with trade unions with jurisdiction in the organization
Intraunit conflict among organizational functional and staff units	Technological component
	Meeting new technological requirements of own industry and related industries in production of product or service
Intraunit conflict among organizational functional and staff units	
Organizational level component	
Organizational objectives and goals	Improving and developing new products by implementing new technological advances in the industry
Integrative process integrating individuals and groups into contributing maximally to attaining organizational goals	
Nature of the organization's product service	

SOURCE: Reprinted, by permission of the publisher, from "What is the Right Organizational Structure" by Robert Duncan, *Organizational Dynamics*, Winter 1979, copyright © 1979 by AMACOM, a division of American Management Associations, p. 62. All rights reserved.

ganization charts and job descriptions. Although charts and descriptions are static representations of the dynamic process of organizational life, they are good first approximations of the formal organizations they are designed to represent.[7]

Formal organizations elaborate, grow, and become more complex. Increased specialization of functions and the addition of new activities may be necessary to meet the needs of a changing environment. Because most organizations are created to last permanently, some managers and employees

---

[7]Hicks and Gullett, *Organizations*, pp. 62–66.

Table 7-2 Classification of Organizational Environments

	Simple			Complex
Static	*Low perceived uncertainty* Small number of factors and components in the environment Factors and components are somewhat similar Factors and components remain basically the same and are not changing *Example*: Soft drink industry	1	2	*Moderately low perceived uncertainty* Large number of factors and components in the environment Factors and components are not similar to one another Factors and components remain basically the same *Example*: Food products
Dynamic	*Moderately high perceived uncertainty* Small number of factors and components in the environment Factors and components are somewhat similar to one another Factors and components of the environment are in continual process of change *Example*: Fast food industry	3	4	*High perceived uncertainty* Large number of factors and components in the environment Factors and components are not similar to one another Factors and components of environment are in a continual process of change *Examples*: Commercial airline industry Telephone communications (AT&T)

SOURCE: Reprinted, by permission of the publisher, from "What is the Right Organizational Structure" by Robert Duncan, *Organizational Dynamics*, Winter 1979, copyright © 1979 by AMACOM, a division of American Management Associations, p. 63. All rights reserved.

view organization structures to be permanent. Resistance to change arises from, among other things, this confusion between the permanence of the organization and its structure.

Structuring Formal Organizational Relationships

Earlier a brief definition of organizational structure as the "design of organization through which the enterprise is administered" was presented. Stated another way, structure may be thought of as the formal arrangements that are established to coordinate all activities in order to implement a given strategy. Thus structure reflects the "anatomy" of a firm through its focus on mechanisms and processes that *link* (both vertically and horizontally) the various parts of an organization. For purposes of analysis, it is useful to classify the major elements of organizational structure as follows:[8]

- Distribution of functions throughout the organization (includes definition of functions to be performed, groupings of functions, and the vertical and horizontal task relationships among functions).
- Vertical and horizontal authority relationships (who has the authority to do what).
- Communication/decision processes (the manner in which formal decisions are made and by whom, supporting informational inputs, and the information systems established to provide the inputs to decision makers).
- Policies (the decision rules or guidelines established in finance, marketing, production, personnel, purchasing, research and development, and other areas; these guidelines tie the performance of specific functions to the overall strategy and objectives of the firm).
- Formal incentive systems (compensation plan characteristics, fringe benefits, incentive or bonus plans, promotion criteria, and other features of the formal reward system used by the organization).

Taken together, these five parts of the organizational structure establish the basic conditions under which organizational members perform their various roles.

THE FORMAL ORGANIZATION: ALTERNATIVE STRUCTURAL FORMS

The following discussion focuses on the three basic structural forms depicted in Figure 7-2 and on the variations, or hybrids, derived from them.

The "Small" Structure

The small structure refers to an organization that is run by one person, with little or no formal operating procedures or division of labor. For example, in a single proprietorship the owner makes all the strategy decisions and is responsible for their implementation. In this organizational structure there is little confusion between authority and responsibility for the functions and activities of the firm because all of these are guided, or performed, by the same person. If the owner chooses to delegate some authority, this will not affect the firm's "small" status because the owner will usually retain final authority. Individual job descriptions may be less specific in smaller organizations because employees generally have to handle more than one aspect of the firm's activities.

---

[8]Robert C. Shirley, "An Interactive Approach to the Problem of Organizational Change," *Human Resource Management*, Summer 1975, p. 12.

Figure 7-2 Alternative structural forms.

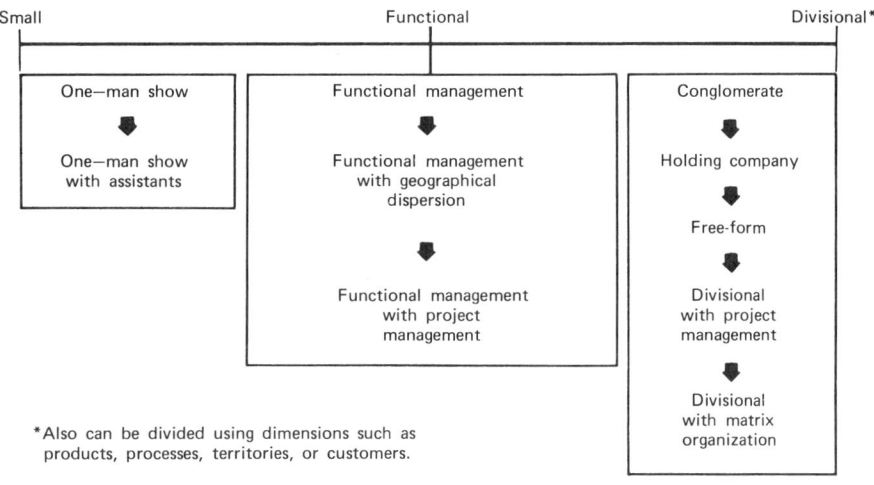

SOURCE: This scheme is basically an adaptation of that proposed by Scott. See Bruce R. Scott "The Industrial State: Old Myths and New Realities," *Harvard Business Review*, 51, 2 (March-April 1973): 141.

Small firms usually have a single product, or a single line of products, with a single channel of distribution. Therefore product/market complexity also will be very simple. This feature allows the sole owner to administer all of the firm's activities effectively. In most cases, an increase in the variety of products offered, and/or an increase in the markets served, would be the main force that could cause the organization's structure to evolve into something more complex. And, this force usually would be accompanied by an increase in size to accommodate a more complex product/market dimension. Thus increases in product/market complexity, sales, and organizational size can all act as catalysts for the emergence of a more formal organizational structure, since one person can no longer make all the management and operational decisions in an efficient manner.

A small organization tends to carry out its activities on an informal basis. For example, research and development, rewards, controls, and other such activities are usually unsystematic and are guided mainly by the manager's "feel" for the situation. However, the lack of a formal system of rewards can be dangerous to the morale of employees, once their number reaches a high point. Also, quality control can be better insured through responsibilities that are established within a formal organizational structure.

There are other disadvantages to the small structure. First, it is very demanding of the owner/manager, who must make a tremendous effort to stay on top of all business operations. Second, as previously discussed, a continuing increase in size will make the structure less efficient—and eventually unworkable. Finally the small structure generally does not facilitate the development of future managers. This can be a critical problem if the owner/manager is forced to be away from the business or if the organization is to grow.

The Functional Structure

The basic characteristic of this form is that tasks are identified and classified according to their *function* (e.g., production, finance). Then functions are combined into major groupings that are the basis for the creation of the firm's major departments. This type of structure allows for flexibility in the medium-sized concern, because functions can be regrouped as they are required by changes in strategy. This structure is also characterized by a number of functional managers (for sales, production, engineering, etc.), who are responsible for all operational decisions within their departments. The efficient use of this type of structure is, of course, highly dependent on the competence and commitment of subordinate managers.[9]

The establishment of a functional organizational structure usually becomes necessary as a small-structure firm grows and as increases in the complexity of business activities create the need for a more formal, systematized approach to major activities and for an increased delegation of decision making throughout the organization. However, the top management will continue to control decisions that involve strategic and coordinative variables (C_1, C_2). Because overall objectives are defined by top management, the functional units must also be organized from that perspective. A typical pattern of a first-order functional department structure might be: engineering, finance, industrial relations, marketing, production, purchasing, and research and development.[10] An organizational chart depicting this pattern of functional departmentation at the M. W. Kellogg Company is shown in Figure 7-3.

The importance of a functional department is usually indicated by the level occupied by its executive officer in the hierarchy of organizational structure.[11] In most industrial firms production, sales, and finance are classified at the highest level because their activities are considered essential to the company's survival. Purchasing and industrial relations may be lower in the hierarchy, depending on management's attitudes toward their value in the achievement of objectives.

The delegation of authority and responsibilities in a firm with functional departmentation may be best understood by looking at the production department of a manufacturing firm. Although the functional objectives of the department are determined by top management's goals for product

---

[9]Robert L. Katz, *Cases and Concepts in Corporate Strategy* (Englewood Cliffs, N.J.: Prentice-Hall, 1970), pp. 503–504.
[10]Ibid., p. 48.
[11]Ibid., p. 101.

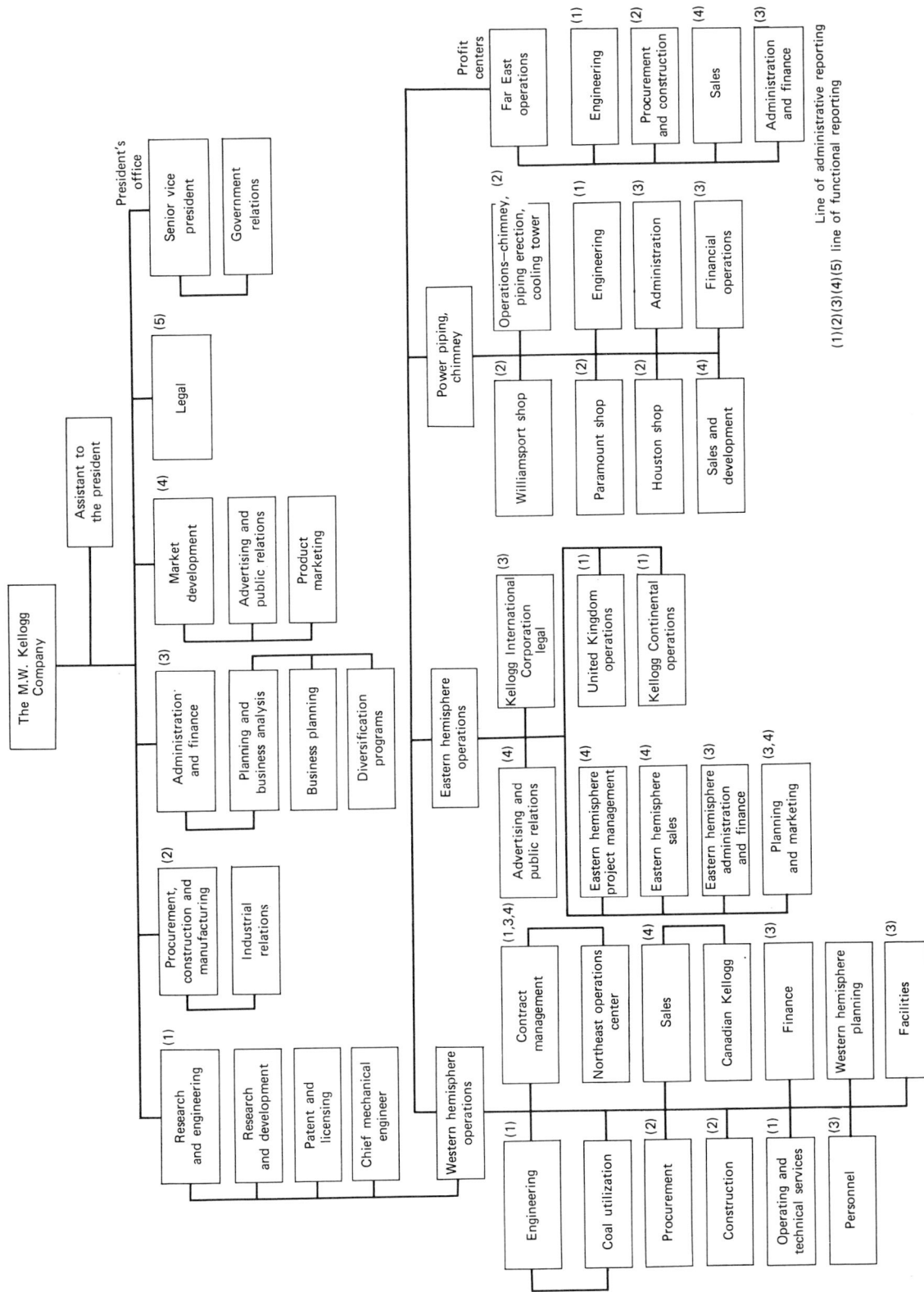

Figure 7-3 Functional departmentation: The M. W. Kellogg Company organization.

quantity and quality, the department management would make all the operational decisions necessary to achieve those objectives. In this case, top management would have overall control of policies but little control over operational activities.

The Divisional Structure

Further growth may create a strain on the ability of a functionally structured organization to achieve corporate goals efficiently and effectively. At this point, corporate structure must be reorganized to take on the characteristics of a *divisional organization*. These characteristics may include product diversification, territorial expansion, changes in customer orientation, and a need for the decentralization of authority so that each operating division can function autonomously under the general direction of top management.[12] Corporate objectives, strategies, and basic policies are generally set by top corporate management for each division. Divisional management then designs its own strategies and operation decisions within these corporate constraints and is evaluated by its effective achievement of corporate objectives, with little top management direction concerning the methods used to achieve them. The descriptors "conglomerate," "free-form," or "holding company" can be viewed as variations in the degree of autonomy and decision-making capacity given to the divisions or subsidiaries of a corporation. For example, Katz diffferentiates the free-form from the holding company by the degree of autonomy the individual units have in making strategic decisions concerning product/market scope, competitive emphasis, performance specifications, and resource allocations. According to Katz, the individual units of a holding company exercise greater autonomy in strategic decisions than do the individual units of the free-form.[13]

Because corporate businesses exhibit varying degrees of diversification, they can be classified as three basic types: "dominant," "related," and "unrelated."[14] "Dominant" business companies derive 70 to 95% of their sales volume from a single business, as is the case with Schwinn and Maytag. "Related" business companies have no single business that accounts for more than 70% of sales (e.g., 3M). "Unrelated" business companies have not necessarily related new business ventures to old ones, and no single business accounts for as much as 30% of total sales volume. Companies of this nature are generally labeled "conglomerates."

Various hybrids emerge from the divisional form of organizational structure. For example, dominant business companies are sometimes managed through a hybrid structure where top management controls the basic business through a functional structure and manages the rest of the organization

---

[12]Justin G. Longnecker, *Principles of Management and Organization*, 2nd ed. (Columbus, Ohio: Charles E. Merrill, 1969), p. 184.
[13]Katz, *Cases and Concepts*, pp. 505–507.
[14]Leonard Wrigley, Divisional Autonomy and Diversification (unpublished DBA dissertation, Harvard Business School, 1970), cited in Scott, "The Industrial State," p. 138.

through product divisions.¹⁵ A number of additional hybrids can result from crossing the divisional form with the functional form and organizing the divisions by products, territories, or customers. Product and territorial patterns are the most common of these hybrids.

Product departmentation. This form establishes each product or product line as an autonomous business entity and is frequently used to make little organizations out of big ones.¹⁶ As such, each smaller organization has its own functional structure for production, sales, finance, research and development, and personnel. Product departmentation at higher levels can reduce the coordination problems of functional departmentation because each product department operates autonomously with its own functional personnel. Thus there would be one marketing manager for each product instead of one marketing manager responsible for all products. However, this can result in a serious coordination problem if there is product diversification. Examples of product departmentation as part of the organizational structure can be found among the largest consumer packaged goods firms, such as Procter & Gamble.

Territorial divisionalization. This form establishes regional offices as autonomous enterprises. The Prudential Insurance Company of America utilizes this pattern, as shown in Figure 7-4. Each regional office has its own set

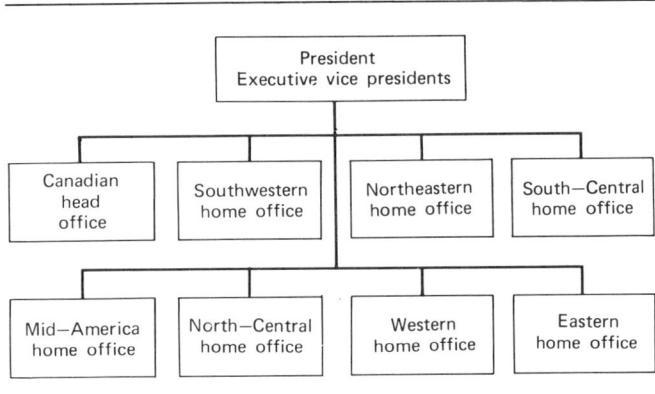

Figure 7-4 Territorial divisionalization: Prudential Insurance Company of America.

SOURCE: Justin G. Longenecker, *Principles of Management and Organizational Behavior* (Columbus, Ohio: Charles E. Merrill Publishing Co., 1969), p. 188.

---

¹⁵Scott, "The Industrial State," pp. 138–139.
¹⁶Henry H. Albers, *Principles of Organization and Management*, 2nd ed. (New York: John Wiley & Sons, 1965), p. 112.

of functional departments and operates under the strategic policies and guidelines established by corporate top management. Geographical location often is "a primary consideration in defining and differentiating executive responsibility."[17] This is usually because there is a major need for knowledge of the local environment, the climate and topography of each region, and the cultural considerations peculiar to each territory.[18]

Basic advantages. The divisional form has several advantages. In a large divisional corporation, especially an "unrelated" business company, each unit can function as an individual enterprise in the open market on a more competitive basis. This structure also simplifies the coordination task of top management, since each division or unit generally is provided with sufficient autonomy to conduct its own business, constrained only by the overall strategic decisions of the firm.

Another advantage of the divisional structure is the ability of top management to capitalize on new developments by creating new divisions. In this way, growth and diversification can be accomplished without distorting the basic organizational structure.[19] When market opportunities arise, a new division, which makes use of the firm's centralized staff and service facilities, can simply be added.

Finally, the ability of top management to draw from a pool of divisional management talent is a major advantage that may be difficult and costly to achieve with other structural forms. In the small structural form, there is relatively little opportunity for management training because of the owner/manager's singular control of all decision making. In the functional form, each manager becomes a specialist in his or her own area but has little experience with other functional areas. A company that is organized in the divisional form allows for a greater breadth of managerial experience. The talents of one manager can be transferred from one division to another because the manager has undertaken multifunctional responsibilities as the director of a fairly autonomous business entity.

Project Management

Project management was developed by the military as a result of pressure to complete tasks more quickly and in a more efficient manner. "The growth in project activity is due directly to the tremendous pressures on time, cost, and performance resulting from rapidly changing technologies in the environment of international tension."[20] After the project management concept was found to be the most effective means available to meet these pressures, whether or not particular firms maintained project management structures

---

[17]Ibid., p. 116.

[18]Ibid., p. 119.

[19]George R. Terry, *Principles of Management*, 4th ed. (Homewood, Ill.: Richard D. Irwin, 1964), p. 428.

[20]Stanley J. Baumgartner, *Project Management* (Homewood, Ill.: Richard D. Irwin, 1963), p. 2.

became a prime criterion for the awarding of government contracts. As a result, the concept filtered into the defense industry first and then into others. Although the full impact of project organization probably has not yet been felt outside the defense industry sphere, companies that utilize this structure have gained some advantages over competitors. In many cases, they have brought new products to market faster than their competition, completed major expansions on schedule, and met crucial commitments more reliably than ever before.[21]

The project management concept (see Figure 7-5) is actually a substructure that is utilized primarily for the ad hoc activities that arise within the firm. It is a temporary structure, because the project organization only lasts until the project is completed.

Figure 7-5 Project management organization.

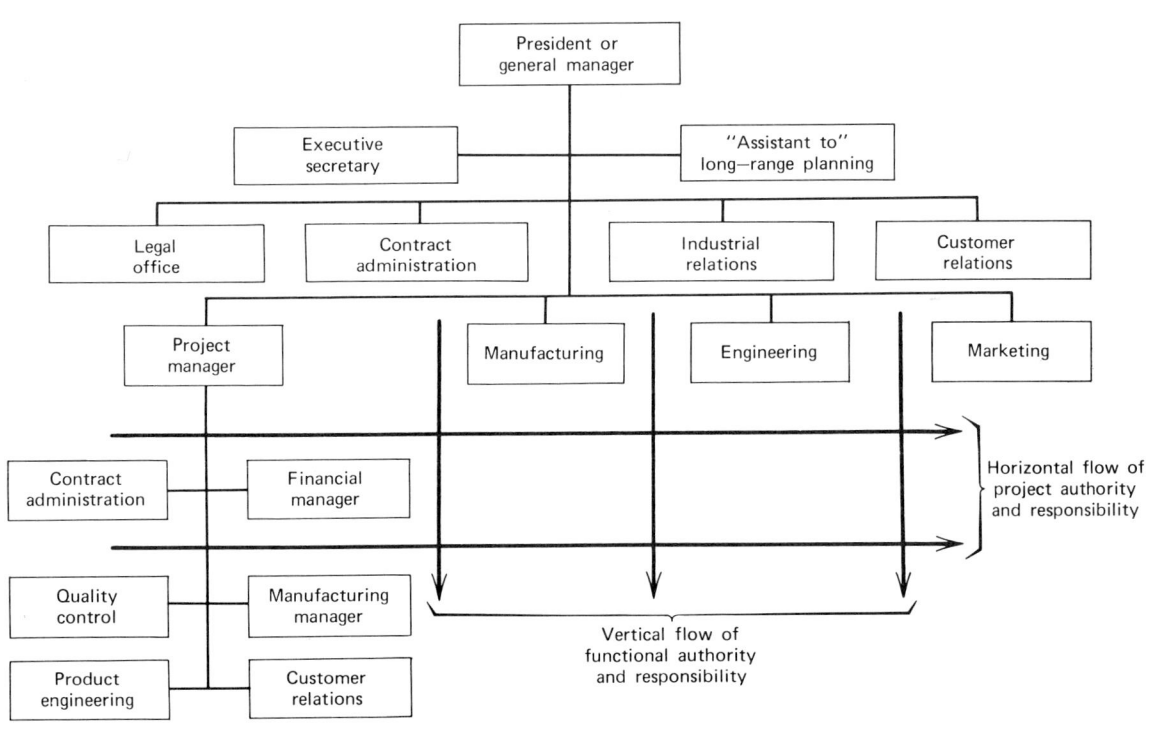

SOURCE: *Management: A Systems Approach* by David I. Cleland and William R. King. Copyright 1972, McGraw-Hill, Inc. Used with permission of McGraw-Hill Book Company.

---

[21]John M. Stewart, "Making Project Management Work," *Business Horizons*, Fall 1965, reprinted in David I. Cleland and William P. King, *Systems, Organizations, Analysis, Management: A Book of Readings* (New York: McGraw-Hill, 1969), p. 292.

There are certain criteria that indicate the need for a project-type structure.[22] The first is the *scope* of the project in terms of the work force, dollars, time, and organizational units required for its completion. It should be larger than any of the firm's previous projects, and it should have a specified completion date. The second criterion is the organization's *unfamiliarity* with the project. This is based on the assumption that unique or infrequent projects are coupled with a high degree of uncertainty about the task to be accomplished. This uncertainty requires that people on lower levels be more precisely informed about the specific tasks they must perform. The third criterion involves the *complexity* of the project in terms of the interdependence of the tasks that must be performed. This necessarily involves the degree to which the project is dependent on several functional areas. Because the integrated effort of these functional areas is necessary for the cost and timing of individual subtasks, project management's emphasis on integrating the diverse activities of these areas will enhance the successful completion of the project.[23] The final criterion is referred to as *stake*. This refers to the adverse effect that failure to complete the job on schedule or within budget might have on the company. This may be in terms of direct out-of-pocket costs or in the form of a lost opportunity caused by delayed production and the consequent loss of sales volume.

Project management evolves with the advancement of technology and the increased complexity of development and manufacturing projects. Because an integrating effort must be made to manage tasks across functional lines in order to achieve objectives, the establishment of a project-type organization insures an integrative focus. Decisions and actions emanating from a number of different functional areas, involvement of personnel at various levels of the existing structure, the necessity for close lateral relationships, and the necessity to consider time, cost, resources, and human factors all require an integrating effort that traditional functional structures generally do not provide.

The Matrix Organization

The matrix organization can be defined as "any organization that employs a multiple command system that includes not only a multiple command structure but also related support mechanisms and an associated organizational culture and behavior pattern."[24]

The matrix form of organization, depicted in Figure 7-6, represents a merger of the project and functional forms.[25] It provides a framework within which an organization can operate continuously on a project-type basis.

---

[22] Criteria from Stewart in Cleland and King, *Systems*, pp. 293–295.
[23] Keith Davis, *The Role of Project Management in Scientific Manufacturing*, IEEE Transactions on Engineering Management, 1962, reprinted in Cleland and King, *Systems*, p. 309.
[24] Stanley M. Davis and Paul R. Lawrence, *Matrix*, (Reading, Mass.: Addison-Wesley, 1977), p. 3.
[25] Cleland and King, *Management*, p. 239.

Figure 7-6 Matrix organization.

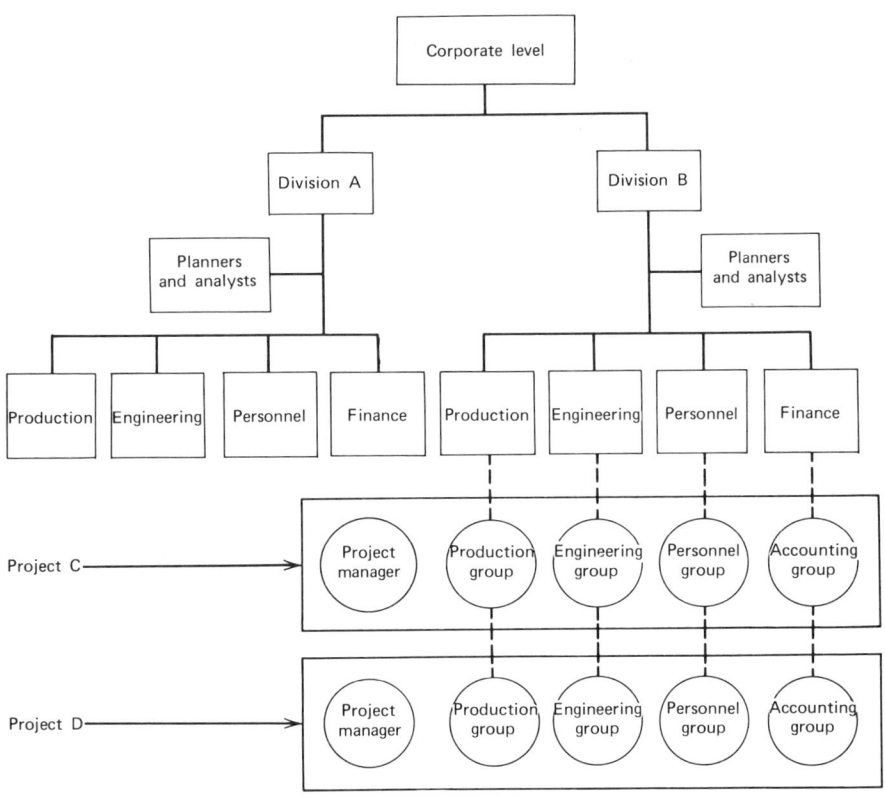

SOURCE: David I. Cleland and William R. King, *Management: A Systems Approach* (New York: McGraw-Hill Book Co., 1972). p. 338.

Unlike the project management concept, which is temporary and only lasts for the duration of the project, the matrix structure is permanent. People may be assigned to different project groups and project managers may change as new tasks are undertaken, but the basic framework or apparatus within which people function is maintained.[26]

The criteria for determining whether the project-type organization is feasible are also applicable here. The firm (or division of a firm) must be undertaking projects with the scope, unfamiliarity, complexity, and functional interdependence that necessitate a focus on timely completion of the pro-

---

[26]This situation can be thought of as being analogous to the traditional functional structure. People are swapped and promoted within the structure while the structure itself does not change.

ject. *However, in order for a company to warrant a matrix structure, it must be undertaking these projects as an everyday part of its business.* This requires that the firm (or division) be a "job-shop" operation—performing, for example, contract work for government or other industrial organizations. In this situation, the production emphasis is on the completion of action or project objectives instead of on the implementation of production programs to increase product volume.[27]

This does not mean that a firm (or division) that produces a standardized product (or products) may not occasionally warrant a project-type aproach. For example, the design and construction of a new plant or entry into a completely new product line may temporarily call for a project team approach. If work performed by an operating division of a company is applied to standardized products or services with high volume, however, there may be no need to consider a matrix organizational design.[28] It can be seen that the essence of a matrix organization is a continuous stream of ad hoc activities superimposed on the traditional functional organization.[29]

The matrix structure evolved out of the need to deal with the complex but recurring ad hoc activities that were first recognized in major military and space projects. The many different projects that were constantly being started and completed required the design of a flexible and adaptable system of resources and procedures to achieve a series of individual project objectives. In addition, this structure was used so that a dual focus could be utilized on the project; for example, within the aerospace industry firms have to concentrate on both complex technical issues and on the unique project requirements of the customer. In addition, as can be seen in Figure 7-6, there are two dimensions of authority and responsibility in these cases: a vertical flow pertaining to the functional organization, and a horizontal flow reflecting the project organization. A coordinating and integrating effort becomes necessary to draw from the various units so that the marketing, financing, and production of the goods can be accomplished. Because of this, the key to effective functioning of both the matrix organization and the project management system is the sharing of authority and responsibility between project and functional managers.

The structure that is produced by the matrix organization is a network of relationships among the participating individuals and teams in the organization. The teams are oriented toward the completion of project goals in a timely manner. With this major focus on the achievement of project objectives, the matrix structure permits a higher degree of specialized talents to be utilized with maximum efficiency of operations.

---

[27] John F. Mee, "Matrix Organization," *Business Horizons*, Summer 1964, reprinted in Cleland and King, *Systems*, p. 24.
[28] Ibid., p. 23.
[29] Cleland and King, *Management*, p. 339.

A prime example of a company using the matrix organization is TRW Systems. The impetus to utilize the matrix-type structure at TRW is derived from the predominant characteristics of the aerospace industry, within which it operates. The industry is basically job shop oriented and subject to frequent changes. One writer described the industry as follows:

> Because of rapid changes in technology, in customer requirements, and in competitive practices, product lines in the aerospace industry tend to be transitory. The customers' needs are finite and discrete. . . . Although the aerospace industry as a whole has grown steadily during the last decade, the fluctuations of individual companies underscore the job-shop nature of defense work. Aerospace industry planners must be constantly aware of the possibility of cancellation or prolongation of large programs.[30]

Another major characteristic of the industry is the complexity of its products. Parts are extremely interdependent, because the functioning of a product (e.g., a rocket) could be jeopardized by a single part. This means that the groups or divisions that design and manufacture the various parts also are highly interdependent. The traditional functional structure lacks the flexibility to meet changing project requirements, technologies, and environmental influences in order to remain viable in this dynamic environment.

The matrix organization and project management supply another means to create hybrid organizational structures. Some authors imply that the matrix structure is an organizational structure continuum.[31] In other words, that the matrix form is really a substructure that causes the organization to become more complex in a hybrid manner. The matrix form grew out of the traditional functional and project management forms and exists within the functional form or, more likely, within a division or a subsidiary of the divisional form. It is within the divisional form that the product/market complexities that warrant a matrix organization usually exist.

Hybrid Designs: Committees and Task Forces

Formal organizations can be found with a wide variety of design "mixtures" or "hybrids." In many cases, the structures discussed earlier may be used in combination. Figure 7-7 is illustrative of an organization using a hybrid of functional, product, territorial, and project structures.

As discussed in Chapter 1, C_1, C_2, and C_3 types of decisions require coordination among departments that have no direct vertical line relationships in the organization. Also, certain tasks and occasions may require commu-

---

[30] T.C. Miller, Jr., and L.P. Kane, "Strategies for Survival in the Aerospace Industry," *Industrial Management Review*, Fall 1965, pp. 23-23. Cited in Gene W. Dalton, Paul R. Lawrence, and Larry E. Greiner, *Organizational Change and Development* (Homewood, Ill.: Richard D. Irwin, 1970), pp. 107-108.

[31] Greiner, "Evolution and Revolution," p. 45, and Cleland and King, *Systems*, p. 279.

Figure 7-7 Hybrid organization design.

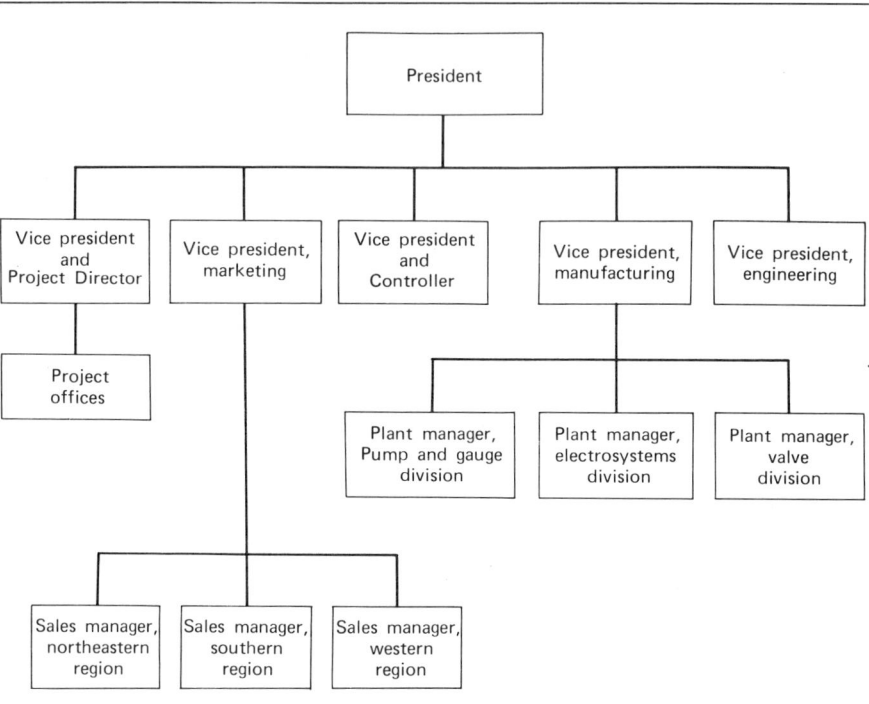

nication and consultation across departments. This requires the formation of committees or task forces to make these decisions. In essence, a committee or a task force results in the creation of lateral relationships in the organization structure.

Committees are used for a variety of purposes in all types of organizations. These may be formal or informal, line or staff, permanent or ad hoc. Committees have an advantage in that group instead of individual deliberation and judgment can be used. Often this device is utilized to counteract the fear of delegating too much authority to a single person. Representation of all the interested parties can be done in order to get more balanced group judgment and a more diversified point of view and also to insure that all groups represented will feel a sense of loyalty and commitment to the decision(s) reached. Better coordination of plans and policies can take place. The disadvantages of committees are their high cost in terms of time and money, indecision due to a lack of consensus, and tendency for a particular individual to dominate all committee decisions. A board of directors and the executive committee are examples of high-level committees in charge of strategic decisions.

THE INFORMAL ORGANIZATION

Invariably, informal organizations arise within the formal organization for a multitude of reasons that may include providing for:[32]

1. Satisfaction of social needs otherwise not satisfied by the formal organization.
2. A sense of belonging and affiliation to satisfy identification and status needs.
3. Knowledge of approved behavior.
4. Sympathetic ear.
5. Assistance in meeting objectives.
6. Opportunities for influence and creativity.
7. Perpetuation of cultural values.
8. Communications and information.

It would be futile for management to oppose or try to abolish informal organizations. If supported, the informal organization can often benefit management by backing the formal organization's goals and providing additional means of communication and social satisfaction.

Top management must understand informal organization characteristics in order to integrate the informal organization into the formal one or develop synergy between both. These characteristics include:[33]

1. Standards of behavior and social pressures to conform to these standards that involve rewards and punishment.
2. An informal leader who emerges from the group and directs members through persuasion and influence.
3. A status system that differentiates the social position of members associated with the groups.

Keys to Linking the Formal and Informal Organizations

As indicated earlier, informal organizations develop to satisfy individual and work group needs unfulfilled by the formal organization. Clear implications emerge from this basic premise. First, the design of formal organizations that meet the basic needs of individuals and groups may preclude the development of informal organizations of the numbers and magnitudes otherwise expected. Second, if the development of informal organizations cannot be avoided, management can get the informal organization to work toward the achievement of formal goals through the use of appropriate incentives. The final part of this chapter deals with needs and motivation as well as leadership as an organizational process important in the integration of individuals and work groups in the formal organization.

---

[32]Hicks and Gullett, *Organizations*, 1975, pp. 108–112.
[33]Ibid., pp. 112–115.

Needs and Motivation

Maslow, Herzberg and McGregor's theories of motivation are outlined in Table 7-3. The thrust of these theories is that effective and efficient organizations satisfy higher-level needs, emphasize motivators (instead of "hygiene" factors), and adopt a Theory *Y* perspective. Modern human resource management theories prescribe job enlargement, job enrichment, and a broad span of management as vehicles for the integration of the individuals and work groups into the formal organization.

Leadership

Internal motivation is based on the individual's needs, wants, and desires. External motivation is provided by the individual's manager or supervisor. Effective leadership should motivate and give direction to the efforts of all individuals in accomplishing the goals of the organization. Indeed, leadership is the ability to persuade others to seek defined objectives enthusiastically. The style of leadership a manager elects to use influences his/her effectiveness as a leader.[34]

Table 7-3 The Relationship of the Theories of Maslow, McGregor, and Herzberg.

These theories each approach motivation from a different perspective, but they all emphasize similar sets of relationships.

Maslow	Herzberg	McGregor
Higher-level needs	Motivators	Theory Y
Self-actualization	Achievement	Satisfaction of esteem and self-actualization needs
Esteem	Recognition	
	Advancement	Responsibility
	Responsibility	Imagination and creativity
	Work itself	Self-direction and self-control
Lower-level needs	Hygiene factors	Theory X
Social	Company policy and administration	Security above all
Safety		Direction preferable
Physiological	Supervision	Threats of punishment needed
	Interpersonal relations	
	Salary	
	Working conditions	

SOURCE: Herbert G. Hicks and Ray C. Gullett, *Organizations: Theory and Behavior* (New York: McGraw-Hill Book Company, 1975), p. 290.

[34]Ibid., pp. 300–301.

Leadership styles range from authoritarian/autocratic to subordinate-centered laissez-faire, as shown in Figure 7-8. According to the modern human resource management theory, subordinate-centered leadership styles are usually more conducive to effective and efficient organizations. Therefore participative management is often prescribed as a vehicle for integrating individuals and work groups into the formal organization.

SUMMARY Corporate strategy cannot be implemented, nor can its objectives be achieved, without proper organizational structure. This chapter has discussed the factors that affect organizational design and alternative structural forms. It should be clear from the discussion that the structural forms are dynamic. They change as an organization passes through its life cycle and as it changes its product and market emphases. The following article provides a discussion of a new and important structural form that may be referred to as a "market-centered" organization. This structural form may supplant traditional functional and product forms of organization in many industries.

Structure-related decisions are very difficult to make and to implement as they affect the human element of the organization. Chapter 8 deals with the problems and dimensions of effective organizational change.

Figure 7-8 The leader can choose which leadership style to use based on the forces in himself, in his subordinates, and in the situation.

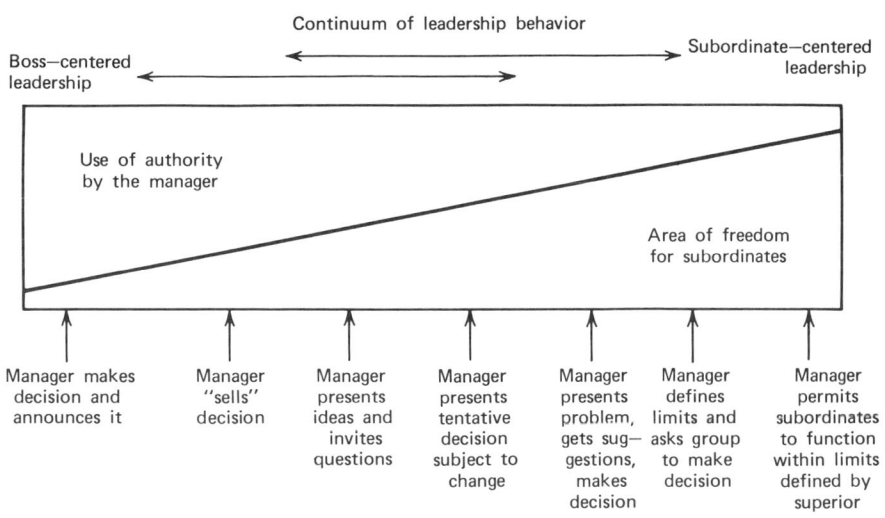

SOURCE: Reprinted from the *Harvard Business Review*. Exhibit from "How to Choose a Leadership Pattern": by Robert Tannenbaum and Warren H. Schmidt (May-June 1973). Copyright © 1973 by the President and Fellows of Harvard College; all rights reserved.

REORGANIZE YOUR COMPANY AROUND ITS MARKETS

Mack Hanan

Throughout the 1960s, market orientation was such a dominant business concept that it is surprising to find, a decade later, that few companies have found a way to organize themselves so that their customers' needs consistently come first. In most companies, the divisional structures are still determined by regions, organized around products, or structured to commercialize a process technology. It has been only over the past few years that a small number of companies have come to realize that:

- There is no substitute for market orientation as the ultimate source of profitable growth.
- The only way to ensure being market-oriented is to put a company's organizational structure together so that its major markets become the centers around which its divisions are built.

Some leading companies are emphasizing growth by gearing their organizational structures to their markets' needs instead of to their product or process capabilities. IBM's data-processing operations are segmented organizationally according to key markets, such as institutions like hospitals and retail establishments like supermarkets. Xerox Information Systems Group, which sells copiers and duplicators, has converted from geographical selling to vertical selling by industry. General Foods has adopted a market-targeting organizational style. Even the strict product orientation of some scientific companies is gradually giving way to a combined product and market orientation. In its electronics product marketing, for example, Hewlett-Packard has created a sales and service group that concentrates separately on the electrical manufacturing market while another group serves the market for aerospace. Still other groups sell to the markets for communications or transportation equipment.

In other companies steps are being taken to orient businesses to their markets. At Mead, broad market clusters are coming into being to serve customer needs in home building and furnishings, education, and leisure. PPG Industries has been examining the benefits of systematizing the marketing of its paint, ceramics, and glass divisions through a home environment profit center whose product mix could resemble the pattern shown in Exhibit 1. Monsanto has organized a Fire Safety Center that consolidates fire safety products from every sector of Monsanto and groups them according to the market they serve: building and construction, transportation, apparel, or furnishings. Revlon is engaged in "Breaking up the company into little pieces": as many as six autonomous profit centers are being created, each of which is designed to serve a specific market segment.

General Electric is well along in constructing strategic business groups for its major appliance and power-generation businesses. For GE, the

---

Reprinted by permission of the *Harvard Business Review*. "Reorganize Your Company Around Its Markets" by Mack Hanan (November-December 1974). Copyright ©1974 by the President and Fellows of Harvard College; all rights reserved.

Exhibit 1 Product mix of a business market centered on the home.

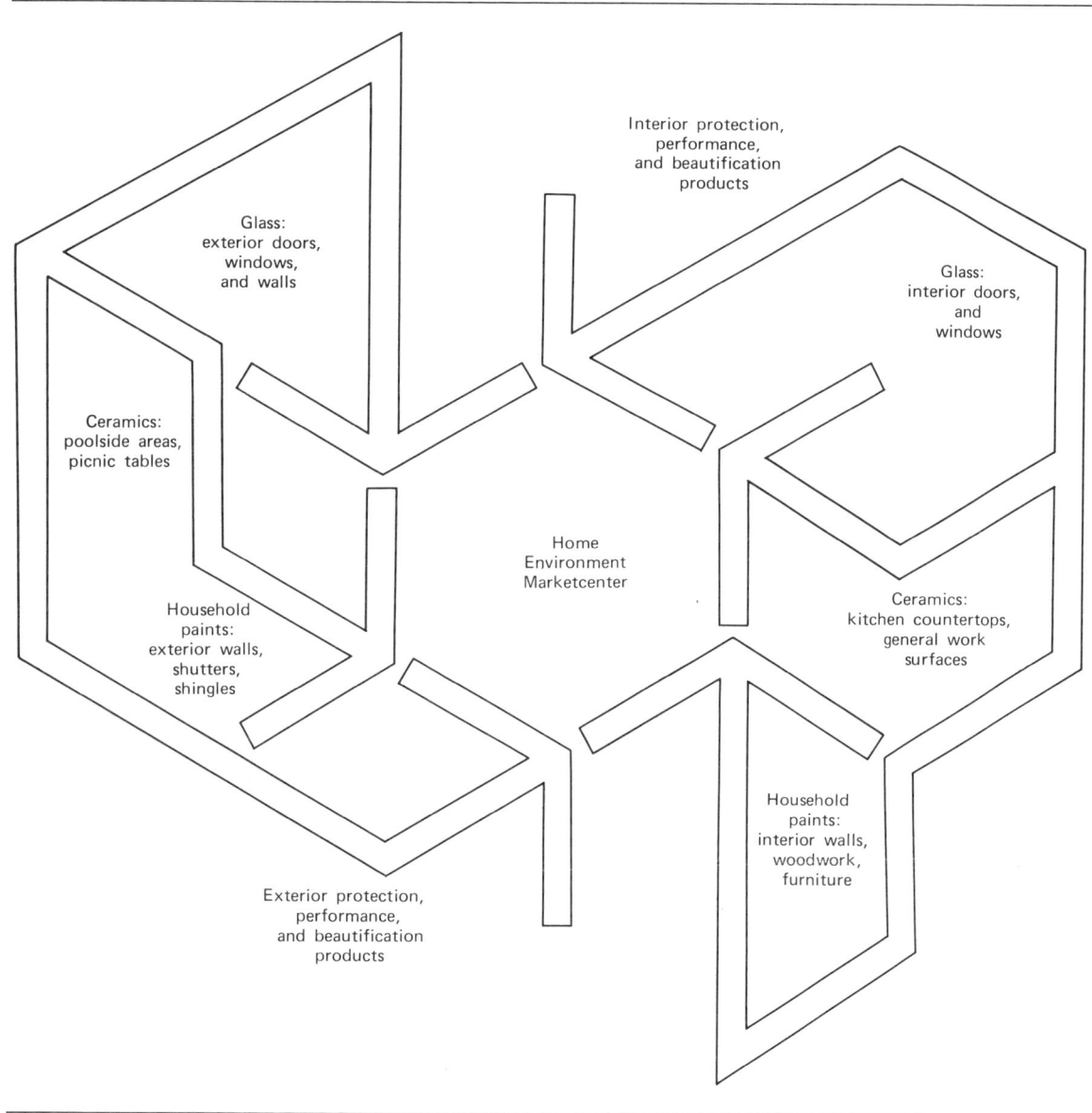

process of reorganizing from a product to a market orientation has been especially difficult. An average department contains three and one half product lines and may serve more than one business or, more frequently, only a part of a major business. Electric motors, for example, are divided among eight departments. Home refrigerators are split between two departments, even though the only significant product difference is the way the doors open. In such a setup, department managers have understandably become oriented to specific product lines rather than to the needs of a total market.

I use the term *marketcentered* (or marketcentering) to describe the wide range of corporate organizational forms that make a group of customer needs, rather than a region, a product line, or a process, the center of a business division. These forms include General Foods's "strategic business units," National Cash Register's "vocations," the "customer provinces" that some high-technology manufacturers are organizing as company-like units to concentrate on serving the needs of specific market groups, and the "financial need groups" through which some progressive banks serve the common financing needs of manufacturers of electronic systems, drugs, cosmetics, household products, and other items.

Marketcentering also describes the way some railroads are grouping their services around the common distribution needs of major customers so that they can provide a unique user-oriented service system for oil, chemical, and fertilizer shippers and a different system for grain shippers. These organizational formats are working so well that more railroads can be expected to adopt them.

WHEN SHOULD AN ORGANIZATION BE MARKETCENTERED?

Marketcentered describes an organization that is decentralized by markets—markets define the business. Organizing an enterprise in this way, which some companies think of as working backward from the points where they deal face to face with their customers, can yield many of the same benefits as decentralizing by processes, materials, or product lines. A marketcenter forms a natural profit center just as readily as does a materials center, such as Continental Can's Metal Operations group. A marketcenter may also be able to dominate the heavy users in its market to such an extent that it becomes the preeminent supplier, like such product centers as The Ansul Company's former Fire Protection Products division.

But marketcentering is not without some costs and inefficiencies. For example, when Coca-Cola was reorienting to its markets in the early 1960s, some of its veteran managers were moved to lament the passing of one of the most cost-efficient mass businesses of all time. Formerly, the company had manufactured a single product, made according to one basic formula and sold at one retail price, which was marketed with great economies in an internationally recognized bottle that conveyed instant product awareness. The managers saw this business give way forever to a diversity of sizes and prices and even to various companion products, all of which bore a considerable burden of their own administrative, operating, and marketing expenses.

Marketcentering an organization may incur other additional costs. In order to zero in on its market, management generally requires its own information bank of customer needs and its own exclusive sales force, which is intensively schooled to apply the data bank's resources to the center's customers. A company that has employed a single sales force before marketcentering may find itself recruiting, training, developing, and fielding several separate sales forces whose compensation plans and support services—to say nothing of product lines and channels of distribution—may be totally dissimilar.

Conditions Favoring Change

When then, does marketcentering become an appropriate form of decentralization? Executives of companies that have been reorganizing around their markets suggested five particular situations that especially favor a marketcentered approach:

1. When market leadership is threatened by a competitor who has achieved sufficient

product parity to deprive the leader of price superiority. Marketcentering can restore a competitive advantage with the more creative marketing techniques it develops from improved knowledge of customer, distributor, and retailer needs.

2. When new-product famine has afflicted the product-development function so that nothing, or only a crop of lemons, is being delivered, or when R & D has been foundering in its resource allocation because of a lack of market direction. Marketcentering can stimulate new-product winners by transmitting current knowledge of market life-styles or emergent needs to technical management. Marketcentering also enables innovative breakthrough thinking to replace a preoccupation with generating only marginal extensions of established product categories.
3. When a product manufacturer desires either to diversify into higher-margin services as a means of broadening his profit base or to market systems of correlated products and services in order to gain a lock on key customers. Marketcentering can group market needs into highly visible targets for systems, enabling the marketer to operate as a one-stop supplier to each center.
4. When a manufacturer who has been selling product-performance benefits shifts his marketing strategy to feature the financial benefits of customer profit improvement. Marketcentering makes it easier to amass the required knowledge of how customers make their profits. Each marketcenter is made responsible for compiling its own data resource.
5. When a marketer desires to attract a more entrepreneurial type of manager. Marketcentering offers candidates an enlarged scope of supervisory duties and full profit responsibility. In a multimarket company, a mobile young manager can often tackle diverse challenges by moving from one marketcentered division to another. He does not have to go to another company in order to obtain variety.

EASING INTO A MARKETCENTERED FORM

A major organizational change like marketcentering can be a shock to any company—especially to the traditional product manufacturer (who, paradoxically, may benefit the most from it). Companies have been experimenting with several ways of easing themselves toward a marketcentered approach, since the change is often best implemented by degrees. Along the way, a company can learn how much marketcentering it can stand at any given time and what particular form it should ultimately have. Three ways of beginning the transition have emerged thus far.

Marketcentering a sales force is the first way. It requires the least up-front commitment and the least alteration in the basic structure of a business. In addition, it succeeds in establishing the central relationship that earmarks all forms of marketcentered organizations: contact between customers with many varying needs and a sales force that can prescribe the most beneficial systems for those needs. In the romantic version of marketing, this interface takes place on a prolonged person-to-person basis in the marketplace. The reality, however, is that customer information is collected and analyzed at a data bank.

This is the approach that NCR has taken. Each sales staff is assigned a well-defined industry group to serve. The company's salesmen are trained to sell systems of different but interrelated products and services in a consultative manner. They consider market knowledge, rather than product knowledge, to be their principal resource.

General Foods has chosen a second way to ease into marketcentering. It has created a separate marketing division to serve each major market. This approach involves reclassifying major markets into new, more comprehensive groups and consolidating similar but differently manufactured products into product families to be marketed to each group. While the NCR sales-centered approach requires a single salesman to serve most or all of a customer's needs with many different products and services, the General Foods approach coordinates a wide range of products that are essentially alike for a single user segment.

The third way is to begin with either the first or second step and then proceed to achieve a thoroughly marketcentered structure by integrating manufacturing and all marketing functions, including sales, into a single division. Both the NCR and General Foods examples lend themselves to this end result, which IBM and Xerox have perhaps most fully achieved.

In the following sections, I shall examine some of the major characterisitics of the NCR and General Foods approaches. Then I shall describe the key criteria of a marketcentered organization, the role of the business manager, and the service systems needed to support that role.

NCR'S APPROACH—
SEPARATE SALES FORCES

NCR has been reorganizing its traditional product-line sales approach into a strategy of "selling by vocation" on an industry-by-industry basis. Each vocation is a broad industry grouping which forms a specific market definable by reasonably cohesive needs. NCR is focusing a separate sales force on each of the following vocational markets: financial institutions, retailers, commercial and industrial businesses, and computer customers in medical, educational, and government offices.

NCR's marketcentered sales organization is enabling the company to be more competitive, especially in the marketing of systems. In each market, the NCR salesman assigned to it can sell coordinated systems of numerical recording and sorting products. Previously, each salesman could sell only his own product line. Also, the decision maker in the customer company could be involved with several NCR salesmen, no one of whom could know the sum total of the customer's numerical control needs, let alone serve them. Under the new system, the same retail industry salesman who sells an NCR cash register to a department store can also search out and serve the store's needs for NCR accounting machines, data entry terminals, and a mainframe computer. If he needs help, he can organize a team with other NCR salesmen that can bring the required strength to his proposal. The product groups he sells are still manufactured separately; the centralized sales approach is the innovation that makes the difference.

By selling groups or systems of products through a single salesman or sales team, rather than selling individual products through many uncoordinated salesmen, NCR believes it can help customers achieve greater profit improvement. It can prescribe systems that solve comprehensive problems which would otherwise remain immune to single product solutions. Management also believes it can expand its profitable sales volume by selling larger packages and insulating its position against competition.

Each vocational market's full range of recording and sorting needs is becoming better known to NCR personnel. In turn, by specializing in seeking out and serving these needs, each of NCR's vocational sales organizations can become known for expertise in its market, almost as if it were an independent specialist company. Moreover, every sales group can utilize the total financial and technical resources of the company for professional counsel and support in developing, prescribing, and installing product systems.

Operations and Options

A vice president of marketing directs NCR's sales organization. The four vocational vice presidents report to him. Regional vocational directors supervise several states, giving a geographic underlay to the organization.

NCR's next step in marketcentering through its sales force is to specialize more precisely. This can logically lead to the appointment of retail specialists within the financial industry sales force, to mention one possibility. As additional ramifications of the new approach become apparent, NCR will be able to reorganize many other aspects of its corporate structure and operations, increasing its market orientation. Among the major options which will be open to the company are decentralizing staff services, bringing R&D and product development activities into closer vocational alignment, adding profit-making services to existing product systems, consolidating advertising and other promotional activities to appeal specifically to vocational needs, and combining the appropriate manufacturing and selling activities in marketcentered divisions.

GENERAL FOODS' APPROACH—SEPARATE MARKETING DIVISIONS

While NCR has been stimulated to reorganize by the increasing preferences of its customers for systems and by the relentless competitive pressures of IBM, General Foods revised its approach because of internal strains and frustrations. In the early 1970s new product winners either stopped coming out of product development at their former rate or carried an unreasonable cost. Better knowledge of the needs of its consumers was obviously required if the company's product developers were to harmonize their technologies with the new life-styles influencing the demand for processed foods. At the same time, the needs of the company's customers at the retail level required new responses. Competitive brands were proliferating, clamoring for shelf and display space, while an increasingly attractive profit on sales was making private-label products more acceptable to the major supermarket chains.

These events combined to place unprecedented strains on the company's divisional structure, which was the legacy of a generations-old policy of acquisition. General Foods's major food divisions—Birds Eye, Jell-O, Post, and Kool-Aid—had evolved historically, each according to the process technology which it brought into the company. As the scope of each division's consumer provinces grew, it was inevitable that one division's consumer provinces would be impinged on by other divisions, and that any given market would be served in a fragmented rather than a concentrated manner. Divisional sovereignties frequently made it impossible for the company to dominate a market that was served by two or more divisions with related product categories but with different styles and degrees of commitment.

Often more damaging for new-product development was the way in which division managers respected a no-man's-land between their provinces, leaving gaps in product categories that could give competitors a clear shot or deny the company a chance to establish a position of category leadership. Beverages are a case in point. They were marketed by three divisions. If they were frozen, they were marketed by Birds Eye. If they were powdered mixes, the Kool-Aid division marketed them. Breakfast drinks had to come from Post. No centralized attack on consumer beverage needs could be made. In a similar fashion, puddings were marketed by two divisions: Birds Eye had jurisdiction over frozen puddings while Jell-O was the steward division for powdered mixes. The pudding market as such had no general representative within the company.

Relating Products to Market Needs

The General Foods approach to marketcentering has been to reorganize its process-oriented divisional structure into separate marketing organizations known as "strategic business units" (SBUs). Each SBU concentrates on marketing families of products made by different processing technologies but consumed by the same market segment. As Exhibit 2 shows, the Food Products division coordinates the marketing strategy for all desserts whether they are in frozen, powdered, or ready-to-eat form. The exhibit also

Exhibit 2 Strategic business centers at General Foods.

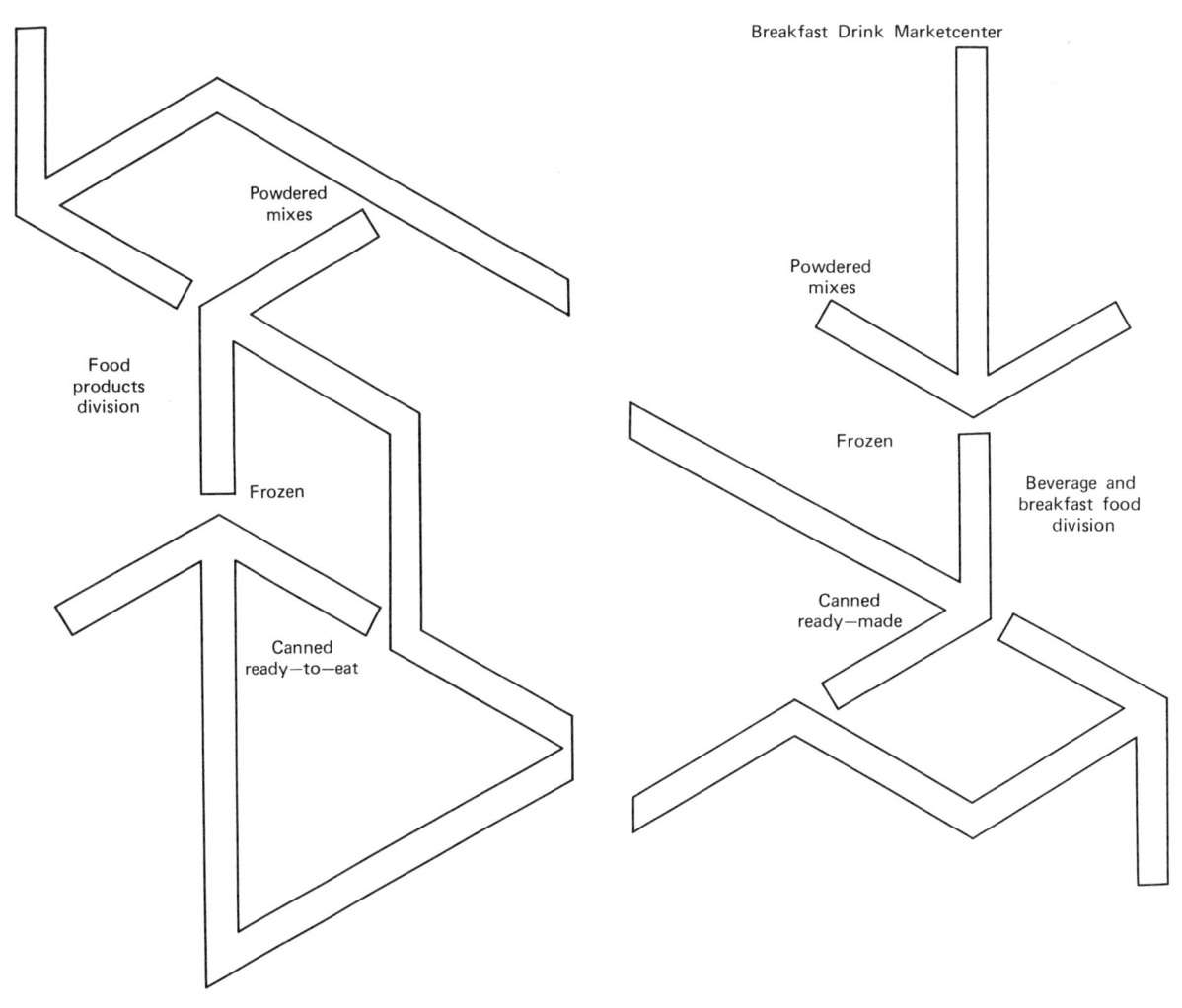

shows how the Beverage and Breakfast Food division markets breakfast drinks of three different processing techniques and how the Pet Food division centers the marketing of freeze-dried, dry pellet, and semimoist dog foods.

This scheme allows each SBU to take an overview of how an entire product family can best be related to the needs of both end users and retailers. Each SBU functions like a division and draws on the full range of corporate technologies. It also derives support services from a corporate pool where market research, production, personnel, new-product development, and sales are consolidated for use by all SBUs. A small amount of product-connected market research and new-product development is still left to the individual SBUs. But their primary mission is to engage in "pure marketing" as much as possible

Exhibit 2 (continued)

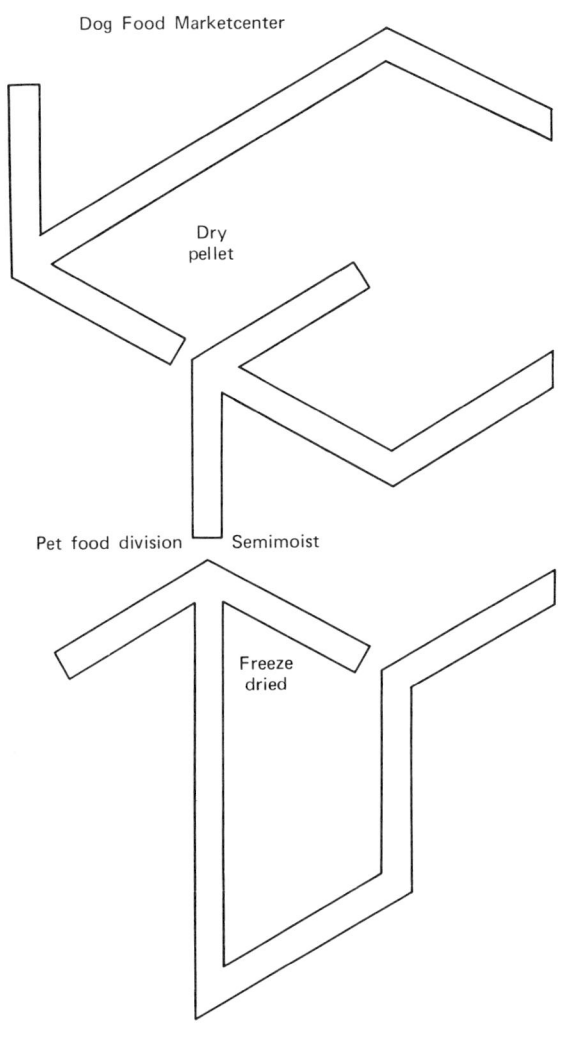

and to concentrate their resources on cultivating the market segments to which they have been assigned.

Among the benefits that General Foods believes it has gained so far from its form of marketcentering are an increasingly productive trade merchandising capability and improved ability to dominate a full consumer-need category at the point of sale—the supermarket. The company has also had better opportunities to aim multiple-product advertising at a single market, with the result that preferences for company brands have risen in certain product categories.

Another benefit has been that new products can be launched with fewer problems of stewardship than before. To take a hypothetical example, suppose that skin care products were to become part of the corporate growth scheme. If one proposed item were to be packaged in frozen form, it would not have to start its market life in the Birds Eye division, as presumably would have been necessary in the past, and therefore labor under the potentially negative connotations of having vegetable origins. Or, if the new skin care product were to be a premoistened patty or a water-soluble pellet, it would not have to be marketed under the umbrella of the Gaines pet food division.

GUIDELINES FOR DEVELOPMENT

In sketching the main guidelines that product- or process-centered companies can use to change to a marketcentered approach, I shall place special emphasis on two areas. One is the key criteria of marketcentering. The other is the role of the manager who runs a marketcenter and the unique aspects of his supportive service system.

Key Criteria

When an organization is fully marketcentered, a market becomes the focal point of every one of the company's major operations. The objective of each business is to become its market's preferred center for fulfilling one or more principal needs. Such a business is the sum of its market-centered divisions and should meet these five criteria:

1. It must be chartered to serve a market which is defined according to a system of closely related needs. This permits the market to be

served by a diversified package of products and services that, taken together, supply a combination of closely related benefits. The business may market two or more related products in a single sale or market a package composed of products and their related services.

2. Because a marketcenter is operated as a profit center, it should be administered by an entrepreneur. I like to call this executive the *business manager* of the organization. Unlike most product managers or brand managers, or even market managers who are merely profit-accountable, a business manager is fully profit-responsible. He enjoys considerable authority in running his business. He commands the key decisions. He sets prices, controls costs, and is charged with operating his marketcenter for a satisfactory profit.

3. Business managers are the chief line officers in their marketcentered organizations. All other corporate functions must be repositioned as satellite supply services that support the business managers' operations. Business managers employ corporate staff services on a contractual basis, which gives them authority to refuse to do business with any service that cannot be competitive in pricing, quality control, or delivery.

4. Once a division is marketcentered, its storehouse of market information quickly becomes its key asset. Through marketcentering, a company grows by basing its future expansion on knowledge about its existing markets. A corporatewide market information center can be set up to store and give access to the market knowledge required by each division, or marketcentered divisions can create their own information centers.

5. Top management must position itself as a holding company or, as it is sometimes called, a central bank. This central bank acts as a council of portfolio managers who centralize corporate policy making and investment funding for their decentralized businesses. Top management's prime concern is usually to manage a balanced portfolio of businesses in which no single investment accounts for more than 50% of total corporate profit, or at least not for long. The business managers consult the central bank when they want money or need advice.

How the Business Manager Operates

A business manager may head up a single, large marketcenter or, if the operations are small or closely related, two or more such centers. His job is to manage the coporate investment in a center so that it will yield the maximum rate of return. At Textron, for example, a minimum pretax return on investment of 25% is mandated for every one of the company's businesses. At ITT, the manager's contribution must fall within the 10% to 12% annual range of increase in earnings.

As a result of his concentration on financial bogeys, a marketcenter's business manager tends to view himself as a profit creator rather than a curator of specific products or processes. He resists becoming addicted to any particular product line or acquiring a reverence for any technological process. "In my marketing mix, I recognize no such thing as an eternal product," one business manager told me. "Nor do I cherish any perpetual promotional appeals for them. Even the customer needs that I serve today will probably prove to be transient. Only my commitment to maximize the long-range profit of my marketcenter is everlasting."

Supportive Systems

While marketcentering decentralizes the management of operations, it centralizes many of the staff services which business managers use. As Exhibit 3 shows, up to four consolidated service functions may revolve around each business manager.

Development services combine new-market research and development with new-product R & D

Exhibit 3 Supporting services available to a business manager.

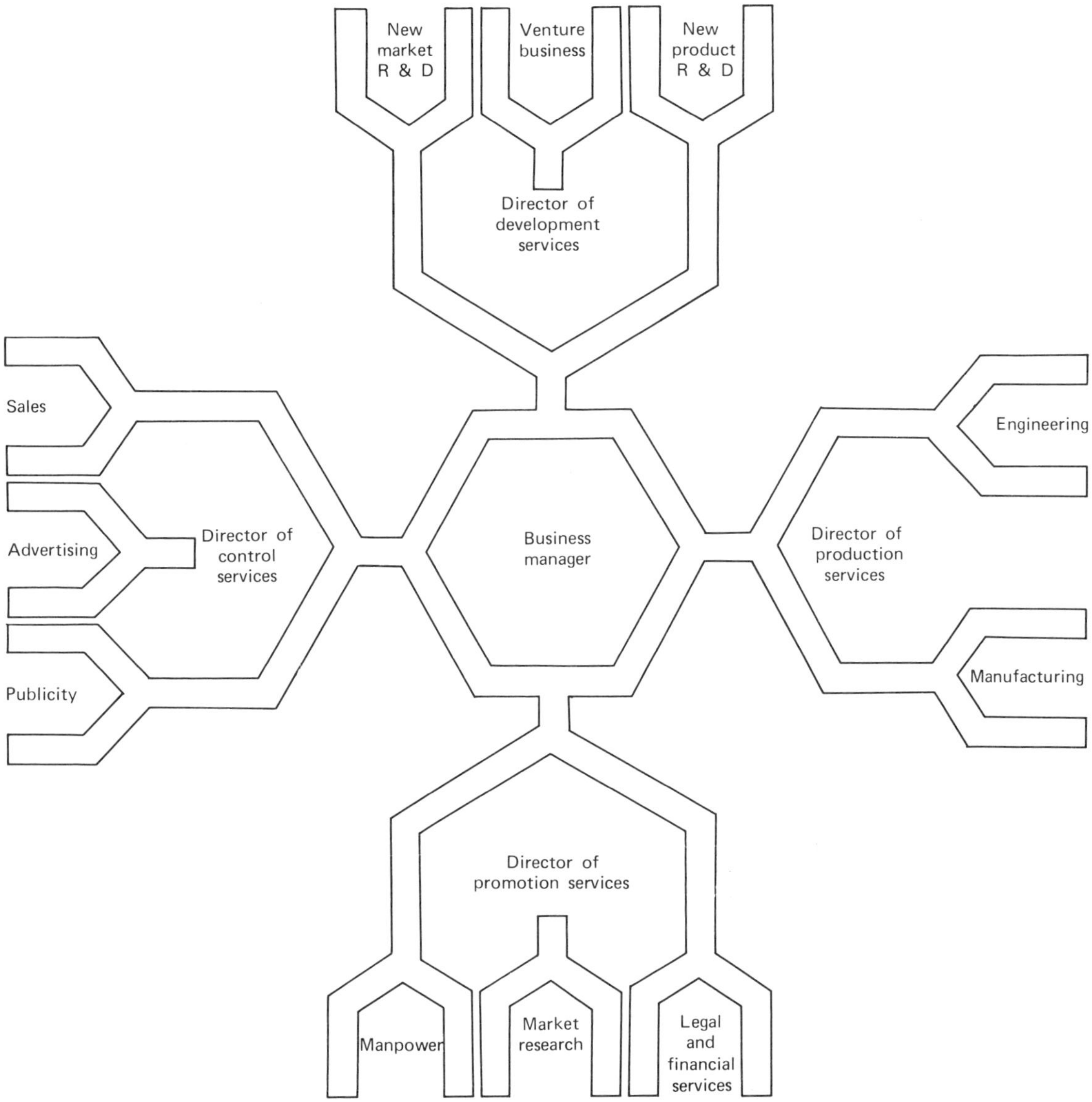

Diagram: A hexagonal central node labeled "Business manager" connects to four directors:
- *Director of development services (top): New market R & D, Venture business, New product R & D*
- *Director of control services (left): Sales, Advertising, Publicity*
- *Director of production services (right): Engineering, Manufacturing*
- *Director of promotion services (bottom): Manpower, Market research, Legal and financial services*

under a single director. In this way, the market orientation of R & D—historically one of the chief stumbling blocks in raising a company's level of consciousness to its customers—is accomplished organizationally. New-market needs, new-process technology, and new-product development are able to interact harmoniously rather than competitively. With marketcentering, the traditional vice presidential functions for marketing and R & D can be subsumed under the director of development's functions. There is generally no need for a vice president of marketing in such an organization because the entire corporate structure is market-oriented and each business manager must act as his own chief marketing officer.

Control services do the basic research to evaluate the effectiveness of established product and service-system marketing. They also provide the necessary recruitment, compensation and motivation, training and development, legal, and financial functions. *Production services* coordinate engineering and manufacturing operations. And *promotion services* combine sales, advertising, and publicity.

These four groups of services are supplied by top management on an elective basis. Whether and when they are used depends on the business manager. Should he elect to contract with the internal services, he negotiates with the service managers as if they were outside suppliers.

Contracting for Service

Any one, or all four, of his company's internal services may be retained, either in whole or in part, by a business manager. As the following position description indicates, the business manager is also chartered to employ outside services whenever he feels they can better help him meet his objectives:

> Through an annual contractual relationship with the director of production services, the business manager acquires a product supply to market. The business manager must, at minimal cost, negotiate for a dependable and sufficient supply of products, manufactured according to marketable specifications, that maintain maximum economies in production without impairing either market acceptance or corporate image.

Since the business manager has ultimate responsibility for profit, he must be free to negotiate with any strategic service that meets his product and market specifications at minimal cost. Much, if not most, of the time, these services will come from inside the company. But he can also buy them from outside and use them interchangeably with, or independently of, internal functions. In either case, the contractual form of doing business acts as his principal instrument of cost and quality control.

The service contract can also be an instrument of top management control. Making the use of internal services optional puts them squarely on their mettle. They must perform for the business managers, competing with alternate sources of supply in cost and quality terms, or be bypassed. If internal services are consistently selected by most business managers, top management can comfortably assume that they are competitive; if the services are rejected, that is a sign that they are not doing the job.

Ensuring Continued Service

From each business manager's point of view, being on the receiving end of a demand-feed schedule with contracted services is an almost ideal situation. Best quality at lowest price, every manager's dream, seems assured. But will there be chaos among the suppliers of services? To discourage an endless series of requests for custom-tailored variations in services, especially in production and promotion, a variance-request control system can be installed. Under this system, market-based justification can be required for all significant departures from contracted specifications.

However, it may be necessary to go further. What can be done to protect an internal supplier of services from having to react simultaneously to short-term strategy changes by several business managers? While a predictable problem area such as seasonal production peaks can be rather simply ironed out in advance, no service can fully anticipate a business manager's midcycle decision changes. He may need to alter his product mix in the face of sudden raw materials shortages. New corporate policies on allocating scarce ingredients or components may shut off his supply. Demand variations among his key customers may dry up one or more markets and force him to shift his product specifications to meet the needs of a previously less important customer group. Such stresses can disrupt R & D priorities, throw off manufacturing runs, scuttle cost estimates, and upset sales and advertising appropriations.

TWO-WAY GROWTH OPPORTUNITY

Some corporate executives feel that marketcentering may come to rank with Alfred Sloan's decentralization of General Motors along market-segmented lines. They see themselves regaining a customer focus that often became blurred by Proctor & Gamble's brand management system. While contemporary with Sloan's market awareness, brand management directed the styles of many corporate formats away from customers and back to products. When product and brand management were imposed on the traditional organization of the manufacturing division and on the pyramidal organization chart, which was adapted for the needs of commercial business from Von Moltke's general staff concept, progress toward marketcentering slowed for half a century.

In the mid 1960s, the beginning of a new thrust toward the customer was signaled by the advent of free-form marketing groups. They were allowed to cut across corporate pyramids whenever unusual market sensitivity was demanded in an operation. A variety of problem-solving task forces and project management teams came into being for much the same reason; they represented jerry-built improvisations to defeat a product-oriented or process-centered organizational system. In other instances, managers have had to depart from the accepted corporate framework and to create highly decentralized conglomerates of market-targeted businesses.

Since it is probable that these dislocations will be with us for some time to come, methods for coping with them are under experimentation. Some companies are establishing resource allocation groups, composed of the directors of development, control, production, and promotion services, who recommend to top management the most favorable distribution patterns in times of materials short-falls. Their suggestions are based on the central criterion of close-in contribution to profit but are naturally conditioned by short- and long-term considerations, such as maintenance of the traditional market position, potential for future growth, and possible preemptive reactions from competitors.

Because a marketcentered company expands chiefly by serving new needs in established markets where it is well franchised, its growth is relatively safe. By asking and reasking the key question, "What *other* needs of the markets we know so well can we serve profitably?" management can develop new business on the basis of the strength of its existing businesses.

Marketcentering a company can give it two-way flexibility for growth. Each of its major markets can be served *intensively*, once it is established as the center of a business. When growth on a broadened profit base becomes desirable, the same markets can be served more *extensively* by searching out their closely related needs and centering new businesses around one or more of them. Through these two approaches, the basic growth strategy of a marketcentered company can be defined as meeting the greatest number of interrelated needs of every market segment it serves.

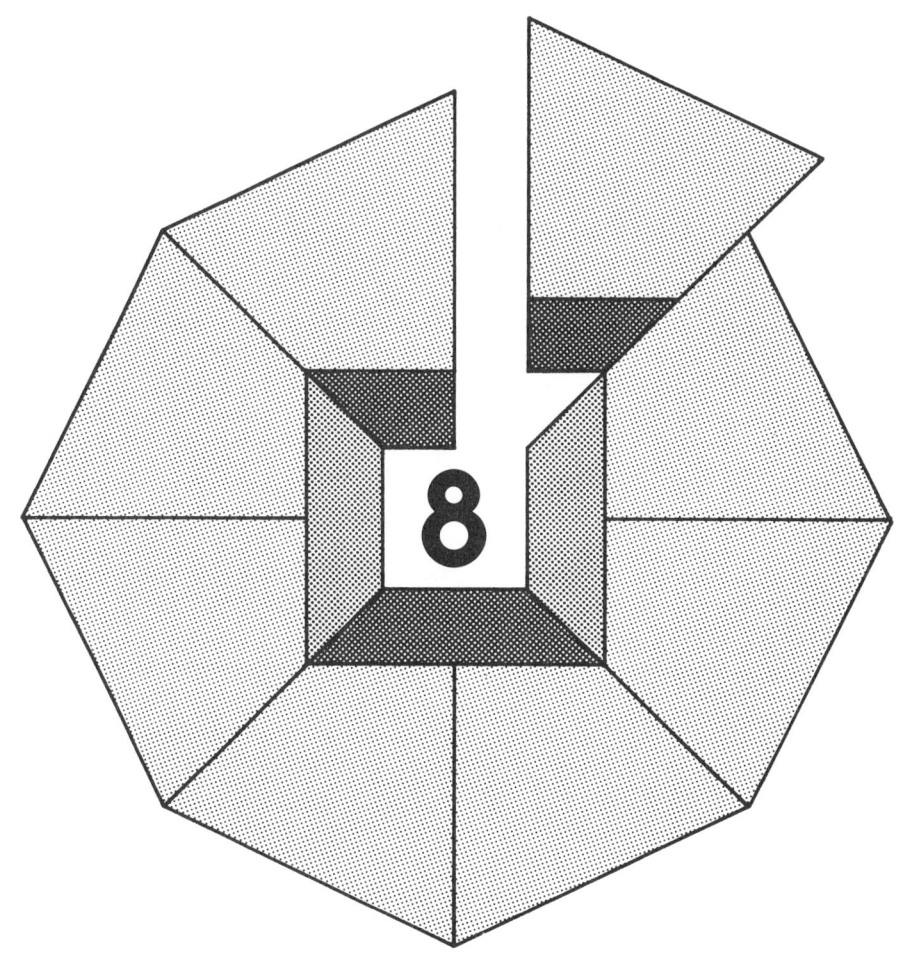

ORGANIZATIONAL CHANGE
an integrated approach

As indicated in Chapter 1, the formulation of recommendations for problem solution in a policy case always signals the need for change in one or more parts of the total organization. This chapter will (1) clarify what is meant by the term "organizational change," (2) delineate the basic elements of the change process, and (3) present a summary of research findings on the reasons for resistance to change. The material should clarify the process of change and point out basic barriers to change as found in various studies.

The emphasis in this text has clearly been on the *formulation* of strategy. However, it is obvious that a well-formulated strategy is of little value unless it is successfully implemented by the organization. Successful implementation in turn depends on the ability of the organization and its members to change obsolete technologies, outmoded behavior patterns, inappropriate organizational structures, or other phenomena. In other words, the organizational arrangements or patterns that were appropriate for carrying out the old strategy are rarely appropriate under new conditions. Consequently, one of the most critical tasks facing top management is the building of a *flexible* organization, particularly in industries where environmental change is rapid and largely unpredictable. Under such conditions the organization's "tolerance for change" may determine its ability to survive in the long run.

THE CONCEPT OF ORGANIZATIONAL CHANGE

An organization has been described as a complex system of mutually dependent parts. It follows logically that the term "organizational change" refers to *an alteration or modification of one or more parts of the system*. What is needed, however, is an operational scheme of organization "parts" so that (1) the focus and direction of the change sought may be clearly identified for any given situation, and (2) the extended and interactive effects of a change in any one part of the system on the other parts may be anticipated and traced.

As discussed in Chapter 1, it is useful to view any organization within the framework of five interdependent dimensions when classifying the information found in a case. This same basic framework also may be utilized to clarify the notion of organizational change. Figure 8-1 summarizes those dimensions and their component parts. Thus organizational change occurs when one or more of the parts outlined in Figure 8-1 are altered or modified in some fashion.

Given this background, we now can proceed to a discussion of the *process* of organizational change. The following sections delineate the major elements of that process and indicate the major variables involved. They place emphasis on conceptualizing and categorizing change activities no matter what their genesis—whether they arise as a result of a changed product mix, a merger, the dissatisfaction of workers, declining profitability, or other sources. However, special attention will be given to the effects of a change in strategy on other parts of the organization.

STRATEGY, STRUCTURE, AND BEHAVIOR: A CASE STUDY OF INTERRELATEDNESS

Changes in an organization's strategic profile usually occur in response to changes in the environment. Once the strategic profile has been altered, it often becomes necessary to change the elements of structure shown in Figure 8-1. Thus structural change will *follow* strategic change, and managers must plan their change programs carefully to insure that needed alterations in structures are not overlooked.

One of the most dramatic illustrations of this phenomenon in the 1970s is the case of American Telephone and Telegraph (AT&T), the nation's fourth largest corporation in terms of sales and the largest in terms of assets. Long a highly regulated corporation, AT&T was attempting in 1979 to adjust its strategy to reflect a series of *deregulation* moves by the Federal Trade Commission. These deregulation actions opened the door for greater competition by making it possible for IBM and others to develop and market telecommunications systems. The increased competition caught AT&T off guard, because its protective "monopoly" for many years had resulted in a less-than-desirable emphasis on research and development of new products. Consequently, this corporate giant had fallen behind the times in technological applications, particularly those involving the use of computers and other sophisticated electronic gear. While not necessarily changing in physical form, the company's products will now take on a new dimension through a focus on the design of communication *systems* to meet the needs of customers. New products are also being developed to meet the requirements associated with the new systems (e.g., new software).

This environmentally induced change in strategy (especially in product mix) has also necessitated a change in structure that has been called the "largest corporate reorganization in history," as evidenced by the fact that over one-third of the work force will be affected.[1] Most fundamentally, the company has begun to structure itself along the lines of its major market segments instead of along functional lines. This move reflects the philosophy of becoming more customer oriented and is consistent with the recent trend noted in the reading that follows Chapter 7.

This massive change in organizational structure will, of course, necessitate a great deal of behavioral change on the part of managers and operating employees, since duties and responsibilities are being altered significantly. AT&T seems to have anticipated such effects:

> In an effort to avoid [chaos], Bell has carefully scheduled a gradual phasing in of the reorganization, working one management layer at a time from the top down. Coordinating the reorganization of the operating companies will be the task of [the new president]. For the next 18 months, the expected duration of the reorganization, that job will take most of his time. "The biggest challenge now is to put the new structure in place and make sure it delivers," he says.[2]

---

[1] "Behind AT&T's Change at the Top," *Business Week*, November 6, 1978, p. 115.
[2] Ibid., p. 117.

Figure 8-1 Summary of the parts of an organization.

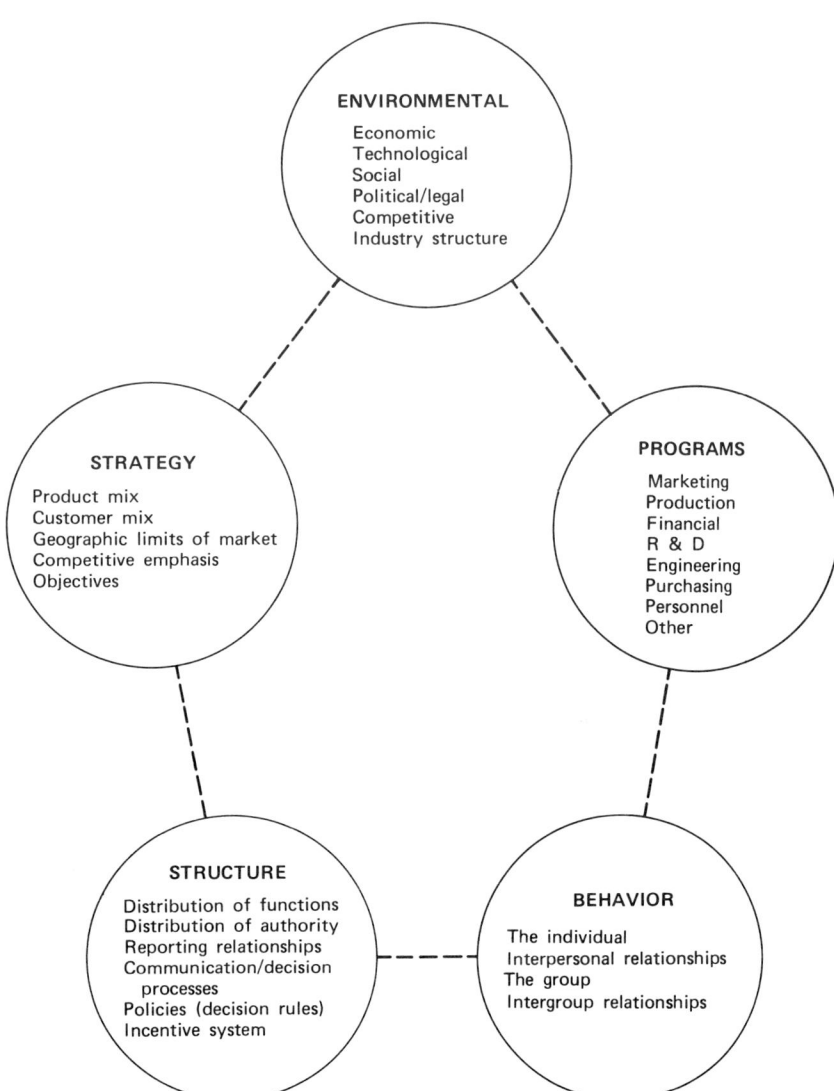

NOTE: Each of the major organizational parts comprises numerous subparts which are not explicitly identified above. For example, the marketing program may be further subdivided into distribution, sales, promotion, and market research. Similarly, numerous subparts of the individual could be listed (for example, his values, sentiments toward work, abilities, desires, overt behavior) to provide a more detailed focus for analytical purposes.

In this case AT&T has clearly recognized that structural change *follows* strategic change and is planning its actions (including the use of the president's time) accordingly. In addition to the focus on structural implementation, however, there is a strong emphasis on *behavioral* change:

> ...Bell still will face a major internal constraint to implementing its new market-oriented strategy: its people. Bell managers have been brought up to prosper in a politically oriented, regulatory environment, where it is more important to get favorable rate increases from state regulators than to provide a service that is tailored to individual customer needs.... With the advent of competition, of course, comes the risk of loss, and that may involve the biggest attitude change for Bell employees. It means that the Bell System will have to generate a new profit motivation, since profits will no longer be guaranteed by regulators.[3]

The company has embarked on a huge retraining program to effect both structural and attitudinal change, including discussion groups to focus on the reduction of anxieties.

The AT&T example clearly illustrates the relationship of strategic, structural, and behavioral change. These interrelationships should be kept in mind as one reads the following sections, which focus on the *process* of change.

THE ORGANIZATIONAL CHANGE PROCESS

Figure 8-2 presents the overall process of organizational change. The following sections examine the major phases of that process and their interrelationships.

Forces Toward Change

Forces toward change are classified as either exogenous or endogenous to the organization. Major exogenous (external) forces that create a need for change are new technology, changing values, and perceived environmental opportunities or constraints (economic, political/legal, and social). These major external forces create the need for internal change, and internal changes can be consciously planned so that the organization will be minimally upset in adjusting to these new external conditions.

Endogenous (internal) conditions that create the need for change may be grouped under the general heading of organizational stress—stress in task activities, interactions, employee sentiments, or performance results. These forces arise internally and are generally associated with inefficiency, morale, or interpersonal problems.

Tension always exists in an organization that is undergoing change. It may be consciously created by management in response to external forces, or it may itself create the need for change in the form of organizational stress of one kind or another. Consequently, recognition of the *source* of the tension makes it easier to predict probable reactions to change by those

---

[3]Ibid., p. 128.

Figure 8-2 The organizational change process.

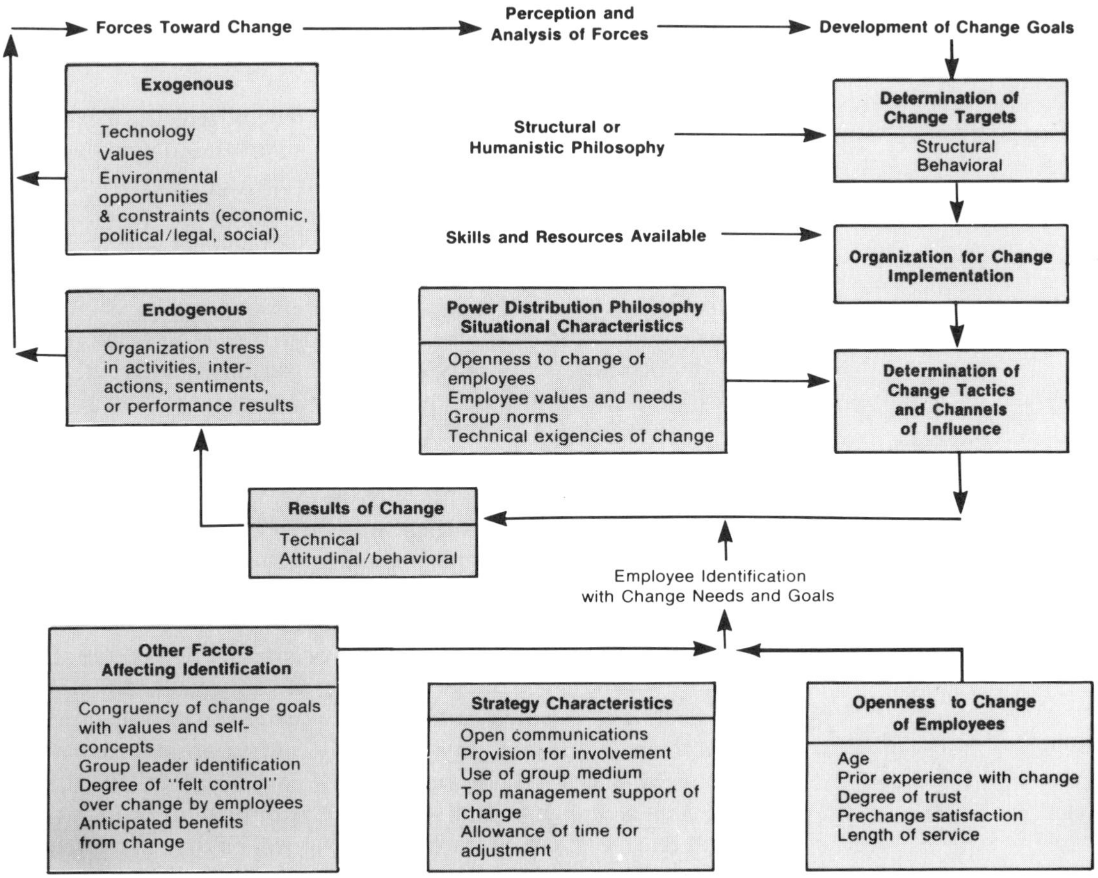

```
Forces Toward Change ────→  Perception and          ────→  Development of Change Goals
                            Analysis of Forces                        │
                                                                      ▼
┌──────────────────────┐                                    ┌──────────────────────┐
│     Exogenous        │    Structural or                   │  Determination of    │
│                      │    Humanistic Philosophy  ───────→ │  Change Targets      │
│ Technology           │                                    │                      │
│ Values               │                                    │  Structural          │
│ Environmental        │                                    │  Behavioral          │
│ opportunities        │                                    └──────────────────────┘
│ & constraints (economic,                                              │
│ political/legal, social)                                              ▼
└──────────────────────┘    Skills and Resources Available ──→ ┌──────────────────────┐
                                                               │ Organization for Change│
┌──────────────────────┐  ┌──────────────────────────────┐     │   Implementation     │
│     Endogenous       │  │ Power Distribution Philosophy│     └──────────────────────┘
│                      │  │ Situational Characteristics  │                │
│ Organization stress  │  │                              │                ▼
│ in activities, inter-│  │ Openness to change of        │     ┌──────────────────────┐
│ actions, sentiments, │  │ employees                    │     │   Determination of   │
│ or performance results│ │ Employee values and needs    │ ──→ │   Change Tactics     │
└──────────────────────┘  │ Group norms                  │     │   and Channels       │
                          │ Technical exigencies of change│    │   of Influence       │
                          └──────────────────────────────┘     └──────────────────────┘
         ┌──────────────────────┐                                         │
         │   Results of Change  │ ←───────────────────────────────────────┘
         │                      │
         │   Technical          │
         │   Attitudinal/behavioral │
         └──────────────────────┘
                                       Employee Identification
                                       with Change Needs and Goals
                                                    ▲
┌──────────────────────┐                            │
│   Other Factors      │ ──────────→                │         ┌──────────────────────┐
│ Affecting Identification│                         │         │ Openness to Change   │
│                      │   ┌──────────────────────┐ │         │   of Employees       │
│ Congruency of change │   │ Strategy Characteristics│         │                      │
│ goals with values and│   │                      │ │         │ Age                  │
│ self-concepts        │   │ Open communications  │ ┘         │ Prior experience with change│
│ Group leader identification│ Provision for involvement              │ Degree of trust      │
│ Degree of "felt control"│ │ Use of group medium  │           │ Prechange satisfaction│
│ over change by employees│ │ Top management support of│        │ Length of service    │
│ Anticipated benefits │   │ change               │           └──────────────────────┘
│ from change          │   │ Allowance of time for │
└──────────────────────┘   │ adjustment           │
                           └──────────────────────┘
```

individuals who will be affected. If internal tension creates the need for change those affected should welcome relief. On the other hand, if the response to external forces disturbs comfortable internal situations, change is more likely to be resisted. Because shifts in the strategy of a firm usually result from changing external conditions, one can expect considerable resistance from individuals whose secure positions might be threatened by the new strategy. As will be discussed more fully, changes in overall strategy have far-reaching effects throughout an organization.

Perception of Forces   How is the need for change recognized by the firm? Changes in exogenous forces are generally perceived by long-range planning offices, research and development departments, or market research units, as discussed in Chapter 2. In fact, the very reason for the existence of these units is to continually monitor and assess changes in external conditions that may signal the need for adjustments in overall strategy or in other parts of the firm. On the other hand, internal organizational stress is generally perceived by individual employees who become aware of poor morale, inefficiency, bad workmanship, or other difficulties.

No matter how the need for change is recognized, the next step in the process shown in Figure 8-2 involves *analysis* of the forces toward change. In the case of a new technological development, for example, analysis must be conducted to decide the feasibility of its application to existing facilities. This will determine whether or not the formal change goal "to utilize new process A in the production of product X" should be established along with its implications for any further changes required in organizational structure and worker skills and attitudes. Or consider the case of newly recognized market opportunities that may be capitalized on by alternative methods. The feasibility of merging with another organization as well as the feasibility of growth through internal expansion may need to be analyzed in depth. The basic reason for the analysis is, of course, to determine what the firm should do in order to respond to changing external conditions. Once this decision is made, change goals then may be developed to guide the adjustments required in the various parts of the organization.

The scheme of organizational parts shown earlier in Figure 8-1 can be a useful tool at this stage of analysis. When one is trying to develop some sort of action plan for responding to external or internal forces, the scheme provides a handy reference for systematizing the approach to the problem. A proposed change in the technology of production (e.g., utilization of some new equipment or process) may be subjected to an evaluation of its extended consequences for other parts of the organization. What will be the effect of such a change on individual skill requirements or attitudes? What will be the effect on task interactions? What will be the effect on production scheduling? What will be the effect on the current piece-rate scheme? In general, what other parts of the total organizational system will be affected by this change in technology? Have the costs and benefits of these *extended effects* of the proposed change been estimated to the maximum extent?

Development of Change Goals

Once the analytical process just described has been completed, the next step (as shown in Figure 8-2) is the development of change goals. Illustrative goals include:

1. *To Diversify into Additional Product/Markets.* Perhaps as a result of changing market opportunities and/or poor performance results in existing markets.
2. *To Merge with Another Corporation.* Perhaps as a result of an objective to increase market share.
3. *To Install Specified Antipollution Devices.* As a result of a new legal constraint requiring such modifications.

4. *To Move Decision Authority Downward.* As a result of organizational stress caused by authoritarian decision making at top levels of management.
5. *To Eliminate Interdepartmental Competition and to Foster Collaboration.* As a result of stress in departmental interactions, perhaps a conflict between the production and marketing departments over levels of finished goods inventory.
6. *To Change the Structure of the Current Distribution Channels.* Because of increased middleman costs, which have contributed to poor performance results.

Although these change goals obviously cover a broad spectrum of change situations, it is possible to classify them in a general fashion consistent with the basic scheme of organizational parts:

1. *Strategic Goals.* Concerned with altering the relationship between the firm and its environment (e.g., revised objectives, new product/market scope). Examples of change goals of this type include goals 1 and 2 above.
2. *Technological Goals.* Directly related to changes in the technology of production, plant and equipment. An example of this type is goal 3 above.
3. *Structural Goals.* Concerned with alterations in reporting relationships, location of functions and authority, communication/decision processes, spans of control, formal incentive programs, and similar aspects of an organization's "anatomy." An example is goal 4 above. Structural change is elaborated on later.
4. *Behavioral Goals.* Aim initially at changing values, attitudes, beliefs, norms, interpersonal relationships, group behavior, intergroup behavior, and similar "humanistic" phenomena. An example is goal 5 above. Behavioral change is also elaborated on later.
5. *Program Goals.* Focus on altering the objectives or structure of the technical implementation plans developed for marketing, production, research and development, and other task areas. An example is goal 6 above.

The various types of goals are *not* mutually exclusive, since two or more may be needed at the same time. Changes in organizational structure and behavior may be pursued in and of themselves, but changes in strategy and technology also will necessitate changes in structure and behavior for their successful accomplishment. For example, the strategic goal of "merger" usually will require some structural changes (e.g., consolidation of some administrative functions) and also some behavioral changes (e.g., transplanting sole identification with one organization to that of a newly merged concern). On the other hand, structural change may be appropriate given an *unchanged* strategy or technology, in order to increase administrative efficiency or effectiveness. The classifications just outlined should pinpoint just what type of change is necessary in a given situation.

Determination of Change Targets

As noted earlier, the initial adjustment or modification of *any* organizational part in response to external or internal forces creates reverberations throughout the total organization. It was also noted that when any of the types of change goals are acted on, eventually some subsequent change along the structural and behavioral dimensions will have to take place. Thus this stage of the change process makes it necessary to determine what must be changed within the organization in order to accomplish the goals established in the preceding step. In the case of a strategic change goal, almost all parts of the organization will require some internal adjustments in order to implement the new or modified strategy.

Figure 8-1 provides a means for structuring an evaluation of the effects of the strategic change on other parts of the organization. As discussed an attempt should be made to predict the effects of such change *before* strategic change goals are established. For example, it has been common practice to evaluate the feasibility of a merger in financial terms only. Yet there is probably no strategic change that promises greater "upset" among employees than the prospect of merging with another company. The attitudinal and behavioral aspects of merger must be anticipated and addressed very early in the process if successful implementation is to occur.

As a concrete example of this phenomenon, consider the following:

> Less than a year after Northwest Industries Inc. played white knight to Microdot Inc., rescuing the company from a hostile takeover attempt by General Cable Corp., Rudolph Eberstadt Jr. left the presidency of Microdot, a company he had helped to found and had headed for 16 years. Eberstadt's departure sent shock waves through the business community, particularly since he and Northwest President Ben W. Heineman appeared to get along very well. Although Eberstadt's reasons for leaving were varied, when asked to sum them up in one sentence, he responds, "I just wasn't used to having a boss."[4]

Although the example involves a chief executive officer, one should realize that managers and employees at all levels can be affected by a merger. Thus it is extremely important to select *individual attitudes* as a change target in order to implement the strategic change goal of a merger successfully.

Organization for Implementation

Decisions on goals and targets of change usually are made by top managers who may or may not be involved in the actual implementation. This task generally falls to the lower-level managers who have direct responsibility for

---

[4]"After the Merger: Keeping Key Managers on the Team," *Business Week*, October 30, 1978, p. 136.

the tasks and for the people who will be affected by the change. On the other hand, major change efforts may require the help of consultants who possess both the necessary expertise and objectivity. For instance, if the firm is seeking to change authoritarian personalities (a behavioral target), outside consultants with extensive background in this particular problem area may be hired. If, however, adequate financial resources are not available for such consultants, the persons responsible for implementation of the change might be the superiors of the authoritarian individuals in question.

Two points are especially important at this stage of the change process. First, those responsible for effecting change must be carefully chosen in light of both the target and the resources available. Second, an explicit definition of their responsibilities and authority to implement change is mandatory in order to prevent subsequent conflict with those affected by a particular change.

Determination of Change Tactics and Channels of Influence

Change tactics and channels of influence refer to the methods used to implement change. Major structural tactics now utilized are (1) direct alteration of structural elements, and (2) training in new task activities and interactions. Behavioral change tactics are those commonly labeled laboratory training, counseling, or therapy. The major channels of influence generally utilized are formal exercise of authority, personal persuasion, and various types of group decision making processes. As indicated in Figure 8-2, selection of the appropriate mix of change tactics and channels of influence depends on three major factors: (1) the targets of change, (2) one's "power distribution philosophy," and (3) various situational characteristics. The interactive nature of the three is evidenced in the following paragraphs, again using merger as a case in point.

In a merger, some direct alteration of structure (e.g., centralization of certain administrative functions) usually would be followed by an appropriate mix of techniques designed to effect desired changes in behavior. Although the selection of behavioral change tactics is assumed to follow the direct changing of structure in this example, this does *not* mean that structural change tactics should be applied without consideration for the individual. This depends on one's "power distribution philosophy." Thus structural change can be accomplished under conditions of mutual goal setting and discussions to better assure acceptance of the change by those most affected. The individuals being asked to change must feel that they have adequate power or control over their own situations.

Other aspects of a merger require behavioral change target selection as the first priority. Assume that the goal sought is related to gaining support for the proposed merger. Structural change is not called for here. The basic goal would be to persuade individuals that the benefits that would accrue to them should make all the adjustments worthwhile. Thus a persuasive strategy may be called for, and the extent of the persuasion required will be a function of the extent to which the benefits are made clear and meaningful to the individuals involved.

As indicated in Figure 8-2, many situational characteristics also determine the nature of the tactics and influence channels that should be used. For example, the extent to which employees are inherently flexible or open to change may determine the success of any change effort. Consequently, some attempt should be made to ascertain employee "states" in this respect so that tactics may be tailored accordingly.[5] Similarly, the extent to which employees identify with group norms will condition the extent to which informal group leaders may be used effectively as channels of influence. Also, a participative approach to change may or may not be appropriate, depending on the values and needs of affected employees. Finally, the technical exigencies of the particular change situation (e.g., how fast must we move?) exert a great influence on the nature of the tactics and channels selected.

The foregoing has indicated the dynamic interrelationship among several major elements of the change process. Perhaps the most important point is that the proper selection of tactics and influence channels is a difficult task and depends greatly on the particular situation. Each change situation requires close scrutiny to ascertain the appropriate tactics and channels to be utilized.

Results of Change and Intervening Variables

The final direct link in the change process reflects the results of change efforts with respect to productivity, morale, and other indicators of performance. The relationship between performance results and the preceding elements of the scheme is extremely complex, however, and is mediated by many other variables. Figure 8-2 indicates three major groupings of such variables: (1) openness to change, (2) strategy characteristics, and (3) factors influencing identification with change needs and goals.

Strategy characteristics ("good" communications, use of the group medium as a vehicle for effecting change, allowance of sufficient time for adjustment, and top management commitment and support) are utilized to try to counteract any possible negative influences of the openness-to-change indicators on the extent of identification with change goals. The latter is also affected, however, by the extent to which (1) change goals are congruent with broader social values (societal and organizational) and with self-concepts; (2) the group or organization leader identifies with the need for change; (3) the employees feel they have a degree of control over the changes affecting them; and (4) the employees anticipate benefits from the necessary changes. The strategy characteristics operate to try to create these conditions, instead of, as in the case of the openness-to-change indicators, trying to *overcome* or counteract any possible negative influences on acceptance of change.

The openness-to-change indicators represent *prior* states or conditions, since they reflect the inherent flexibility of affected employees. Thus, in effect, they constitute parameters at this stage of the process. On the other hand, the group of "other factors" that influence identification represent

---

[5]Factors associated with "openness to change" of employees are discussed more fully in the final section of this chapter.

variable states that may be *created* by change agents. Therefore both classes of variables, as well as any of the individual variables within each class, operate to determine the extent of acceptance of change, and their influence on such acceptance may be modified by the strategy characterisitics shown in Figure 8-2.

Even though management may be successful in cultivating employee identification with change goals, the ultimate success of any change program is, of course, the extent to which the goals themselves are accomplished. This is frequently very difficult to determine because causal influences other than those consciously designed in the change program may affect the end result.

Additional Remarks

The individualistic nature of change situations makes it impossible to specify a normative model that will apply in all cases. The major point is to recognize that mediating influences such as those just discussed do exist and do modify the degree of success that can be achieved with any change program.

One final point should be noted with respect to the interrelation of the major elements of the model. Although a definite sequential pattern of the elements is evident both in the model (Figure 8-2) and in the discussion, an attempt also has been made to indicate the interactions among the major elements. Thus it was shown that the selection of tactics and influence channels requires a situational assessment of several factors, many of which may involve trade-offs. Similarly, the selection of change goals obviously does not result from a simple sequential process of perception, followed by the analysis of change causes and conditions. A complex process involving the consideration of various alternatives and associated combinations of resources required to adjust to change forces must take place before any final decisions are reached. However, reference to a sequential process will help to identify the basic interrelationships. More detailed interactions then can be developed to guide the implementation of change in any given situation.

RESISTANCE TO CHANGE

Much empirical research has been conducted on factors causing resistance to change. This section summarizes the major findings into three categories: (1) openness to change of employees, (2) method of implementation of change by management, and (3) other factors affecting the extent to which employees will identify with the goals of change.

Openness to Change

The major findings to be discussed here refer to the *flexibility* of employees, relative to their ability to accommodate change. The importance of looking at "individual openness" is indicated by Edgar H. Schein:

> . . .*flexibility and capacity to change ultimately rest with the human resources of the organization. If the managers and employees are themselves flexible, the organizational blueprint can be consciously and rationally altered in the face of changing external situations . . . The psychological prob-*

lem . . . becomes, therefore, how to develop in its personnel the kind of flexibility . . . needed. . . .[6]

Three major indicators of openness to change have been identified for this discussion. First, the individual's *prior experience with change* has been found to be related to how well he or she will accept the need for changes. Individuals who have become accustomed to change will be more receptive than those who have worked in very stable and unchanging environments. However, Floyd C. Mann and Franklin W. Neff note that:

Major changes create a climate in which additional change can often be introduced without materially increasing problems. With the unfreezing of an organization, it is often possible to make changes which have been postponed because of the impact that such a single change would have. . . .[7]

Thus an organizational climate that has been characterized by some unpredictability is generally better suited for the creation of flexibility and openness towards change on the part of employees. It should be noted, however, that prior *negative* experiences with change may contribute to change resistance in the same fashion as no prior experience with change does.

A second major influence on individual openness to change seems to be the *degree of trust* in top management, or in whoever initiates the change. The reputation of top management for fairness and honesty will be a primary factor in determining the response of employees to any plan for change. Based on a detailed analysis of four case histories, Mann and Neff conclude that reactions to organizational change are very much related to trust in management. Moreover, the degree of trust is significantly influenced by (1) the amount of information about the change provided to employees, and (2) the amount of participation employees feel they will have concerning the changes to be made.[8] One can generally infer from case materials whether or not top management does have the trust of employees. A decision then can be made as to whether one feels that the proposed recommendations will be feasible and acceptable to lower-level employees.

A third major indicator of the extent to which employees are likely to be receptive to change is the *degree of satisfaction with existing conditions.* Of course, employees who are dissatisfied with the situation generally will tend to welcome change. On the other hand, a comfortable and satisfactory condition of equilibrium may exist, which will cause employees to resist disruptive changes. It is possible, however, that a high state of morale or satisfac-

---

[6]Edgar H. Schein, *Organizational Psychology* (Englewood Cliffs, N.J.: Prentice-Hall, 1965), p. 16.
[7]Floyd C. Mann and Franklin W. Neff, *Managing Major Change in Organizations* (Ann Arbor, Mich.: Foundation for Research on Human Behavior, 1961), p. 48.
[8]Ibid., p. 70.

tion with existing conditions also may contribute to *acceptance* of change. The same management responsible for creating those satisfactory conditions may command the respect of employees and thus their willingness to accept changes that promise to make things even better.

Finally, *parochial self-interest* of employees may result in considerable resistance to change. Consider this example:

> After a number of years of rapid growth, the president of an organization decided that its size demanded the creation of a new staff function—New Product Planning and Development—to be headed by a vice president. Operationally, this change eliminated most of the decision-making power that the vice presidents of marketing, engineering, and production had over new products. Inasmuch as new products were very important in this organization, the change also reduced the vice presidents' status which, together with power, was very important to them.
>
> During the two months after the president announced his idea for a new product vice president, the existing vice presidents each came up with six or seven reasons the new arrangement might not work. Their objections grew louder and louder until the president shelved the idea.[9]

Method of Implementation of Change

As discussed earlier in this chapter, the manner in which change techniques are implemented in a given situation is a function of the targets selected, one's "power distribution" philosophy, the results of a situational assessment of employee openness to change, the values and needs of employees, and the technical exigencies associated with particular change objectives. Certain common denominators related to successful implementation can be identified, however, and are discussed here.

First, the importance of frequent, open, and well-timed *communication of information about change* is well documented. Harriet O. Ronken and Paul R. Lawrence note that open communication is especially important during a period of change because:

> ... the social factors (such as membership in a group, the chances of working with people with complementary frames of reference, the assurance of durable and satisfying relationships, etc.) which would otherwise enhance the individual's ability to give and receive communications accurately are themselves upset during periods of change and uncertainty.[10]

There are two important points here. Management must effectively communicate the reasons for change to affected employees, as well as the benefits that should accrue as a result. Also, management must keep employees informed as to the progress of any change efforts and solicit the advice of the people affected concerning the best ways to make the changes.

---

[9]John P. Kotter and Leonard A. Schlesinger, "Choosing Strategies for Change," *Harvard Business Review*, March-April 1979, p. 107.
[10]Harriet O. Ronken and Paul R. Lawrence, *Administering Change* (Boston: Harvard University, Division of Research, 1952), p. 318.

Second, means must be provided to allow affected employees to be *involved*, or to *participate*, in both the planning and the implementation of the change process. The implication of all the studies and writing on participation is that greater identification with change needs and goals can be instilled in this way. However, much evidence exists to indicate that a participative approach is not appropriate for all employees and all situations and may, in fact, be resisted by some employees—findings to date again indicate the need for a *situational* approach in the choice of implementation tactics related to participation.

Closely related to the desirability of participation in many situations is the *use of the group* as a vehicle for gaining acceptance of change. The basic rationale here is that the attitudes of individuals are anchored in a "social matrix" of co-workers, family, friends, and reference groups. Thus the influence of the group as a whole may be used to persuade reluctant individuals. Use of the group mechanism also permits the interchange of ideas and misgivings about change objectives and procedures that might otherwise never be identifed.

The fourth requisite for effective implementation of change techniques is related to the timing of change, particularly the *period allowed for adjustment* to new structural and behavioral patterns. Usually, too little attention is given to the fact that much time is required to alter behavior patterns and to learn new skills. It is also important to allow time for a gradual accommodation to the idea of change before introducing it.

The final requisite for effective implementation is related to the *commitment and support by top management*. Employees will not support a major change effort if they do not perceive a real commitment to what is being attempted on the part of top management. If such a commitment is not visible, then employees will naturally attach less importance to the change goals.

Table 8-1 provides an overview of methods for dealing with resistance to change.

Effective methods of implementation frequently can overcome any negative influences of those factors discussed earlier under the concept of "openness to change." Other factors can influence the acceptance of change goals, however, and these are discussed in the following paragraphs.

Other Factors Affecting Acceptance of Change

Identification with, or acceptance of, the goals of change is partially a function of the openness to change of employees and of the manner in which change techniques are implemented. Certain other factors can contribute to acceptance of change, as well.

One particularly important influence on the acceptance of change is the *extent of identification by the group leader with the goals of change.* Here, the key implication seems to be the need to instill a "total organization" view in formal or informal group leaders, as distinct from a "subsystem" view. The following observation by Robert H. Guest is particularly appro-

Table 8-1 Methods for Dealing with Resistance to Change

Approach	Commonly used in situations	Advantages	Drawbacks
Education + communication	Where there is a lack of information or inaccurate information and analysis	Once persuaded, people will often help with the implementation of the change	Can be very time-consuming if lots of people are involved
Participation + involvement	Where the initiators do not have all the information they need to design the change, and where others have considerable power to resist	People who participate will be committed to implementing change, and any relevant information they have will be integrated into the change plan	Can be very time-consuming if participators design an inappropriate change
Facilitation + support	Where people are resisting because of adjustment problems	No other approach works as well with adjustment problems	Can be time-consuming, expensive, and still fail
Negotiation + agreement	Where someone or some group will clearly lose out in a change, and where that group has considerable power to resist	Sometimes it is a relatively easy way to avoid major resistance	Can be too expensive in many cases if it alerts others to negotiate for compliance
Manipulation + co-optation	Where other tactics will not work, or are too expensive	It can be a relatively quick and inexpensive solution to resistance problems	Can lead to future problems if people feel manipulated
Explicit + implicit coercion	Where speed is essential, and the change initiators possess considerable power	It is speedy, and can overcome any kind of resistance	Can be risky if it leaves people mad at the initiators

SOURCE: Reprinted by permission of the *Harvard Business Review*. Exhibit from "Choosing Strategies for Change" by John P. Kotter and Leonard A. Schlesinger (March–April 1979). Copyright © 1979 by the President and Fellows of Harvard College; all rights reserved.

priate here, and his basic reasoning may be applied to various levels within an organization:

When an organization is a subordinate unit to a larger organization and when the patterns of internal relationships within the subordinate organization are similar to those linking it to the larger, changes leading to more successful performance within the subordinate organization will take place after there has been a change in the patterns of relationships (interactions and sentiments) linking the larger to the subordinate organization.[11]

Thus it is helpful to convince formal or informal group leaders of the desirability of any proposed change so that other employees will be more receptive.

Another important influence is the *extent to which change goals are congruent with larger social values and with individual self-concepts.* With respect to congruency with social values, two different perspectives may be taken. First, Cyril Sofer has noted the importance of making sure that change goals are congruent with the cultural norms or values of the *organization* as an entity. In the study of changes required in internal operations of three British hospitals after the nationalization of health care delivery, he found that:

A variety of formal rules have been changed without corresponding adjustments occuring in the internal social structure and in the whole "culture" of the hospital. . . . A whole body of informal relationships, traditions, and values remains out of gear with formal arrangements.[12]

Second, the perspective on congruency with social values may take the total *society* as its reference point. Such a perspective is illustrated by Guest's observation that:

The process of successful change in a hierarchial organization will start and continue to the extent that the members perceive the behavior of superiors, peers, and subordinates to be more in keeping with the norms of behavior in the larger culture.[13]

With respect to the need for congruency of change goals with an individual's self-concept, Mann and Neff conclude the following:

A person who has worked in one job for a long time usually has come to see his job performance as consistent with the kind of person he sees himself to be. A major change in the way he is required to perform his job is likely to

---

[11]Robert H. Guest, *Organizational Change: The Effect of Successful Leadership* (Homewood, Ill.: Richard D. Irwin and The Dorsey Press, 1962), pp. 153–54.
[12]Cyril Sofer, "Reactions to Administrative Change," *Human Relations, 8,* 1955, p. 313.
[13]Guest, *Organizational Change,* p. 117.

conflict with his concept of himself. A new adjustment, requiring some modification of his self-image, will have to occur before he will be effective and satisfied.[14]

A third major influence on acceptance of change is *the employee's evaluation of his control over the change situation*. This feeling of control will be influenced by the amount of information an employee has about the change and the amount of participation he or she feels will be permitted.[15] This supports the use of two devices discussed earlier: (1) clear communication of change goals and rationale and, frequently, (2) a participative approach to involve affected employees in planning and implementing change.

Finally, a fourth major class of influences on acceptance of change goals encompasses the *employee's anticipated benefits from the change*. The list of anticipated benefits relevant to change acceptance covers the major dimensions of morale or job satisfaction (pay, duties, working conditions, chances for personal growth and development, and relationship with supervisor). If employees perceive positive effects of change on these various dimensions at the time change plans are made known, positive attitudes are likely to be expressed about the change goals.

SUMMARY

The first part of this chapter outlined the major phases of the organizational change process. Each phase was discussed in some detail to provide some general guides for understanding the numerous complexities of change.

The next part of the chapter examined reasons for resistance to change. It found that a greater ability to adjust to change is usually found in employees who exhibit the following characteristics:

1. They have had frequent and positive experiences with change.
2. They trust the top management personnel or others who initiate major changes.
3. They are dissatisfied with existing conditions (unless a satisfaction with existing conditions is reflected by a high degree of trust in top management).

The chapter also showed that certain characteristics related to the manner in which change techniques are implemented tend to increase the probability of acceptance to change:

1. Open and well-timed communication of information about changes.
2. Provision of means by which employees can participate in both the planning and implementation of change (depending on various situational characteristics).

---

[14] Mann and Neff, *Managing Major Change*, p. 23.
[15] Ibid., p. 70.

3. Use of the group as a vehicle for influencing positive attitudes toward change.
4. Allowance of sufficient time for adjustment to required changes.
5. Evidence of commitment and support of proposed changes by top management.

Although these characteristics of the change implementation process may serve to overcome resistance among employees who are not as open to change (e.g., those who may have experienced negative effects of major changes in the past), certain other factors also were seen as conditioning the final extent of acceptance of change in any given situation:

1. The extent to which group leaders identify with the need for changes affecting group members.
2. The extent to which change goals are perceived by employees to be congruent with larger social values (both within and outside the organization) and with individual self-concepts.
3. The employee's evaluation of his or her control over the changes.
4. The employee's anticipated benefits from proposed changes.

INDEX

Aggregrate output: description of, 214-215
   determinants of, 215-216
   planning of, 215-216. *See also* Production/operations function

Break-even analysis, 124-128
   break-even point, 125
   fixed costs, 124
   total revenue, 125
   variable costs, 124
Break-even point, calculation of, 125

Capability audit, *see* Resource audit
Case analysis, 2-17
   framework for, 3-5
   stages of, 5-17
     analysis of data, 9-15
     classification of data, 5-9
     formulation of recommendations, 16-17, 117-124
     identification of problems, 15, 109, 117
Competitive advantage, 71-74
Computer simulation, 2-3
Corporate strategy, *see* Strategy
Credit decisions, 167-168

Discounts, 165
Distribution channel structure, 162-163
Dividend payment, level 132-135
     description of, 132
     determinants of, 132-135
     stability of, 132-133
     stockholder preferences for, 135. *See also* Financial function
DuPont system of financial control, 122

Environmental forces: analysis of, 51-54
   impact on strategy, 41-51
   types of: competitive, 44-45
     economic, 41-44
     political/legal, 50-51
     social, 46-48
     structure of industry, 45-46
     technological, 48-50. *See also* Strategy

Facilities layout, 208-211
   determinants of, 209-211
   process layout, 209

product layout, 209. *See also* Production/operations function
Financial analysis, 103-136
   action plans in, 117, 122-124
   diagnosis of problems in, 109-117
   financial statements in, 104
   industry averages in, 108-109
   leverage indicators in, 105-107
   liquidity indicators in, 105-107
   ratio analysis in: Dun & Bradstreet Ratios, 110-116, 118-121
     types of ratios, 105-108
   trend analysis in, 108
Financial function: decision variables in, 129-136
   description of, 128-129

General managers: definition of, 1n
   perspective of, for problem solving, 9-15
   tasks of, 1, 11, 15

Informal organization, 251
Inventory levels, of raw materials and work-in-process, 216-218
   description of, 216
   determinants of, 216-218. *See also* Production/operations function

Job design and process planning, *see* Process planning and job design

Leadership, 252-253

Manufacturing decisions, 224-231
   alternatives in, 225-228
   design trade-offs in, 225-227
   limitations on, 230
   policy determination of, 228-229
Marketing, 139-196
   basic approach to, 140-141
   core elements of, 139
   environment of, 139, 142-143
   functions of, 139-141
   gaps, 139-141
   institutions, 139-141
   mix, 140
   multidimensional view of, 139
   organization of, 149, 254-265
   of organizations, persons, and social causes, 141-142

themes of analysis in, 140
tools of analysis, 142-143
Marketing audit, 150-154
Marketing information systems, 159-162
Marketing management: definition of, 140
tasks of, 143
Marketing planning, 172-178
Marketing strategy, 144-149, 160-161
Market research, 53, 159-162
Matrix organization, *see* Organizational structure

Needs and motivation, 252

Organizational change, 267-284
concept of, 267
forces causing, 268-272
goals of, 271-274
implementation of, 274-275, 279-280
openness to, 277-279
process of, 271
resistance to, 277-283
targets of, 274
Organizational decisions: functionally dependent, 12-14
functionally independent, 14-15
multifunctional coordinative, 11-13
strategic, 6-7, 11, 38-39
Organizational dimensions, 5-11
behavioral, 8-9
environmental, 5-6
program, 7
strategic, 6-7
structural, 7-8
Organizational environments, 236-237
classification of, 237
components of, 236
Organizational structure, 233-265
alternative structural forms, 238-239
characteristics of, 235-237
design of, 234-235
market-centered, 254-265
multidimensional view of, 233-234
types of: divisional, 242-243
functional, 240-242
hybrid designs, 249-250
matrix organization, 246-249
product departmentation, 243
project management, 244-246
"small" structure, 238-240
territorial divisionalization, 243-244

Personal values, 77-84
impact on strategy, 77-81
resolution of conflicts in, 81-84
types of: culturally derived, 77-80
organizationally derived, 80-81. *See also* Strategy
Physical distribution, 168-170

Plant location and capacity, 201-208
description of, 201-202
determinants of, 202-208
objectives of, 201-202. *See also* Production/operations function
Price determination, 164-165
approaches to, 164
determinants of, 164-165
objectives, 164
Process planning and job design, 211-214
description of, 211
determinants of, 211-214
impact of technological change on, 212-213. *See also* Production/operations function
Product life cycle, 159-161
Product planning, 179-196
Product research and development, 157-159
Production/operations function: decision variables in, 201-219
description of, 199-200
types of systems, 200-201
Production smoothing, 214
Profit Impact of Marketing Strategy (PIMS), 146-148
Project management, *see* Organizational structure
Promotion, 165-167
determinants of, 167
objectives of, 165-166
product publicity as form of, 166

Raw materials inventory, *see* Inventory levels
Resistance to change, *see* Organizational change
Resource audit, 69-71, 85-101

Social responsibility, 46-48. *See also* Environmental forces
Strategic decisions, 6-7, 11, 38-39. *See also* Strategy
Strategy: definition of, 37-40
determinants of, 39-40
impact of environmental forces, 41-51
impact of personal values, 77-81
impact on manufacturing function, 220-231
process of formulation of, 55-67
adaptive mode of, 57-59
entrepreneurial mode of, 55-57
planning mode of, 59-61
strategic decisions identified, 6-7, 11, 38-39
Synergy, 74-77

Working capital, level of, 129-132
cash flow forecast of, 130
cash management of, 130
cash preference of management, 130
determinants of, 130-132
impact of credit on, 131. *See also* Financial function
Work-in-process inventory, *see* Inventory levels